THERE'S A SILVER LINING

An evocative Blackpool saga, full of warmth and colour...

It's 1918, the war is finally over, and Sarah Donnelly and her cousin Nancy are filled with hope for the future. Sarah awaits the return of her cousin Zachary whom she has adored since childhood, but Zachary returns shattered by the horrors of war and can barely face his family. Sarah throws herself into her job at Donnelly's tea rooms, and eventually decides to set up in business on the North Shore, running her *own* tea rooms. Meanwhile, Nancy has chosen to follow her mother on to the stage, where her youthful naivety soon lands her in trouble.

THERE'S A SILVER LINING

THERE'S A SILVER LINING

by

Margaret Thornton

Magna Large Print Books
Long Preston, North Yorkshire,
BD23 4ND, England.

British Library Cataloguing in Publication Data.

Thornton, Margaret
    There's a silver lining.

    A catalogue record of this book is
    available from the British Library

    ISBN   0-7505-2192-9

First published in Great Britain in 1995 by Headline Book Publishing

Published in Large Print 2004 by arrangement with
Headline Book Publishing Ltd.

Magna Large Print is an imprint of Library Magna Books Ltd.

Printed and bound in Great Britain by
T.J. (International) Ltd., Cornwall, PL28 8RW

For my grandchildren. As Hetty says in this book, to have grandchildren is to be given a 'second chance'. To Amy, Lucy, Sarah and Robert, with my love and thanks for all the joy they have brought to me.

Chapter 1

Sarah Donnelly peered through the top-floor window of Donnelly's Department Store, craning her neck upwards. Between the roofs of the buildings across the street the Irish Sea could be glimpsed, greyish-blue with tiny white-capped waves on this calm sunny November morning. But it was Blackpool Tower, that huge ironwork structure dominating the landscape, that was the focus of Sarah's attention now, as it had been to visitors and residents alike for the past twenty-five years. There was definitely something going on up there, right at the top.

Sarah's neck was beginning to ache with bending back so far. 'Yes, it is. I do believe it is,' she whispered to herself. 'It's a Union Jack.' And a Union Jack could mean only one thing: the war was over!

There had been rumours for the past week or so, which they had hardly dared to believe were true. Then it had been reported in the newspapers a couple of days ago that the Kaiser had abdicated and fled Germany; a new regime, a republic, had been formed there. And now, if the flag fluttering from the top of the Tower were to be believed, the Armistice had been signed.

Sarah rushed along the corridor into the room next door. Edwin Donnelly turned round from the window of his office as his daughter entered.

11

He, too, had been peering upwards.

'Oh … sorry, Father, I forgot to knock.' Sarah put a hand to her mouth, but she didn't look at all contrite; neither, judging from his benign expression, did Edwin expect her to be. 'But I've just noticed–'

'Yes, so have I.' Edwin Donnelly grinned widely at her. 'The Union Jack at the top of the Tower. I've been expecting it all morning, looking out for it. I had a feeling it would be today. It's happened, my dear. The war's finally over.' He smiled fondly at Sarah and she thought she could see just a trace of moisture in the corner of one of his warm hazel eyes.

She smiled back at him, feeling her own deep brown eyes fill up with tears. This time, though, they were not tears of sadness, such as they all had shed many times over the past four years, but tears of joy … and of hope.

Sarah dashed forward then, flinging both arms around her father. 'It's all over, at last. What a blessed relief.'

Edwin Donnelly held her closely for a moment or two, then released her. 'You'll be wanting to go and celebrate, won't you?' he said gently. 'Off you go and join the rest of the crowds in Blackpool. I daresay they'll be making for Talbot Square, like they always do.'

Sarah nodded. She wasn't much of a one for crowds, but today was different. 'Thank you, Father,' she said. 'I would like to see what's happening out there.'

'I don't suppose we'll do much trade this morning,' Edwin went on. 'And if it's really true,

12

then we'll be shutting shop this afternoon. Folks'll have too much on their minds to be bothered with shopping. Besides, it calls for a celebration. It does that!'

In Bank Hey Street, outside the store, there was a feeling of anticipation, of barely contained excitement, as people hurried towards Talbot Square. It was always said that bad news travelled fast; it seemed now that good news did too, for already streamers of red, white and blue were strung across several shop fronts, and flags were flying above windows and doorways, although it couldn't have been more than an hour since the news had come through.

'Yes, it's true. It's a fact. They heard it at the *Gazette* office nobbut an hour ago…'

'Aye, they've signed it…'

'Thank God for that. Thank God, that's all I can say…'

Sarah listened to the comments of the crowd all around her as she stared towards the Town Hall doorway. And when the Mayor, Alderman Parkinson, came out to give the official announcement the crowd went wild with joy. His voice could scarcely be heard above the tumultuous shouts and cheers, but they managed to get the gist of his message. Marshal Foch had accepted the German surrender. They had signed the Armistice agreement and the Great War was over. There was to be a Thanksgiving Service at St John's Parish Church at 12 noon – that would be in about half an hour's time – and, later that afternoon, further celebrations would take place in Talbot Square. And all the shops in the town were to close at 1 p.m.

'Hello there, Sarah. I thought I might see you here.' Sarah turned at the sound of the familiar voice. It was her cousin, Nancy, pushing her way towards her.

'Isn't it exciting?' Nancy's green eyes were shining with happiness. 'One of the neighbours told me the news when I was scrubbing the front doorstep, and Mam said I could come and see what was happening. She didn't seem all that thrilled herself – she just went on blackleading the stove. Still ... I expect she was thinking.' Nancy's eyes grew serious for a moment.

Sarah nodded gravely, then reached out and touched her cousin's arm. 'Yes ... Maybe she thinks she hasn't very much to celebrate.' Sarah was recalling, with a pang of grief that momentarily lessened her elation, how Uncle Albert – Aunt Hetty's husband and Nancy's father – had been killed in Ypres, getting on for two years ago.

'We've got to look forward though, now, haven't we?' said Nancy, smiling again. 'Shall we come back this afternoon – and I'll see if our Joyce'll come as well. Your father'll let you off, won't he?'

'Of course. Hasn't the Mayor just said that all the shops'll be closed? I'd better go now and tell him that it's official.'

'I'll walk back with you,' said Nancy, linking arms with her cousin.

The two girls crossed Talbot Square, dodging between the now dispersing crowds and walked back arm in arm along Market Street. 'He'd have been closing whether or not,' Sarah went on, 'but at least he'll know that somebody else'll not be

14

pinching his trade. You know what shopkeepers are like. It's every man for himself... Not that you could honestly say that about Father. He's a wonderful boss. I don't suppose there's a better store to work for in the whole of Blackpool than Donnelly's. The girls are all very contented. I don't think I've ever heard anybody complaining.'

'Well, you wouldn't, would you?' Nancy retorted. 'You're one of the top dogs. You're Uncle Edwin's righthand man ... well, woman at any rate. They're hardly likely to let you hear them grumbling, are they? I daresay you're right, though. It's well-known in Blackpool that Donnelly's is a good place to work. The hours are reasonable and the pay's not bad, and most of the girls reckon that it's a cut above being in service. Or working in a boarding house,' Nancy added, grinning. 'You're lucky, aren't you, Sarah?' she continued. 'Being the owner's daughter, I mean. You're sure of promotion, whereas the other girls'll have to fight tooth and nail if they want it. Well, look at you. You've got it already.'

Sarah smiled, confident that Nancy, in spite of her words, was not envious of her cousin's position. 'Not for much longer though,' she reminded her. 'When Mr Middleton comes back from the war, that'll be the end of my Under Manager's position. Father said it was only temporary. It's only right that when the men come home they should get their old jobs back. We've only been standing in for them.'

'I don't see why it's right,' Nancy objected. 'Women are as good as men any day.'

'Nancy! How can you say such a thing?' Sarah

15

turned startled brown eyes on her cousin. 'After all that the men have been doing for us for the last four years. And a lot of them never even coming back at all. You wouldn't have wanted to go and fight in a horrible war, now would you?'

'No, of course not.' Nancy frowned. 'I didn't mean that. I was only trying to say that women can do a job of work – well, some jobs at any rate – as well as the men if they put their minds to it. And don't forget, we've got the vote now. Women are beginning to count for something at last, and about time too.'

'What do you mean, *we?*' Sarah laughed. 'It'll be a long time before you and I can vote, Nancy. It's only for women over thirty, and then they have to be householders. That's a nine-year wait for me, and how long for you?' Sarah grinned at her cousin. 'Twelve years, isn't it?'

'All right, all right, I know it's a long time. But I daresay there'll be another Act of Parliament before that. I shouldn't imagine for one moment that I'll have to wait twelve years. Anyway, what are you going to do, Sarah, when you have to hand back your job to that Mr Middleton? Are you going to be a sales assistant?'

'I don't know,' Sarah replied thoughtfully. 'I have a feeling that Father would like me to go into the Fashion Department. There are a lot more ready-made garments than there used to be, and more and more women are getting interested in buying fashionable clothes. At least they will, when they're there for them to buy … *and* if they have the money,' she added quickly. 'It's not a fair sort of world, is it, Nancy? There

16

are those who have a lot, and others who have hardly anything at all. Some poor women won't have any money to spare for fancy clothes, especially if their husbands have been killed.'

'Like Mam,' said Nancy flatly, and Sarah at once felt guilty.

'I wasn't really thinking about Aunt Hetty,' she replied, squeezing her cousin's arm. 'Your mother'll be all right. She was upset, of course, when Uncle Albert was killed, but she's a fighter, isn't she? I've often heard my mother say that she's a born survivor. Aunt Hetty's got the boarding house, after all, and look how she's kept it going all through the war – with your help, of course. No, I was thinking of the thousands of women who have been dependent on their husbands for every penny.'

'Mmm … Mam's not exactly short of a bob or two, as Gran would say,' Nancy replied, 'and she's certainly got plenty of guts. The women'll have to get jobs, won't they, if they've no men to look after them. A lot more women have been going out to work during the war, so it won't be very much different now.'

'Doing men's jobs though,' Sarah pointed out. 'There have been women bus conductors and ambulance drivers, even painters and plumbers, as well as women in banks and offices. But all those jobs'll go back to the men now … like mine,' she added quietly. 'There's not much scope for women round here, Nancy, no matter how badly they might need a job. There are no mills in Blackpool and hardly any factories. There's only the boarding-house trade and the shops ... and very few shops as good to work for as Donnelly's,' she concluded, going back to her original theme. 'Yes, I realise I'm very lucky.'

Sarah was deep in thought as they approached Donnelly's Department Store at the corner of Bank Hey Street, in a prime position near to the Tower. Not that the position had been of such supreme importance in 1865 when the store was founded, as the Tower had not then been built. The town-centre site had, however, from the very beginning attracted shoppers who liked value for their money – and which northern folk didn't? – combined with the courteous and friendly service for which Donnelly's soon became famous.

The business had been started by George Donnelly, the grandfather of Edwin, as a small lock-up shop known as Donnelly's Draper's, and had been developed and expanded mainly by William Donnelly, Edwin's father, who had died only a couple of years ago. It was still a family-run firm controlled largely by Edwin, the owner and Managing Director, helped, during the absence of the menfolk, by his wife Grace and his daughter Sarah.

Strictly speaking, Sarah was not Edwin's daughter; she was the daughter of Grace and Walter Clayton, Grace's first husband, who had died when the little girl was only two years old. Sarah could scarcely remember her real father. At times a shadowy image flickered across her mind, a hazy memory of a deep booming voice and a burly figure holding her tightly in his arms. For Walter Clayton had loved his little daughter dearly. Her mother, Grace, in her gentle way, had always assured her of that, even though she had always, also, encouraged Sarah to look upon Edwin as her father. Sarah hadn't needed any persuading. She loved Edwin as though he were her own flesh and blood, a love which was readily reciprocated.

It was of Edwin that Sarah was thinking now as they approached the store. How glad Father would be to see Mr Middleton back, along with some of the heads of Department who had been away serving King and Country for the past four years. It couldn't have been easy for him, the only man in a store full of women, apart from the few young lads they employed who were too young to join up; he couldn't have missed the resentful looks which had, at times, been cast in his direction, for Edwin Donnelly, for all his forty-nine years, was very youthful-looking.

There were many who had wondered why he, too, wasn't in khaki. The white feather that had fluttered from an envelope which Sarah had opened one morning about a year ago had been eloquent confirmation of that. She had quickly destroyed the evidence and the virulent accompanying letter, but had felt sure that it wasn't an isolated incident. Other missives must surely have reached their intended source.

How vile it all was, and how vile was war. Thank God it was all over. The prayer of thanksgiving that Sarah uttered in her mind now was not just idle words: she really meant them. Thank God that Father had not had to go. Another few months and he might have been forced to join up – and how he would have hated

19

that! Sarah couldn't have borne it, if anything had happened to Father … or to Zachary. Thank God, too, that Zachary was safe and in a little while would be coming home to her. She felt her heart leap with gladness at the thought of it.

'What *will* you do though, Sarah, when Mr Middleton comes back?'

Sarah blinked rapidly. She had been miles away hardly aware that her cousin was speaking to her. 'What will I do? I'm not sure. At least, I have a vague idea, but I'll have to discuss it with Mother and Father first. I don't really want to go into the Fashion Department.'

'Ah, I see … secrets. You're not going to tell your little cousin, then?'

'There's nothing to tell, not yet.' Sarah smiled. 'Besides, whatever I do, I don't suppose it will be for very long. I can't see myself somehow as a career woman. All I want really is to have a happy marriage, like Mother has. That's all I've ever wanted. And Zachary will be home soon, won't he?'

Sarah knew she hadn't imagined Nancy's tut of exasperation, nor the heavenward glance of her green eyes. Nancy was impatient, Sarah knew, at her cousin's affection for Zachary Gregson, even though Zachary was Nancy's own brother.

Hetty Gregson opened the door of her North Shore boarding house, Sunnyside, to find her mother standing on the doorstep.

'Haven't you heard, our Hetty?' Martha Makepeace stared in surprise at her daughter's soiled apron and grimy hands. 'What d'you think you're doing, blackleading the stove on a day like this? Don't tell me you haven't heard!'

'Heard what, Mam?' Hetty put her hands on her hips, looking a trifle belligerently at her mother. She knew very well what Martha was on about, for hadn't they all been expecting the news for days, and hadn't Nancy dashed out like a whirlwind only half an hour since – but a stubborn streak made her play her mother along. 'Tuesday's my day for the back kitchen, you know that, and the stove won't clean itself, more's the pity. Now, what am I supposed to have heard?'

'It's over. The war's over, lass.' The two women stared at one another for a few seconds, then Hetty dropped all her notions of pretence and flung her arms round her mother. The tears ran down her cheeks, mingling with those of the older woman, as she breathed the heartfelt words, 'Thank God … Oh, thank God.'

'Aye. Mrs Collins from next door just popped in to tell me on her way back from town.' Martha gently pushed Hetty away from her and quickly dabbed at her eyes – she was not a one for a great show of emotion – then followed her daughter along the dark passage into the living room at the back of the house, the 'kitchen', as it was generally called. She sat down in an easy chair at the side of the fire.

'There's a Thanksgiving Service at St John's at twelve o'clock, according to Mrs Collins. The Mayor has just said so. Apparently the town's agog with the news already – flags are flying and folks going mad in Talbot Square. I wondered if

21

you'd like to come along with me, to the church?'

'You reckon I've something to be thankful for then, do you?' Hetty's green eyes narrowed as she looked unsmilingly at her mother.

'Yes, I do. I do that!' Martha's tone was emphatic. 'We should all find time today to thank God that it's all over and that there's better times to look forward to. The fellows haven't been fighting for nowt, you know. It's to make a better world for all of us.' Martha's glance softened as she looked at the lowered head of her daughter, at the grey hairs now liberally sprinkled amongst the once bright auburn. 'I know you're upset about your Albert, love,' she said more gently, 'and you're bound to be thinking of him today of all days. But it's getting on for two years now…'

'That doesn't make it any easier, Mam. I still feel bitter about it at times. It wasn't as if he had to go. He was nearly forty when he joined up. He could have waited until they made it compulsory.'

'Now, that wouldn't have been like Albert at all, would it? He felt he had to go and do his bit – although I know it must make you a bit resentful when fellows like Edwin Donnelly have gone and missed it all.'

'No. Funnily enough I don't feel like that at all about Edwin,' replied Hetty. 'He was a few years older than Albert anyway, and he'd have hated it – Edwin, I mean. He's such a gentle soul, he wouldn't have wanted to hurt a fly, let alone try to kill his fellow men.' Hetty gave a shudder. 'And he did feel it, about not going. Our Grace told me. He had a couple of white feathers in the post a year or so ago and he nearly went and enlisted then. But Grace persuaded him not to. She reckons that if he'd been a lot younger and he'd been called up then he'd have become one of them "conchies"; or else they might have made him a stretcher bearer – they didn't have to fight. Anyroad, it makes no odds now, does it? It's all over and he hasn't had to go.'

'He's made our Grace happy, I'll say that for him,' said Martha, staring into the fire. 'Aye, he's a fine young man is Edwin Donnelly, though I was dead against him at first.'

'Not so much of the young, Mam.' Hetty was smiling now. 'He'll be fifty in a year or so, will Edwin, and Grace and me are no spring chickens neither. What do they say – "fair, fat and forty"?' Hetty patted her spreading hips beneath her flowered apron. 'And to think that I once had a nineteen-inch waist.'

Martha nodded curtly. 'It beats me how you've managed to put so much weight on, our Hetty, what with the war and the rationing an' all. To say nothing of all the chasing about that you do.'

'Can't resist nibbling, that's my downfall,' Hetty confessed. 'When I make a batch of scones or cakes I always have to eat one, fresh from the oven. But I gave up sugar in my tea ages ago.'

'A fat lot of good it's done you,' said Martha tartly.

Hetty grinned good-naturedly although she was aware of the heartache deep inside her. She knew only too well that her waistline had spread considerably of late, especially since Albert had been killed at Ypres in 1917. One might have thought that she would have lost weight – some

23

women she knew had gone to skin and bone grieving for their loved ones – but Hetty had sought consolation in the biscuit tin or the pudding basin. Like her mother, she was a good cook, a talent she hadn't really known she possessed until she and Albert took over his mother's boarding house a couple of years before the war started. Now, with Albert no longer around to tell her how pretty she looked, Hetty had ceased to care much about her appearance. The mirror told her that she was still, at forty-one, an attractive woman, her green eyes just as sparkling and her complexion just as smooth as when she was eighteen or so. But her hair, although it still curled alluringly in a style that was not altogether fashionable, now had a pepper and salt appearance, with as much grey as auburn. And as for her figure, well, there was very little she could do about that and a cursory glance in the mirror now and again was all that she allowed herself, she who had once spent much of her time preening.

'Well, are we going or aren't we?' Martha persisted. 'Come on, lass, make up your mind.'

Hetty gave a sigh, just a small one. 'All right, Mam, I'll come with you. In spite of everything I suppose I do have something to be thankful for, don't I? Zachary's come through it safe and sound. I can't tell you how relieved I'll be to see him home again.'

'You're not the only one,' said Martha. 'I reckon that lass of our Grace's'll be pleased to see him, too. She's always been potty about our Zachary, ever since she was a little lass.'

'Yes ... Sarah,' said Hetty slowly, her green eyes momentarily thoughtful 'I only hope...' She stopped suddenly. 'Well, never mind. I'll just go and wash my hands and put my coat on, then we'll be off.'

'What was that you were saying about Sarah?' asked Martha. 'You hope what?'

'Nothing, Mam. It was just something that crossed my mind, but it isn't important.' Well, it is really, she thought to herself, but she hadn't time to discuss it with her mother or even to think about it just at the moment. 'Yes, I'm certainly thankful our Zachary's come through it all in one piece.'

St John's Church, in the centre of Blackpool, was packed, not only with the usual parishioners but with others who seldom set foot inside a place of worship or who, like Martha Makepeace, usually worshipped elsewhere. Martha was a dyed-in-the-wool Methodist and proud of it, but today was a special day and one had to compromise a little.

She nudged Hetty after they had settled themselves in the high-backed pews and bowed their heads in a brief moment of prayer. 'Look, there's our Grace. Can you see her, two rows in front? At least, I think it's Grace. It looks like her hat.'

As if aware of their scrutiny, the woman in the close-fitting green hat with a petersham bow at the side, turned round and raised her hand in greeting. She smiled serenely at her mother and sister and Martha thought how kind the years had

25

been to her elder daughter. Grace was forty-two now, just a year older than Hetty but, unlike her sister, she was still as slim as ever and her dark hair was scarcely touched with silver. Martha had worried about Grace's thinness when she was a young woman and about her recurrent bouts of bronchitis. But there had been no sign of a cough at all since Grace had married Edwin, soon after the turn of the century, and the radiance that had shone from her then was still a part of her even now. Martha often thought that if ever there was a truly happy woman then it was Grace. Her marriage to Edwin Donnelly had certainly been made in heaven, in spite of the fellow being a Roman Catholic. It was a great pity they hadn't had any bairns of their own... Still, it hadn't to be, and Edwin loved Sarah as though she were his own daughter.

The congregation was silent, listening to the words of the Reverend Little, the vicar of Blackpool; there were a few whispered 'Amens' and more than a few tears wiped away.

'Our day has come,' he intoned, 'the day when every man, woman and child who has done anything at all can thank Almighty God that they have been allowed to save democracy...

'Go mad with joy if you like,' he continued, 'but remember this: every man and woman of you must stick behind the Prime Minister until peace is declared – and the salvation of democracy and civilisation is made secure for all time...'

Martha and Hetty declined to join the revellers in Talbot Square later that afternoon, as did

26

Grace, but Sarah was there. So were Hetty's two girls, Nancy and Joyce. The three cousins had always been good friends and they stood together now, arm in arm, one little family unit amongst the crowd of thousand upon thousand that thronged the area outside the Town Hall. From the promenade railings right up to the junction of Clifton Street and Talbot Road, where Yates's Wine Lodge dominated the corner, it was one solid mass of people jammed closely together. Sarah, clinging tightly to her cousin Nancy, felt quite frightened once or twice, as though she could hardly breathe, but she wouldn't have missed this celebration, not for anything. They had been waiting for it for so long.

It was an occasion that she would never forget. Amongst the crowd Sarah could see hundreds of soldiers. She wondered what they were doing there, whether they happened to be home on leave or whether they were some of the lucky ones, stationed nearby, who had never gone abroad. Not like Zachary; he had been serving on the bloody battlefields of the Somme for the last two years, ever since he was nineteen, but he had been spared, thank God. She stole a glance at Nancy and Joyce, knowing that there must be a certain sadness mingled with their joy today at the thought that their father would not be returning. But Nancy turned and grinned at her and Joyce appeared happy enough, staring around at the crowds that surrounded them. Maybe they had done all their weeping for Uncle Albert and were now rejoicing, as Sarah was, that at least their brother would soon be coming home.

There were several young men there, too, in the bright hospital blue; such men had been an all-too familiar sight for the past year or so. Some were on crutches, some with their arms in slings – many, indeed, with an arm or leg missing – and some with hideously scarred faces. The ones who were in Talbot Square today, though, were obviously well on the way to recovery. It was no place for anyone on crutches; they would have been swept aside by the sheer weight of the crowd. And how thankful these lads must feel, knowing that now they didn't need to return to the scenes of carnage.

The crowd was waiting for the Mayor to appear on the dais outside the Town Hall: a tremendous cheer went up when he finally arrived, complete with purple robe and gold chain. There was Alderman John Bickerstaffe, too, the first Chairman of the Blackpool Tower Company, a familiar figure in the town with his ruddy face and white imperial beard and peaked sailor's cap. Today he sported a Union Jack across his chest, tucked into his waistcoat. At a signal from the Mayor the music began, played by the combined bands of the RAMC and the King's Lancashire Military Convalescent Hospital. Thirty thousand voices were raised, and hearts and spirits were raised, too, as they sang the familiar songs; 'Goodbye Dolly Gray', 'It's A Long Way To Tipperary', 'Pack Up Your Troubles'…

…and 'Keep The Home Fires Burning', the song that had become very popular of late, expressing as it did all the yearning of the lads for the comforts of home, and the anguish of the

28

women who waited for them.

'There's a silver lining,
Through the dark cloud shining,
Turn the dark cloud inside out
Till the boys come home.'

As Sarah sang she felt a lump in her throat and tears misting her eyes. She blinked them away; today was not a day for sorrow. She was aware of the crystal clear voice of Nancy next to her. She had heard her cousin sing a few times at chapel concerts and she thought again what a lovely voice Nancy had. Aunt Hetty had once been a singer – had performed, in fact, in one of the sea-front public houses; Sarah had often heard her mother talk about it. Nancy must take after her.

'You're trilling away like a songbird,' Sarah said to her cousin now, lessening for a moment the emotional atmosphere.

Nancy's green eyes danced with delight. 'Just try stopping me,' she grinned.

Sarah thought, not for the first time, how Nancy was the image of her mother, although much slimmer than Aunt Hetty, of course. She had the same sparkling green eyes, and the same auburn hair, pushed under her round hat now, but escaping in curling tendrils round her ears and forehead. Joyce, the younger sister, resembled her late father, dear old Uncle Albert. She was a much more solid girl in every way than her sister. Joyce's figure was stocky, as Albert's had been, and her mid-brown hair that refused to curl and her square-shaped face were his too. Her grey eyes were candid and clear and you always felt that you could trust Joyce, just as you had been able to trust Uncle Albert. It wasn't that you couldn't rely on Nancy, but she was a much more mercurial person. Up one minute and down the next, as changeable as the wind.

As for Zachary, he didn't resemble his sisters at all. Sarah knew that her cousin, with whom she had fallen in love as a child and still loved, had inherited the curling black hair and dark eyes and the swarthy good looks of his father, Reuben Loveday. Reuben was a gipsy whom Hetty had married when she was nineteen, but he had died tragically only a couple of years later.

How different we all are, thought Sarah. As for herself, she knew that she was very much like her mother. She had Grace's delicate features, dark curling hair and dark brown eyes, and – so she had been told – the same gentle disposition. Sarah was flattered when people said she resembled Grace because she thought her mother was a truly wonderful person.

The Mayor was waving his cocked hat now and calling for three cheers for the King. Then, three cheers for the boys at the Front, for Marshal Foch, for Lloyd George... And a moment of silence for the men who had fought and died: 'the heroes we shall never see again'.

Every head in the crowd was lowered, just as, a few moments later, every head was raised at the sound of a loud droning overhead. The singing of 'Rule Britannia' was almost drowned by the engine of the monster airplane that was wheeling gracefully in a circle, not far above the rooftops.

'It's been a wonderful day,' said Nancy happily. She could hardly keep still for excitement. 'I don't want it to end. Come on, girls, what shall we do? Where shall we go?' She turned to Sarah. 'Our place or yours?'

'Let's go and have a walk on the prom,' Sarah suggested, 'then we'll go back to our house and I'll make us some tea. I made a huge Dundee cake last night, a new recipe I got from Mrs Jolly. I'd like you to try it – tell me what you think.'

'You and your baking!' Nancy poked her cousin in the ribs, none too gently. 'Honestly, if we had somebody to cook for us, like your Mrs Jolly does for you, I'd be only too happy to let them get on with it. You Donnellys don't know you're born.'

Sarah pulled a face at her cousin, then grinned. There was no malice in Nancy's remark, at least she didn't think so. It was just the way things had worked out. While Grace had married a man who was what Grandma Makepeace would call 'well-heeled', Hetty's second husband Albert had been just an ordinary sort of chap who worked for a firm of joiners. And whereas Hetty had always had to work hard in the boarding house, Grace, in her later years, had become more of a lady of leisure.

'Mmm, not bad,' Nancy pronounced, an hour or so later, as the three girls sat in Sarah's bedroom munching the Dundee cake and drinking tea. 'Nearly as good as Gran's, I would say.'

'Thank you kindly,' Sarah said. 'I take that as a compliment. There's no one to touch Grandma Makepeace for cakes and pastries. She had a stall on Burnley market at one time, so Mother tells me.'

31

'She's had a lifetime at it,' said Joyce, 'so she should be good, but you're doing quite well yourself, Sarah.'

'I don't know why you bother, though,' Nancy commented, placing the china cup and saucer on the corner of the dressing-table and leaning back against the pillow propped up on the bed. 'You've a cook to do all that sort of thing for you. Why waste your time baking cakes and suchlike when Mrs Jolly can do it for you? I wouldn't, I can tell you!'

'I enjoy it,' said Sarah simply. 'Like you enjoy singing. We're all different, Nancy.'

'You might not enjoy it as much if you had to do it for a living, like Gran,' remarked Nancy. 'And Mam as well. Honestly, Sarah, you are lucky.'

Sarah could see Nancy's eyes travelling round the room as she spoke, taking in the modern oak dressing-table with the oval mirror, the matching wardrobe and the low bed which had been bought to replace the old high brass bedstead. Sarah knew that she was lucky in having parents who could afford to give her the best of everything ... but there were certain disadvantages as well.

'And a fire in your bedroom whenever you want it,' Nancy went on, eyeing the glowing coals in the green tiled fireplace, an exact match with the pale green walls and the paisley patterned eiderdown and curtains. 'Talk about luxury! Honestly, you don't know you're born.'

Nancy had made a similar remark earlier in the day and Sarah answered it now. She didn't want her cousins to think that she took everything for granted. 'I know I'm fortunate,' she said. 'I know

32

only too well that Mother and Father indulge me. They always have done...' She gave a slight sigh. 'But I can't really do much about it, can I? That's why I've tried to work hard at the shop, to repay Father for all he does for me. But I don't like it when people are – well – envious of me. It's just the way things are.' She looked at her cousins somewhat apologetically.

'But we're not envious of you,' said Joyce quickly. 'Are we, Nancy?'

'No ... we'd just like to scratch your eyes out,' said Nancy, but she laughed good-humouredly and the other two girls laughed, too. 'Like you say, Sarah, it's just the way things are. But Joyce and me, we've never really had a proper bedroom to call our own, have we? And we've always had to share. We've slept in every blessed room at Sunnyside since we moved in there, and in the summer we're always stuck up in the attic so that the visitors can have the best rooms.'

'But you'll have a better room in the winter, surely?'

'Huh! Don't you believe it. Mam always uses the winter months to decorate and we're usually up to our eyes in paint and paste – at least, I am. Joyce works for Gran across the road now, of course.'

'And it's pretty much the same there,' agreed Joyce. 'Visitors in the summer, decorating in the winter, and so it goes on. Still, it's the life that most folks in Blackpool live, those in our line of business, that is. And I'm sure there are no better digs anywhere in Blackpool than Sunnyside and Welcome Rest.'

'Spoken like a true boarding-house keeper,' quipped Nancy. 'I can see you'll be a regular Blackpool landlady before you're twenty, our Joyce.'

'I could do much worse,' said Joyce evenly. 'It's a good job that some of us are content.'

'Oh, don't mind me, I'm contented enough,' said Nancy. 'Till something better comes along...'

Sarah had been thoughtful while this exchange was going on. Now she spoke. 'Don't bicker, you two,' she said, looking earnestly at the two sisters. 'If only you knew how much I've envied *you* at times.'

'Us? Good heavens above! Why on earth should you envy us?' said Nancy, her green eyes opening wide.

'Well, not exactly envied you,' Sarah went on, 'but I've wished that I wasn't an only child. Mother and Father are so protective of me, whereas you two ... and Zachary ... have always had so much more freedom, or so it seemed to me.'

'We've had to fend for ourselves a good deal more,' nodded Nancy. 'I'd agree with that. But Mam's always tried to keep us on the straight and narrow – and Dad did too,' she added, a sad expression crossing her face just for an instant. 'But you can't envy us having a brother! Our Zachary's a pain in the neck, isn't he, Joyce?'

Joyce smiled. 'Sarah doesn't think so. But I daresay he's different with her. We're only his sisters.'

'To be treated with the contempt that women-folk deserve.' Nancy's voice was a trifle bitter.

'Our Mam's spoiled him rotten. Anyway, never mind about Zachary. Let's talk about something interesting. Shall we go out again tonight, girls? It isn't every day we can celebrate the war ending...'

Sarah joined in the conversation, but she was still thoughtful, her mind on their two families. They had always remained friendly, even though Grace had 'gone up in the world', and the three girls spent a lot of time together. And Sarah hoped that, before long, the ties between the two families would be even closer. When Zachary came home...

Chapter 2

Martha Makepeace's parlour had changed very little in the last twenty-three years. Looking round at the flocked wallpaper, almost hidden by the wealth of pictures and family photographs, at the plush-covered armchairs and the cast-iron mantel shelf overflowing with ornaments and knick-knacks, Hetty recalled how it had been her mother's ambition when she first arrived in Blackpool, to have a posh parlour that would compare favourably, if not outdo, that of her friend and neighbour, Alice Gregson.

It had been in 1895 that the Turnbull family, as they were then, had moved to Blackpool from Burnley and opened their boarding house, 'Welcome Rest'. The business, in Martha's capable hands, and helped by Grace and Hetty, had soon thrived and it wasn't long before Martha had been able to furnish the parlour of her dreams. Hetty remembered how delighted her mother had been when the sideboard had arrived from the saleroom in Church Street – a huge mahogany piece with turned spindles and elaborate carving and a mirror set in the backboard. And there it still was, dominating the small room, the embroidered runner on its top almost covered by a fruit bowl, two large copper lustre vases with painted flowers, and yet more family photographs. Martha had been a widow then and it was five years later that she had married George Makepeace, a widower who had lodged with her for a few years.

'Sunnyside', the boarding house of which Hetty was now the landlady, was directly across the road from Welcome Rest. But there was not, nor had there ever been, any rivalry between the two concerns, save that of friendly comparison. There was ample room in Blackpool for any number of boarding houses and the holiday trade had not suffered to any great extent during the war years, as one might have expected it to do. Hetty often popped across the road during the evening for a cup of tea and a chat, and it was this matter that they were discussing now, on the evening of Armistice Day.

'We'd better prepare ourselves for an influx of visitors next summer, our Hetty,' said Martha. 'I reckon they'll come flocking back in their thousands now that this blessed war's over.'

'We haven't done too badly though, Mam, all things considered,' replied Hetty. 'There have been almost as many visitors the last couple of summers as there were in peacetime, after the troops had gone from here.'

'Aye, we were glad of the troops, and those Belgian refugees that they billeted on us, though they didn't pay us all that much. It was better than nothing though, I suppose. They were a real caution and no mistake, those refugees,' Martha recalled smiling. 'Still, live and let live, I always say, and I didn't mind giving a few of them a roof over their heads, poor souls. It must have been dreadful for them, driven from their homes with nothing but what they could stand up in. That Kaiser's got a lot to answer for. I notice he's keeping his head down at the moment and he might well an' all.'

'I've heard that a lot of the boarding houses on the Isle of Man have gone out of business,' said Hetty. 'The steamers stopped running there, you know. So we've been lucky in a way, Mam, because we got their trade as well as our own.'

'Yes ... not much consolation for them though, is it?' Martha nodded grimly. 'I'd never want to prosper at someone else's expense. Let's hope they get their visitors back now the war's over. We benefited from Scarborough's bad luck an' all, after they had that attack from the German Navy. Folks started coming to the west coast instead of the east. Still, it's all over now and we can look forward to peace, thank the Lord.'

'Yes ... peace,' said Hetty slowly. She gave a little frown. 'There was something I didn't quite understand when the vicar was speaking this morning. Do you remember? He said something about us all sticking together, with the Prime Minister, until peace is declared. But I thought it had been – they've signed the Armistice, haven't they? I thought peace had been declared already.'

'It has as far as I'm concerned,' said Martha. 'I don't understand it at all. I know they do a lot of talking and laying the law down, these top brass.' She turned to her husband. 'Do you understand it, George? We are at peace now, aren't we?'

'As near as makes no difference,' said George Makepeace. 'From what I can make out, Germany will have to sign a peace treaty, because they've been defeated, and it'll only be truly official once that's been signed and sealed. If you ask me, I can't see them taking too kindly to it.'

'Why not?' asked Martha, alarmed. 'I'm sure they must be glad it's over, same as we are.'

'Oh, I daresay there'll be all sorts of conditions they have to agree to. Handing back territories that they've been keen to hold on to, and limiting the size of their army – all that sort of thing.' George pursed his lips. 'Like I say, I can't see Germany being very keen on being made to toe the line. They've always wanted to be top dog. Still, time will tell.'

'Anyroad, there'll never be another war, will there?' said Martha. 'We can rest assured on that score. They're calling it the war to end all wars, aren't they, George?'

'That's what they say. But like I've just said, time will tell.' George looked serious for a moment as he stared into the fire. Then he looked up and smiled at Martha and Hetty. 'It's over though now, isn't it, and we can all look forward to your Zachary coming home.'

As Hetty smiled back at him she felt a real surge of affection for this man who had been such a good friend to her for the past twenty years or so. Not exactly a father; Hetty could remember her own father who had died when she was ten, and George had never tried to take his place. But he had been a tower of strength to both her and Grace over the years, as he had been to Martha, and a doting grandfather to Martha's grandchildren. His blue eyes, always a noticeable feature in his ruddy face, were a little

39

less bright now and his coarse wavy hair was entirely grey, but he was still very active for his years. He must be about sixty-six now, Hetty guessed. He was a couple of years older than her mother, whom she thought was sixty-four or thereabouts: Martha was always a little cagey about her age. Hetty wondered how much longer George would go on working at Pickering's, the joinery firm belonging to Albert's uncle, who had also been Albert's employer. Surely not for much longer, and it must be time, too, for her mother to think about giving up the boarding house.

Hetty thought that her mother looked tired. Martha's dark hair, drawn back in a bun, a style that she hadn't changed over the years, was nowhere near as grey as her husband's, but the lines of her forehead and round her mouth were more prominent now and there was no longer the same spring in her step. Hetty knew better, however, than to tell her mother that she should rest; Martha would be very quick to deny any suggestion of tiredness. But she did try to broach the subject casually.

'You're talking about next summer's visitors, Mam,' she said. 'I was thinking you might have called it a day by then. Have you never thought of selling up and going to live in a little place like Alice and Henry did?' Hetty's in-laws, Alice and Henry Gregson, had retired from their boarding house before the war – that was when Hetty and Albert had stepped into their shoes – and gone to live in a small terraced house at Layton. 'It's only a ten-minute tram ride away, up Talbot Road, and it's really handy for the shops and everything.'

'You don't need to tell me, 'cos I know,' replied Martha sharply. 'I've been up to see them often enough, haven't I? What Alice Gregson chooses to do and what I do are two different things, and there's no chance of me giving up for a while yet, my girl. I shall know when the time has come and it hasn't come yet, I can assure you. Besides, Alice had been doing it a lot longer than me and she'd made her pile long ago. Very comfortable is Alice Gregson.' Martha looked enquiringly at her daughter, her head on one side. 'Anyroad, why are you wanting me to give up? After my trade, are you – is that it?'

The twinkle in Martha's eye told Hetty that her mother was only joking. She laughed. 'No, Mam, not at all. As a matter of fact, I've got something different in mind for next summer. I've been meaning to tell you about it, see what you think…' Hetty paused, setting the china cup and saucer on the spindle-legged table beside her before she went on. 'I've been thinking about taking stage people in instead of ordinary visitors. "Pros", they call them. Quite a lot of the boarding houses in Blackpool do it and it can be quite lucrative, especially if you get the ones who are here for the whole season… What's the matter, Mam? You don't look very keen on the idea.'

'It's nothing to do with me, lass. It's your business and you must run it how you think best. I was only thinking that you might find they're more trouble than what they're worth. They're a rum lot, you know, Hetty, stage folk.'

'Yes, I do know, Mam.' Hetty grinned. 'I worked with some of them if you remember.'

41

'Oh, that was ages ago,' said Martha dismissively. 'You were nobbut a giddy lass. I should hope you've got a bit more sense now than you had then. No, they're a law unto themselves are stage folk. Coming in at all hours and wanting meals cooking at goodness knows what time. From what I've heard, they don't have their proper meal until they've finished at the theatre, and if there's two houses it can be getting on for midnight before they get themselves home. I don't think you realise what you'd be taking on, Hetty. What gave you the idea, anyway?'

'Oh, I had a couple staying here earlier this year,' Hetty replied. 'They were appearing at the Palace Varieties. A middle-aged couple; he was a baritone and his wife did musical comedy numbers. They were normal enough, Mam, not much trouble at all. They had a midday dinner, same as the other guests, and then I made them some sandwiches when they got in, about eleven o'clock. And I started thinking then that it might not be a bad idea to take more of them in, when the war finished. I'm my own boss now, Mam, now that Albert's gone, and I've got to do what I think is best all round.'

'Hmmm … can't say I ever saw you kow-towing to Albert,' said Martha pointedly. 'You were always a one for getting your own way. How will you go about it, then? You haven't any contacts, for a start. You don't know anybody who's on the stage.'

'I'll put adverts in the stage magazines,' said Hetty. '"Comfortable digs – home comforts, good cooking" and all that – and see what happens. I shall have to keep on with the ordinary visitors as well for a while, though, till I see how things go.'

'You'll find it hard work coping with both of 'em,' Martha told her. 'It'll be nearly as bad as the old lodging-house system. There's a lot of landladies round here still do that, but I decided when I first came here that I'd run a boarding house and not a lodging house.'

Hetty smiled to herself, remembering how her mother had always bristled at the very suggestion that she might be a lodging-house keeper and not a boarding-house landlady. There was a distinct difference between the two. The keeper of a lodging house let rooms to the visitors who brought their own food in for the landlady to cook. Some landladies provided such items as bread, milk and potatoes, hot water for tea, and the use of the 'cruet' at an extra charge. Some even went so far as to provide a pudding for those who wanted it; others were known to clean their visitors' boots or wash their clothes, all for a suitable payment added to the bill at the end of the week. The boarding-house landlady, however, which was what Martha had always proudly called herself, provided all meals – cooked breakfast, midday dinner and high tea – at a fixed rate and a fixed menu. It had been quite an innovative idea back in 1895, when Martha had first come to the town. Now, more and more lodging-house keepers were seeing the wisdom of it and were changing their ways and their names accordingly, although there were still very many who were sticking to the old system.

'Aye, I could never understand why Alice kept

on with the old idea as long as she did,' Martha said ruminatively. 'More trouble than what it was worth, I always thought, cooking a bit of this and a bit of summat else for fussy folk. I remember Alice telling me once that she had a couple staying with her from one of the inland towns – Bacup, I think it was – and they were in the tripe-dressing business. And that was all that they brought with 'em for Alice to cook.' Martha chuckled, shaking her head then wiping the tears of merriment from her eyes. 'Tripe! Would you believe it? A tin trunk full of tripe.'

Hetty laughed too. 'I daresay I'll cope, Mam,' she said. 'I usually do. I just feel as though I'm ready for a change, and there's little else I can do, is there? I've got to stick with the boarding house – it's one of the few ways of making a decent living in Blackpool. If I make enough, I might even be able to buy it off Alice and Henry. That's what I'd really like to do.'

At the moment Hetty was paying rent to her in-laws for Sunnyside, whereas her mother now owned Welcome Rest, the property she had at first only rented when she came to the town.

'Yes, you give it a try, lass,' said George now. 'You don't know what you can do till you try, and if anybody can make a go of it I'm sure you will, Hetty. You've always been one to be ready for a challenge. What does your Nancy think about it? Does she think it's a good idea, taking pros in?'

'I haven't discussed it with her yet, George,' Hetty admitted. 'It's only a vague idea at the moment, but I can't see that she'll raise any objections. She's always seemed happy enough, working in the boarding house. I don't know what I'd have done without her, to tell you the truth. She's worked like a Trojan these last few years, ever since she left school. But I must admit that I wonder sometimes if she might want something a bit different now that this lot's over. She might want to spread her wings – and who could blame her?'

'Not much scope though, is there?' said Martha. 'What is there in Blackpool except the boarding houses and the shops? And she's not trained for 'owt else, is she? Same as Joyce, but she seems happy enough an' all, working for me. Leastways, I've not heard her complain. You've got a couple of grand lasses there, Hetty, although I know you think that the sun shines out of that lad of yours.' Martha looked at her keenly.

'Yes, I know they're good girls, Mam,' said Hetty, not replying to her mother's comment about Zachary. Her son, her firstborn, was her favourite child. She didn't admit it to anyone but herself, but obviously her mother had noticed it. She loved her two girls – of course she did – but there had always been something special about Zachary, resembling, as he did, her beloved Reuben who had been taken from her so very tragically in the early days of their marriage.

Hetty pushed thoughts of Reuben – and Zachary – to the back of her mind now, concentrating instead upon her youngest child. Joyce, the younger of her two daughters, was sixteen. She was the one that Hetty always thought of as the most complacent and biddable of her three children. 'It was good of you to find a job here for

45

Joyce,' she said now to her mother. 'I can't imagine how she'd have gone on if she'd had to work with our Nancy. Nancy tries to boss her around, you know. And Joyce is so easygoing, she tends to get put on. Yes, it's much better for her working here. It gives her a bit of independence.'

'Joyce is like her father,' said Martha reflectively, 'and not just in looks either. She's a real thoughtful lass. And it's never been a question of finding her a job, Hetty. I've really needed her this last couple of years, I can tell you. I'd have had to employ a lass from somewhere or other, and it's better to keep it in the family if you can. Like the Donnellys do. Sarah's working hard at the store, isn't she? They tell me Edwin 'ud be hard pressed to manage without her, although I always thought it was a rum sort of job for Sarah. And our Grace has been doing her bit an' all since the war started.'

'Hmmm… We can't all be born with a silver spoon in our mouths though, can we, like the Donnellys?' There was a decided edge to Hetty's tone and Martha looked at her in surprise.

'That's not like you, our Hetty. What's up? You've never been jealous of our Grace before, and I'm sure she's never made you feel that she's any different because she married a fellow with a bit of brass.'

'I'm not jealous, Mam,' said Hetty. 'You should know me better than that. I've never been envious of our Grace, not ever, but I can't help thinking that life is unfair sometimes. Look at me – I'm only forty-one and I've already lost two husbands. I should think I've had more than my

46

fair share of trouble if anybody has.'

'So has Grace,' said Martha quietly. 'She lost her first husband – Walter Clayton – very tragically too, just like you did.'

'She never really loved him though, Mam, not like I loved Reuben. It was never what you would call a love match. And it left her free to marry Edwin … like she should have done in the first place.'

'Aye, well, I must admit it's all worked out for the best,' said Martha. 'And I'm sorry about Albert, lass – I am that. I know how you must be feeling. But you've got to try and count your blessings, like I had to do when I lost your father. I said to myself, I've got a couple of grand lasses here, and I've got a strong pair of hands and I can work for my living. And you take after me in that respect, Hetty love. I've never known you to be down-hearted for long. You've got your grand little family, same as I had, and they'll be a blessing to you, you'll see.'

'I know that, Mam,' said Hetty with a pensive smile. She was thinking that her mother had had her share of heartache with herself and Grace, as well as the joy, but that was what motherhood was all about. No doubt she, too, would experience sorrow as well as happiness with her own three. She had already spent two agonising years worrying about Zachary. 'I know they'll be a blessing to me – take no notice of me, I was just being silly – but I want the best for them all, you see. And I sometimes think that they won't get the best out of life by working in a boarding house. The two girls, I mean: Zachary's got his job on the railway to go back to. He should be all right; it's what he always wanted to do, to be an engine driver.'

'The lasses'll be all right, too. I shouldn't worry if I were you,' said Martha. 'They'll find their own feet, both of them. And if they want to spread their wings a bit you'll have to let them. I never stood in your way, did I, when you wanted to go and sing in that there Tilda's Tavern!'

'No, you didn't, Mam,' said Hetty, grinning at her mother. 'I was a proper little minx, wasn't I? But it never amounted to much – my stage career.' She laughed. 'I went and got married.'

'And no doubt that's what your two lasses'll do, when the time comes,' Martha said reassuringly. 'And what better career can there be for a woman than being married? It's what we were created for, Hetty, to look after the male of the species.' Martha got up and crossed the room to take her husband's cup and saucer from him. She laid a loving hand on his shoulder, looking at him fondly. 'And he looks after me an' all, don't you, George? Aye, I've had two good husbands, and that's a lot more than some poor women can say.'

'So have I,' said Hetty, 'but some of the girls today don't see things just like we do, Mam. They don't all want to get married. Some of them want a career of their own. Besides, haven't you thought? There's not going to be enough men to go round. It's very sad – tragic, it is – but it's true. So many of the young men – young fellows of Zachary's age – have been killed. There are going to be a lot of girls left on the shelf, I'm afraid, over the next few years.'

'Aye, you're right.' Martha shook her head ruefully. 'Unclaimed treasures, I've heard 'em called.' She gave a little chuckle, but it was a somewhat mirthless sound. 'Not that it's any laughing matter.'

'They may not look at it like that, though,' Hetty went on. 'Like I was saying, some girls today want their own career and not marriage. Our Nancy and Joyce were talking to Sarah today, after they'd been to the celebrations in Talbot Square, and they said that Sarah seemed very secretive about something or other – something to do with her job – but she wouldn't say what it was. Sarah only took on the Under Manager's job to help Edwin out during the war and she'll have to give it up when Mr Middleton comes back.'

'It's no job for a young lass anyway,' said Martha firmly, 'being in charge of a department store. Our Sarah's too gentle to boss folks around. Anyroad, you can't say that she doesn't want to get married. That lass is cut out for marriage if ever anyone was. I can just see her with three or four bairns. A real motherly sort of girl, Sarah is.'

'The husband has to come first, Mam.' Hetty nodded meaningfully. 'I only hope our Zachary feels the same way, because the girl has set her heart on him, there's no doubt about that.'

'Aye, she wears her heart on her sleeve all right,' Martha agreed. 'Why? Don't you think that Zachary...?'

'I don't know, Mam.' Hetty shook her head. 'That's what I was thinking about this morning when you mentioned Sarah. You know I'll never hear a wrong word about Zachary, but I

49

sometimes wonder if he's as keen on the idea as she is. They've been as thick as thieves ever since they were children and we've always assumed they'd make a match of it. But our Zachary can be a dreadful tease.'

'He can that,' said Martha feelingly. 'You don't need to tell me. I know he had Joyce in tears time and time again when she was a little 'un, pulling her hair and calling her a cry-baby. And I remember him putting a spider in her bed, that was when they were staying with me once. I didn't half give him what for. He never got away with much with your Nancy though. She'd give him a clout round the ear soon as look at him. Aye, I know what you mean about Sarah and Zachary. I've thought so before, but I didn't like to say anything. She's a sensitive lass.'

'I just hope he'll be kind to her, that's all,' Hetty fretted. 'She's a lovely girl, and so trusting. But I'm sure he will be. He'll have grown out of his mischievous ways while he's been in the Army. And it was just devilment, that's all it was, like all little lads get up to. His heart's in the right place, I'm sure of it. And Sarah would be so good for him…'

'But would he be good for her? That's more to the point,' said Martha drily. 'I don't want to see her get hurt.'

'Oh, he wouldn't hurt her,' said Hetty, almost too quickly. 'I've told you, Mam, all his naughty tricks were just playful, nothing else. He'll have grown up by now, you'll see.'

'Aye, so you keep telling me,' said Martha, with an eloquent glance at her daughter. 'Let's hope

50

he has.' But her tone softened as she went on speaking. 'At all events, it'll have been no picnic for him this last couple of years, poor lad. I'll bet he's seen some sights he'd sooner forget. And happen a lovely lass like Sarah'll help him to put it all behind him. And that's what we've all got to do now, to look forward…'

Hetty's thoughts were still with Zachary as she sat at her own fireside an hour later. She poked at the lumps of coal to coax what little warmth she could out of the dying embers, knowing that soon she must leave the comfort of the living room for her chilly bedroom … and her lonely bed. After two years she still missed Albert and the gnawing ache inside her seemed, at times, to get worse and not better. It had been exacerbated today, of course, by the scenes of rejoicing all around her, but she couldn't have been so churlish as to let her mother go to the service on her own. Time is a great healer, well-meaning friends had told her, but Hetty sometimes wondered if it was.

Over the years she had come to love Albert, her second husband, with a deep and enduring affection. There had never been the same passion and ecstasy that she had felt for Reuben, but her second marriage had been good, had become the bedrock of her existence and she missed Albert now far more than she could say. The cheerfulness that she assumed when she was with other people sometimes gave way, when she was alone, to feelings of grief and despondency.

But, as everyone kept reminding her, she must

try to look forward, especially to Zachary coming home. Zachary... She felt her heart surge with tenderness now, at the very thought of him, just as it had done when she had had her first glimpse of him, a tiny red-faced bundle with his father's smouldering dark eyes and black curly hair, placed in her arms by the midwife. She had adored him then as she did now. She couldn't help loving him although she had begun to realise, to her dismay, as he grew up that, though he resembled his father so much in looks, he failed to take after him in disposition. Reuben had been the kindest of men, warm-hearted and loving, with none of the deviousness of which his race, so often unjustly, were accused. Zachary, though... There was a hard, unfeeling streak in the lad which Hetty had, over the years, tried to ignore, to excuse, to deny. She had made excuses because she loved him, possibly more than he deserved, blind as so many women through the ages have been blind – or have pretended to be – to the imperfections of the beloved. And she feared that Sarah's love for her cousin was of the same intensity as her own. She prayed that the girl wouldn't get hurt; she had hinted as much to her mother tonight, something she had never done before.

Hetty, too, recalled an incident with a spider, as well as the one that had been put in poor Joyce's bed. She had caught six-year-old Zachary with a jam jar upturned over a large spider, watching the demented creature scuttling round and round in circles. Just as she opened her mouth to shout at him he lifted the jar and the spider scurried away across the table top, only to be pounced on by her son, who then proceeded to pull off its legs, one by one. Hetty loathed spiders, but that wasn't the point; it was the glee on Zachary's face that she had found hard to come to terms with. She had shouted at him, and, if she remembered rightly, given him a clout across the face; then she had quickly put the insect out of its misery and tried to forget about the incident. As she tried to forget about the kitten whose tail he had trodden on and the little lad across the road whose best marble Zachary said he had 'only borrowed'.

When it came to their own girls, though, she hadn't been able to make convincing enough excuses either to herself or to Albert. Her husband, she remembered, had given the lad a good hiding when he had splattered ink all over Joyce's drawing book, and another time when he had kicked Nancy on the shin. Nancy, though, as her mother had said, was usually well able to stand up to him. Albert's chastisement of the lad had been the cause of a bitter quarrel between Hetty and her husband, because seldom would she lay a finger on her son.

'You spoil him rotten,' Albert had told her, 'and you'll rue the day, you mark my words. You'll live to regret it if you don't take a firm line with him.'

But never could Hetty regret for one moment giving birth to Zachary, although she sometimes feared that he was taking after Reuben's cousin, Drusilla.

Hetty's thoughts had been wandering off at a tangent, as they often did when she was on her own, and now, at the thought of Drusilla, a coldness seemed to fall over the room, and over Hetty's heart as well. She gave a shudder and glanced round nervously, as though she could almost sense a malign presence there with her. That was the effect Drusilla had always had upon her, though she hadn't thought of her, not consciously, for ages. The gipsy girl, with her imperious manner, her calculating, all-seeing, all-knowing stare and her jealousy of Hetty and Reuben's love for one another had many times filled Hetty with foreboding. And Hetty had been convinced in her own mind, though she had never been able to prove it, that Drusilla had had something to do with Reuben's untimely death. It had been strange that Drusilla had disappeared the self-same day and that Hetty had heard nothing of her since that time. She had been reminded of her though, occasionally, by Zachary's roguish ways and she found herself, now, remembering the gipsy girl more acutely than she had done for years.

You're getting fanciful, she told herself. Stop all this nonsense. Make yourself a cup of tea and think of something else. It was being alone that did it, but she hadn't had the heart to tell Nancy and Joyce not to be late tonight, the night that heralded a lifetime of peace for them all. She got up from her low chair and crossed the room to switch on the electric light. She still found it difficult to believe she possessed this luxury, and its harsh radiance now flooded the room, dispelling the dark shadows. Hetty had been sitting in the semi-darkness with only the glow from the fire and the gleam of the gas lamp in the street to illuminate the room. She usually found that the gloaming was a comfort, but tonight the shadows were menacing and unfriendly.

Half an hour later she padded across the cold linoleum of her bedroom and clambered into her equally cold bed. The sheets felt chilly and she didn't dare stretch her toes to the bottom of the bed – not yet – but the feather mattress moulded itself around her ample curves and she knew that in a few moments she would begin to feel warm. One had to be thankful for small mercies.

Hetty forced her mind towards pleasant thoughts. She was looking forward to next summer and her new venture as landlady of a theatrical boarding house. It would be hard work, but a change and, above all, a challenge – and that was what she needed. Come to think of it, why wait for next year? Some theatres in Blackpool were open all year round, not just during the summer season, and theatre folk were always looking for good lodgings. She wouldn't wait till the spring; she would put an advert in the stage magazines next week...

Chapter 3

Grace Donnelly smiled contentedly to herself as she walked up Church Street towards her home on Park Road. This was in the residential part of Blackpool, an area of quiet tree-lined streets and spacious villas, away from the busy noisy town centre with its bustling shops and markets and rows and rows of boarding houses. And yet it was within walking distance, only a ten-minute walk away from Donnelly's store, at the brisk pace that Edwin always took. For this reason he had never owned a carriage; besides, the cost of horses would have been prohibitive. Grace wondered, however, if he might let himself be persuaded to buy a motorcar before long, especially now the war had come to an end. His business acquaintances were always telling him he should move with the times, but Edwin, like Grace herself, was usually quite content to take life as it came, at a nice even pace.

There were smiles on many faces this morning, as well as on Grace's, everyone still basking in the general euphoria that had swept across the nation yesterday with the announcement of the Armistice. The windows of Donnelly's store were now gay with red, white and blue garlands, and a large picture of King George and Queen Mary was prominently displayed near the doorway. Edwin had been very keen, on hearing the news of peace, to make sure that his store was as quick off the mark as his competitors, even though he had had a total hatred for war.

Yes, I think our store looks as well as any of them, thought Grace, as she peered in the windows of the shoe shops, the ironmongers, the drapers and confectioners and chemists that fringed Church Street, the main shopping street leading out of Blackpool. This was one of the main tram routes, too, heading for Marton, then taking a circular route back to the town centre. Grace could have ridden home on one of the huge 'Dreadnought' trams which could carry over a hundred passengers, but she preferred to walk if the weather was fine, as it was today.

The area where the Donnellys lived was known as the Raikes Estate, because it had once been the site of the Raikes Hall Pleasure Gardens, the vast entertainment centre that had been the focus of much of the social life in Blackpool in the last quarter of the nineteenth century. Then had come the Tower, the Big Wheel, the Winter Gardens, attractions that had proved too great for the Raikes Hall, or Royal Palace Gardens, as they were sometimes called, to withstand. They had been forced to close down, and now the site was covered with sturdy semi-detached houses of shiny red Accrington brick with impressive ball-topped gateposts and immaculate front gardens; as well as the slightly more imposing detached residences on the fringes of the estate, in one of which the Donnellys lived.

Grace regretted the demise of the Raikes Hall Gardens. She had spent many happy hours there as a young woman when they had first moved to

Blackpool. She had, she recalled, even seen Blondin the world-famous tightrope walker, perform there, but that had been before she had known Edwin.

Now, after eighteen years of marriage to Edwin Donnelly, Grace smiled because she was still so happy. At times she found it hard to believe that she lived in such a grand residence with a cook to prepare their meals and a maid to do the housework; she, Grace Turnbull as was, who had been brought up in a two-down, two-up terraced house in a cobbled street in Burnley and worked long hours at the cotton mill. But it wasn't because of her grand house and affluent lifestyle that she was happy. Grace often thought that she would be happy anywhere with Edwin, even in the same tiny house she had lived in as a child. But she didn't voice her thoughts; people didn't believe you when you talked like that, they just thought you were showing off. Grace was happy because she knew she was married to a wonderful man. She loved him now just as much as she had when they were first married, and she knew that her love was returned.

Their only disappointment had been that Grace had never borne Edwin any children, any living children, that is. In the first year of their marriage she had miscarried and this had happened again, two years later. This second time, after she had carried the child for six months, Grace had nearly died. The miscarriage had left her severely damaged internally and the doctor had told them that it would be impossible for her to bear any more children. Grace had been devastated at the news; there seemed to be no explanation, especially as she had given birth to Sarah, Walter Clayton's child, with very little difficulty. But time had healed the sadness for both of them and she knew that Edwin couldn't possibly have loved her more had she given him a dozen babies.

And Sarah meant so very much to both of them. She had grown into a lovely girl and Grace never ceased to be thankful that Edwin had taken to her right from the start. The three of them were now a self-sufficient family and Grace had long since ceased to worry, or even to think about, her former desire to bear Edwin's child.

Apart from this, she had never known one moment of unhappiness with Edwin – not since their marriage, that is, although there had been times before that when she had experienced sorrow because of him. But she never thought of those times now.

She had been working with him in his office for an hour or two this morning, helping him with the accounts and the ordering of stock, as she had done throughout the years of the war in the absence of the male heads of department. Now, with the coming of peace, Grace was ready to relinquish her position in the store as her husband's helpmate and assistant. She had never seen herself as a career woman, had never really wanted to be one, although she had been happy to do her bit, as most women had, during the difficult days of war. Marriage was Grace's true vocation, and it was to that end that she intended to put all her energies now, and to her work at the local church and with charitable organisations. She was on the committee that helped to raise money for the local hospital and another for war widows and orphans. Grace was often amused at the thought of herself as a lady of leisure, a middle-class lady, just like her mother-in-law, Clara Donnelly, concerning herself with good works and charity.

She turned in at the gate of Copper Beeches. Grace had secretly thought it somewhat ostentatious to give their house a name, but it had been Edwin's idea and she had agreed without demur as she did with most of his suggestions. It was an apt name, she thought now, admiring the huge tree which grew by the front gate, far enough away from the house to prevent it from taking the light. The tree was, by now, almost denuded of its dark reddish-brown foliage which lay in piles around the base of the trunk and over the well-tended lawn. As were the trees which grew at the end of the rear garden, another copper and two ordinary beech trees, a constant delight to Grace throughout the year with their variegated colours and welcome shade. Hard work for Mr Williams, though, she mused, eyeing the fallen leaves; for that was another luxury that the Donnellys could afford, a gardener who came twice a week to tend the lawn and the flower beds.

As Grace stepped into the hallway, through the door with its stained-glass panel, she sniffed appreciatively. It was obvious that Mrs Jolly had been hard at work, preparing the lamb casserole for a light lunch that Grace had discussed with her earlier this morning. There was no 'green baize door' here to keep the kitchen smells away from the rest of the house. Grace would have hated that; she always thought it was a constant reminder to servants that they must 'know their place', and she had never fully got used to the idea of servants. She would rather have done all the work – especially the cooking – herself, as she had been brought up to do and as her mother and sister still did, but Edwin had insisted that she should have some help.

She took off her green ankle-length coat with the fur collar and her close-fitting green hat and placed them on the hall chair. She would just go along and see how Mrs Jolly was getting on with the lunch preparations. Wednesday was half-day closing at the shop so Edwin and Sarah would both be home at lunchtime. And this morning Sarah had told Grace that she would like to have a chat with both her parents after lunch. She had some plans, she said, that she wanted to discuss with them.

'A *cook?* You're telling us you want to be a cook?' Grace's eyebrows almost disappeared under her curly fringe as she stared at her daughter. 'Good gracious, Sarah. I don't know what to say, dear, I really don't. It seems ludicrous. Most girls nowadays are dead against going into service – they'll do anything else rather than that, it seems – and there are you, actually *wanting* to do it!' She laughed and shook her head.

Sarah had decided to broach the subject of her culinary ambitions to her parents that very

61

afternoon and the three of them, having finished their lunch, were sitting in the drawing room.

Sarah laughed too, knowing that her mother was laughing not at her, but with her. Mother would always listen, would sympathise and give advice and would never, never ridicule her or pour scorn on her ideas. 'Yes, I know it sounds mad, Mother,' she said, 'but you know how much I enjoy cooking and I'm good at it, too – you must admit that I am – and I feel that I'd like to try to do something in that line for a living, instead of just as a hobby.

'I don't mean like Mrs Jolly does,' Sarah went on hastily. 'I think even you would object, wouldn't you, Mother, to me becoming a household cook. Not that there's any shame in it,' she added, 'but it wasn't quite what I had in mind. Let me try to explain…'

Sarah had begun by telling her parents that although she was willing to carry on with her office job at the store for the time being, until Mr Middleton came back, what she had in mind for the future was something quite different. She was aware that some of her ideas might be somewhat startling to her parents, which was why she didn't quite know how to begin, how best to explain her tentative plans. And so she had blurted it out impulsively: 'What I would really like more than anything else, is to try my hand at cooking.'

Even as she said it, Sarah knew that it wasn't, in fact, what she wanted 'more than anything'. What she wanted, more than anything, was Zachary. But Zachary was still far away in France and Sarah knew that, until such time as the two of them could be married, she had to have some sort of employment, and cooking was the thing that she enjoyed most of all.

The plans she had in mind were concerned with Donnelly's store. She turned to her father. 'I was wondering if we could develop the tearoom on the top floor. It's quite a popular place, isn't it? And it used to be even more popular before the war, when Gran used to do the baking for it. I'm sure it could be again, once things start getting more plentiful. That was why Gran stopped baking, wasn't it, because she couldn't get the ingredients.'

'Yes, it was,' Edwin agreed, 'and also because she'd done it for so many years and I think she was getting a little tired. Not that she would admit it, mind you, but it was becoming a bit too much for her, running the boarding house *and* baking for Donnelly's as well. And it's never been the same, I can tell you, since she gave it up.'

Martha Makepeace had supplied Donnelly's tearoom, ever since the late 1890s until the early years of the war, with her delicious homemade cakes – Eccles cakes, feather-light sponges, parkin, Dundee cake, almond tarts, to name but a few – for which she had once been renowned on Burnley market. And Sarah knew, as her father had just said, that the tearoom had never been quite the same since she had finished. It wasn't just the shortage of ingredients, although that, admittedly, had played its part. The women who had done the baking since had not had Martha's flair. Donnelly's tearoom had continued to thrive throughout the war years more because of the pleasant surroundings and the friendly service than because of the quality of its food.

And Sarah knew that this could be improved upon. 'I wondered if I could take over the baking,' she said. 'You've never had anyone really reliable, have you, since Gran finished? And I know I could do it, perhaps not as well as Gran, but I'm quite good.'

Edwin looked puzzled. 'Do the baking at home, you mean, like Grace's mother used to do, and then have it collected by the vans? I suppose so...' He pressed the tips of his fingers together, looking at them contemplatively. 'Where would you work, though? Mrs Jolly might not want you messing about in her kitchen.'

'Hardly messing about, father.'

'No ... no, I didn't mean that. I put it badly. But Mrs Jolly's very busy, you know, cooking for us. It's a full-time job and I can't see that there'd be room for the two of you.' He smiled. 'You know what they always say about two women in one kitchen.'

'Yes, I know it's difficult.' Sarah frowned slightly. 'I thought that maybe I could work in the evening, when Mrs Jolly's finished for the day, then I wouldn't be in her way. She usually finishes washing up about half-past seven, so I would have plenty of time then.'

The Donnellys dined early, because Grace liked to ensure that Mrs Jolly had as much time to herself as possible. Some of Grace's acquaintances on the various committees on which she served, had endless trouble trying to find and hold on to a decent cook. They were forever

64

complaining about the succession of unsuitable women who passed through their kitchens, a problem that Grace didn't have. But Sarah knew that that was because her mother was an unusually kind-hearted and considerate employer who wasn't above putting on her own apron and giving a helping hand when it was needed. Just as Sarah had been encouraged to do since she was old enough to help.

It was from Mrs Jolly, as well as from her grandmother, Martha Makepeace, that Sarah had acquired her love of cooking. It had always been a delight to her, as a tiny girl, to stand by the huge scrubbed pine table and watch Mrs Jolly at work. In her starched white apron and cap, the rosy-cheeked cook rolled out pastry for apple pies, or stirred a dark brown mixture for Christmas puddings and cakes, or wiped the tears from her merry blue eyes as she skinned onions ready for pickling.

'Now, don't get in Mrs Jolly's way,' her mother used to say. 'She's quite enough to do without having to see to you as well.'

But to Mrs Jolly Sarah had never been a nuisance. When she was only four or five she was making her own gingerbread men with currants for eyes and candied peel for a nose and mouth, helping to shell peas and top and tail gooseberries, and making a special wish as she stirred the fragrant fruity mincemeat in the massive brown bowl. As she grew older she had progressed to Victoria sponges, scones, custard tarts and maids of honour, and the cakes and pastries that graced the tea table on a Sunday afternoon, when Mrs Jolly was having a well-earned rest, were often of Sarah's making.

Sarah could see, however, that helping out occasionally and making a few cakes for a family tea was a very different thing from the large-scale baking that she would have to undertake to supply Donnelly's tearoom.

'I would have a few hours each evening when the kitchen is free,' Sarah went on now. 'And then there's Mrs Jolly's half-day, when we usually "make-do" for our meal. I could make good use of that time.'

'But you're not going to have any time to go out with your friends, dear, if you're working in the evenings,' Grace protested. She was looking concernedly at her daughter. 'And what about the daytime? Have you thought what you'll do then? I can see it's a good idea about the baking and I know you'd do it very well, but your working hours would be all upside-down, wouldn't they?'

'You know I don't go out very much in the evenings, Mother,' said Sarah. 'I'm not much of a one for gadding about. I've hardly been out at all since … for the last year or two.' She had been going to say, 'since Zachary joined up', but decided not to. She sometimes noticed a tiny flicker of unease cross her mother's face when she mentioned her cousin and she didn't want to talk about Zachary now. 'And I intend to keep myself busy during the day as well,' she continued. 'I thought I could lend a hand in the tearoom. I could act as supervisor, if you think it's a good idea, Father. There's never really been anyone in charge, has there? Just a woman to see to the tea and coffee, and a waitress.'

'It's all that's been necessary, Sarah, and we've had to cut down on staff lately, as you know. But if you think it warrants it, yes, I'm quite willing for you to take charge of the tearoom. And I can see we may well have a lot more customers before long when the news gets round that none other than Sarah Donnelly herself is doing the baking.'

Sarah felt that her father was humouring her, even patronising her slightly; she could see a twinkle in his golden-brown eyes. She didn't want to be indulged, as though her ideas were just a childish whim to be treated with amusement.

'I can see difficulties, though, with the kitchen arrangements,' Edwin continued. 'Like your mother, I don't really like the idea of you working in the evenings. I know you don't go out a great deal, but there may come a time when you would want to?' He looked at her quizzically. 'It would be far better for you to do the baking during the day, if we could come to some arrangement. But I can't quite see how...'

Her father was playing right into her hands. Sarah had been wondering how to introduce the other ideas she had about Donnelly's tearoom. Now he had given her an opening.

'I told you I'd like to develop the tearoom,' she said, 'and I don't just mean by selling more cakes and pastries. I wondered...' She took a deep breath. 'I wondered if it would be possible to do the baking on the premises, eventually, I mean. If we were to make a kitchen up on the top floor, then I'd be able to work during the day. We could extend the area where they make the tea and coffee. It's only a little cubbyhole at the moment, but it could be made into a proper kitchen, with a storeroom and a cooker and a much bigger sink for washing up. And then we might be able to be a bit more adventurous than just serving cakes and scones. We could serve proper midday meals, and afternoon teas and–'

'Hold on a minute.' Edwin held up his head, breaking into Sarah's excited talk. He was smiling, though. 'You're going too fast for me. What you're suggesting, as far as I can see, would be a restaurant – a full-scale restaurant – not a tearoom. I'm not sure that Donnelly's could cope with that.'

'I could cope with it, Father – I know I could. Not on my own, of course. I'd have to have one or two staff working with me in the kitchen, preparing the vegetables and doing the washing up and all that. But I could be responsible for planning the menus and for most of the actual cooking.' There was a moment's silence as both her parents stared at her. 'I know I could do it...' Sarah's voice petered out uncertainly, not because she was doubtful of her own capabilities, but because of her parents' reaction.

Edwin shook his head confusedly. 'I don't know, Sarah. I really don't know. If – and I only say *if* – we were to make a kitchen up there on the top floor, then the seating area would have to be enlarged as well. And that would mean taking some of the space that the household department occupies.' He rubbed his chin contemplatively. 'It's certainly a startling idea, but I can't help wondering if it's too startling. There are already several restaurants in Blackpool which cater so well in that direction. There's Jenkinson's in Talbot Square, for instance, and that's only a stone's throw from our store. Donnelly's has always been a department store and I've never visualised it being anything else but that. It would need careful consideration.' He turned to his wife. 'What do you think, Grace?'

'I think it's a good idea for Sarah to do something she really wants to do,' replied Grace. 'And I can see she's heart and soul behind this idea of baking for Donnelly's. I'm not quite so sure about the meals, though. Three-course lunches, I daresay you have in mind, hadn't you, Sarah? Soup, and roast meat and two veg, and a pudding to follow – that sort of thing?'

Sarah nodded. 'Good old-fashioned Lancashire cooking to start with, that the folks round here like. They don't go in much for fancy stuff, do they? But perhaps after a while we could be a bit more adventurous...'

Grace laughed. 'Not so fast, Sarah. You're wanting to run before you can walk. As I was saying, I like the idea of you baking for us. It was very clever of you to think of it. Your father would have found you a place somewhere in the store when Mr Middleton takes over his old job, so it's far better for you to do something you're really keen on. But I don't know about the three-course meals – not yet. Let's take one step at a time, shall we? We can perhaps compromise a little.' She turned to her husband. 'Maybe we could make a larger kitchen area, like Sarah has suggested, then she could do most of the preparations there. And we could start by serving more substantial afternoon teas – a range of sandwiches, perhaps, as well as cakes and scones – then just see how it goes. I could even go in and lend a hand myself. I'd like that, Edwin. I've always had a soft spot for the tearoom. Of course you know that, don't you, dear?'

Sarah noticed her mother and father exchange what she termed to herself as one of their 'soppy' looks. It was something they quite often did and it rendered them oblivious, for the moment, to their surroundings, to Sarah – to anything, in fact, but one another. It was a piece of family lore how Grace and Hetty Turnbull, visiting Blackpool in the spring of 1895, had gone into Donnelly's tearoom to partake of morning coffee and how Edwin Donnelly, the owner's son, had seen them there and promptly fallen in love with the elder girl. It had been Hetty who had been the most alluring, the pretty and provocative one, Grace had always hastened to add, but Grace's quiet charm and her air of serenity had captivated Edwin. There had been several ups and downs, however, Sarah gathered, before the two of them had finally married.

Aunt Hetty must have been a good deal slimmer than she is now, Sarah thought amusedly, recalling the frequently recounted incident. Her mother and father, though, were probably very little changed since that day over twenty-three years ago. Edwin was still a handsome fellow – Sarah could quite understand why her mother had fallen for him – with his golden-brown hair,

70

now flecked here and there with grey, that flopped over his brow, and his thin, almost gaunt features which gave him a very appealing ascetic air. His long-limbed handsomeness was accentuated by the pin-stripe trousers and morning coat which he always wore in the store and which he hadn't yet changed out of.

The looks that he and Grace were exchanging now were of perfect understanding and Sarah, for a brief moment, felt a flicker of jealousy. If only Zachary would look at her in that way… But he would – she knew he would – when he came home and they got to know one another again. It had seemed such a long time and Sarah had to think very hard to recapture in her mind the glances that had passed between them. She remembered the desire in his black eyes … but that had only been that one time, just before he had gone overseas. At other times there had been impishness in his glance – Zachary could be a terrible tease – and friendliness and wayward charm, and a boldness that she knew others thought of as insolence. But had she ever seen love there, such as she had seen in the way her father looked at her mother? Zachary did love her, Sarah was sure of that; why else would he have asked her to marry him, not once, but twice? Sarah liked to hug the remembrance of those words closely to herself. She hadn't told another soul about Zachary's proposals of marriage, although she knew that some members of their family assumed that the two of them would marry one day; they had been inseparable ever since they were children.

'Yes, I think that's the best idea, Grace,' her father was saying now. 'Sarah shall have her kitchen at one end of the tearoom. I'll make arrangements for that as soon as I can, then we'll see how things go. Will that do for you, Sarah?'

'Yes, Father. Thank you very much.'

'Maybe by the time it is ready to be used Charlie Middleton will be back home again, then you'll be able to move in there and start your baking.'

'How long do you think it is likely to be before he … before the men are back?' Sarah asked. She wasn't really thinking of Mr Middleton, though, and obviously, from the understanding look that he gave her, her father knew that.

'Who can tell?' Edwin gave a slight shrug. 'Charlie was one of the lucky ones. He never had to go overseas. He's somewhere up in Scotland as far as I know, so he may be home fairly soon. But as for the ones who are serving abroad – I suppose it could take several months.'

'Months?' repeated Sarah, feeling her face drop. 'As long as that? He … they won't be home by Christmas, then?'

'I very much doubt it.' Edwin smiled sympathetically. 'Never mind, my dear. The fighting's over and that's the important thing. At least we know that our boys are out of danger now. And there's so much for us all to look forward to – so very much.'

'Yes.' Sarah nodded resignedly. 'If you're agreeable I'll start my baking straight away, in the kitchen here, like I suggested. I won't wait for the one at the store to be ready. You know what Gran

72

always says: "Never put off until tomorrow..."'

'Yes, all right, dear.' Grace's smile was full of encouragement. 'You know your father and I will do our best to support you as much as we can in what you want to do. We've always tried to do that in the past.'

But would they always support her in the future, Sarah wondered to herself – not, at that moment, thinking of her culinary aspirations. As far as Donnelly's tearoom was concerned, so far, so good. If she were honest with herself, Sarah acknowledged that she hadn't really expected to get any further than this today. It was quite encouraging that she had already got the promise of a kitchen to work in and permission to use the one at home in the meantime. Father and Mother, though they tried to move with the times, couldn't be expected to be as modern in their ideas as were the up and coming generation; herself and her cousins, Nancy, Joyce ... and Zachary.

Sarah glanced round the drawing room where they were sitting. Her mother was the most unpretentious of women, but if Grace could be said to have any pride at all then it was in her drawing room, the room that she had furnished to her own taste soon after they moved into the house. It was, Sarah thought, as different as it could be from Grandma Makepeace's over-furnished parlour, or from the shabby, but comfortable, living room where Aunt Hetty usually entertained. It was an elegant room with a spacious feel to it – absent were the knick-knacks and ornaments and clutter beloved of the women of Grandma's generation – with pale green walls and a white ceiling with the plasterwork delicately picked out in gold. The oak floor, which showed beyond the edges of the plain, floral-bordered carpet, gleamed with constant polishing, as did the walnut piano which Grace occasionally played, and the corner cabinet where she kept her best china. The only ornaments displayed on the Adam fireplace were a pair of Chelsea birds – brightly coloured bullfinches – and a porcelain mantel clock decorated with flowers. Grace was sitting on the gold brocaded chaise longue, an article of furniture intended for reclining – but it was very seldom that Grace did that – while Sarah and her father sat on the matching armchairs. The only really modern article in the room was the gramophone, one of the very newest models with the horn, hidden away in its walnut cabinet. The older one, with its nickel-plated flower horn that the Donnellys had bought about ten years ago, had now found its way into Sarah's bedroom.

'People are always telling me I must move with the times,' said Edwin now, smiling. 'It looks as though I shall have to stop being such an old fogey, doesn't it?'

'No one could ever accuse you of that, Father,' said Sarah kindly. 'I suppose it's true, though, that you'll have to keep well-informed about modern business trends if you want Donnelly's to hold its own. After all, we'll be in the 1920s soon.'

'Donnelly's will do all right,' said Edwin, nodding confidently.

'Of course it will, dear,' said Grace, adding her support to his remark as she always did. 'It looks as though there are going to be changes all round, from what I hear. Our Hetty was telling me the other day that she had some plans of her own for the boarding house. Nancy hasn't said anything to you, has she, Sarah?'

'No, Mother, she hasn't mentioned anything,' replied Sarah. 'What sort of plans?'

'Oh, something about taking pros in – you know, theatrical people – instead of ordinary holidaymakers. Obviously she hasn't discussed it with Nancy yet, so you'd better keep it under your hat, dear, till she knows about it.'

'Mmm... Sounds interesting,' said Sarah. 'And if I know Nancy it'll be just up her street. She's always in Sharples' Music Shop looking at the latest song-sheets, and she can't keep away from the song-booths. It would be strange, wouldn't it, if she wanted to go on the stage, like Aunt Hetty did?'

Grace gave a knowing smile. 'The same thought struck me. I wondered if history might well repeat itself, especially when I heard Hetty's idea about the stage folk. And do you know, I don't think it has occurred to our Hetty at all. Now, dear,' Grace leaned forward eagerly. 'Tell your father and me about some of the things you'd like to bake for Donnelly's. I'm sure you must be bursting with ideas...'

Chapter 4

The folks who come to Blackpool certainly know how to enjoy themselves, thought Nancy Gregson as she walked along the promenade arm in arm with her sister, Joyce. She often thought how lucky she was to be able to live in Blackpool all the time instead of only visiting the place once a year like the holidaymakers did. It wasn't very often that she and Joyce went out together, but it was such a glorious afternoon that even her industrious sister had been persuaded to put aside the job of work she was doing for Gran and come for a walk on the prom. Nancy had been surprised, when she went across the road to Welcome Rest, to find her sister knee-deep in sewing, or so it had seemed to Nancy.

'Thursday is supposed to be your half-day, like it's mine,' Nancy had told her. 'For heaven's sake, put those rotten old pillow-cases away and come out with me.' She turned to her grandmother. 'You're a proper old slave-driver, Gran,' she chided, with a twinkle in her eye.

'We'll have less of your cheek, young woman … and less of the "old" an' all,' Martha replied, grinning at Nancy. 'You're right, though, Nancy love. I've just been telling Joyce to put that sewing away and go and get some fresh air into her lungs. The sewing'll keep for another time.'

Joyce carefully cut the thread with her tiny

76

scissors and put the needle back in the quilted top of the work-box. Then she folded the pillowslip neatly and put it on top of the pile of several others. She was adding lace to the edges of plain cambric pillow-cases, a touch of luxury that Martha thought her guests would appreciate now that the days of austerity were officially over. 'I like to complete a job once I've started it and I've only a couple more to do now,' Joyce said. 'I wanted to finish them before I went out, but it'll do tomorrow. To what do we owe the honour of your company, anyway?' She raised her eyebrows with a certain amusement. 'You usually go out with Sarah on your half-day, don't you?'

'Sometimes.' Nancy shrugged. 'But it seems as though Sarah's too busy these days in her new kitchen to be bothered with half-days and such like. She's dashing around like somebody demented. I've told her she'll wear herself to a shadow if she doesn't watch out.'

'It's doing well, though, the tearoom at Donnelly's, now it's been extended,' Martha commented. 'I popped in the other day for a cup of tea and an Eccles cake, something I very rarely do, mind you, but I wanted to see how our Sarah was shaping up. Like you say, Nancy, she was hopping up and down like a flea on a flitting, but she's making a go of it, I'll say that for her. And I couldn't have made that Eccles cake any better myself.' Nancy knew that from her grandma that was praise indeed.

'So you thought you'd make do with me, eh, seeing that you can't have Sarah.' But Joyce smiled good-naturedly. 'It's a good job I know you, our Nancy.'

'It was Mam's idea really, that I should come and ask you,' said Nancy, unaware that she might be adding insult to injury. 'She said I'd to make sure you took a bit of time off and got out into the fresh air.'

'All right then,' said Joyce. 'I know when I'm beaten. Where are you thinking of going – round the shops? Or shall we have a walk on the cliffs towards Bispham?'

'Too quiet up there,' said Nancy dismissively. 'I like to see a bit of life. I thought we might go the other way … past the Tower and along Central Beach,' she added with an air of nonchalance.

'Oh yes, I see,' said Joyce, a knowing little smile curving her lips. 'I wonder why? It couldn't be anything to do with a certain Mr Barney Bellamy, could it?'

'Who told you?' Nancy's chin tilted aggressively. 'I mean … what on earth are you talking about? I only said I wanted to walk along Central Beach. I didn't say anything about… Who told you, anyway?'

'It was Sarah,' Joyce admitted. 'You were telling her about it, weren't you?'

'And she went and told you! So now the whole world knows,' said Nancy with an exaggerated sigh. 'I would have thought that Sarah would have had a bit more sense than to go blabbing about everything I do. I shall know to keep my mouth shut in future. I'm surprised at Sarah. You can usually trust her with a secret – not that there *is* any secret,' she added hastily.

'What are you bothering about then?' said Joyce

78

laughing. 'Oh, come on, Nancy. Don't be so huffy. Sarah only told me there was a new song-booth opened along Central Beach and that you'd been there a time or two. And she mentioned the fellow's name because it sounds so funny. Barney Bellamy. You must admit it's a comical name.'

'I don't see anything funny about it.' Nancy was feeling peeved. She had been looking forward to going along this afternoon and seeing Barney again. He might give her one of his dazzling smiles, like he had done last week. It had been her secret... Now Joyce had found out about it and was laughing at her and it was all spoiled. She pouted at Joyce, but when she saw her sister's clear grey eyes looking back at her she knew she couldn't really be cross with her. It wouldn't do any harm to pretend to be cross though.

'I'm sorry,' said Joyce, simply. 'We weren't really talking about you. I know it must seem like it, though.'

'Forget it,' said Nancy, shrugging her shoulders. 'It doesn't matter.'

'Don't pull your face like that, Nancy, it'll freeze,' put in Martha sharply. 'And who the heck's Mr Barmy Bellamy when he's at home?'

The girls looked at one another and burst out laughing.

'Barney, Grandma, *not* Barmy,' tittered Joyce.

'He's a man who runs a song-booth on Central Beach,' explained Nancy.

'Well, he's got a right barmy name and no mistake, whoever he is,' said Martha. She picked up the pile of pillow-cases that Joyce had finished. 'Come on, the pair of you, or you'll have it dark.

You'd best make the most of your freedom while you can. In another few weeks we'll all be rushed off our feet, so off you go and enjoy yourselves.'

Nancy certainly intended to do that. Her anticipation and excitement grew as they walked southwards along the promenade. Soon they would be there...

It was a glorious afternoon in mid-May and, as Gran had said, in just a few weeks' time Blackpool would be bursting at the seams with holidaymakers. If this sort of weather continued they could very well be packed out for Whit Week. Hetty's idea of taking in 'pros' had meant that there was not as much room for the ordinary visitors, but several 'regulars' had made a firm booking before they completed their last year's holiday: many visitors did, returning year after year to the same 'digs'.

'It must be like one long holiday living here,' one of the visitors had once remarked to Nancy. And there was some truth in that, Nancy thought now, glancing across the tramtrack at the afternoon sun glinting on the sea and the crowds of holiday-makers thronging the sands. The tide was far out today and the visitors had congregated, like sheep, as they always did, on the stretch of beach between North Pier and Central Pier. Come mid-July or August, you wouldn't be able to put a pin between them. If only they were to move further north or further south then they would have loads of room to spread out; it must be the herd instinct, Nancy supposed, that made them always want to cram together like sardines in a tin.

There was, indeed, no place on earth like

Blackpool and Nancy couldn't imagine living anywhere else. She captured the holiday feeling every time she walked on the prom. All the same, it was blooming hard work in a boarding house. Up every morning before six; breakfasts to cook, as well as dinners and high teas; beds to change; furniture to polish; bathrooms and lavs to clean; shopping to be done – every day – to ensure that the produce was fresh... The list of jobs was endless. Not that Nancy did it all herself, of course not. She doubted that there was a landlady in the whole of Blackpool who worked harder than Hetty did, unless it was her gran across the road. During the height of the season, which would be upon them in a few weeks' time, they employed a couple of girls from the mill towns – from Burnley or Bolton or Blackburn – to help with the heavy work and to serve in the dining room. This was the job that Nancy liked best, waiting at the tables and chatting with the guests, although she could turn her hand to anything, like all daughters who had been brought up in the boarding-house business.

Nancy suspected that before long they would really have their work cut out, when the 'pros' arrived at the beginning of June. Hetty's idea had got off to a somewhat hesitant start. She had had a few bookings from theatrical folk throughout the winter and spring, which had kept them ticking over nicely; artistes who were doing a week at the Palace Varieties or at Feldman's Theatre near Central Station. But in June she had a whole troupe – nine or ten of them – who had booked in for the entire season. They had a three-month contract for a summer show on the North Pier. Nancy thought it would be exciting seeing them in such close proximity and getting to know them. Even cooking meals for them at all hours of the day or night, which was what her gran said it would entail, would, she thought, hold a certain glamour.

Nancy and Joyce crossed the wide expanse of road by the Palatine Hotel, on to Central Beach, the stretch of promenade that was usually called the 'Golden Mile'. The sideshows, oyster stalls, itinerant hawkers and musicians that thronged the area had, years ago, in the 1890s, plied their trade on the stretch of sands opposite. There had been, as her Grandma Makepeace had told her, 'no end of argy bargy' because the Central Beach landladies feared that the tone of the place was being lowered and that the 'better class' type of visitor would no longer feel inclined to come to Blackpool. In 1897 the Corporation did, at last, succeed in clearing the beach of the most disreputable of the quacks and charlatans, but the appetite of the ordinary visitors to Blackpool, for stalls and sideshows and amusements, remained. All that happened, in effect, was that the beach traders, banned from the sands, moved themselves across the road to the front gardens of the Central Beach houses. And there they had stayed, blocking the view of the Irish Sea, attracting the 'common herd' and irritating the less accommodating neighbours. There was little, however, that anyone could do about it. The Golden Mile, as it had come to be called, was here to stay.

Vulgar and coarse as it may have been, and many of the North Shore landladies from the posher end of the town deemed it to be so, the area had always held a fascination for Nancy. Less so for Joyce, but she had come along to please her sister, as she invariably did. Nancy held her head high sniffing the mixed aroma of fish and chips, vinegared shrimps, oysters, strongly brewed tea, mint rock and – less appealing – the scent from bodies pressing close to her, for this stretch was always crowded. Not only were her nostrils assailed, but her eyes and ears as well, by the riot of colour and the clamour and confusion all around her. Palmists' booths; racks of saucy postcards; amusement arcades with their penny slot and What-the-Butler-Saw machines; rock stalls, fish stalls, tea stalls, and sideshows with startlingly lurid posters and raucous showmen inviting you to step inside. You could be titillated by the sight of the Plate-lipped Savages from Darkest Africa; Jolly Alice, the Fattest Woman in the world; giant rats; giraffe-necked women; men with no arms … if you were so inclined – but Nancy, who was somewhat squeamish about such things, was not.

Her consuming interest at the present time was in the song-booth run by Mr Barney Bellamy, and she had her ears strained now for the sound of the tinkling piano and the voices of holiday-makers raised in song, with Barney's rising lustily above them all. She hardly dared to look as they approached, staring instead around her with an air of nonchalance, pretending an interest in the donkeys on the sands or the Punch and Judy show. Then she felt Joyce nudging her. 'Is that him?' she asked. 'Is that Barney Bellamy?'

So Nancy looked. 'Yes, that's him,' she said casually, though her pulse had quickened and she felt her heart thumping against her ribcage. 'Let's go and join in, shall we? It's ever such good fun.'

There he was, swinging his cane, in his red and white striped blazer and his straw boater at a jaunty angle over his sleek black hair. He was leading the singing, prancing up and down in front of the crowd while his assistant, a similarly dressed young man, though not possessed of the same vivacity, was turning over the pages of a massive book suspended from a stand so that the onlookers could read the words. It was a rather silly song – many of them were – about Kissing Pretty Katy in the Kitchen, but the crowd was joining in heartily with the chorus. There was sometimes a girl there as well, in a red and white striped dress, who sang the more plaintive numbers – Nancy liked those best – but she didn't seem to be there today. The idea, of course, was to sell the sheet music which was displayed all round the walls of the booth, racks and racks of it.

They had finished that song now and Barney was coming round thrusting the sheets of music under the noses of the crowd, many of whom, on being asked to part with their money, were drifting away.

'Come along, ladies and gentlemen, "Katy in the Kitchen", only threepence a copy. Two for a tanner. "Katy in the Kitchen" and "Love Me Just a Little", both for sixpence. Now, I can't say fairer than that, can I? Two for the lady over there… Thank you, madam.'

He hadn't noticed her yet. There was quite a crush round the upright piano, but Nancy pushed forward, dragging her uncomplaining sister with her as she tried to get a place nearer the front.

'This one sounds nice. Much more my cup of tea,' she whispered to Joyce as the pianist started to play a lyrical melody. He certainly knew how to coax music from the yellowing ivory keys – the piano had seen much better days – did this third member of the team, similarly dressed in striped blazer, natty bow tie and straw boater.

Barney's assistant had turned over the pages of the giant book and was now pointing with his cane to the words of the new number, while Barney himself was singing the song in his somewhat nasal tenor voice.

'A pretty girl is like a melody, that haunts you night and day…' he sang, mouthing the words exaggeratedly and rolling his eyes expressively at the crowd. 'Come along, ladies and gentlemen,' he admonished when he came to the end of the song, 'sing up! You're not trying at all.'

'How can we? We don't know t'tune properly yet,' argued an amused voice from the crowd.

'Aye, sing it again, Barney lad. It's the first time we've heard it…'

'But it won't be the last, I can assure you.' Barney waggled his cane vehemently in their direction. 'One of Mr Irving Berlin's, this is. From *The Ziegfeld Follies*. All right, Charlie. One more time, *if* you please! A pretty girl…'

This time Nancy joined in, her sweet clear voice

contrasting oddly with the more raucous tones of the folk around her. A few people turned to smile at her and Nancy smiled back disarmingly.

'...A pretty girl is just like a pretty tune.' She sighed contentedly as they came to the end of the number. 'Nice, isn't it? Lovely words and a lovely tune, too. But I must admit it might sound better if we could hear Chloe sing it. That's the girl who's usually here,' she added. 'She sings ever so nicely. Of course, I know it's really a man's song, with it being about a pretty girl and all that, but I didn't feel that Barney got the best out of it.'

'I'm surprised to hear you say that.' Joyce grinned at her. 'I thought he was the bee's knees as far as you were concerned.'

'Oh, he's good. You've got to admit he's good.' Nancy gave a satisfied nod. 'But he's much better with the humorous numbers – you know, like that Katy thing he just sang. He's a real scream at times, I can tell you. But Chloe would have got that last one over real well. I wonder where she is?'

'Perhaps that's your answer. She must have left.' Joyce pointed towards a notice, untidily scrawled in pen and ink, that was pinned to the wall near them. *Wanted, young lady vocalist,* it read. *A few hours a week. Good pay. See Mr Barney Bellamy.*

'Oh, I see.' Nancy was thoughtful. 'I wonder where she's gone? Perhaps she's got another job.'

'It's not really any of our business, is it?' Joyce replied. 'Shhh … I think they're going to sing it again. Come on, Nancy, let's be hearing you. I hope you've had your birdseed?'

And this time Barney did notice her, looking in her direction and giving her a beaming smile and a saucy wink. Nancy fumbled in her handbag at the close of the number, taking out her purse and searching for a tiny silver coin.

'What are you doing?' hissed Joyce. 'You're not going to buy a copy, are you?'

'Of course I am. Why shouldn't I? 'Tisn't fair, anyway, to come along and enjoy ourselves and then not buy the music.'

'You've not bought any the other times you've been here, have you?'

'No, but I'm going to today.' Nancy shut her handbag with a decisive click.

'Why? What would you do with it? You've never learned to play the piano.'

'No, but I can sing the words. And we've got a piano, haven't we, for the visitors to play? And Mam can pick out a tune with one finger, and so can I, after a fashion. Anyway, I'm buying it and that's that. Actually, I wanted to ask him something,' Nancy added slowly. 'And I can't very well ask him, can I, if I don't buy his music.'

'What do you want to ask him?' Joyce was looking at her suspiciously.

'About that, there.' Nancy nodded in the direction of the notice. 'I wanted to ask him if he'd consider me. As his lady vocalist.'

'*You?*' Joyce stared at her in disbelief.

'Yes ... me. Why not?' Nancy stuck out her chin aggressively. 'Come on, why not?'

But Joyce looked too dumbstruck to answer.

Joyce stayed close by Nancy's side – not too

close, but close enough to hear what was going on – while she talked with Barney Bellamy. There was a lull in the proceedings after the Pretty Girl song, and most of the crowd drifted away so Nancy was able to chat quite freely to him.

He was forty, if he was a day, Joyce thought, as she observed him, trying to make her scrutiny as unobtrusive as possible. Prominent blue eyes which he used to great effect to attract a crowd, sleek black hair combed sideways beneath the brim of his straw boater, dazzlingly white teeth – so white that they surely couldn't be his own? – that he displayed frequently in a flashing smile, and lips that were just a shade too red. The fellow had a certain charisma and assuredly knew his business, but what on earth did Nancy see in him? To start with, he was old enough to be her father and he seemed so ... so false, somehow, so phoney. But Joyce knew that she mustn't make rash judgements. The fellow might be quite all right really. He was talking very politely to Nancy, his head on one side, listening to her and asking questions.

'So you think you'd like to come and sing for us, do you? Well, I'm quite willing to give you a try. An audition first of all, of course. But I've heard you singing in the crowd and you've a very nice little voice. I say little because your voice isn't too strong, is it? But very clear. Very sweet and clear. Have you had any experience?'

'I've sung at chapel concerts,' said Nancy. 'And I sing at home sometimes for the visitors. We have a boarding house,' she explained.

'Very good training, chapel concerts. I thought

88

the pair of you might be visitors when I saw you there in the crowd. But, come to think of it, you've been here before, haven't you?' Nancy nodded. 'Yes, I always remember a face, especially one as pretty as yours.' Barney rolled his eyes and Nancy flushed slightly and lowered hers. 'And what about your friend here?' Barney raised his eyebrows at Joyce. 'You don't fancy yourself as a vocalist? A bit too shy, perhaps.'

'No, I'm not shy,' Joyce answered confidently. She wasn't at all shy. 'But I'm not a singer. Nancy's the singer and I've just come along with her. She's my sister, by the way, not my friend.'

'Not your friend? Tch, tch, tch! What a thing to say! It's to be hoped she's your friend as well as your sister, isn't it?' Barney's over effusive manner was getting on Joyce's nerves and she found herself answering more sharply than she'd intended.

'Of course she is! And I want to make sure she doesn't do anything silly.' She tried to give Nancy a meaningful glance, but Nancy wasn't looking.

'I'm sure she won't do anything silly.' Barney turned away from Joyce. 'Now, young lady – Nancy, isn't it? – how would it be if you come along when we're nice and quiet, early tomorrow afternoon, perhaps, and sing a couple of songs for me. Then I can see how you're going to shape up. You won't be nervous, will you, singing in front of all these people? Can't do with any modest violets here, you know.'

Nancy shook her head.

'No? That's fine then. Now, tell me, always supposing we took you on, what hours could you work?'

Joyce wandered away while the two of them were talking. She had heard enough and was beginning to feel very irritated with her sister. And what on earth was Mam going to say about it all? Obviously Nancy hadn't given any thought to that. Joyce pretended to study the sheets of music in the racks, watching them surreptitiously from time to time through the mirror on the back wall, strategically placed to make the booth appear larger. Nancy was pretty, there was no doubt about that, and would definitely be a crowd-puller, provided she could make herself heard. She was looking up coyly at Barney now, her green eyes alight with enthusiasm. Her auburn hair, worn rather longer than was fashionable at the moment, curled charmingly beneath the brim of her round straw hat. Neither of the sisters had had their hair cut yet in the modern style, although Joyce sometimes wondered about her own tiresome locks, straight and refusing to curl. She stole a glance at herself now, viewing with resignation her mid-brown hair, falling like a curtain on either side of her square-shaped face, and speculated briefly on whether she should have it lopped off. Then she looked away again hurriedly. There were other more important matters to think about at the moment, like Nancy and this dratted Barney fellow.

The whole idea was ludicrous, of course, and Mam was sure to think so when she heard about it. And what on earth could Nancy see in such a phoney as he was? Joyce knew, in all fairness, that her sister hadn't had much experience of men, that she hadn't, therefore, anyone with whom to compare Mr Barney Bellamy. What chance had any of them had, for the last five years, to learn anything about the opposite sex? Joyce herself, of course, had been too young. She was still only seventeen, but Nancy at nineteen would most likely, if it had been a normal world, have had a young man or two by now. As it was, the only men they had met had been the ones, at chapel mostly, who were too old to join up or the young lads who were too young. All the young men of Nancy's age had been away serving King and Country and many of them, like Father, would never be coming back.

Zachary would be home next week though, all being well; and that should bring a smile back to their mother's face, Joyce reflected ruefully. Both she and Nancy paled into insignificance in Mam's eyes when Zachary was around: it had always been so. Still, it would be good to see her brother again and maybe Mam would be so delighted to have her family complete again – well, almost complete – that she would just smile approvingly on Nancy's crazy idea. Joyce hoped, for all their sakes, that it would be so. Nancy could be a holy terror if her plans were thwarted.

'You don't like him, do you?' Nancy stormed at her sister the minute they walked away from the song-booth. 'I can tell you don't. You looked at him as though he was something the cat had dragged in.'

'I don't think I did,' replied Joyce evenly. 'And I neither like nor dislike him. How can I when I don't know him? And neither do you,' she added pointedly. 'And have you thought what Mam will say about this notion of yours to be a lady vocalist?'

'Oh, she won't mind,' said Nancy airily. 'She can't very well object, can she? She did the same thing herself when she was a girl.'

'You're telling me you want to sing in a song-booth? On Central Beach? I've never heard such nonsense in all my life!' Hetty stood up and gave the fire a vicious jab with the steel poker. The coals fell apart, bursting into flame, and Hetty sat down again, staring as if mesmerised at the blue and yellow tongues of fire. The evening had turned chilly as it frequently did in May, but Hetty often felt cold now, even in the warmth of the day. She had done ever since Zachary went away and more particularly since the shocking news about Albert came. She was aware of her elder daughter's eyes boring into her, but she refused to look at her.

'It's quite out of the question,' she went on. 'How can you go singing when you've a job to do here? I don't pay you to do nothing, you know. We'll be rushed off our feet in a few weeks' time, especially when the theatre folk come. No, you can't go, and that's my last word on the subject.'

'Well, I like that!' Nancy put her hands on her hips, staring sullen-faced at her mother. Her green eyes glinted dangerously and Hetty was startled, when she finally looked up at her daughter, to see the identical face glowering at her that had often looked back at her from the mirror; when she was younger, that was, and when she was in one of her fits of pique. 'You of all people,' Nancy stormed, 'telling me I can't go and sing. I don't know how you dare. It's ... it's laughable, it is really. And you're being totally unreasonable, Mam. Surely you can't have forgotten–'

'That'll do, Nancy!' Hetty snapped at her daughter, but not as angrily as she might have done. 'That's quite enough. If your father was here you wouldn't have dared to speak to me like that. And I haven't forgotten anything. I know exactly what you were going to say – that I was a singer myself when I was a girl. Well, yes, I was, but it was different altogether. It was a proper show, in an entertainment room – like a music hall really, not a ... a tuppence-ha'penny song-booth on the Golden Mile.'

Hetty's tone was disparaging, although she didn't really look down her nose at the Golden Mile as she knew many of her fellow boarding-house keepers did. She thought the place had a certain dissolute charm; but it had flashed into her mind at that moment that Drusilla, Reuben's cousin, had run a fortune-telling booth there, after she, along with many others of her ilk, had been moved off the sands by order of the Blackpool Corporation. Hetty felt a tremor of foreboding now as she always did when she thought about the gipsy girl.

'It's a perfectly respectable song-booth.' Nancy's tone was surly. 'You should see the crowds they get in there. They're packed out every day. It isn't as if I'm asking for the moon,' she went on moodily. 'I'll still do my rotten old jobs here if that's what you're worried about. It'll only be a couple of hours a day, and not every day either. I should have thought you would be pleased to see me get a chance like this.'

'I've said no, Nancy,' repeated Hetty, but not so convincingly now. She sighed inwardly, trying to fathom out in her own mind why she was being so intractable with this daughter who reminded her so much of herself. Perhaps that was why? 'I just don't think it's a very good idea,' she finished lamely.

'Oh you! I might have known you would go and spoil everything!' Nancy turned on her heel and flounced towards the door. She stopped with her hand on the door knob to fling one last accusation at her mother. 'If it was something our Zachary wanted you'd say yes, wouldn't you? Well, your precious Zachary'll be home soon, won't he, so perhaps you'll be satisfied!'

'Nancy...' Hetty half-rose from the armchair, but Nancy had gone. Hetty heard her feet stomping up the stairs, then her bedroom door slamming. Hetty sighed dejectedly and her shoulders slumped as she stared again into the flickering flames. It would be best to let her daughter cool her heels. Perhaps in the morning they might be able to talk things over a little more rationally. Hetty knew that she might have to climb down and try to see this thing from Nancy's point of view. That parting shot about Zachary had gone home and she didn't want the girl to think she was being victimised. Zachary... The thought of his homecoming next week brought a glimmer of a smile to her lips and Hetty closed her eyes, thinking of how it would be.

'Why did you say no?' Martha Makepeace carried on drying the breakfast pots while she talked with her daughter. 'I can't really see as how there'd be much harm in it, our Hetty.'

'But a song-booth, Mam – and on the Golden Mile of all places. Not a very nice place, is it? It's just about the worst part of Blackpool. There's all sorts of strange folk hanging around down there.'

'It's nobbut a stone's throw from the place where you did your singing.' Martha gave a curt nod.

'But Tilda's Tavern was a proper entertainment place,' Hetty persisted. 'And Central Beach was a good deal more respectable in those days than it is now. I tell you, I don't like it, Mam. And I don't like the sound of that Barney Bellamy either.'

'Eh, dearie me, Hetty. You can be an awkward madam at times, but then you always were.' Martha shook her head, but she was looking fondly at her daughter. 'You seem to have clean forgotten about a lot of things. About how you went mad to go and sing at that there place – there was no holding you – and your Nancy's only doing the same. Surely you can see that.'

'Of course I can,' said Hetty indignantly. 'And that's why I'm so much against it – because I can remember what it was like! It needs a lot of nerve to stand up and sing in a place like that, and a fair amount of talent, too. And, quite honestly, Mam, I don't think our Nancy has got what it takes…' Hetty's voice petered out. 'That's the top and bottom of it. I don't think she's got the stamina for it – not the guts nor the voice or anything – but I can't very well tell her that, now can I? I

95

daren't tell her. She'd really go off the deep end.'

'Are you sure that's the real reason?' Martha was looking at her shrewdly.

'Of course I am. What other reason could there be?'

'You couldn't be the tiniest bit … jealous? Wishing you were her age again, perhaps? Wishing it was you…'

'Of course not! What a ridiculous idea. I wouldn't go back on the stage now if you were to give me a gold clock. No …I'm worried for her, Mam. I really am.'

'I don't know as you need to be. She's a sensible sort of girl is Nancy, at least she can be when she tries. I don't think she'd do anything silly. And I think she's got a very nice little voice. She sings lovely in the chapel concerts.'

'That's just it, Mam. A *little* voice. Very sweet and clear, I grant you, but you need a strong voice to sing in public. I don't think she'll be able to make herself heard. And she's not all that sensible, either. Our Joyce is the level-headed one, for all she's two years younger. Oh, I know that Nancy likes to pretend that she has loads of self-confidence – that's why she bosses Joyce around so much – but she hasn't, not really. Underneath it all she's so thin-skinned, very easily hurt. I fear for her at times.'

'You'll have to let her make her own mistakes. Like you did,' Martha added pointedly. 'And I seem to remember you saying, not so long ago, that if she wanted to spread her wings then you would let her. You've changed your tune very quickly.'

'But I wasn't thinking of her going on the stage, Mam. I meant if she wanted to do some other sort of work, in a shop, perhaps, or an office, rather than the boarding house.'

'If you take my advice you'll let her have a try at this singing lark,' Martha said sagely. 'Singing in a song-booth is hardly going on the stage, is it? She'll soon give it up, believe me, if she can't cope with it. And you can always nip along, can't you, and have a word with this Barney chap if you feel worried. I did, you know, when you were so set on going and singing for Joss Jenkinson.'

'If I remember rightly, Mam, he came to see you,' said Hetty. 'Very respectable, Joss was. I'm sure I don't know whether this Barney fellow is. Our Joyce said he looked as though he were wearing make-up!'

'I expect it's so they can see him clearly,' said Martha calmly. 'Anyroad, our Hetty, if he's the sort that wears make-up you won't need to worry about him chasing after Nancy, will you?'

'Mother, really!' Hetty smiled in spite of herself at the wicked gleam in her mother's eye. 'I didn't think you knew about things like that.'

'You'd be surprised at what I know, lass,' said Martha evenly. 'Now, are you going to let that girl of yours have her head?'

Hetty could almost hear her mother's unspoken words, 'like I did with you', and when she replied it was with a nod, albeit a reluctant one. 'I suppose so. I'll go back and tell her in a minute that she can go down and see that Barney fellow this afternoon. She's sulking at me just now, polishing the brasses as though her life depended on it. I shall go and see him myself though, like you suggested. I know Nancy'll think I'm treating her like a child, but I'm not bothered. I want to know what sort of a fellow he is. I do care about Nancy. I love them all, you know, Mam,' she added, almost defiantly.

'Of course you do, dear. Nobody's saying you don't, are they?'

'No, but Nancy accused me of showing favouritism to Zachary, that's all,' said Hetty in a small voice.

'Ah well, there you are then,' said Martha quietly.

There was no need for her to say any more. Hetty opened the back kitchen door. 'I'll go and tell her, Mam,' she said. 'I'll tell her she's got my blessing. Although goodness knows what she's letting herself in for.'

Chapter 5

Sarah could scarcely contain herself for excitement although, to watch her at work in the tearoom, no one would know it. She was so busy that there was no time to gaze into space and dream, which is what she felt like doing. But the thought of seeing Zachary again in two days' time was like the thought of birthday presents and Christmas gifts and Sunday School treats all rolled into one; lovely exciting things to be looked forward to and savoured and dreamed about, but the thought of Zachary coming home surpassed them all.

The extended tearoom, with her parents' blessing and co-operation, was already thriving. Father had been as good as his word; the new kitchen with two gas stoves and a large sink, walk-in pantry and more than ample cupboard space had been ready early in the New Year. That was when Sarah had become, officially, the Manageress of Donnelly's tearoom, for by that time Mr Middleton had come home from the Army and she had relinquished her job as her father's deputy. Now she had two assistants working with her in the kitchen, helping her with the baking of cakes, scones, biscuits, pies and pastries for which she was already becoming renowned, and making mounds of appetising sandwiches each day for the very popular afternoon teas. There were now three waitresses instead of the former one, smartly dressed in maroon frocks with frilly white aprons and caps, and they were kept busy most of the day from ten o'clock in the morning until the store closed at five-thirty.

Her father had proved adamant, though, about his refusal to serve midday dinners. He felt that it wouldn't be fair on rival establishments who were in the catering business exclusively rather than just dabbling in it as the Donnellys were. Every man to his trade, was what he thought, but Sarah only partially agreed with him. She was inclined to think more along the lines of every man for himself, especially these days with shops diversifying and opening all sorts of new departments. However, she had to admit that she had quite enough to cope with at the moment and she would never have dreamed of getting involved in a serious argument with her father.

Zachary had never been much of a letter-writer, Sarah thought fondly now as she spread out the flimsy yellowing epistles – a pitiful few of them – on the paisley eiderdown that covered her bed. He would be the first to admit that he was no scholar, but then he hadn't had the chances that she had had. Sarah had been educated at a private school, at Father's insistence, and had stayed there until she was sixteen, whereas Zachary, Nancy and Joyce had gone to the local board school and had all left at fourteen. Zachary had gone into a job he enjoyed, though, one he had always wanted to do, which was something that a lot of young men didn't achieve. His job as a fireman and trainee engine driver had never involved much book learning, Sarah reflected as she fingered his letters, but she wouldn't have him any other way, not her Zachary.

It seemed as though he didn't know how to express himself in words. There had never been any suggestion in his letters, for instance, that he was missing her, although she had told him so frequently in her numerous letters to him and she was sure that he must have felt the same. He had written mainly about the conditions in the trenches, the mud and the squalor and the frugality of the Army rations. She drew one of the letters from its envelope.

'....*Most of the fellows in here are suffering from trench foot, which is what I have got and why I am in this place.*' (Zachary had been in hospital at that time.) '*It's because we have to stand up to our knees in water... I've no news really but I hope I'll get a letter from you soon. Yours sincerely, Zachary.*'

'Yours sincerely' indeed, she thought, shaking her head over the signature. But he probably thought that was what you should always put at the end of a letter. She looked at another one.

'...*Sorry I haven't written for a while, but I've been rushed off my feet since I was promoted. I'm sending you one of my photos. Please send me one of yours. All the chaps have photos pinned up. They help to make the place look more like home...*'

The sepia photograph of Zachary in his uniform, the corporal's stripes prominent on the arm nearest to the camera, was one of Sarah's greatest treasures. He looked serious, though, unlike her memories of the happy laughing lad she had known, his dark eyes startled – almost fearful – and his curly hair cut short above his ears. No, he may not have known how to express himself in his letters, but he had sent her that photo. And he had sent her a beautiful embroidered card; *From your Soldier Boy,* the inscription read. She picked it up now, running her finger over the colourful raised flags of Great Britain, France and Belgium intertwined with flowers. And at Christmas he had sent her a lace-edged handkerchief with *Souvenir de France* embroidered in the corner with the flags of the allied nations.

Not all that much to show for two years at the Front, a dozen or so letters, a photo, a hand-kerchief and an embroidered card, but for Sarah they were more than enough. Because she had her memories as well; those two precious remembrances of Zachary asking her to marry him, and nobody could take those away from her.

She knew, in her heart of hearts, that she couldn't really count the first occasion because they had been only twelve years old at the time. They had all gone on a picnic to the sandhills at Squire's Gate, herself, Mother and Father, and Aunt Hetty, Uncle Albert and the three Gregson children. It had been a sunny Sunday afternoon in high summer and, if she remembered correctly, they had been celebrating Joyce's seventh birthday.

They had travelled part of the way along the sea front in a horse-drawn landau and the rest of the way on the electric tram. It had been a wonder-fully happy day, full of fun and laughter, and if she closed her eyes Sarah could bring to mind even now the essence of it all. The cry of the seagulls wheeling overhead, the splash of the waves in the distance, the prickly feel of the star grass against her bare feet and the gritty taste of sand in the salmon sandwiches. The ginger beer that the children drank had been slightly warm, but nonetheless delicious, and Uncle Albert had given her a sip of his bottle beer. She had pulled a face at the bitter taste – how could anyone drink stuff like that, she had asked – and everyone had laughed. Everyone except Zachary, she remembered now with a stab of unease. He had been staring into space, not taking part in the general jollification that Uncle Albert had instigated. Uncle Albert had always been at his best when he was surrounded by his family, full of quips and jokes and nonsense.

'Stop your tomfoolery, Albert!' Aunt Hetty often used to say to him, laughing herself. But invariably, when his father started his larking around, Zachary would be, like the late Queen, Not Amused.

For all that, it had been a happy day. The grown-ups had been content to relax on the sandhills on their tartan travelling rugs. Mother and Aunt Hetty had removed their flat straw hats as a concession to the informality of the occasion, but had kept the hot sun from their faces with large parasols. The children, however, had been anxious to get the full benefit of the sea. Even though they lived at the seaside, outings such as these were quite rare, especially for the Gregsons who were involved in the boarding-house trade. Sarah wondered, fleetingly, what Aunt Hetty had

103

done that day to ensure her visitors were cared for; she had no doubt come to some arrangement with the staff she employed. Oh no... Sarah remembered now; that occasion – it must have been about 1909 – was before Aunt Hetty took over Sunnyside. Uncle Albert's mother, Alice Gregson, had still been running it then although Hetty had gone in frequently to help, both there and at her mother's place across the street. It was amazing how one's mind could veer off at a tangent when one started reminiscing...

The four of them, with warnings from their parents to stay close to the edge and to mind the jellyfish, had careered off across the dunes to the stretch of sand leading to the sea. The ridges left by the tide dug into their bare feet and they yelled with mock agony at the pain. They hadn't, Sarah recalled, been very suitably clad for the occasion, but they had had to make do. Zachary had rolled up his knickerbockers to the knee and the girls had tucked up their dresses as best they could for a splash and paddle in the waves.

Then she and Zachary, the eldest two by a few years, had wandered away together as they usually did on such occasions, leaving Nancy and Joyce to play together. They walked northwards, keeping close to the edge of the sea. In the distance they could see the ironwork struts of the three piers jutting out over the ocean and, a couple of miles away, the tall finger of the Tower pointing upwards into the cloudless blue of the sky.

'My father used to live not far from here,' Zachary said, gesturing towards the Star Inn which stood on the seaward edge of the sandhills. 'Over there, near where the Pleasure Beach is now. That's where my mam first got to know him.'

Sarah stared at him in puzzlement. 'Your father? Oh yes, I see. You mean Reuben … the gipsy.'

'Yes, my father,' Zachary answered, his chin tilted defiantly. 'There was a gipsy encampment there, and stalls and sideshows and roundabouts and all that. Mam's told me all about it. He lived in a caravan – they called it a vardo – that's until he married my mother.'

Sarah had felt disturbed to hear Zachary talk like that. She had known, of course, that Uncle Albert was not his real father, just as Edwin Donnelly was not hers. But always, from being a tiny girl, she had thought of Edwin as her father and had been encouraged to do so by her mother. She had assumed that it would be the same with Zachary and Uncle Albert. After all, it was so long ago. Her mother had told her that Reuben Loveday, Aunt Hetty's first husband, had died tragically, although she had never explained exactly how, when Zachary was only two years old. Surely he couldn't remember him, except perhaps in a distant sort of haze, like she remembered her own real father, Walter Clayton. It was obvious, though, that Aunt Hetty must have talked about him to her son and strived to keep his memory alive. Sarah had felt unaccountably cross with Aunt Hetty just then; she considered that she was doing poor Uncle Albert a disservice by harping on about Reuben. Uncle Albert had been a wonderful father to Zachary, just as he had been to his own two girls. Uncle Albert was a love.

'I'd like to live in a caravan, a big green one like my father lived in, with fancy patterns painted all over it,' Zachary had gone on. 'I get fed up living in a house sometimes, 'specially a poky one like we live in.' The Gregsons had lived at that time in a small terraced house near to North Station. 'You're real lucky, Sarah, living in a mansion like you do.'

'I don't think Mother and Father would call it a mansion,' Sarah replied.

'Well, I would! 'Tis, compared with ours. And just for three of you.'

'You'd find a caravan even smaller then, wouldn't you?' said Sarah prosaically. 'There's not much room inside them. They have beds that fold up against the wall because there's hardly any space to move around.'

'How'd you know that?'

'Oh, I read it somewhere, in a book I borrowed from the school library, I think.'

'Huh! No doubt you did.' Zachary didn't have much patience with reading. He scowled now and kicked impatiently at the waves, splashing droplets of water all over Sarah's muslin dress.

'Look out, you silly fool! I'm drenched now.' Sarah pushed at him in fun and he pushed her back, grinning at her, his good humour magically restored. Zachary was like that, up one minute and down the next.

'You could sleep outside though, under the stars,' said Zachary, returning to the subject of the caravan. 'Mam says that my father never got used to sleeping in a proper bed and he never liked the doors being shut. Just think, Sarah...' He seized hold of her hand. 'We could have a big green caravan and a horse to pull it and we could travel for miles and miles. Just you and me. Right away from Blackpool, right as far as ... Bristol, or ... or Plymouth.'

Zachary's geographical education was limited and Sarah guessed that these were two towns that he just happened to have heard of. In reality he hadn't travelled any further than Preston, eighteen miles away. Sarah's own knowledge was not much better, although the Donnellys had been on family holidays to Morecambe and Southport, once as far as Scarborough, and on day trips to the Isle of Man; and she read avidly about distant and exotic places – London, Paris, even New York, far away across the Atlantic Ocean – in the school library books she devoured.

'It sounds very nice, Zachary,' she replied, though not very convincingly. She was not altogether sure about horses and caravans. But if Zachary was with her ... and that was what he had said, wasn't it? 'Just you and me.' She felt her heart give a funny sort of jump at the thought of being alone with Zachary for ever and ever, not for just a few minutes as they were now. She stood still and turned to look at him. 'You mean ... for you and me to go away together? For us to–'

''Course I do. We're going to get married, aren't we, Sarah?' His black eyes burned intently into hers and Sarah knew at that moment that the twelve-year-old lad most certainly wasn't jesting; he seemed, indeed, in that instant to have become a man. And Sarah looked at him and knew that she loved him; she had loved him ever since.

'Yes, we'll get married, Zachary,' she said, knowing beyond all doubt that it would be so. They looked steadily at one another for a few minutes, unsmiling, then Zachary leaned forward and kissed her gently on the lips. His mouth felt soft and warm against her own, but it had been the most fleeting touch, an ephemeral moment that afterwards, Sarah wondered if she had imagined.

'That's all right then,' said Zachary. 'But we won't tell 'em, will we? Not yet. It'll be our secret. We don't want all that lot knowing our business. Come on, let's go back.' He suddenly grabbed hold of her hand, pulling her back towards the sandhills. 'Mam said we might have time to go on the roller coaster at the Pleasure Beach before we go home. Let's go and ask her.'

Zachary was a young lad again and Sarah ran with him, shouting and laughing as he almost pulled her off her feet, the sea breeze tangling her hair and catching at her throat. Then she had sat close beside him on the roller coaster, burying her head against his shoulder and screaming as her stomach turned somersaults at the undulations of the truly frightening ride. At least, it would have been frightening if Zachary hadn't been with her; Sarah wouldn't have dared to venture on to it at all if Zachary hadn't convinced her that there was nothing to fear. And he had put his arm round her and held her close for the very first time that day.

He had never again mentioned the marriage proposal – for that was what Sarah had considered it to be – but as they grew into their teens the two of them became closer and the family seemed to assume that Sarah and Zachary were inseparable. Some of them, like Grandma and Grandad Makepeace, made jokes about it, although Nancy would often tut with impatience whenever Sarah mentioned Zachary; Nancy didn't seem to get on very well with her brother. And Sarah sometimes noticed, to her consternation, a flicker of disquiet cross her mother's face when she watched the pair of them together.

Not that there had ever been much opportunity for them to be really alone together. On family outings, like the visit to the sandhills, they usually managed to snatch a few minutes away from the rest of the crowd and, as they grew older, Zachary had kissed her a few times, tentatively, experimentally. But, most of the time, the family was there in full force.

When Zachary started work on the railway he had a little more money to spend, but not much opportunity to spend it, because his job as a fireman often took him away from home. Sarah remembered, however, how he had gloried in his independence on the few occasions that he took her to the cinema or the music hall, buying her ice cream or chocolates like a real man of the world now that he no longer had to rely on his parents for a shilling or two pocket money each week. Their friendship had been one of affection and innocence, a natural development from their proximity as devoted cousins, until that day in June 1916, just before Zachary went overseas.

The family had seemed to understand their desire to be alone together, and for once there had been no suggestion of a family outing. Besides, with Uncle Albert away at the Front the heart had gone out of such gatherings. By mutual agreement Sarah and Zachary wanted to avoid the town centre that day; the milling crowds that thronged the prom and the streets nearby, the clanging trams, the raucous shouts of the stall-holders, the screech of the seagulls, all the multifarious ingredients that together made up the extravaganza that was Blackpool. Instead they boarded a tram from Talbot Square which took them along Whitegate Drive to Marton. They stopped at the Cherry Tree Gardens Inn for a refreshing drink of lemonade and then wandered inland towards Marton Moss.

Although it was only a mile or two from the centre of Blackpool, you felt you were in the heart of the country here. It was an area of whitewashed thatched cottages, solitary farm-steads and mile upon mile of greenhouses where the 'Moss' folk grew their famous tomatoes and tilled a living from the fertile soil. Zachary had lived in this part of the Fylde when he was a small boy, Sarah had heard her mother say, but she wasn't sure where and she didn't ask him now. He seemed preoccupied and she didn't want to encourage him to talk about his gipsy father. Such reflections only served to make him maudlin and disgruntled and Sarah wanted today, their last day together for who could tell how long, to be a happy one.

It was little wonder, though, that Zachary was preoccupied; he had much to make him so. In a couple of days' time when he returned to his camp in the Midlands he was to be sent overseas. Sarah, in spite of her closeness to him, wasn't sure how to deal with this situation, whether to talk about it openly or to ignore it completely and talk about something else. But about what? It seemed, as the afternoon drew on, as though they had little idea of what to say to one another. They had chatted quite easily on the tram and in the inn about Sarah's new job, helping her father at Donnelly's and about the visitors who were staying at Sunnyside and Welcome Rest; the war had, surprisingly, made very little difference to the holiday trade.

But now, as they walked hand in hand along a rutted country lane, between hedges white with hawthorn blossom and, here and there, clusters of sweet-smelling honeysuckle and wild roses, all conversation died. Sarah, for the first time in her friendship with Zachary, felt ill at ease, embarrassed at the silence that had sprung up between them. She searched frantically in her mind for something to say to restore a feeling of normality to the tension that surrounded them. She turned her head to look at him, smiling at him uncertainly, but he didn't smile back. His black eyes were unfathomable, but Sarah thought she could see a glimpse of something there that she would never have associated with Zachary; fear, or if not outright fear then most certainly alarm.

In Zachary, of all people – her intrepid, devil-may-care cousin who had never seemed to be afraid of anything or anybody.

They were at that moment passing a gate which led into a wood and Zachary, still unspeaking, pushed at it, gesturing Sarah to follow him. It was just a small copse at the edge of a field, but the beech and sycamore trees in their early summer foliage provided a welcome shade from the heat of the afternoon sun. The place was deserted. Since they had left the Cherry Tree Gardens and ventured on to the Moss about half an hour ago, they had seen scarcely another soul, just a farmer on a tractor who had called a cheery 'Good day!' and a few folk in the cottage gardens, their backs bent over the straight rows of vegetables.

Zachary took her hand again, leading her into the middle of the thicket, and they stopped by a wide-spreading sycamore tree. Firmly he pushed her back against its broad trunk and took hold of her shoulders. She could feel the heat of his hands through her thin cotton blouse, and his grip on her upper arm was so strong that she feared he would leave a bruise there. As she looked again into the depths of his dark eyes she realised that he was holding on to her so tightly in order to stop himself from trembling, because the look she could see there now was unmistakably one of terror.

Suddenly his head dropped down and his arms, too. He seized hold of both her hands, then he leaned towards her, burying his head against her breast. 'Oh, Sarah ... Sarah,' he whispered. 'I'm so frightened. You won't tell any of them, will you? But I'm so scared – scared out of my mind and I don't know what to do. I feel like running away. Come with me, Sarah. Let's run away.'

She wrapped both her arms around him then, holding him close, feeling the rapid beat of his heart against her own as she stroked his black curly hair; it felt strong and wiry and a little oily. 'We can't, Zachary. You know we can't,' she said softly, feeling that she was years and years older than this wretched, frightened lad, instead of a few months younger. It was useless, though, to tell him not to be afraid, that there was nothing to be frightened of. Didn't the long columns of the dead and wounded in the regular bulletins from the Front prove that such words would be pointless, would, in fact, be a downright lie? She tightened her hold on him, feeling that she wouldn't be able to bear it if anything happened to Zachary. Tears were pricking her eyelids even now, but she hastily blinked them away. Now was no time to start weeping; she had to give Zachary all the support she could.

'I know you're afraid, love,' she breathed, 'but who wouldn't be? It's nothing to be ashamed of, being afraid, but of course I won't tell them. I won't tell another soul. We'll just have to pray that it will all be over soon. It's the same for everyone, Zachary. We're all up to our necks in it, one way or another. You'll have to try to keep cheerful, won't you, for your mother's sake. Just think what it's like for her. Your father's there already and now you're going.'

Zachary nodded numbly, for once not reminding her that Albert was not his father. 'Yes, I

113

know … I know. Perhaps when I get over there with all the other lads it won't seem so bad. It's the waiting, Sarah, that's what's making it worse. We've only been playing at it till now. Now it's going to be for real.'

'I know, love,' said Sarah. 'But they'll all be feeling the same as you, you can be sure of that. At least you've had the courage to admit it. Thank you for telling me, Zachary.'

When he looked at her again, some of the fear had gone from his eyes and there was a sort of blind resignation there. 'Just hold me, Sarah,' he murmured, so quietly she could scarcely hear him. 'I won't feel so frightened if you … hold me.'

Gently but firmly then he pulled her to the ground, to the patch of soft grass beneath the sycamore tree. And when she glanced at him again a moment later there could be no mistaking the expression in his dark eyes now. It was one of stark desire, something Sarah had never seen before, but which she instinctively recognised.

'Sarah … Oh, Sarah.' Zachary reached out and touched her breast and she felt his trembling fingers fumbling at the pearl buttons of her white cotton blouse. Unashamedly then – for didn't she love Zachary with all her heart? – she helped him and he pushed away the constraining fabric exposing her small breasts. She caught her breath as he laid his head on the softness between them, then gently fondled her, pressing his lips against her nipples. She almost shouted out with desire as he kissed her again – never before had Zachary kissed her in this way – but when she felt him reaching for her skirt, pulling it above her knees and stroking her thigh, then she came to her senses.

'*No!*' The single word sounded like a whip-crack in the silence. 'No, Zachary, we can't. We mustn't.' Sarah sat bolt upright as she pushed him away, tugging down her crumpled skirt, pulling her blouse back on to her shoulders. 'Whatever were we thinking about? You know it's wrong. We can't.'

The sideways look that Zachary gave her from beneath his thick eyelashes was half-defiant, half-ashamed. 'I don't see why we can't. It's all right,' he mumbled. He looked away, seemingly embarrassed as she frantically tried to fasten the rest of the buttons on her blouse and push her hair back into place. When he looked at her again his eyes were pleading, like a small pup that had been scolded, she thought. 'I don't see why it's so wrong,' he said. He hesitated. Then: 'We're going to get married, aren't we, Sarah?'

Those were exactly the same words that he had used when he was twelve years old, was Sarah's immediate thought, before her heart gave a tremendous leap that he had said them again. He had asked her to marry him.

'Yes, we'll get married, Zachary,' she replied, just as she had done on that occasion some seven years before. 'But that's no excuse for us to … you know,' she added, somewhat discomfited. The fact that he had mentioned marriage again didn't prevent her from feeling guilty about what she had so nearly allowed him to do.

'All right then. If you say so.' Zachary smiled at her as disarmingly as ever and she felt her heart melt with love for him. 'I'm sorry, Sarah love.' He lifted her hand to his lips and teasingly kissed the tip of each finger. 'I know I shouldn't have... Am I forgiven?'

Sarah nodded. 'Of course you are.'

'Let me kiss you then. Just ... kiss you, that's all.'

He kissed her then, tenderly at first then more fervently. She felt her mouth open beneath his as she gloried in the intoxicating feeling of her love for him, at the same time wanting to cry out with despair because he would soon be leaving her.

Abruptly he let her go and stood up, holding out a hand to help her to her feet. 'Come on. We'd better be getting back. You know how they worry and we don't want to give them any cause for alarm.'

Sarah detected a note of derision in Zachary's remark, but she didn't comment. She knew, though, that there might well have been plenty of cause for alarm if she hadn't put a stop to Zachary's embraces when she did.

Even now, two years later, the memory of that encounter was enough to bring a guilty flush to Sarah's cheeks. But, at the time, she had excused herself with the thought that their lovemaking, abortive though it was, seemed to have momentarily stilled Zachary's fear. He had been as carefree as ever on the tram journey home, and when he had departed for his camp two days later he had said goodbye with a cheery wave and scarcely a backward glance. So, though it may have been wrong, Sarah liked to feel that she had helped her cousin to forget his fears, if only for a little while.

And in two days' time he would be home again. Sarah lifted up the sepia photograph and held it to her lips. She closed her eyes, imagining how it would be, how he would look, what he would say to her, what she would reply... And trying to stifle that tiny niggling cloud of doubt at the back of her mind.

Chapter 6

'Of course we must put the flags out. It's not every day we get the chance to welcome a soldier home from the war.' Martha had unearthed a box of red, white and blue bunting and some Union Jacks from the attic and she was spreading them out on the clipped rag rug in front of the kitchen fire. 'They're a bit dusty and I know some of 'em have seen better days, but I'll give 'em a shake in the backyard and when they're strung up nobody'll know as they're not new.'

They look as though they've come out of the Ark, Hetty thought, casting a critical eye over the streamers. They had certainly been around since the time of the old Queen's Diamond Jubilee – the same year that both Zachary and Sarah had been born – and they had come out again for both Coronations, 1901 and 1911. And again last year when the Armistice was signed, although Martha hadn't gone mad on that occasion. She'd just put a couple of flags over the front door, preferring to wait until the family really had something to celebrate – as they had now. But surely Zachary's homecoming was worth more than a few shabby old streamers...

'Yes, they're all right, Mam,' said Hetty, not wanting to offend her mother, 'but I think I've got some over the road that might be a bit newer. I seem to remember that Alice bought some for

King George and Queen Mary's Coronation and they've never been used since.'

Hetty certainly hadn't felt like celebrating on 11 November last year and she was doubtful even now about decking the street with flags. Martha, however, seemed set on the idea so Hetty decided that if they were to do it then they would do it properly; there would be no half-measures. 'I'll have a look for them when I go back,' she declared. 'I mustn't be long either before I get myself moving. I'll have that lot from the theatre coming in before I can turn round, all wanting their supper.'

'Oh aye, your pros,' said Martha, nodding. She let go of the flags, wiping her hands on her flowered apron. 'Aye, they're a bit dusty and that's a fact,' she said, flopping down in the sagging easy chair at the side of the fire. 'How are you getting on with them? Your pros, I mean.'

'Oh, fine, Mam. I think it's going to work out just fine. But then I never had any doubt but that it would.'

'Yes, I've got to admit, our Hetty, that if you set your mind to something then you make a go of it,' said Martha. 'Don't work too hard, though. You don't want to go wearing yourself out.'

'You're a fine one to talk, Mam,' Hetty laughed. 'How many times have I heard you say that hard work never killed anyone? And it doesn't seem like hard work when you're enjoying it, like I am. They've only been here a few days, but I can see that it's going to be just the job. They're a grand crowd and Sid and Flo make sure that they toe the line and don't cause us any unnecessary

119

work. That's the couple that stayed with me before, d'you remember? That was what gave me the idea in the first place, knowing Sid and Flo. He's a baritone singer and she does musical-comedy numbers.'

'And they're in charge of the company are they, this Sid and Flo?'

'No, not exactly. It isn't really a touring company as such, Mam, but from what I can gather, the lot that are staying with me all have the same agent so they tend to get block booked. And they've all been booked for the pier show so they'll be here all summer, till about the middle of September.'

'And how many of them are there?'

'Ten altogether, five men and five women – I say women although some of them are only young lasses, not much older than our Joyce. I'd have a fit if I thought that either of my two girls were touring around like those lasses are. Sleeping in different digs every week and mixing with all sorts of rum folk.'

'But they're here for a good stretch now, from what you say?'

'Yes, about fourteen weeks all told, but it's quite another matter in the winter when they're touring. It's a different theatre every week then, and not all of 'em out of the top drawer neither. And some pretty lousy digs an' all sometimes, from what Flo tells me. No, Mam, I wouldn't want any lass of mine doing it.'

'You wouldn't have said that when you were Nancy's age,' said Martha, grinning. 'I remember you as if it were yesterday, all dolled up in that green frock singing them Gilbert and Sullivan songs. You were as pretty as a picture. I shouldn't be telling you this, it'll make you swelled-headed, but you were a bonny lass and a lovely singer too.' Martha's eyes grew misty for a moment. 'I don't suppose you'd have minded rotten digs and third-rate theatres so long as you could have gone on singing.'

'But I married Reuben, didn't I, Mam?'

'Aye, so you did, love.' Martha looked at her fondly.

'And now I'm getting old,' Hetty sighed. 'I've told you, I wouldn't go back to the stage, not for any money, and I wouldn't want Nancy to do it neither. That's why I gave way in the end about this song-booth business, so she wouldn't start getting any even barmier ideas.'

'And you were quite satisfied in your own mind, weren't you, after you'd seen that Barney Bellamy fellow?'

'Yes, like I told you, he's harmless enough, Mam. And she's only doing three afternoons a week. Apparently he's got another young lass singing there as well, so they're doing it between them. It suits me because I need all the help I can get just now and it seems to have satisfied our Nancy, so that's all right. She's working like a real good 'un at the moment, I must admit, making up for the time she's not here. And I've got the two lasses from Burnley helping out for the summer as well…'

Hetty's mind had been set at rest when she had ventured down on to the Golden Mile and met this Barney Bellamy whom she had heard so much about. He was, as she had told her mother, harmless, and Hetty considered herself to be a good judge of character. His appearance was somewhat larger than life, flashy and flamboyant – it was little wonder that the matter-of-fact Joyce had been daunted by him – but Hetty guessed that it was largely an act that he put on to attract a crowd. She learned, by tactical questioning, that he was married with grown-up children and that his wife was staying in Blackpool with him for the season. They were looking for something more permanent than their temporary digs and he was keeping his fingers crossed that the position, as manager of the song-booth, would be permanent too.

'It's a job, love,' he had told Hetty, spreading wide his hands and raising his eyebrows, 'and that's what a lot of chaps 'ud give their eye-teeth for these days, isn't it? I'd always fancied meself as a singer and it's better than selling matches and bootlaces on street corners, dear. Now don't you go worrying about your Nancy. I'll take good care of her. Got a daughter the same age, I have, and she'll come to no harm with me.'

Hetty had believed him, realising that Nancy had been attracted to this dazzling character because she was virtually starved of male company. She had lost her father, of whom she had thought the world: could it be that this Barney represented a father figure to her, albeit a very different one from Albert? And she had had no opportunity yet, poor lass, to meet any young men. Yes, she felt that Nancy would be safe enough with Barney and it would perhaps help her to get this singing nonsense out of her system.

Martha cut across her rambling thoughts. 'So everything in the garden's lovely then, is it?'

'Seems like it, Mam.' Hetty smiled at her mother, feeling a good deal more contented than she had for a long while. 'And it certainly will be tomorrow, when our Zachary gets back.'

'Yes, it'll be grand to see him again,' said Martha. 'It's taken a long time for them to get themselves moving, I must say. Seven months it is now since the war finished, and still the lads are not all home. A damned disgrace, I call it. You'd think when they've been serving their King and Country for more than four years that the least they could do was to send them home when the fighting stopped.'

'I'm sure they'd agree with you love.' George Makepeace put down his copy of the *Blackpool Gazette* which he read from cover to cover every night and leaned forward earnestly. 'But it's not as simple as all that. I told you that Germany wouldn't take too kindly to signing the peace treaty, didn't I? Well, I was right. They're kicking up a fuss now about this Treaty of Versailles, and a lot of our lads – those that you say should be coming home – have been sent to Germany with the Army of occupation. I suppose the chaps in charge reckon that if the Germans are threatened with occupation by Allied troops then they may decide to toe the line in the end.'

'Mmm ... I see,' Hetty nodded. 'So I suppose I must be thankful that our Zachary hasn't been sent over there. And what exactly is Germany objecting to? Do you know, George?'

'Oh, territory mainly. That's what wars are all about in the main, isn't it? Which bit of land belongs to who.'

'And what does it matter anyway?' put in Martha gruffly. 'I'm sure it's not worth fighting about.'

George looked at his wife affectionately. 'I'm inclined to agree with you, love. But then we're not politicians, are we? Anyroad, they've to give Alsace and Lorraine back to France – there's been arguments about that bit of territory for ages – and they're to lose quite a chunk of land to Poland as well. And on top of all that, Germany has to surrender her Navy and destroy all her warplanes and promise to keep only a small Army, not more than a hundred thousand men. And they've been told they've to pay for the cost of war – more than six thousand million pounds – seeing as how it was them that started it.'

'But it wasn't them, was it?' argued Hetty. 'It all started in Serbia, with that Archduke fellow being shot.'

'Aye, well, that's what the Germans are saying. They're feeling sore that they're being blamed for it, and a lot of folks are thinking that if they ever get their chance they'll take their revenge. Apparently Lloyd George is predicting that there'll be another war because of it all,' George added gravely.

'For heaven's sake, let's drop all this talk of war,' said Martha, tutting impatiently. She picked up a Union Jack and waved it defiantly in front of

George's face. 'It's all over now – and we won, didn't we? And I'm sure there'll not be another one, not in our lifetime anyway, so you can stop all your gloomy talk, George. Our Hetty's lad's coming home tomorrow, so let's start thinking about that. We'll give him a real good hero's welcome with this lot, I'll tell you. What time will he get here, Hetty – have you heard?'

'There's a train gets into North Station at four o'clock,' said Hetty, 'and he's hoping to be on that one. I'll be able to go and meet him before I start getting the visitors' teas. I've got a couple of regulars in this week as well as the stage folk, but there'll be plenty of time.'

'Then I'll come with you,' said Martha decidedly. 'And our Joyce can come along too. What about Nancy? Will she come or is she singing tomorrow? It'll be nice for the lad if both his sisters are there to welcome him. And I daresay Sarah'll come along, won't she?'

'Yes, you can be sure that Sarah'll be there.' Hetty smiled. 'I don't think even her new café would stop Sarah from being there to meet our Zachary. I'm not sure about Nancy, although tomorrow's not one of her days at the song-booth...'

Hetty was not at all sure, in fact, about the homecoming that they were preparing for Zachary but she didn't want to disappoint her mother who was getting carried away on a rising tide of exuberance. There would be ... how many? – she counted in her head – five women, if her mother had her way, at the station to meet Zachary. Maybe he would prefer to see just

125

herself … or Sarah? Strangely enough, Hetty was not jealous of her niece and the love that she so openly displayed for her cousin. Hetty knew that Sarah could be the making of Zachary and she felt that, when the time came, her sister's lovely girl was the only person with whom she would willingly share her son's affections. But how did Zachary feel? Hetty had never really been sure. And how would he feel tomorrow when greeted with such an overwhelmingly feminine reception committee?

Hetty stood up abruptly and was surprised to feel that her knees were trembling a little. 'I'd best be off now, Mam. It's getting late. We'll get these flags strung up in the morning, then we can sort out who's going to the station and all that.'

Hetty suddenly realised that she was nervous at the thought of seeing her son again after more than two years. He had been on leave from the Front only once, and that had been soon after Albert was killed. She knew that Zachary, too, had lost several of his close pals. The war had brought changes for them all and it was quite possible that it would have changed Zachary as much as anyone. Hetty knew she must be prepared for that. But he would be glad to be home again and Hetty was going to do everything in her power to make sure that his homecoming was a memorable one.

Zachary Gregson felt his eyes closing as the train drew out of Preston Station on the last lap of his journey home. He felt as though he could sleep for a week, but he couldn't allow himself to doze

126

for many minutes at this particular stage of the journey or else he would miss it altogether. He had looked forward to it for so long, his first glimpse of Blackpool Tower, and as the train rattled through Kirkham he forced himself to keep his eyes open although they so desperately wanted to close.

It had been a hell of a journey; the train-ride across France and Belgium to the Hook of Holland and then the cross-Channel steamer to Harwich. Zachary had been as sick as a dog and he vowed that never again would he go on a ship of any kind, not as long as he lived, not even a rowing boat on a park lake. He had been sick travelling to Dover that very first time, he remembered, but that had been due to fear rather than the turbulent sea; a fear that he had never managed to conquer, not in two and a half years.

If he had known how indescribably dreadful it would be, then he would never have... Never have what? he asked himself. Never have gone? But what choice did he have? What choice had any of them had? He had enlisted when he was seventeen, knowing that if he didn't do so he would soon be conscripted anyway. The only alternative was to say that you were a 'conchie' and that took a different kind of courage, a moral fibre that Zachary knew he didn't possess. Most of the time, though, he had managed to keep his fear, if not completely under control, then at least hidden from the eyes of his colleagues. Being afraid wasn't something that the lads had talked about very much; mostly they had concealed it beneath a screen of banter and bravado.

'It's nothing to be ashamed of, being afraid,' Sarah had told him, that time in the wood on Marton Moss when his nerve had given way. 'They'll all be feeling the same as you.'

And Zachary knew that most likely it was true, although they never actually said so. His best mate, Jim, had been afraid and Zachary had never even realised it. Jim had been a down-to-earth Yorkshire lad with an easy manner and an infectious grin, always ready with a quip and a joke … or so it seemed. But one night his nerve had snapped completely and he just ran away. Ran and ran and ran, as far as he could, before 'they' finally caught up with him. Rumours filtered back that he had been found hiding in a wood, that he had been court-martialled… Leastways they had never seen him again and Zachary knew only too well why that was. Jim was a deserter, wasn't he? And everyone knew what happened to deserters…

But it was all over now and soon he would be home. The actual fighting had been over for ages, of course, and all they had been doing for the last seven months mounted to sweet fanny adams. The boredom had been preferable to the terror, infinitely so, but there were still nights when Zachary awoke in a blind panic, the sweat streaming from every pore of his body as he buried his head in his arms hiding from imaginary shellfire. It took only the slightest unexpected sound to bring on one of these panic attacks. It had happened, to Zachary's consternation, on the journey across England. He had been dozing and had been unprepared for the sudden banging of the carriage door. The short sharp sound had startled him into instant wakefulness and the shielding of his head with his arms had been a reflex action. Most of the people in the compartment had looked away embarrassed, but one middle-aged woman had smiled at him.

'Don't worry, lad, I know just how you're feeling,' she said. 'Both my lads were at the Front for two years. And they're both safely home now, thank God.'

Zachary had nodded an unspoken thanks. But how could she possibly know how he was feeling? How could anyone know who hadn't been there?

He blinked rapidly now in an effort to keep his eyes from closing and focused them on the sepia photographs opposite, just below the luggage rack, of northern seaside resorts: Morecambe, Southport, Llandudno – but not one of them a patch on Blackpool, he thought with a sudden surge of nostalgia. He was wide-awake now and he eagerly scanned the horizon for that first tantalising glimpse of his home town. It shouldn't be long now, just after the next hill... Yes, there it was! Blackpool Tower, welcoming him back after all his long time away. The rest of the people in the compartment didn't seem to have noticed or at least weren't showing any glimmer of interest. Zachary knew that holidaymakers, children in particular, often played that game on the journey to the coast; who could be the first to spot Blackpool Tower – the sign that their holiday was really beginning. Zachary and his sisters and his cousin, Sarah, all being sand-grown, had played it in reverse, so to speak; the sight of Blackpool

Tower meant to them that they were home again. And even after Zachary had gone to work on the railway, fulfilling his boyhood ambition, he had never done a journey on that line without looking out for the familiar landmark.

He humped his kitbag off the rack as the train drew into North Station, then, looking in the fly-blown mirror, adjusted his cap atop his black curls. His hair was a little longer now than it had been on the photograph he had had taken in France, the one he had sent to Sarah, and his eyes had lost the startled look that the camera's flash had given them. He couldn't help noticing, though, that he looked much older now than his twenty-two years, with quite pronounced lines around his mouth and eyes. Unless it was the poor quality of the glass, of course. He frowned at his reflection, then, putting his head on one side, tried to grin. The other occupants of the carriage had gone out into the corridor so there was no one to watch his antics.

'Come on, Zachary lad. Best foot forward,' he whispered to the pale face that looked out at him from the mirror. 'They'll all be waiting for you...' And he felt his heart quail at the thought.

There was a squeal of brakes and a hiss of steam as the train pulled up at the barrier – Blackpool North was the end of the line – then the banging of doors as the passengers alighted. Zachary couldn't see as far as the barrier because of the cloud of thick grey smoke billowing from the engine. He felt it now entering his nostrils and catching at the back of his throat, a soot-laden acrid taste and smell, like none other in the world; a danger, no doubt, to the chest and lungs, but Zachary was used to it and he revelled in it.

He experienced a moment's joy now, as he started to walk along the platform, at the thought that he would soon be returning to the job he loved and to his beloved engines. Zachary had had only one or two stabs at driving before he joined the Army. His real job had been that of a fireman and he had driven only under the supervision of the proper engine driver, but he hoped that before long he would become a full-fledged engine driver himself. He knew how lucky he was to have a job to return to; it was more than many of his pals from the trenches could say. One of the good things about the war – and there had been very little that was good, God alone knew – had been the sense of purpose and the comradeship. They had all been in it together, and for many of the lads that Zachary met in France the war had provided an escape from the drudgery of a life in the city slums or from a hand-to-mouth existence as a farm labourer. Lads such as these were now very uncertain as to the future. Lloyd George had promised that postwar Britain would be a land fit for heroes to live in, whereas, in reality, all that some of them had to return home to was the dole queue.

Yes, Zachary was lucky; he had his steady job and a comfortable home – his mother looked after him as though he were the Prince of Wales – so he didn't waste too much of his time thinking about the poor sods who were less fortunate than he was. That was their look-out, wasn't it? You had to take care of Number One in this life and that was what Zachary intended to do right now. He had done his bit – and more – for the last three years and no one could say that he hadn't. Now it was time for Zachary Gregson to start living.

First of all, though, he had to get through the ordeal of meeting his family. If he knew his mother, she would have got them all there in full force – probably the town band as well – his gran, his sisters ... Sarah, maybe? As Zachary approached the end of the platform he could just make them out through the haze of smoke. Yes, there they all were. There was his mother, right at the front near to the barrier, with the rest of the family grouped behind her. Zachary's eyes flitted from one to another as he strode along, feeling that his smile was painted on his face, like that of a ventriloquist's dummy. They were waving to him, his mother, Grandma, Nancy, Joyce ... and Sarah. No, Sarah alone was not waving, but she was smiling, more with her eyes than with her lips. She was obviously so happy to see him and Zachary, as he looked at her, felt a stab of guilt. What the hell was he to do about Sarah?

My poor Zachary, he looks years and years older, was Sarah's immediate thought as she watched the slightly-built figure striding towards her, getting nearer and nearer. He lifted his hand in greeting and his eyes met hers, but only for a brief moment before he looked away again to acknowledge the rest of his family. That moment was enough, though, to start the warning bells ringing in Sarah's brain, for Zachary looked sheepish, ill-at-ease; if it wasn't such a ridiculous thought Sarah might even imagine that he wasn't pleased to see her. He must be weary though; it had been a long journey and it was probably just that he was feeling tired. As she stood back, listening to him greeting his mother and gran and sisters, she convinced herself that that was all it was. Her poor love was tired. She could hear him saying so...

'Hello Mam, hello Gran... Grand to see you. And Nancy and Joyce. All the family, eh? Aye, I'll say I'm tired. More than twenty-four hours I've been on the move. Had to wait hours at Crewe. All I want now is me bed! Aye, I could sleep for a week.'

At last he came over to Sarah. She had been standing there quietly, back from the rest of the group, feeling that this, when all was said and done, was Aunt Hetty's moment. Poor Hetty had lost one fellow at the Front; she should have a few moments in which to welcome her beloved son who, Sarah knew, had always meant all the world to her, possibly more so than ever now.

'Hello there, Sarah.' Zachary was smiling at her and the uncomfortable look in his eyes had vanished; maybe she had only imagined it. He stooped to kiss her cheek. 'Glad you could come. How've you been? I expect you're busy with your new café, aren't you, now the season's started?'

Sarah nodded happily. She didn't really want to talk about the tearoom, but more important issues between herself and Zachary would have to wait until they were alone together; they couldn't be discussed with all the family around them.

With his mother and gran and sisters there Zachary wouldn't even get a chance to tell her that he had missed her and that he was glad to see her again. But he would do, she knew he would, when they had a chance to be on their own.

It was only a five-minute walk from the station to Aunt Hetty's boarding house and after the first minute or two conversation died. Sarah, giving a stealthy glance at Zachary walking at the side of her, noted that his smile had gone now; his mouth was set in a grim line and his dark eyes looked bleak. It was strange, and a little frightening, too. He had seemed so cheerful – quite normal – when he had greeted her at the station, but now, only a couple of moments later, he looked as though he was shouldering all the troubles of the world.

Zachary became aware of Sarah looking at him and his dark brows met together in an expression of annoyance. 'What's up?'

'Nothing … nothing at all.'

'Then why are you staring at me like that?'

'I'm not staring. I'm just looking at you. I was thinking you looked tired, that's all.'

'So would you be tired if you'd been on your feet since this time yesterday. What the hell d'you expect? Of course I'm bloody tired!'

Sarah bit her lip and looked away and when Zachary spoke again his tone was more gentle. 'Sorry, Sarah. I didn't mean to snap at you,' he mumbled, casting a half-glance over his shoulder. 'I wasn't really prepared for the … er … reception committee.' He pointed backwards with his thumb.

'It's all right, Zachary. I understand.' Sarah tried to smile at him, at the same time flicking away from the corner of her eye the odd tear that had formed there at his harsh words. He was making amends now, though, wasn't he? He was as good as saying that he wished there had only been her there to meet him. And she must try to be patient and tolerant with him. He had been through such a lot, poor love.

As they turned the corner by the station wall, into the street which held the boarding houses that belonged to Hetty and Martha, Zachary stood stockstill. 'Bloody hell, Mam. Why didn't you hire a brass band while you were at it, and the town crier an' all?' Zachary's eyes were blazing with fury. 'What the hell d'you think you're playing at, making a bloody fuss like this?'

Sarah, glancing at Hetty, thought that her aunt looked as though she had been hit over the head. She was staring open-mouthed at her son, an expression of bewilderment and hurt creeping across her bonny face. She had looked so delighted, so radiant at seeing her son again. But now...

'I'm sorry, dear,' Hetty stammered. 'I didn't realise. I thought you would–'

'That'll do, Zachary. There's no need to speak to your mother like that.' Martha Makepeace stepped forward, putting a protective hand on her daughter's arm, while the three girls stopped in their tracks, too embarrassed to say anything. A few holidaymakers, returning from the beach to their boarding houses, were giving the little party some curious looks.

'And watch your language an' all,' Martha went on. 'We don't want any of your soldier's talk here, thank you very much. And you don't need to go blaming your mother either for this lot.' She pointed down the street. 'If you want to know, it was my idea. We were only doing what we thought was right, giving you a proper welcome back from the war. We thought as how you'd be pleased. We *are* proud of you, you know,' she added more softly.

'I know, Gran. I'm sorry.' Zachary shuffled his feet and hung his head. 'It's ... it's very nice. I just don't like a lot of fuss. You know me.' He gave an uneasy little laugh. 'All I want is a bit of peace and quiet.'

And Sarah, staring wistfully at him, longing to take him in her arms and comfort him, thought again how desperately tired he looked, and old and ... bewildered.

'All right then, lad. We'll leave you alone in a little while,' said Martha brusquely. 'But I daresay you wouldn't say no to a cup of tea, would you? And some of our special cakes. Sarah here's been right busy. She's getting to be as good as her old gran in the kitchen, I can tell you.'

Gran seemed somewhat mollified, Sarah was glad to see, as they all set off walking down the street again towards Sunnyside, Aunt Hetty's place, where they had laid on a bit of a 'spread' for Zachary. Aunt Hetty, though, had hardly spoken since her son's outburst, except to mutter a few words of apology. They really had made the street look gay and colourful. It was a pity that Zachary was too tired, or fed up, or something, to appreciate it. Red, white and blue bunting was zig-zagged across the street between the two boarding houses, which were directly opposite one another. Union Jacks fluttered from the upstairs windows and over the front doors, and a painted sign *Welcome Home Zachary*, which Hetty had painstakingly executed, hung in the window of Sunnyside.

Zachary nudged Sarah's arm as they turned in at the gate and gave her a conspiratorial glance, casting his eyes heavenwards, as he looked at the fruit of their labours. She was elated at his touch, out of all proportion, and her heart surged anew with her love for him. She felt that she was the only one who really understood how he was feeling. But did she? *Did* she know what he was feeling? Again that tiny niggling doubt was clouding her mind.

Zachary pulled off his boots and tossed them into a corner of the bedroom then flung himself down on his bed. He lay there, hands behind his head, staring up at the ceiling. Thank God they had all gone and he could have a moment's peace. He had told his mother he was going to have an hour's kip, but Zachary was wide-awake now. He reached in his pocket for his packet of Wills' Woodbines and, taking out his matches, lit a cigarette. Mam didn't approve of smoking in the bedroom – at least, she hadn't at one time – but what the hell! A fellow was entitled to do as he liked in his own room. And a pretty poky room it was an' all, right up in the attic with a sloping ceiling and a view of the backyard and the dustbins and the outside lav. The best rooms were occupied by the visitors, of course, as they always had been, and these new folk, the pros, that his mother was now catering for. Still, after the trenches it was heaven, or it should have been, but Zachary was feeling disgruntled and depressed and weary of his family already ... and he had only been home for an hour.

He had felt claustrophobic in their presence before, but now it seemed even worse. All those damned women! Already he was missing the companionship of his mates in France, but maybe it would be better when he was able to return to work – next week, all being well. And at least it was the sort of job that kept him away a good deal. Sometimes, even before he had joined the Army, Zachary had considered leaving home and getting digs – Mam did fuss so; it was enough to drive a fellow crackers at times – but what would be the point? It would cost a lot more than the few shillings which was all that Hetty would take from him. Besides, she was a damned good cook, and though the room was not exactly Buckingham Palace, he could do a lot worse. Yes, Zachary Gregson knew only too well which side his bread was buttered.

He would have to put his foot down, though, about all those family get-togethers, 'the gathering of the clans', as George Makepeace sometimes called them. Zachary intended making his own amusements now. He would no doubt meet lots of fellows of his own age on the railway. And then there was Phyllis... He had discovered, to his amazement, that she lived only a few miles away in Preston. He intended looking her up; she had been a promising lass, very promising indeed. Zachary would have no time now for childish pursuits like chapel concerts or trips to the countryside with Joyce and Nancy ... and Sarah.

Again he felt a pang of guilt as he thought about his cousin. What the hell was he to do about her? But then, why should he feel guilty? He had done nothing wrong and surely she wouldn't be such a fool as to imagine that he had really meant it? It wasn't as if he had actually proposed. No, of course she wouldn't. Sarah was a sensible lass. He had got a bit carried away that day and Sarah had been so kind and understanding. What had happened had been inevitable ... but she hadn't let him go the whole way, had she? And when he came home on leave from the Front, just that once, Sarah had been ill in bed with the flu and he had hardly seen her. He really was very, very fond of her – she was a good-looking girl, too, that any fellow would be proud to have on his arm, but damn it all, she was his cousin! She was part of the whole Donnelly–Gregson setup from which he so badly wanted to break away.

Besides, he knew now that Sarah wasn't the right sort of girl for him. Probably she never had been. She was too sweet, too trusting. The way she turned those soulful brown eyes on him made him feel like a heel at times. Zachary wanted a lass with more spirit, more verve and vitality. A much more brazen and shameless lass than Sarah was, although he didn't let this thought come to full fruition. More like Marie, the young French barmaid in Amiens who had taught him more than he had ever known – or dreamed of – before. Or Phyllis, the pert little nurse who had looked after him in the hospital when he was suffering from trench foot. He had seen her a few times afterwards and she had been a willing pupil to some of the tricks he had learned from Marie. Phyllis was a Lancashire lass. She was home now, in Preston, only eighteen miles away, and she had seemed very keen for Zachary to look her up once he got home…

But first he would have to tell Sarah that the two of them were not … that he wasn't going to… Oh hell, what on earth was he going to say to her? But perhaps he wouldn't need to say anything. Perhaps she would already have realised. Zachary puffed away at his Woodbine, filling the room with a haze of blue smoke. He would just have to play it by ear. He'd take her to the cinema, perhaps tomorrow – Mary Pickford was on at the Imperial in *Less Than Dust,* he had noticed on a hoarding on the station wall – and then see if he could lead round to it, gradually like…

Chapter 7

She would not cry. She was most certainly not going to cry now. Mother would be expecting her to go down in a few moments and chat for a little while, as they always did in an evening, before they went to bed. Sarah shut her eyes tightly, so tightly that she could see red and black patterns swirling around, in an attempt to stem the threatening tears. She wiped away the traces of wetness from her long eyelashes and started to breathe deeply, trying, so very hard, to keep calm, not to give way to the heartbreak that she was feeling deep inside. For that was what Zachary had done: he had broken her heart.

And yet, had it been such a complete surprise? If she were honest with herself, and Sarah believed in being honest, she had realised the moment she set eyes on Zachary at the station, even before, maybe, that things were not the same. He had been odd, distant, never looking her straight in the eye; then there had been that awful scene in the street when he had first noticed the decorations. And he hadn't written to her for ages, not what you could call a proper letter; only a note, such as he might also have sent to Aunt Hetty, telling her that he was, at last, coming home.

Idly she traced the pink and green paisley pattern of her eiderdown with one finger, sighing deeply. Yes, she had known, deep down inside, for a long time, but she hadn't wanted to face up to it. Now there could be no more pretending. Sarah was trying to be realistic and she was aware that uncertainty could be the worst agony of all. So, even though it hurt like mad and she felt that she would never be the same again, it was far better to know that there was no hope at all than to go on deluding herself.

Ironically, he had seemed different, much more like the old Zachary, when he had popped into the tearoom that morning. Sarah had felt her heart leap at the sight of him, not in uniform today but in a tweed jacket she had remembered him wearing before he joined the Army. There hadn't been much time to chat; the tearoom was busy, as it always was at eleven o'clock in the morning, but Zachary hadn't wanted to linger anyway.

'Hello there, Sarah.' He had smiled disarmingly at her when she went over to him, showing a set of large even teeth, slightly yellowed with nicotine. 'You're busy, I see.' He glanced round at the customers at the neighbouring tables, mainly women taking a break from their shopping. 'Jolly good. Keep up the good work. I mustn't hinder you. I only popped in to ask you if you fancied going to the pictures tonight. Mary Pickford's on at the Imperial in *Less Than Dust* – how about it?'

'That would be lovely, Zachary,' Sarah replied eagerly. Mary Pickford, 'The World's Sweetheart', with her simpering girlish sweetness and fluttering eyelashes was not a particular favourite of Sarah's, but she knew that the men liked her, and

142

she was only too delighted to be going anywhere with Zachary. He seemed much more at ease today, thank goodness. 'Thank you,' she said. 'I'd love to go.'

'Right then, that's settled.' Zachary put both hands on the table in a gesture of finality. 'I'll see you outside, shall I, about a quarter to seven?'

'Yes ... that's fine, Zachary.' Sarah hesitated only fractionally. After all, the Imperial cinema was only a few minutes' walk away from Aunt Hetty, boarding house in North Shore. It wouldn't make sense for Zachary to come all the way to Park Road to call for her. She could easily get a tram into town or walk if it was a nice evening. All the same it might have been more gentlemanly... Sarah pushed the intrusive thought away. 'Yes, I'll see you at a quarter to seven. Now I really must get back to work. Stay and have a cup of coffee, won't you? I'll send one of the waitresses across.'

'Very well, if you insist,' Zachary smiled, almost as though he were humouring her, Sarah couldn't help thinking. When she glanced across a few moments afterwards, he had drunk his coffee and gone.

His jovial manner of the morning had been shortlived, for when she met him at the appointed time at the cinema on Dickson Road, Sarah could tell at once that it was not going to be a carefree evening. Again, Zachary seemed unwilling to make eye-contact with her, and in the darkness of the picture house he made no attempt to take hold of her hand, as he always used to do on their outings in the past. He did, somewhat grudgingly, buy her an ice cream at the interval, but as Sarah licked the delicious creamy confection from the little wooden spoon she might just as well have been eating tasteless gruel. She felt relieved when the lights dimmed again, but the tension between them was mounting until it was a palpable thing, like a thick creeping fog, obscuring all light and warmth.

He took her arm when they left the cinema. 'Come on, Sarah. Let's go down to the prom ... take a look at the sea.' His voice sounded strained and unnatural; as for Sarah, she couldn't even trust herself to speak. She nodded numbly.

In silence they crossed the tram-track by the Carlton Hotel and walked across to the promenade railings. The sky was almost fully dark and there was only a slight crescent of a moon. The sea was calm for once, with no foam-capped waves dashing against the sea wall, but it looked black and menacing. Sarah shivered, but she knew that it was as much from her fear of what was to come than because of the chill of the evening.

'Cold?' Zachary looked at her now, his face troubled, eerie-looking and tinged with yellow in the dim electric light.

'A little,' Sarah replied, turning up the collar of her coat, although nothing could ease the coldness inside her, this feeling of fatality. She turned to face Zachary, forcing him to look at her. 'You've something to tell me, haven't you?' she said.

'What d'you mean?' Zachary's tone was evasive and again he glanced away, feeling in his pockets for his packet of Wills' Woodbines. He took out a

144

cigarette and lit it, cupping his fingers round the silver lighter. Sarah could see that his hands were trembling. He drew deeply on the cigarette then puffed out a circle of smoke. It rose slowly in the still evening air. 'What d'you mean?' he said again. 'If I had something to tell you, I'd say it, wouldn't I? I don't know what you're talking about.'

'I think you do, Zachary. You've hardly spoken two words to me all evening, except when you've had to. It can only mean that you've something … important to say. Doesn't it?' Sarah glanced sideways, almost afraid of the look she might see on Zachary's face and of what he might say in answer to her question. But she had to know. She couldn't carry on with this nagging uncertainty any longer.

Zachary shrugged and shook his head. He stared out to sea for a few moments, not looking at her. Then, 'It's not the same, is it?' he said, still not glancing in her direction. 'You and me. It's not the same.' His words were muffled and indistinct, but Sarah heard them only too well.

'It's still the same for me, Zachary,' she said, as calmly as she could. 'I still feel the same as I always did. I still … care very much for you. I've thought about you – prayed that you'd come home safely – all the time you've been away. Nothing has changed … not as far as I'm concerned.' But Zachary had changed, she thought. He didn't love her any more. But then, had he ever really loved her? 'You don't care for me any more,' she said in a quiet voice. 'Is that what you're trying to say?'

'Of course I care, Sarah.' He turned then,

staring at her almost savagely. 'I've always cared about you and I always will. But, damn it all, you're my cousin. We can't … it just isn't possible. We only – you know – got friendly like, because we grew up together. We didn't know any better.' That really hurt and Sarah felt herself wince. She turned away, willing the tears not to fall.

Zachary touched her hand then as it lay on the iron railing, the first time he had done so all evening, but she made no response. She felt too wretched to speak. Anyway, it was up to him to talk now, to explain to her about his change of heart. At least he owed her that much.

'I mean – we didn't know anyone else,' he stumbled on. 'We were thrown together, you know we were. It was only natural we should … get friendly. One thing leads to another, doesn't it?' He gave an embarrassed little laugh.

'Then it didn't mean anything? All the times you kissed me. That time when you wanted to … to make love to me. You didn't mean it.' Sarah's voice was flat and emotionless as she gazed out at the distant horizon, almost indiscernible, where the black brooding sea met the darkening sky.

'Of course I meant it!' Zachary almost shouted. 'I wanted you, Sarah. I've told you – I cared for you, I still do, but I was upset, that time when … you know I was. I was going abroad to God knows what–'

'Yes, I remember, Zachary,' said Sarah evenly. 'You asked me to marry you.'

'Oh, damn it all, Sarah!' Zachary's voice was harsh and he snatched his hand away from her.

'You couldn't have taken me seriously. I was all worked up; I didn't know what I was saying. Anyway, we were only a couple of kids.'

'We were nineteen. Plenty old enough, I would have thought. And it wasn't the first time you had said it.'

'Now you're being ridiculous! You mean – that time at the sandhills?' Zachary's eyes were incredulous, slightly mocking. 'Good God, Sarah, we were only twelve years old, or thereabouts. Fancy taking any notice of what a twelve-year-old kid said to you. You must be mad!'

Nevertheless you remembered, thought Sarah. You knew only too well what you said, Zachary Gregson, and exactly how old you were at the time.

'Anyway, you're my cousin,' he repeated moodily. 'Cousins can't get married. It would be like marrying one of my sisters. It just wouldn't do.'

'Queen Victoria married her cousin,' said Sarah, but as soon as she spoke the words a feeling of hopeless resignation came over her. Why on earth was she arguing with him? What was the point? He didn't love her – he most likely never had – and she did have her pride. Even though she was hurting like mad she had her pride.

'It's different for that lot,' said Zachary sulkily. 'Royalty aren't like us ordinary folks. Anyroad, you deserve somebody better than me, Sarah. I'd've thought you might have met somebody else while I was away, a pretty girl like you.'

He was trying to get round her now, 'soft

147

soaping' her, as Grandma Makepeace would say, but she could see through him. She was beginning, to her amazement – and to her dismay – to see through Zachary more and more. It was as though the scales had suddenly dropped from her eyes. But the heartrending part was that she knew she still loved him, even though he was not the honourable young man she had once thought him to be. *Love is not love Which alters when it alteration finds.* The words of a Shakespeare sonnet, learned at school, flashed through her mind then. Yes, she still loved him, silly fool that she was, but she was damned if she was going to let him see it; not any longer. She had already made her feelings far too obvious.

'What chance have I had to meet someone else?' she asked, as casually as she could. 'All the men have been in the Army, or have you forgotten?' A sudden thought struck her. 'Is that what it is? You've met someone else yourself, have you, Zachary?'

'No, of course not.' His reply came too quickly and was not convincing. 'What gave you that idea? What chance have I had, either, to meet girls?' He looked away, discomfited by Sarah's searching glance. She was getting the measure of Zachary now and, in spite of herself, was not averse to seeing him squirm a little. 'Anyroad, you can't expect a fellow to behave like a hermit,' he mumbled. 'Not in France. It was hell, Sarah, in them trenches.' His voice broke with emotion.

'I'm sure it was,' she replied, feeling a surge of sympathy as she watched a sudden expression of anguish cross his face. 'You're home now. You'll

148

have to try and forget about it, put it all behind you.'

He nodded. Then, 'I'm sorry if I upset you,' he said, more contritely. 'I didn't want to. I didn't know how to tell you, but I've known for ages that it just wouldn't do … you and me.'

'All right, Zachary,' she replied trying to speak calmly. 'I think we've said all there is to say. Now, I'd better be going home. Mother and Father don't like me to be too late.'

'I'll come with you, see you home.' Zachary took hold of her arm.

'No, please don't.' She pulled away from him. 'Just see me to the tram-stop. I'll be all right. It's only a few minutes' walk from the stop at the other end. We've had to get used to doing without male escorts for the last few years,' she added, trying to sound casual.

'If you're sure then…'

'Quite sure, thank you.'

'We'll still be friends, though, won't we, Sarah?'

'If you like…' Sarah's airy tone belied the turmoil that she was feeling inside her. She wanted to burst into tears, to run away, sobbing, to the security of her home, to people who truly cared for her. Or else to fling herself against Zachary's shoulder, begging him to change his mind. But that would be no use. She had to maintain some dignity to cover up the pain she was feeling. She looked him straight in the eyes now, though it hurt like mad to do so. She found, too, that he was unwilling to meet her gaze, staring out to sea, at the ground, anywhere but at her.

'But there won't be much time,' she said, struggling to keep her voice calm, 'for us to be ... friends. We'll both be busy, won't we? You're going back to work next week, and I'll be rushed off my feet at the tearoom when the season starts in earnest. I won't have much time for ... for anything else.'

That would be the antidote, she thought as they crossed the wide stretch of promenade towards the tram-stop. Work, work and more work. So that she wouldn't have time to think, to feel, to agonize over Zachary Gregson.

As Sarah sat alone in her bedroom an hour or so later she doubted that anything would help to dispel the utter dejection that she was feeling. She had her job which would occupy her mind as well as her body. She would work as she had never worked before ... but would it be enough to help her to forget Zachary? Sarah doubted it.

She knew that she was lucky, as Nancy often reminded her, to have such a luxurious room to retire to at the end of each day. She glanced round now at her costly possessions: the tortoiseshell-backed mirrors and brushes, with her initials embossed in silver, which adorned her dressing-table; the silver-topped scent bottles and hair tidy; the Dresden shepherdess and the delicately enamelled boudoir clock which sat on the mantelpiece; the set of leather-bound books – classics such as Dickens and Trollope – tooled in gold. All were gifts, many of them from her loving parents on her twenty-first birthday. On a low chair, which Sarah had used as a child, sat her teddy bear, now bald in patches from frequent cuddling, and her favourite china doll, Belinda, with her broderie anglaise dress and bonnet and satin slippers. Ned, her rocking horse (on which Zachary had played the part of a dragon-slaying knight, she recalled bitterly) stood in a corner. The Gregson children had loved him, taking turns to clamber on his back for rides every time they came to visit.

This room had seen so much fun and happiness but now, as Sarah looked around, it seemed for the first time ever to be claustrophobic. She found herself wishing that she could escape – from this room which held so many memories, from the home in which she had lived, doted upon and indulged, since her childhood – even, she thought guiltily, from her parents. She had found a certain independence in her work at the café, but was it, she began to wonder, enough of a challenge? She was still working for her father and she was still living at home. She caught a glimpse of herself in the dressing-table mirror. Pensive and somewhat puzzled brown eyes stared back out of a heart-shaped face that was slightly paler than usual.

'Come on, snap out of it!' she said to herself, trying to smile at the sad-looking girl who was gazing at her so plaintively. 'You don't really want to leave here; you're just feeling sorry for yourself, because of Zachary.'

Sarah rose to her feet, knowing that she could put off the evil moment no longer. She would have to go down and tell her parents that it was all over between herself and Zachary. They would find out sooner or later, even if she were to say nothing at all, but Sarah had never had secrets from her parents in the way that some girls did. Always they had listened to her and sympathised and understood.

'Hello, dear,' said Grace, smiling warmly as Sarah entered the drawing room. 'Did you have a nice evening? Didn't Zachary come back with you?'

Sarah didn't answer either of her mother's questions, not straight away. She glanced across at the empty chair opposite Grace. 'Where's Father? He's not gone to bed, has he?'

'Yes, dear. He had a slight headache so he decided to have an early night. Nothing to worry about – just eyestrain, I think. He's very naughty, he doesn't like wearing his spectacles. Come and sit down and have a cup of tea.' Grace put her hand on the silver-plated teapot which stood on an occasional table at her side. 'This is still hot. Mrs Jolly insisted on making it only ten minutes ago, although I'm always telling her that I'll see to our bedtime drinks.'

'No thanks, Mother. No tea.' Sarah sat down on the gold-brocaded armchair opposite Grace. Tea would only serve to keep her awake, not that Sarah expected to sleep much that night anyway. She was relieved in a way that Father wasn't there. One pair of sympathetic eyes upon her would be quite enough to deal with. 'I want to tell you something, Mother,' she began.

'Yes, dear. What is it?' A faint flicker of alarm crossed Grace's face as she looked at her daughter, although she was still smiling. 'Something to do with you and … Zachary?'

'Yes.' Sarah hesitated, then: 'It's over, Mother. Between me and Zachary. We've decided not to go on seeing one another, not like we used to, I mean. It's finished.'

If only Mother didn't look so gratified, thought Sarah, as she watched the expression of unease on Grace's face change to one of relief. What had she thought Sarah was going to blurt out? That they were getting engaged, planning to get married very shortly? And now, in finding out that the news was the other extreme, her mother was obviously relieved. Sarah felt hurt and aggrieved, but it was the reaction she should have expected. She had always known that her mother was none too keen on Zachary.

But Grace's words were sympathetic. 'Oh dear, how upsetting for you, darling. I'm so ... I do know how you must be feeling.' Sarah was aware that her mother had been going to say, 'I'm sorry,' but had bitten back the words. Because she wasn't sorry, not at all. 'Do you want to talk about it, dear? Or perhaps you'd rather not. Either way, I'll understand.'

'There's really nothing much to tell,' Sarah replied, looking down at her lap, pleating and unpleating the soft, pale-green material of her woollen dress. 'We found that we've both changed while he's been away. It doesn't seem the same any more. It's the war, I suppose. We've all changed.'

Sarah wasn't going to admit to her mother that this had been all Zachary's doing – that he had, in effect, jilted her. No, far better to let Mother think it had been a mutual agreement to call it a day. Then no blame would fall on Zachary.

'Never mind, dear. Perhaps it's all for the best,' said Grace gently. 'I know you were fond of him. It's only natural, with you growing up together, that you should spend so much time with one another.' That was just what Zachary had said, earlier that evening. 'But I daresay you've grown apart now. You've both grown up. There will be all kinds of new experiences ahead – for both of you. Try not to let it upset you too much.'

'I won't. You're right, Mother – we've got to look ahead,' said Sarah indifferently. Then she raised her eyes, looking keenly at Grace. 'You never liked him, did you?' Her words were spoken in a tone of resignation. 'You never cared for Zachary.'

'Of course I like him, dear. I'm very fond of Zachary. He's my nephew, isn't he? Of course I'm fond of my sister's boy.'

'But that's the only reason why, isn't it? If he wasn't your nephew you wouldn't like him at all, would you?'

Grace was silent for a few moments before she answered. 'I'm not sure, dear,' she said at last. 'I must admit that I've always liked the two girls more. Both Nancy and Joyce are worth a dozen of Zachary, in my opinion.' Sarah flinched involuntarily and looked downwards again, clasping her hands together tightly. 'I'm sorry, darling,' said Grace, very sympathetically. 'I don't want to hurt you, to rub salt in the wound, as it were. I've always tried not to criticise Zachary to you, knowing how you felt, but you did ask me, didn't you?'

Sarah nodded, not looking at her mother.

'To tell you the truth, I've always thought that our Hetty spoiled that lad, and I know that Albert thought so as well, but it was no use talking to Hetty; she wouldn't listen. Not that I ever tried to say anything to her. I wouldn't – you know that, dear – but I do know that Albert thought she was making a rod for her own back in indulging him so much.'

'You think Zachary's been spoiled?' Sarah looked across at her mother then, shaking her head slightly. 'I don't see how you can say that. We're the ones who are wealthy, aren't we – according to Nancy, at any rate.' She gave a sad little smile. 'Nancy's often told me that I don't know how lucky I am. She thinks I was born with a silver spoon in my mouth, as they say. Nancy would no doubt think that I was the one who's been spoiled. We've always had more of this world's goods than the Gregsons, haven't we, Mother? Some would say it wasn't fair.'

Grace's brown eyes, so like her daughter's, were serious as she looked at Sarah, but full of warmth and tenderness. 'Your father and I have always given you the best of everything, because we could afford to do so. I make no apology for that; but that isn't to say that we spoiled you. In my opinion, children are only spoiled when their characters are marred because of over-indulgence. It's far worse to let children get away with bad behaviour, to refuse to correct them, than it is to spend money on them.'

'And you think Aunt Hetty's done that … with Zachary?'

'I'm afraid so, dear.' Grace sighed. 'At least, I used to think so when he was a little boy. It may well be that he's different now. I expect his war experiences will have changed him. No doubt that's why you found you didn't get on so well, because you're both different now. But I'm sure it will all be for the best, Sarah dear.'

Sarah was feeling much calmer by now. Mother always had that effect on her and she knew that what her mother said made sense, even though it was almost impossible to believe at this moment that the break could ever be 'for the best'. 'Tell me about Reuben,' she said suddenly. 'What happened to him?'

Grace looked startled. 'About Zachary's father? It's all a very long time ago. We don't talk about it any more, it was so upsetting for poor Hetty.'

'But Aunt Hetty's not here, is she? And I would like to know. No one's ever told me what really happened; it all seems to be shrouded in mystery.'

'And so it was, dear.' Grace frowned and her eyes clouded over for a moment. 'It was a complete mystery at the time; nobody ever got to the bottom of it… Reuben Loveday was a splendid young man. He was a gipsy – of course you know that, don't you? – and I must admit we were a little prejudiced at first because of this. Your gran certainly was. But we were proved wrong because he was a wonderful husband to Hetty and they were so happy together. And Zachary is the very image of his father, he's so much like him that it's uncanny. I'm certain that that's why Hetty spoiled him, and perhaps we shouldn't blame her. Zachary didn't inherit his father's disposition, though, more's the pity.' Grace looked apologetically at her daughter. 'I'm sorry, darling, but he didn't.'

'Go on, Mother,' said Sarah unemotionally. 'Tell me what happened.'

'They were living in a little cottage on Marton Moss, Reuben, Hetty and Zachary – he was about fifteen months old then. Reuben used to go round the markets, selling wooden things that he carved, and sometimes Hetty and the child went with him. They travelled in a neighbour's pony and trap. Well, the morning that the tragedy occurred, Reuben turned back to get something he'd forgotten. He was gone such a long while that Hetty went home to look for him and she found him lying on the hearthrug with his head against the steel fender. He was ... dead.'

Sarah gave a gasp of horror. 'Oh no! Poor Aunt Hetty. Whatever had happened?'

Grace shook her head. 'As I said, they never knew. The doctor thought he'd had a dizzy spell and tripped over the hearthrug, then hit his head on the fender. The coroner gave a verdict of misadventure.'

'How terrible!' breathed Sarah. 'And ... where was Zachary?'

'With his mother, until a kind neighbour hurried him out of the way. He wouldn't remember any of it; he was too young, fortunately. And, as far as I know, Hetty's never told him the full story. He's never said anything to you, has he, dear?'

'No, not a word. Not about all this, but he has talked about his father.'

'Don't ever tell him, Sarah. It's probably better that he shouldn't know, not all the tragic details.'

'I'm not likely to tell him now, am I?' said Sarah ruefully.

'No ... probably not. But that wasn't all, you see. Hetty was convinced that there was someone else there when Reuben died.'

'You mean that he might have been *murdered?*' Sarah was appalled at this story that she was hearing for the first time. 'But ... who?'

'Reuben had a cousin, Drusilla, and the girl was very jealous of Hetty. Hetty got it into her head that Drusilla was somehow involved in all this. But it was more than likely that she was just being fanciful. I remember that Hetty used to be frightened to death of Drusilla at times. And there was no sign of a struggle or anything, so it's more than likely that it was just an accident.'

'A very tragic one,' said Sarah. 'And now Aunt Hetty's lost her second husband. She's not had a very happy life, has she?'

'She's been happy for a lot of the time,' replied Grace. 'I'm sure she'd be the first to tell you that. I've heard her say many a time that she's had two good husbands. I know they both brought her a lot of happiness – and that's what life's all about, isn't it? Joy and sorrow, sunshine and shadow... Like your Grandma Makepeace is fond of saying: "Every cloud has a silver lining." And you'll be happy again before long, Sarah, you can be sure of that.'

'I hope so,' said Sarah, looking pleadingly at her mother. Her heartache about Zachary had temporarily abated whilst she was listening to the sad story of his father. Now she could feel it all flooding back. 'Oh, I do hope so.'

Grace's look of complete understanding went a long way towards convincing Sarah that eventually it would be so.

Chapter 8

'Aw, go on, Sarah. Come with me, there's a love.'
Nancy looked beseechingly at her cousin on the
other side of the table. 'You can't sit around
moping for ever, you know, about that flippin'
brother of mine. I've told you – he's not worth it.
Come with me to the show. It'll do you good and
you'll enjoy it. I know you will.'

'Sit around? I like that, you cheeky madam!'
Sarah grinned. 'We've been rushed off our feet in
here, ever since the end of May. We've hardly
time to catch our breath, let alone sit down.'

'Then what d'you think you're doing, sitting
down now?' Nancy retorted.

Sarah laughed. 'I can't win with you, can I?
You've an answer for everything. I'm just joining
my cousin in a cup of tea while there's a lull in
the proceedings. I don't see that anyone can
object to that. I'm due for a tea break, anyway.'

'And nobody can object, that's for sure,' said
Nancy. 'You're the boss, aren't you. You can crack
the whip, do as you please. It's all right for some
folk. You should be thankful you don't have to
put up with what I do, always at Mam's beck and
call.'

'Then what are *you* doing here, drinking tea in
the middle of the afternoon?' Sarah responded to
the twinkle in her cousin's eye. She knew only
too well that Nancy pleased herself pretty much

what she did a lot of the time, and Nancy knew it too. Aunt Hetty certainly couldn't be branded a slave-driver.

'I'm shopping for Mam, of course,' Nancy replied, giving an exaggerated sigh. 'I've only sat down for a minute to rest my weary bones. And I've come to ask you to go to the show on the pier with me. I've got complimentary tickets. Sid's given them to me. They always hand them out for first house on a Monday.'

'Why didn't you ask Joyce to go with you? She might be offended at you asking me.'

'Oh, Joyce has already seen it. We both went a fortnight ago. But it's worth seeing again. Go on, come with me, Sarah.'

Sarah hesitated for a moment, then, 'All right, I will,' she replied. She nodded decidedly. 'Why not? I think I deserve a treat. First house, you said? That's rather early, isn't it? What time does it start?'

'Six o'clock. It's about two hours long. And the second house starts at eight-fifteen. They're usually fairly full up for that, so that's why they give out tickets for the first performance.'

'Six o'clock ... I'd have to get my skates on,' Sarah reflected. 'We don't finish here till half-past five, and then I'd have to get home and back. I can't go in my working clothes. Oh, I don't know ... I'm not going to have enough time.'

'Of course you are!' Nancy was adamant. 'You've said you'll come with me, and I'm not going to let you back out now. Take some time off, for goodness sake. I've told you, you're the boss.'

'Yes … why not?' said Sarah again. 'I'm sure Maud will be only too happy to be left in charge, and the other girls are all good workers. I'll go and ask them now, while you drink your tea.'

'You *tell* them, not ask them,' said Nancy grinning. 'Go on – crack the whip, Miss Donnelly.'

'They'll be only too happy to oblige,' beamed Sarah, when she returned to the table a few moments later. 'What do you think of the cake, by the way? Do you like it?'

'I'll say I do. It's scrumptious,' said Nancy, licking her lips and wiping a few stray crumbs from her mouth with a paper napkin. 'Another new recipe, Sarah?'

'A new old one, you might say,' Sarah smiled. 'Good old Mrs Beeton. This one's flavoured with real orange juice. We've started serving a lemon cake and a coffee one as well, but I think the orange one is proving the most popular. I wanted to know what you thought of it.' Enthusiasm crept into Sarah's voice as she spoke about the vocation that enthralled her so much. Her work at the tearoom had proved to be a lifeline, preventing her from drowning in the depths of the despair that had overcome her, at first, at Zachary's faithlessness.

'I think you've worked wonders in here,' said Nancy, gazing round admiringly. 'Everyone says so. Donnelly's Tearoom's more popular than it ever was, and that's saying something.'

'Yes, I'm very pleased at the way things have worked out,' said Sarah modestly.

It was now the end of June and takings were up

fifty per cent on the same time last year. Sarah's father had professed himself delighted at how well it was all going and he gave his daughter full credit for the changes she had instigated and for the way in which she controlled her staff, kindly, yet with an air of authority. Sarah had surprised herself that she was able to take charge in the way she had done. The two women who helped her with the baking and preparation, and the three waitresses, all respected her and never tried to argue with her or to shirk their duties, even though most of them were many years her senior. They had fallen over themselves just now to fit in with her arrangements, when she had suggested, diplomatically, that it would be helpful if she could finish an hour earlier. With one voice they had told her to 'get along and enjoy herself'.

Glancing round now at the refurbished tearoom, Sarah couldn't help but feel gratified, and ever so slightly smug, although this was not her nature. Her father had been extremely co-operative, providing her with a large kitchen and moving much of the household department down to the basement, in order to accommodate more seating for the café. Maroon velvet curtains, an exact match to the waitresses' dresses, hung at the large windows. The customers fortunate enough to procure a window seat could see, about fifty yards away, the busy promenade, the golden sands and the sea and, if they craned their necks, the top of Blackpool Tower. The carpet was maroon, too, floral-patterned and with a thick pile, and on the oak-panelled walls there hung prints of country scenes; bluebell woods, greystone farmhouses and cascading waterfalls. On each of the small round tables, which would seat no more than four, was a dazzling white damask cloth and, in the centre of each, a small vase of fresh flowers, roses and sweetpeas at the moment, in this time of early summer.

'You look like a dog with two tails,' teased Nancy, smiling at her cousin, 'and well you might an' all. I'm real glad for you, Sarah.' Nancy leaned across the table and took hold of her hand. 'I'm glad things are going so well for you now, after ... well, you know.'

'I'm not hurting any more,' said Sarah quite calmly. 'Honestly, I'm not. You said earlier that I was moping around, but it's not true. I haven't had time to mope.'

'That's the spirit,' said Nancy. 'You forget all about that bloomin' brother of mine, there's a good lass. I've said to our Joyce many a time that he's not good enough for you. Just forget him.'

Sarah doubted that she would ever do that, but what she had said to Nancy was more or less true. She wasn't hurting any more, at least not with the same intensity. She had had a good cry, that first night, and then she had tried to put it all behind her, throwing herself into her new work with a singlemindedness that had worried her parents at first, until they had seen that it was her way of coping with her unhappiness and that it was proving to be her salvation.

'How is Zachary?' asked Sarah now. She had only seen him once, and only very briefly, since that night about five weeks ago when they had parted. She had called at her Aunt Hetty's and he

164

had just been on his way out. He had been casually friendly, but with a certain wariness in his eyes and, as for Sarah, she had tried to act as though nothing untoward had happened. It had hurt though, seeing him again, and for a moment the memories had started flooding back, but she tried to stifle them. It was far better when she didn't see him at all.

'He's all right, I suppose.' Nancy shrugged. 'We don't see all that much of him. He's on shifts, so it's very much a case of now you see him, now you don't. He doesn't spend much time at home: Mam complains he's treating the place like a café, just has his meal then he's off out again. She says he stayed overnight in Preston a couple of times when he was on that run; with a friend, he said, but he didn't say who. Secretive so-and-so, our Zachary is, when he wants to be.'

'Preston?' Sarah frowned. 'I wonder who he knows in Preston. Perhaps somebody he met during the war. A lad from his regiment, maybe?'

'What's it to you?' said Nancy. 'You're not bothered, are you? Never mind our Zachary. Tell me more about this restaurant of yours. Any more new ideas, apart from these gorgeous cakes?'

Sarah nodded. 'Plenty of ideas, but not all of them feasible, I'm afraid. It isn't really a restaurant, you see, much as I would like it to be. It's just a café – a tearoom – and Father is quite determined that he doesn't want it to be anything else. I'd love to serve midday dinners – proper three-course meals – but he won't hear of it; so I have to make do with sandwiches and light refreshments. I'm always trying to think of ways of varying them, making them interesting.'

'I should think you've got enough on your plate,' commented Nancy, 'without bothering with three-course meals. I say, that's good, isn't it? "Enough on your plate?".' She laughed. 'I didn't realise I was a comedian, an' all. Honestly though, Sarah, you're a real glutton for punishment. Anyroad, you'd better be getting off home soon, hadn't you, and putting your glad rags on? And I'd best be moving as well or Mam'll be in a real old flap. See you outside the pier, shall I, about ten to six? Can you manage that?'

'Of course I can,' Sarah smiled. 'I'm looking forward to it. Thanks for asking me.'

The promenade was unusually quiet when Sarah arrived at the entrance to North Pier at the arranged time. Blackpool promenade was never entirely deserted during the season, but early evening was the time when there was a temporary lull, the holidaymakers, in the main, having gone back to their lodgings to partake of high tea. The people that were on the prom seemed to be all, like Sarah, heading towards the pier.

She read the posters on the hoardings as she awaited her cousin. Top of the bill was Charlie Chinn, 'A Cheerful Chap in Comical Capers', and below him, in slightly smaller letters, Sidney Marchant, 'Singing the Songs you Love to Hear'. That would be Sid, the person who had given Nancy the tickets and who seemed to be in charge of the group staying at Aunt Hetty's; but Sarah knew that his real name was Morris, not

Marchant. Florence Fairbrother, 'The Night-ingale of the North'; that, no doubt, was Flo, Sid's wife, who also must have changed her name to look more imposing on the billing. Mervin the Marvel and Maria... They certainly believed in alliteration. Sarah was just reading about the North's greatest Magician and Illusionist when she heard Nancy's voice behind her.

'Sorry I'm late. I knew you'd be here before me.'

Sarah turned and smiled at her cousin who was dashing towards her, one hand clinging on to her little green hat with a shallow brim which was threatening to blow away in the brisk breeze. 'You're not late, are you? I hadn't noticed. I was busy reading the poster. They're all staying with you, are they, all these people?'

'Most of them, not all,' replied Nancy. 'We'll get a programme inside the theatre, then I'll be able to tell you who's who. Come on, let's get through the turnstile. Whoops!' Nancy gave a yell as a strong gust of wind pulled again at the brim of her hat. 'Gosh! That was close. I nearly lost me best titfer in the Irish Sea.'

Sarah laughed, likewise hanging on to her close-fitting hat with one hand and endeavouring to cling to her skirt with the other. Her dress was whipping round her legs, revealing her calves almost up to the knee. But she should have known what to expect; it was very often like this on Blackpool prom. It was a good job that the show they were going to see was in the theatre at the landward end of the pier and not in the Indian Pavilion at the seaward end, or they would

167

be blown to bits before they arrived.

'What a rush it's been,' sighed Nancy, as they sat down in their seats, four rows from the front. 'I had to help Mam set the tables for tea when I got in and prepare the salad. I thought I'd never make it.'

'I thought you were cutting it a bit fine when you were sitting there nattering to me,' said Sarah. 'Have you some other visitors in, as well as the stage folk?'

'Yes, we've eight more in this week – all regulars, so Mam didn't like to disappoint them. Some of them have been coming every year since goodness knows when. The pros take up four bedrooms, so we've still quite a bit of room, and Mam and I share sometimes, when we have to.'

'You've certainly got your work cut out at Sunnyside,' said Sarah. 'Aunt Hetty must be rushed off her feet. And you, of course. How on earth do you manage, with your singing job as well?'

'Oh, fine,' said Nancy, nonchalantly. 'It's only three afternoons a week that I'm singing at Barney's – Tuesday, Thursday and Saturday – and I fit my work at home in around it. Mam's very obliging now she's got used to it.'

'I'm sure she is,' said Sarah. She grinned slyly at her cousin. 'And only this afternoon you were making her out to be a slave driver.'

'Oh well, you know me,' said Nancy airily. 'You'll have to come down the Golden Mile and listen to me. You haven't been for ages.'

'Yes, I'll try and get there soon. It's just that I've been so busy. But no more so than you and Aunt

168

Hetty, obviously. You were telling me about getting the tea ready… What about the stage folk, then? Does your mother have to prepare a separate meal for them?'

'Sometimes she does, but they're all pretty accommodating; they try to fit in with our regular mealtimes. They have their midday meal with the other visitors, except when there's a matineé, then they only have a snack. They don't like too much before a performance. And Mam prepares mounds of sandwiches and cakes for them when they get in about eleven o'clock at night. We just leave them to it and go to bed as a rule, but I know they sometimes stay up till the early hours laughing and carrying on. Flo's asked me to join them once or twice. They're a grand crowd. Anyway, let's have a look at the programme, then I can tell you the ones that I know.'

'Sid and Flo, of course…' Nancy ran her finger down the page. 'And Charlie Chinn, the comedian – he's staying with us. And Mervin and Maria; he's the magician and I'm telling you, Sarah, I'm blessed if I can see how he does all them tricks. Marvellous, he is. And Maria – well, she's his lady friend, the current one, that is.' Nancy lowered her voice. 'According to Flo, there's a different Maria every season, but this one acts more like she was his wife.'

'They share a room then, do they?'

'Good gracious, no! Mam wouldn't allow any funny business like that. And Sid won't, neither. He sorts out the room arrangements. No, Maria shares with the other girls. Look – there they are on the programme – Ivy, Rose and Rita; they do a song and dance act. Then there's Albertino, the Wonder Juggler – his real name's Albert Smith – and Clive Conway.' Nancy added this last name as though it were an afterthought. 'He's a singer and tap-dancer,' she said, in such a subdued voice that Sarah stole a sideways glance at her. She was looking down at the programme, smiling secretly to herself.

'And that's all,' she added, a few seconds later. 'There are a few others in the show as well, but I don't know them.'

'Mmm … it looks as though it'll be a good little show,' Sarah remarked.

'Don't let Sid and Flo hear you call it a little show,' warned Nancy. She gave a tut of mock indignation. 'They think it's the Ziegfeld Follies, I can tell you! And it *is* jolly good. Anyway, you can see for yourself now. It's starting…'

The red plush curtains were drawn back to reveal a garden setting. Trees and flowers and a rose arbour were painted on the flats at each side of the stage and from the centre appeared seven girls. They were clad in flimsy floaty dresses of a gauzy material which displayed a good deal more than a glimpse of ankle which was all that well-brought-up girls were supposed to reveal. 'The Rainbow Revellers' they were called on the programme, and their dresses were of the seven colours of the rainbow. They flitted as daintily as butterflies to the music of Grieg's *Morning*, then, at a sudden chord from the five-piece orchestra, their mood changed and they gave a spirited rendering of 'Oh, You Beautiful Doll', arms waving and legs high-kicking in unison while the feathers on their heads dipped and swayed.

'Good, aren't they?' whispered Nancy. 'But they're not staying with us.'

Sarah had no time to reply before Charlie Chinn (the Cheerful Chappie) came bounding on to the stage. His costume of loud green-checked suit with an enormous flower in the buttonhole, vivid yellow shirt and shaggy ginger wig with a tiny bowler hat perched on top proclaimed to the audience, if they were ever in doubt, that this was the funny man of the show. And he was funny, too. His deadpan expression had you smiling before he even spoke and Sarah found herself laughing uproariously at his jokes, even though she had heard some of them before, and tapping her feet as he broke into his final song, 'Wait Till the Sun Shines, Nellie'.

'He's a caution, isn't he?' she remarked to Nancy as he rolled off the stage. 'I'll bet he's good fun to have around.'

'He's a bit of a misery actually,' Nancy hissed behind her hand. 'Forever complaining about his digestion. He can't eat this and he can't eat that. He drives Mam barmy. Shhh ... here's Sid.'

Sidney Marchant, the singer of popular ballads ('the songs you love to hear') was only adequate as a baritone, slightly off-key at times, but the audience loved him. Probably because, as Nancy whispered to Sarah, he was a 'real lovely man', and this came over in his performance. He was as stockily built as a bull terrier and he stood in the centre of the stage, legs apart, fists clenched and his forehead beaded with perspiration as he sang of the roses blooming in Picardy. His rendering

171

of 'Because' (you come to me ... with naught save *lo-hove*...) might have brought the house down, Sarah thought, if the theatre had been full. As it was, there was the sound of appreciative applause as Sid left the stage and a shout from the back of 'More, more!'

Sarah wasn't particularly interested in the trick-cyclist, clever as he undoubtedly was, nor the lady with the performing poodles because they were not among the pros at Aunt Hetty's. But she declared herself to be delighted at the other acts. Florence Fairbrother was, on the whole, a more talented singer than her husband, but her heaving bosom and suggestively rolling eyes as she exhorted the audience to 'Follow the Merry Merry Pipes of Pan' would have had Sarah and Nancy in fits of laughter a few years back. As it was, they controlled themselves admirably, just exchanging sly grins and the tiniest giggles.

Albertino, the Wonder Juggler, had Sarah on the edge of her seat as she watched the coloured balls and skittles, then massive dinner plates, whirling through the air; and she avowed she was as mystified as Nancy when Mervin the Marvel made Maria vanish in a puff of smoke before their very eyes.

'You can do as well as that,' Sarah murmured as Ivy, Rose and Rita – billed as The Tantalising Trio – went into their song and dance routine. Their voices harmonised well and their dancing was passable, but none of the trio seemed particularly gifted. They were just three very pretty and personable girls.

'D'you really think so?' said Nancy, beaming

with pleasure.

'I'm sure of it,' replied Sarah. 'You could knock spots off them, any day.'

Sarah couldn't help but notice a change in Nancy's demeanour, a heightened awareness of what was taking place on the stage, when Clive Conway came on. 'The Boy with Flashing Feet' it said on the programme, and that was no exaggeration. Sarah had never imagined that feet could move so fast, darting about like quicksilver, two patent leather pumps on the end of well-shaped legs. He was in evening dress, complete with top hat and cane, and was elegance personified. There was no doubt that Clive Conway was an extremely handsome young man – and he looked as though he knew it, too – if somewhat dandified, with eyes of startling blue and blond curls which appeared to be plastered to his head. Sarah found herself wondering, as she stole a surreptitious glance at her cousin, if this fellow had supplanted Barney Bellamy in Nancy's affections. Barney, she knew, was now more of a father figure to Nancy than a prospective beau. Clive Conway, however, could be no more than twenty-eight or so, and Sarah could well understand that he might turn a girl's head, especially an impressionable girl such as her cousin. His eyes were flirtatious, full of 'come hither' glances, as he asked the audience 'Who Were You With Last Night?'

Nancy gave a sigh of sheer delight as he left the stage and turned to Sarah, no longer bothering to feign disinterest. 'Terrific, isn't he?' Her eyes were shining as brightly as emeralds. 'Oh, I do

173

think he's talented. The best of the lot, in my opinion.'

'Yes, he's very good,' Sarah admitted. 'What's he like, though? As a person, I mean. Is he …nice?'

'Of course he's nice. Very friendly – unaffected, you might say.' Sarah doubted this, judging by Clive Conway's haughty stance as he strutted off the stage, but she didn't comment. 'He gets on well with everyone,' Nancy added.

The lights were going up now, signalling the end of the first part of the show. 'So you're seeing how the other half lives,' Sarah remarked, 'having all these folk staying with you. D'you ever feel like joining them?'

'What, me? Chance'd be a fine thing!' But Nancy sounded wistful. 'No, I'm quite happy singing at Barney's … at the moment, anyway. I've had some jolly good numbers and I'm not as nervous as I was at first. Honestly, Sarah, I was scared out of my wits when I first started there, but I never let on to anyone. And they're a good crowd that you get down the Golden Mile, just wanting to enjoy themselves and have a laugh. I suppose they're not too critical,' she added thoughtfully.

'They won't give you the bird, you mean?' Sarah laughed.

'Perish the thought!' Nancy gave a mock shudder. 'Flo's been telling me tales of the rough audiences they've had sometimes. Not often, mind, just occasionally when they've been working the inland towns.'

'But not in Blackpool?'

'No, of course not in Blackpool. Folks here just want to have a good time.'

Sarah looked round at the theatre, the Eastern Pavilion, as it was called. It had been built about sixteen years ago, in 1903, and Blackpool was justifiably proud of it. It didn't have the grandeur of the Opera House, which was part of the Winter Gardens building, nor the cosy intimacy of the Grand Theatre in Church Street, but it was quite splendid for all that. The roof was held up by intricately carved pillars, and elaborate chandeliers of an Eastern design hung from the ceiling. Their seats were in the front stalls, and from the fourth row they had an excellent view of the stage. It was not a very large theatre; there was just one floor, no circle or gallery, and it was, on this Monday evening, only about half-full. Sarah guessed that most of the people would be, like herself and Nancy, complimentary ticket-holders.

The only fault that Sarah could find with the theatre was the seats. They were hard wooden benches, not the comfortable plush seats to be found in the town's rival theatres. She was by now wriggling around in some discomfort.

'These benches are a bit hard on your bottom, aren't they?' she remarked to Nancy. 'We should have brought cushions. Why didn't you warn me?'

Nancy giggled. 'Never thought of it. Come on, let's go and get an icecream and stretch our legs. When the second half starts you'll forget all about your numb bum!'

The second half of the show was very much the mixture as before – the same acts, but with different costumes and different songs. The finale was what might be called the *pièce de résistance* of the evening, a Celebration of Victory. It was now some eight months since the war had ended, but the country was still rejoicing. Only that week a special Children's Day, with races and competitions, was being held in the town and a full-scale Peace Celebration and Parade was planned for September. In the Winter Gardens Pavilion a Victory Revue was being staged, complete with a Flying ballet, while here, on the North Pier, the artistes were performing, twice-nightly, their own more modest celebration.

Florence Fairbrother and Sidney Marchant, separately and then in duet, sang songs from *Merrie England,* that essentially British light opera; and when the whole company joined in the singing of 'O Peaceful England' Sarah was sure that there couldn't be a dry eye in the house. Hers were unashamedly moist.

Then the audience was invited to join in the perennial favourites 'Let the Great Big World Keep Turning', 'Dolly Gray', 'Tipperary' ... and 'Keep the Home Fires Burning'.

'There's a silver lining,
Through the dark cloud shining...'

Sarah sang the words feeling happier than she had felt for ages.

The stage was a riot of red, white and blue; the buntings and streamers and Union Jacks which fluttered from all four corners, the sequin-bedecked costumes and the feather headdresses of the dancers, the evening gowns, suits, top hats and striped waistcoats of the assembled company were all in the same patriotic colours. Sarah clapped till her hands were sore, as did Nancy at the side of her, then they all stood to sing 'God Save the King'.

'It's been a glorious evening,' said Sarah, as they walked over the wooden planks of the pier to the turnstile. 'I'm so glad you asked me to come, Nancy. I wouldn't have missed it for anything.'

'Knew you'd like it,' said Nancy, a satisfied note in her voice, 'and it's good to see you enjoying yourself again.'

They stood for a few moments at the promenade railings, gazing out towards the horizon. Over there, somewhere, but not visible now, was the Isle of Man. The sky was still quite light, but the sun was beginning its descent over the sea, painting the sky in glowing colours of scarlet, yellow and orange. Every warm colour imaginable, thought Sarah, remembering the poetic names in the paintbox she had possessed as a child – vermilion, crimson lake, burnt umber, yellow ochre – and all these hues, and more besides, were to be seen in the evening sky. The low hanging clouds below the ultramarine of the sky were edged with silver, and tiny circlets of gold glimmered like sovereigns on the darker blue of the sea.

If Blackpool could be said to have any true beauty then it was undoubtedly in its sunsets. Sarah wondered, as she stood there, feeling completely at peace with herself, if a sight such as this could be matched anywhere in the world.

The cloud really did have a silver lining, just as they had been singing about in that song. Sarah, for the first time for ages and ages, felt an uplifting of her spirit and a desire to look forward to a future of which she was no longer afraid.

Chapter 9

Zachary flung another shovelful of coal into the boiler, then stretched, easing his aching back. It certainly was back-breaking work. Surely there could be few jobs to match it for sheer physical labour, except for working down the mine, of course, or as a navvy on the railway, but Zachary didn't mind the hard work. He welcomed, in fact, the toil that each new day brought, because with the work came a respite from his agonising thoughts which, when he was idle, gave him little peace. And the dreams, too, which seemed to be getting worse instead of better.

He drew a large khaki handkerchief, a reminder of the trenches, from his pocket and wiped the sweat from his forehead. 'That should see her up the next hill,' he remarked to Alf, the driver, on the footplate beside him.

'Aye, she's pulling nicely now, lad,' replied Alf. 'Not too little and not too much. That's the secret wi' t'coal. But you're learning fast. Aye, you are that! You'll be ready to take a turn at my job afore long.'

Zachary was gratified to hear that. It had been his childhood dream to be an engine driver, to be in charge of one of those great locomotives that ran all the way from Preston, down to London, or up to Edinburgh or Glasgow. Before he went into the Army he had gone part way to realising his

179

ambition. He had started as a humble cleaner in the locomotive sheds, as all the lads did, then he had worked as a relief fireman and later as a fireman in his own right, with the occasional spell of driving, under the supervision of the engine driver. But the war had put paid to his training and, at the moment, he was a fireman again. He was watching carefully though, watching and learning and hoping that before long the coveted driving job would fall into his hands. In the normal course of events it could take several years, but many of the lads, firemen and trainee drivers like himself, had not been as lucky as Zachary; they had not returned. And so Zachary's turn for promotion might come all the sooner.

An engine was a remarkable piece of workmanship, Zachary thought now, as he watched Alf pulling at the levers and working the gears. It was almost human ... almost like a woman. You had to know just how to treat her, just how much to give her before she would respond. Zachary knew that if a locomotive lost steam on an incline it was the very devil of a job to ease her into motion again. Similarly, if a woman lost interest there seemed to be nothing you could do to re-ignite the spark. Sometimes, though, it was the fellow that lost interest.

Phyllis had been a case in point... Zachary had really believed he was on to a winner with the pert and pretty little nurse he had met during his spell in the French hospital, and finding out that she lived in Preston, only eighteen miles away, had seemed too good to be true. He had stopped off there a couple of weeks ago on his way back home from Crewe, taking a change of clothes with him in an overnight bag. He had spruced himself up in the station waiting room and, feeling well pleased with his appearance – his soft felt hat and double-breasted pinstripe suit with matching waistcoat – had set out to meet Phyllis Ogden as arranged, near the clock on Fishergate.

But it hadn't been the same. Right from the moment he set eyes on her Zachary had a feeling it wasn't going to work. Phyllis was different, somehow. As he walked towards her he couldn't help thinking how ordinary she looked; just like one of the many girls you passed in the street every day and wouldn't give a second glance. He had thought she was a stunner when he had known her in France. Maybe it had been the uniform, the crisp white apron and starched headdress and wide black belt, all giving an air of severity. A uniform always did something for a girl. Now, without it, she was quite commonplace.

'Luvly to see yer, Zachary,' she said, as he dutifully bent and kissed her cheek. 'I thought as I was goin' t' be la-ate, but I was 'ere afore you, after all. Cum on. Me mam and dad are dyin' to meet yer.'

Zachary felt himself cringing inwardly. Surely she hadn't sounded like that when he had known her in France? He had known straightaway, of course, that she was a northerner, as he was. Maybe the over-broad vowel sounds had sounded comforting when he was so far away from home, but now – well – they were just grating on him. He felt his heart sinking to the soles of his shiny black boots as he walked with her to the small terraced

181

house on the outskirts of Preston where she lived with her parents. He tried to tell himself not to be such a snob. He had a Lancashire accent himself and he wasn't ashamed of it; so had his mother and his sisters and his grandmother ... not Sarah, though, he found himself thinking irrationally. Why then, was Phyllis's accent annoying him so much?

'What's up with yer?' She dug him in the ribs. 'Cat got yer tongue? Nivver thought as 'ow you were the quiet sort, Zachary Gregson.'

He had smiled, winningly he hoped, and assured her that he was just tired after a hard day's work, and then they had gone on to talk about acquaintances that they had both known in France. It wasn't the same, though, now they were distanced from them by both time and space and Zachary was beginning to realise that he had very little in common with the girl who was walking by his side, glancing at him bemusedly from time to time. Except for ... *that,* of course. Phyllis had been an extremely provocative young lady, arousing him as few girls had ever been able to do, apart from Marie, the French waitress. It was sure to be all right when it came to that.

Zachary, however, was doomed to disappointment. But what else could he have expected, he thought bitterly, as he lay on the lumpy flock mattress in the Ogdens' tiny box-room. Mr and Mrs Ogden, nice folk, reminding him of his own Grandma and Grandad Makepeace, were very protective of their only daughter, whom they had obviously had very late in life. They professed themselves delighted to meet ''er young man',

182

but he knew that he would have to keep his distance from her. He had managed to inveigle her down a back alley on the way home from the cinema earlier, but apart from a few passionate kisses and the odd bit of groping he hadn't got very far. Phyllis on home ground was a very different kettle of fish from the sexy little nurse he had met in Amiens. Even Charlie Chaplin had failed to amuse him that evening and Zachary was glad to depart for home in the morning. At his next visit, a week later, he told her that he didn't think it was much use continuing their friendship and, to his relief, she hadn't argued.

Since then Zachary had thrown himself wholeheartedly into his work, trying to forget, if he could, all about women. They were nothing but a blasted nuisance when all was said and done. Sarah, from all accounts, was behaving as though she could manage very well without him; running round like a scalded hen in that Donnelly's Tearoom she was in charge of, according to Gran. Zachary felt peeved at Sarah's indifference, though he knew he had no right to do so. The one and only time he had seen her, since they split up, she had smiled at him so charmingly that he had almost been tempted to ask her out again. But he hadn't. He knew that Sarah Donnelly, with her refined ways and her uncompromising respectability, was not the girl for him. One day he would find what he was looking for, but at the moment he wasn't even looking.

Work was the thing, he said to himself, jumping down from the footplate as the train drew into

Preston. There was a few minutes' wait here, time for a bit of spit and polish before starting that last leg of the journey. He rubbed away diligently at the brasswork round the wheels and tender, admiring the smart maroon livery which was a significant feature of the London Midland & Scottish rolling stock. He ran his hand caressingly along the shiny paintwork of the engine. She really was a majestic creature, full of life and fire and strength, more than a match for any woman. And it was he, Zachary, who had brought her to this state of gleaming magnificence. Zachary was not alone in feeling a pride in his work, the same was true of the majority of railway workers. It was a matter of honour to them that their particular train should run exactly to time – not a minute early, not a minute late. The management demanded this, and punctuality was not only a duty but a challenge in the average railway man.

The guard waved his green flag and blew his whistle as Zachary climbed back into his cab. In less than an hour he would be home, by mid-afternoon, if he was lucky, in time for a kip for an hour or so before tucking into one of his mam's enormous high teas.

'Zachary? *Zachary!* For goodness sake, what d'you think you're playing at?' Zachary woke with a start from what, for once, was a dreamless nap, to see the irate figure of his mother standing on the clipped rag hearthrug, hands on hips, her green eyes blazing with annoyance. 'I've only just washed them chairback covers, only this morn-ing, and there you are leaning your mucky head

184

on them. And look at your boots an' all, covered with engine grease and mucking up my carpet.'

'Pardon me for breathing, I'm sure!' Zachary drew his long legs towards him now and sat bolt upright, staring back defiantly at Hetty. There was a smear of oil on the carpet, to be sure, he noticed as he cast a surreptitious glance downwards. But what the hell? It was a shabby old carpet square anyway, ready for the dust heap in his opinion. 'I've only just this minute sat meself down, and here you are screaming at me like a fish-wife. It's a pity if a fellow can't have a bit of comfort in his own home...'

'You've been here half an hour and more, Zachary Gregson! I heard you come in when I was in the back kitchen. But I thought you'd gone upstairs for a lie down, like I've told you to do many a time. Bed's the place for sleeping, not down here, and you've got your own room.'

'Ye-eh, I have, haven't I?' Zachary scowled. 'And a right poky little place it is an' all, up in the attic. If you must know, Mam, I was too tired when I came in to traipse up all them stairs. But I'll go now.' He gave an exaggerated sigh and rose to his feet. 'I can see you want to get rid of me.'

'I never said that.'

'But you meant it. Oh yes, you meant it all right. You're frightened of your stage folk – your "pros" – coming in here and seeing me in all me muck.'

'That's not true, my lad, and well you know it. None of the visitors ever come in here, into our living room, not unless they're invited.'

'I'll move out altogether if you like.' Zachary's

185

tone was aggrieved as he stood, leaning against the mantelpiece, idly kicking at the brass fender. 'I could get digs, easy as not. Some folks 'ud be glad of a lodger that pays his way every week, on the nail. In a regular job an' all.'

'Don't talk such damned nonsense, Zachary! You know your home's here, until such time as you – well – get yourself married.'

Zachary realised that he had gone too far. His mother's use of a swearword, albeit a mild one, told him very clearly that she was more than usually angry with him, and he knew, too, that what he had said wasn't entirely true. The amount that Hetty took off him each week couldn't really be said to be paying his way. But she riled him so much. Ever since he came home it had been the same, argument after argument, but he couldn't seem to stop himself.

'Lodgings, indeed. Whatever would folks think if you went into lodgings! Nobody knows better than I do that it's a poky room,' Hetty went on, more calmly now, 'but that's the way it is when you've got a boarding house. The best rooms are for them that pays most.' Her meaningful glance was not lost on Zachary. 'Our Nancy and Joyce have always been in the same boat, but I've never heard either of them complaining.'

'Joyce isn't here now, is she?' said Zachary sullenly. 'She's sleeping at Gran's. So that's another room for you to let, Mam. More profit for you to rake in.'

'Don't be so damned cheeky.' Hetty's voice was not raised, in fact he could scarcely hear her, but Zachary knew from the grim set of her mouth and the blank look in her eyes that he had not only enraged her but hurt her as well.

'I'm sorry, Mam,' he mumbled. 'Didn't mean it.'

'No, I don't suppose you did, lad.' Hetty's green eyes were expressionless and her tone apathetic as she looked across him. 'I don't suppose for one minute that you ever mean half of what you say.'

Zachary didn't answer the double-edged remark. He looked the other way, towards the mirror over the mantelpiece and as he did so he noticed the ticket that was lying there. He picked it up, reading the lettering on it. *Follies of 1919, North Pier Pavilion.* 'What's this?'

'It's a ticket, what does it look like?' his mother snapped. 'A complimentary one. They give 'em out for Monday nights. Our Nancy went a couple of weeks ago, in fact she's been twice. She took Sarah with her last week.'

'Oh, she did, did she?' said Zachary, feeling a touch of pique, as he always did whenever Sarah's name was mentioned.

'Yes, she did!' Hetty's eyes were blazing now. 'After you threw the poor girl over like a … a worn-out coat. It's a good job somebody's concerned about her. I've been ashamed to look our Gracie in the face after what you did to that poor lass.'

'Is that what Aunt Grace said? That I … threw her over?' said Zachary tentatively. He had always been aware that his aunt was none too keen on him being friendly with Sarah, although she had tried hard not to show it. He knew, intuitively, that his aunt didn't, in fact, like him very much,

187

but strangely enough, that didn't alter his regard for her. He had the greatest respect for his mother's sister. Grace Donnelly was a truly gracious woman, the personification of her name, and Zachary didn't wish to go down any further in her estimation.

'No, she didn't say that,' Hetty replied, in answer to his question. 'You know your Aunt Grace never says anything wrong about anyone. She's said very little to me, except to tell me how well Sarah's doing at the café. And I'm jolly glad she is, too. Like I was glad when she went to the show with our Nancy. Better than staying at home fretting over you.'

'She wouldn't do that, Mam. I told you – it was mutual, like. We decided we didn't want to go on seeing one another.'

'Aye, so you said,' replied Hetty flatly. 'You can have that ticket if you like,' she went on, more agreeably. 'It's for two, although I don't know who you could take with you.'

'What about you, Mam? Get your best bib and tucker on and we'll make a night of it.' Zachary smiled disarmingly, trying to make up to his mother for his unkind words, even if it was only with a free ticket.

'Don't talk wet! How can I go out at six o'clock with all the teas to see to?'

'No … I suppose not.' Zachary tried to look as though he were disappointed. 'I think I will go though, Mam. I'll go on my own.'

'You'll have to get a move on then, if you want some tea before you go. Get on with you, shape yourself.' She pushed at him, smiling for the first

188

time since she had come into the room. 'Go and get them mucky clothes off.'

Zachary found himself enjoying the performance much more than he had anticipated. He had been exhausted when he came in from work and his angry exchange with his mother had been largely a result of his fatigue. But the bracing sea air had revived him and the light comedy and musical acts were proving to be a pleasant diversion from vexing thoughts about Phyllis and Sarah, and from fears of the horrific dreams that night-time might bring.

Most of these folks, up there on the stage, were staying at Sunnyside, although he hadn't paid much attention to them until now. As far as Zachary was concerned they were, by and large, nothing but a nuisance, taking up the best rooms and occupying the bathroom when he was wanting a bath. Now, however, all decked up in their stage attire, he was seeing them in a different light.

He had seen the one they called Flo talking to his mother on a few occasions and he had thought her a very ordinary little person. But now, in her purple satin evening gown with sequins sparkling on her ample bosom, she looked positively regal; she was quite a nice singer, too. It was as though, along with her stage name and her costume, she had put on a different personality as well. It was the same with all of them and Zachary, expecting to be bored or, at the most, temporarily distracted from his worries, found himself fascinated.

It was when 'The Tantalising Trio' came on that

he really sat up in his seat and began to take notice. Ivy, Rose and Rita – they occupied the large room in the attic opposite to him and he had caught sight of them on occasions on the stairs or scurrying to the bathroom clad in dressing-gowns and slippers. It was a room which wasn't often used for guests, but as it was one of the largest in the house, taking up the whole front width of the building, Sid had said it would be fine for the four young ladies – the 'Trio' and Maria, the magician's assistant, who shared with them. These three girls looked startlingly different in their stage get-up. The fishnet tights, short frilly skirts and tight-fitting bodices left little to the imagination, and Zachary's eyes were out on stalks as he watched them.

The girl in the centre – Zachary thought she was the one called Ivy – now she really was a stunner. Her blonde hair stuck out from her head like a dandelion clock and her wide red mouth, continually smiling, revealed dainty white teeth. And Zachary had never seen such long, shapely legs; he found himself licking his lips appreciatively as he watched them swaying from side to side, twisting and twirling and kicking. Come to think of it, he had hardly ever seen a girl's legs at all. Girls were usually decorously covered from neck to ankle in demure blouses and long skirts and on the odd occasions when a girl had divested herself of some of her clothing he hadn't wasted time looking at her legs.

'By the light ... of the silvery moon,
I love to croon...'

The Trio sang teasingly, temptingly ... and Zachary felt as though Ivy's big brown eyes, a startling contrast to her wispy blonde curls, were gazing straight into his. It was, of course, doubtful if she could make out his features at all from up there on the stage, with the spotlight shining on to her face, but Zachary smiled back at her and he made up his mind that before long he would make the acquaintance of that young lady who occupied the room opposite his own. He hadn't realised that untold pleasures might be in store for him.

The dream was always the same, only varying in its intensity and gruesomeness; tonight it was more than usually horrific. He was in the trench, shielding his head and his ears from the deafening bangs going on all round him, and when he did dare to lift his head, there, at eye-level, were hundreds and thousands of feet, clad in heavy boots, marching past him, *stamp, stamp, stamp,* in a never-ending line. Zachary knew that they were the feet of dead soldiers, the thousand upon thousand of young men who had perished there in the trenches, and he knew, too, that very soon he might be numbered among them.

The scene always changed then, incoherently, as was the way of dreams, and he was there with his pick and shovel, dragging the stinking bodies from the barbed wire, flinging them into the pit. And always, always the mud, seeping round his ankles, up to his knees, his thighs. Zachary struggled to break free, to escape from the

191

hideous scene, but always the clinging, cloying mud held him back. It was when the rats appeared, enormous malevolent creatures, scurrying from amongst the remains of his dead comrades, that Zachary always woke.

The nightmare had been worse than ever this time and he found himself sitting bolt upright in his bed in a blind panic. Sweat streamed from every pore, his limbs were shaking and the muscles in his neck were so taut that he could scarcely move his jaw. He glanced round fearfully, wondering for a moment where he was, then he breathed a long shuddering sigh as he made out the familiar outlines of his wardrobe and chest of drawers and saw the faint glow of moonlight through the thin cotton curtains at his window. He was here, at home; he was safe and they couldn't get him, not this time. He started again, cowering back against the pillows, as the door opened and a gowned figure crept in; then almost cried with relief as he recognised the concerned features of his mother.

She sat on the edge of his bed and placed her hand upon his own which was clinging tightly to the eiderdown. 'Zachary, Zachary love, whatever's to do?'

'What ... what d'you mean, Mam?' Zachary's voice, to his own ears, sounded husky and unreal.

'I heard you shout. I went down to make a cup of tea – I couldn't sleep – and I heard you.' She put her hand on his forehead. 'You're sweating, lad. You're not ill, are you?'

'No ... not ill, Mam. It was a dream, that's all. A nightmare. Didn't realise I'd shouted.' Zachary wondered how many times he had shouted out before, and why his mother had never heard him. But it had been more than usually terrifying this time.

'About France, you mean?'

Zachary nodded. 'Aye, about France, the trenches. It's always the same.'

'You mean it happens a lot?'

'Quite a lot. Some times are worse than others. It was ... bad tonight.'

'But Zachary, love, why have you never told me?' Hetty's eyes shining silver, not green, in the half-light, were clouded with anxiety. 'I'm your mother, aren't I? Surely you could have said something. You know I'll always listen.'

'Dunno, Mam.' Zachary gave a slight shrug. 'I daresay I've not wanted to talk about it. It's too horrible to talk about. I keep thinking it'll all go away.' His voice was rising hysterically. 'But it doesn't, Mam, it doesn't. In fact it's getting worse.'

'Shh. Hush, lad. It'll be all right.' Hetty's tone was soothing and her hand on his brow felt cool and comforting, the way he remembered it being when he was a little lad, ill with the measles. He experienced a slight pang of guilt, recalling that he hadn't really talked to his mother about anything at all, let alone his nightmares, since returning from France. He hadn't felt like talking to anyone and his mother had aggravated him with her continual fussing and fidgeting. Now, however, he felt glad of her soothing presence.

'D'you want to talk about it, dear?' she said now.

Zachary stared at his mother, almost pleadingly. He hadn't wanted to discuss anything with her for ages, not since he was a little boy. He hadn't even considered her very much of late; she was just his mother, there to cook his meals and wash his clothes. Now, looking at her troubled face, he was beginning to realise how much she cared for him and how much she wanted him to confide in her.

'It's so real, Mam,' he began. 'Just as though I was back there. Sometimes I think I am. That must be when I ... when I shout. I can see them all again, all the pals that I lost, and I want to run away, but I can't because of the mud. It's the mud, Mam, that I can't stand, weighing me down, stopping me from getting away. And that awful stink in my nostrils – I could be sick just thinking about it. And the rats...'

He heard his mother draw her breath in sharply, and glancing across at her he saw that her eyes had filled up with tears and a look of horror had replaced her earlier expression of concern. Zachary remembered then, with a stab of remorse, that his mother had lost her husband in such horrible circumstances as he was describing. Albert, his step-father, with whom he had seldom seen eye to eye, but who, nevertheless, had been a grand fellow, had been killed at Ypres. Self-reproach did not come easily or often to Zachary, but he knew now how painful it must be for his mother to listen to his memories.

'I ... I don't want to go on talking about it,' he said hurriedly. 'I'd rather try to forget about it, if you don't mind. But thanks for listening, Mam, and for coming in to see me.' He reached over and squeezed her hand in an unaccustomed gesture of tenderness.

Hetty seemed to regain her composure quite quickly, though her eyes, when she smiled at him, still held a trace of sorrow. 'I think you ought to see a doctor,' she said quietly. 'I'd no idea you were suffering like this. I feel dreadful that I didn't know ... my own son, an' all. I'd have got the doctor round sooner if I'd realised.'

'What the hell can a doctor do for me?' A touch of Zachary's old belligerence showed as he answered his mother. 'I'm not ill. It's just my head that's full of horrible scenes.'

'It's a sort of illness, Zachary. In your mind, though, not your body.'

'You mean I'm going barmy or summat?' Zachary glared at Hetty.

'No, of course I don't mean that. Don't be so touchy, love. Anyroad, it's nothing to be ashamed of. I knew your nerves were in a bit of a state. I've seen you jump when there's a sudden noise – it's them shells, isn't it, in the trenches? – but you've seemed better these last few weeks. I'd no idea about the nightmares, though. Go and see the doctor, there's a good lad.'

'I don't see what he can do, Mam,' Zachary repeated. 'He can't make it all go away.'

'He could happen give you something to make you sleep. It's worth a try.'

Zachary nodded gratefully. 'Aye, perhaps you're right. I'll go when I'm on late shift, later this week.'

Dr Holgate had seen many young men over the

last few months in the same state as Zachary Gregson. 'Shell shock' was the term now being used by the medical profession; it was the result of being bombarded night and day for months on end by shell and mortar attack. This young man, however, said that that aspect wasn't too bad now. Sudden bangs didn't alarm him in the way that they had at first. It was the recurring nightmares, the inability to clear his head of the gruesome sights that he had been a part of for so long and which now still came back to haunt him. And not only at night; sometimes they would recur during the day when his mind was empty of other matters.

'Suppress these thoughts,' counselled the doctor. 'Chase them away when they come. Don't let them take control. You must keep your mind occupied so that they can't take over.' At least this fellow had a job to absorb his body and mind, the doctor thought, which was more than a lot of poor devils had. Thousands had come home to a dole queue.

'I'll give you a sleeping draught,' he said. 'That should help you at night. And during the day, just keep busy if you can, that's the secret. Chase the goblins away and after a while they'll stop bothering you. Your memories will fade … it'll just take time.' Dr Holgate gave a brief nod and smiled, sympathetically yet dismissively. He had many other patients to see, several of them, he didn't doubt with similar problems. As an afterthought he added, 'Have you a young lady?'

'Er, no. Not at the moment.' Zachary sounded surprised.

'Then get yourself one, that's my advice. A handsome lad like you shouldn't have any trouble. Get a nice young lady and all your nasty dreams will vanish.'

Zachary made up his mind to act upon the doctor's advice as soon as possible. It had been in his mind, in fact, before his visit to the surgery. For the last couple of days he had acquainted himself with the movements of the girls in the room opposite his own, especially Ivy, the tall one with the blonde hair and brown eyes. He had smiled at them more amiably when he had seen them, calling a cheery 'Good morning' or 'Good afternoon', as the case might be, instead of nodding morosely, which is what he had usually done in the past. He knew that they were in the habit of going out at about two in the afternoon and he waited now, his own door ajar, for the door opposite to open. He hoped they wouldn't be too long; he was due to start work at three o'clock, but he didn't want to change into his working clothes until he had made his date with the delectable Ivy.

She stared at him in some surprise, her delicately arched eyebrows raised, as he stepped forward into her path. 'Ivy ... it is Ivy, isn't it?'

'Yes.' She motioned to her friends to go on ahead. 'And you must be Zachary, although we haven't been formally introduced.'

Her voice was clear and well-spoken, without the broad vowel sounds that Zachary was so used to hearing in the girls he met. A little self-consciously he found himself wiping his hand across his trousers before holding it out to this delightful girl. 'How do you do, Ivy. I've been wanting to see you.'

'How do you do, Zachary.' Ivy's tone and her faint smile both held a trace of amusement.

'I've been wondering ... would you like to go out with me sometime?' Zachary was trying not to sound too eager – it was never a good idea to sound too enthusiastic – but it was hard to keep his tone casual.

'I'm very busy. Two performances each evening and matinées twice a week doesn't leave very much time for going out.' Ivy didn't sound regretful, only matter-of-fact, and Zachary's impatience got the better of him.

'What about Sunday then? You can't be busy on a Sunday. We could catch a tram to Squires Gate ... or go up to Fleetwood, anywhere you like.'

'No, I don't think so.' Ivy smiled brightly, but there was no doubt that she was giving him the brush-off. 'But thank you for asking me.'

Never had Zachary felt so humiliated as he watched her turn on her heel and hurry away to catch up with her friends.

Chapter 10

Sarah decided to walk northwards when she alighted from the tram at Talbot Square. It was a glorious summer evening, with the promise of daylight until ten o'clock or later, and much too nice to stay indoors. Besides, she had a slight headache which she must clear before going to bed. It was vital that she be in tip-top health for tomorrow, the start of the August Bank Holiday weekend, which was always one of the busiest Saturdays of the year, and her first in charge of Donnelly's Tearoom. She wanted business to be booming tomorrow, to justify her father's faith in her enterprise and to justify, too, the not inconsiderable sum he had invested in the venture.

She crossed the tramtrack by North Pier and walked past the Hotel Metropole on Princess Parade, named after Princess Louise, the daughter of Queen Victoria, who had opened it in 1912. In the Parade Garden was a small marble obelisk – a temporary one, Sarah had heard, to be replaced at a later date by a more significant memorial – inscribed *The Blood of Heroes is the Seed of Freedom*. Poor Uncle Albert, she found herself thinking, as she looked at the wreaths of flowers at its base; there were usually several such tributes left there by grieving relatives. She was sure that Uncle Albert had never really wanted to be a hero; he would surely much rather have been here, the jovial laughing person she remembered, in the midst of his loving family, instead of being revered now as one who had given his life for his country.

But life had to go on, as they were continually being reminded by both preachers and politicians. One had to look to the future, and the future of Blackpool, in this summer season of 1919, seemed assured as the leading holiday resort in the north of England. The visitors had flocked there in their thousands this summer and they were still coming. Many of them travelled by the railway, as holidaymakers had done for over half a century, but the railway monopoly was now being challenged by the development of motor transport. Many of the visitors to Blackpool were day-trippers who came to the resort in chara-bancs. Sarah's Grandad Makepeace, who was always well-informed about such matters, had told her that there was a load of war-surplus motor vehicles now appearing on the second-hand market. Many of these were being snapped up by ex-servicemen who knew how to drive and maintain them, and they were exchanging the lorry chassis for a charabanc body and running trips to the seaside.

'They tell me that the Preston to Blackpool road is getting that busy they're going to have to widen it,' Grandad Makepeace had said. 'To sixty feet! Just imagine that. They say it's the busiest road in t'country.'

'That's all very well,' his wife had replied with a sniff, 'but the folks that are coming here in them there charabancs are only day-trippers. They don't spend so much brass in the town, not like the folks who stop for a weekend or more. A lot of 'em bring their own sandwiches and a flask of tea an' all – you can see any number of them sitting on the seats along the prom – so they're not spending so much as a penny piece in the town. Folks like that aren't going to help Blackpool's economy now, are they?'

George smiled. 'You wouldn't begrudge them their day out, would you, Martha? It's happen all that some of 'em can afford, a day trip on a charabanc.'

'No, I suppose not.' Martha laughed. 'Take no notice; it's the boarding-house keeper in me talking now. Of course I don't begrudge working folk their bit of pleasure. I remember when our Grace and Hetty were little, just after Fred died. I couldn't have afforded even a day out, we were that hard-up.'

'And look at you now, Gran, positively coining it in,' Sarah had teased her grandma. 'And some of these day-trippers, as you call them, do find their way into our café. I can tell from their conversations that they're only here for the day, and they seem to think they get good value for money at Donnelly's.'

'Well, that's all right then.' Martha had grinned. 'And I'm ever so pleased that you're doing well, Sarah. I am that.'

Sarah was tempted to call and see her grandmother and granddad now. They lived only a few minutes' walk inland from Lansdowne Terrace which she was now passing, but she thought better of her idea. They would only detain her and, much as she loved them, Sarah

201

had decided she must have a good breath of sea air this evening, something she all too seldom found time to do. Besides, there was the odd chance that she might run into Zachary if she ventured too near to Welcome Rest, her grandma's domain. She was recovering very nicely and she didn't want to suffer a setback.

This part of the promenade between Cocker Square and Gynn Square, a mile or so to the north, had once been private land, known as the Claremont Park Estate. Sarah's gran had told her that there had been toll-gates at either end in the 1890s, when Martha and her two daughters had first come to Blackpool, charging 1d for pedestrians and 3d for carriages. Very little profit had been made, however, and now the area was free for everyone to walk there; both the working-class folk who stayed at the boarding houses in the area around North Station, and the wealthier visitors who frequented such places as the Imperial Hotel, one of Blackpool's most prestigious buildings.

Sarah walked briskly now, for a fresh breeze was blowing in from the sea. She would just go as far as the cliff gardens to the north of Gynn Square, she decided, and then turn back. She leaned against the railings at the top of the cliffs, gazing at the sea far below and at the newly constructed sea wall. This strong concrete structure would, it was hoped, deal successfully with the problem of erosion which had been the plague of this part of the coast for many years. Sarah recalled that when she was a little girl, Uncle Tom's Cabin had stood just about here, right on the cliff edge. She remembered the wooden figures of Uncle Tom,

Eva and Topsy standing up there on the roof; she remembered, also, having a drink of sparkling lemonade when she had been taken there on a family outing. She could taste its tangy freshness and feel the bubbles fizzing up her nose even now, as she thought of that happy occasion. Zachary had been there, too, as he invariably was on these jolly family get-togethers. Memories of him had a habit of creeping up on her unawares, just when she thought she was starting to forget; she tried, now, to push him from her mind. Uncle Tom's Cabin, alas, had been closed in 1907 for reasons of public safety and all buildings were now constructed on the other side of the tramtrack, away from the perils of the marauding sea.

Sarah turned now, deciding to head for home, for she was feeling suddenly very chilly. This often happened in Blackpool; you set off glorying in the sunshine and then, before you could say 'Jack Robinson', a creeping little wind would blow inland from the sea lowering the temperature in a matter of minutes. Sarah was glad, however, of the chilly wind which drove her off the promenade, for without it she might never have seen the shop.

It stood on the corner of Warbreck Road, opposite the old whitewashed building, the Gynn Inn, which had occupied that site for as long as anyone could remember, certainly since the mid-eighteenth century. The shop which was now the focus of Sarah's interest, however, was of later construction, possibly mid-Victorian, she thought, like the rest of the buildings on Warbreck Road. It was an area that Sarah didn't often frequent, being more than a mile from the town centre, too far to wander to on the odd occasions when she had time to browse around the shops. This one looked in a sorry state: the paintwork was faded and peeling, the downstairs windows were so grimy you could scarcely see through them, and the lace curtains which hung at the windows of the top two storeys were dirty and torn. But it was the large sign in the window, declaring that the premises were *To Let*, that had attracted Sarah's attention and the reason why she was standing there now, on the pavement outside, deep in thought.

She hadn't really been aware that she so badly wanted a business of her own; at least, she had never allowed the idea to take a firm hold in her mind. But now, as she gazed at the dilapidated premises at Gynn Square, Sarah realised that it was what she wished for above all else. She wanted to be boss in her own restaurant and, what was more, this was just the kind of place she wanted. It would be ideal; far enough away from the town centre and other rival establishments, and yet in the middle of a growing residential area.

Sarah shaded her eyes with her hand, peering, as best she could, through the filthy glass to the gloomy interior of the shop. What she could see was far from prepossessing; cracked linoleum only partially covering the wooden floor, wallpaper, once gold-embossed, but faded now and in place hanging in tatters, and, at the far end, a long mahogany counter. Sarah guessed that it might once have been a café of some sort, but she couldn't remember it. The premises would be ideal, though… A *frisson* of excitement gripped her as she gazed upwards at the top two storeys. It couldn't be better; attic rooms to convert into living premises and a first floor which could be made into a proper restaurant. She took a note of the name and address to contact and then set off down Warbreck Road towards the town centre, her head positively buzzing with ideas.

'Good gracious, Sarah! You certainly don't let the grass grow under your feet, I'll say that for you.' There was an unmistakable edge to Grace Donnelly's voice that Sarah had never heard there before.

She looked at her mother in some surprise, and slight consternation, too. She hadn't expected her to raise any objections. Mother was usually so amiable, always ready to listen and advise.

'What's the matter, Mother?' Sarah asked now. 'You sound as though you don't entirely approve.'

'I neither approve nor disapprove, Sarah.' Again that scarcely discernible tetchiness, but Sarah, who knew her mother so well, was acutely aware of it. 'You've sprung all this on your father and me without any warning,' Grace continued. 'We need some time to digest it all. It isn't even as if you've had a good look at the premises yet. They might be unsuitable – entirely unsuitable.'

'I've told you, Mother. I've got an appointment with Mr Butterworth to look over them tomorrow, my half-day. I wouldn't have done that without telling you both about it, you know I wouldn't.'

Sarah suspected that her parents – her mother in particular – might be a little peeved that she had progressed even this far in her negotiations for the property in Gynn Square without telling them. It had been on her way down Dickson Road, near to her gran's boarding house, that Sarah had realised that the name Butterworth on the *To Let* notice rang a bell in her mind. That was the man, surely, who had been her grandmother's landlord, until Martha, when she realised she was making a success of the business, had bought the property from him. Sarah couldn't rest until she knew and she had called at her gran's that very evening to find out more about him.

'Charlie Butterworth? Yes, he was my landlord when we first moved here,' Martha had told her. 'But this one that you're referring to will be his son, Ernest. They own quite a lot of property in this area and as far north as the Gynn.'

Both Martha and George Makepeace had shown an interest in Sarah's news and Martha had said she would contact young Mr Ernest Butterworth the next day and put in a good word for Sarah. 'Charlie Butterworth was always a decent sort of chap as landlords go,' she had said, 'and his son's pretty much the same, I believe. Not out to fleece you, like some of 'em are. Ooh … I say, Sarah, it would be real grand, wouldn't it, if you could get your own place! And right on Gynn Square, too. The posher end of Blackpool, that is. There's folks up there that aren't afraid of spending a bob or two.'

Sarah laughed. 'We're crossing our bridges a bit too soon, Gran. Let's wait and see how things go, shall we?'

But Sarah, in spite of her words, was finding it hard to curb her excitement. She had done so, with some difficulty, all over the busy Bank Holiday weekend and now, telling her parents about it all for the first time, she had hoped for a more positive reaction. Mother looked, and sounded, a trifle piqued and Father had said nothing at all yet, just looked at her contemplatively.

'I'm sorry,' Sarah said now, feeling, moment by moment, more deflated. 'Maybe I shouldn't have said anything to Gran before I told you, but it was with her knowing Mr Butterworth. I wasn't trying to be secretive.'

'It isn't that,' said Grace. 'I wouldn't be so petty as to make a fuss because you told somebody else first. You should know me better than that, Sarah. No ... it's your father I'm concerned about.' Grace's eyes softened, as they always did, when she looked at her husband. 'He's invested such a lot in this scheme of yours, the tearoom at the store – and it was entirely your idea, Sarah, to have it enlarged, you can't deny that – and now you're telling us that you're wanting to be off, flying your kite elsewhere. Haven't you given any thought to what's going to happen to Donnelly's?'

'Of course I have, Mother. I wouldn't be leaving straightaway, would I, and the staff there are all very good, quite capable of carrying on without me.'

'All the same it was your venture. And now you're leaving us in the lurch.'

'Oh, steady on now, Grace. I think that's being a little unfair.' Edwin Donnelly spoke for the first time. His hazel eyes were serious, but still very affectionate as he regarded his wife. 'Sarah has trained the tearoom staff so well that, like she says, they could very easily take over. The one called Maud, she's a first-class worker, isn't she?' He looked enquiringly at Sarah, who nodded her agreement. He made a steeple of his fingers, then tapped them together thoughtfully as he leaned back against the gold brocade of the armchair. 'I'm not going to say that we wouldn't miss you at Donnelly's, Sarah. You've done a wonderful job there, but there's no reason why the café shouldn't continue in the same way, now that you've done the groundwork. And I can quite understand that you want to spread your wings, go for your own place. I admire your spirit, my dear.'

Sarah smiled her thanks at her father, but her mother was refusing to meet her eye.

'But, there again,' Edwin continued, 'we mustn't be too hasty. Like your mother says…' he cast a slightly apprehensive glance in Grace's direction '…the premises may be … er, unsuitable. We won't know till we've seen them. We'll have to take a good look over them, find out if there are any snags.'

Sarah couldn't help but notice her father's use of the pronoun 'we.' So she wasn't altogether surprised when, looking at her decidedly, Edwin said, 'I'll come with you tomorrow, Sarah, when you go to Gynn Square. They won't try to pull the wool over your eyes if I'm there as well. Yes, we'll go together, my dear.'

If Sarah was disappointed that she wasn't to be allowed to act for herself, to make her own decisions, then she didn't show it. 'Thank you, Father,' she said, smiling at him gratefully. It had been second nature to Edwin, for so long, to cosset and protect his only daughter that she couldn't expect him to break the habit of a lifetime now. 'I'll be glad of your advice,' she added, with a sidelong look at her mother. It was Grace's attitude that was worrying her now.

Grace gave a sigh and an almost imperceptible shake of her head and when she looked towards her daughter her eyes were now more puzzled than annoyed. 'It doesn't seem all that long since we had this sort of conversation before,' she remarked, 'sitting in this very room. You remember,' she nodded at Sarah, 'when you were full of ideas for Donnelly's Tearoom. It's not a year ago...'

'And look what she's achieved in those few months.' Edwin sprang to his daughter's defence. 'You've got to admit it, Grace.'

'I'm not denying it.' Grace's voice was expressionless. 'I'm only saying that it isn't all that long since. And you can't expect your father to sink any money into this venture of yours. That's if it comes off,' she added, almost to herself. 'He's already spent enough on the tearoom at the store. It'll be up to you, Sarah, to see to the financial side.'

'Of course I wouldn't expect Father to help!' Sarah was feeling quite angry now, something she had never felt before in her dealings with her mother. 'I've got my own money, haven't I? The money that Grandad Donnelly left me. And I've saved up quite a lot while I've been working for Father. You needn't worry, Mother. I won't come sponging on you, not on either of you.'

'Your mother didn't mean it like that,' said Edwin gently, but Sarah noticed that he cast an admonitory glance at his wife. 'We know you've never been an avaricious sort of girl, don't we, Grace?'

Grace looked up and nodded and Sarah was pleased to see a look of quiet understanding pass between her parents. They never stayed at variance with one another, not for more than a moment or two.

'And we'll be so pleased if this all works out for you dear.' The lines round Edwin's mouth and eyes, much more pronounced of late, wrinkled as he smiled at Sarah, then at his wife. 'Won't we, Grace?'

Sarah was pleased to see her mother smile, albeit faintly, as she echoed her husband's words. 'Of course we'll be pleased, Edwin.'

'Grace, my dear, what a lovely surprise.' Clara Donnelly rose to her feet, somewhat stiffly, as her daughter-in-law was shown into the drawing room by the maid. Leaning forward, she kissed her affectionately on both cheeks. 'I was only thinking this morning that it was quite a long time since you paid me a visit, and here you are.' She lowered herself, with more than a little effort, into the maroon velvet sofa and patted the cushion at the side of her. 'Come and sit down, dear, and tell me all your news.'

Grace smiled warmly at this woman of whom she had once been so much in awe. Clara Donnelly had been instrumental, many years ago, in keeping Grace and Edwin apart. But that was ancient history, best forgotten, and the two women had been good friends for a long time. Indeed, Grace often found that if she had a problem then it was Clara Donnelly that she chose to share it with, rather than her own mother, who rarely seemed to have the time to sit and chat.

Clara had lived alone since the death of her husband a few years previously, still at the large house on Whitegate Drive. It was too big for her now, but Grace supposed that her memories were precious and that that was why she stayed. Her live-in maid and cook-cum-housekeeper saw to her needs and Edwin popped in at least once a week to see how his mother was faring, Grace a little less frequently. Clara must sometimes feel lonely, Grace thought now, with a surge of compassion. Her other two sons lived away from Blackpool and, at all events, had never shown as much solicitude for her as Edwin did. Grace felt sad at the thought of her mother-in-law growing older, becoming gradually more crippled by rheumatic joints, unable to go out and about as much as she used to. She made up her mind that she must visit Clara more often – there was no reason why she shouldn't do so – and to ask Edwin, too, if he could see his way to take his mother out, at least once a week, in the new Humber saloon he had recently acquired. Clara, at the time Grace had first got to know her, had led a very active social life, was on numerous committees, always attending whist drives, concerts and social gatherings, and a pillar of her local Catholic church. Now, she could hardly hobble as far as the local shops, certainly not without her stick, although Grace knew that she still attended Mass, conscientiously, once a week, driven there and back by one of the other parishioners.

The years had taken their toll of Clara Donnelly, perhaps not surprisingly, as she was now in her late seventies. Her once dark hair was completely silver and her long aristocratic features had sharpened, giving her a gaunt, almost emaciated look. Her piercing blue eyes, once so bright, had faded, but they were kinder now, much more tolerant and gentle. For though the years may have played havoc with Clara Donnelly's looks, her disposition had undergone a change for the better. She had become a much nicer person than the imperious, snobbish character that Grace recalled from twenty-odd years ago and Grace now had a deep affection for her.

The surroundings had changed little, Grace reflected. The subtle elegance of the room – the deep-buttoned velvet furniture, gilt-framed mirrors and delicate cream-coloured walls and ceiling – was the sort that didn't alter a great deal with the dictates of fashion.

'Now, what have you to tell me?' Clara put her head on one side, peering enquiringly, and a little short-sightedly, at Grace. There was a trace of haughtiness in her glance – old habits died hard

– but Grace was no longer afraid of her. 'How's that lovely daughter of yours – still working hard at the café?'

'Sarah ... Yes, she's still hard at it. She's a worker all right, is our Sarah. I have to grant her that.' Grace hesitated, staring down for a moment at the deep pile of the carpet before looking Clara straight in the face. 'It's Sarah I wanted to talk about really, Mother-in-law. We've had a row ... well, not really a row, more of a disagreement.'

'Well I never! You do surprise me. I can't imagine you falling out with anybody, Grace, let alone with Sarah. She's such a biddable sort of girl. And as for you, well, you don't like arguments, do you, my dear? If ever there was a peacemaker, then it's you.' Clara frowned. 'Whatever was it all about? Do you wish to tell me, or not?'

'Of course I want to tell you – that's the reason I came. Not the only reason,' Grace added hurriedly. 'I wanted to see how you were, too, of course. But this business with Sarah, it's been on my mind and I have to tell somebody. You see, I feel that I was entirely to blame. I was really sharp with her – quite horrid, I know – and now I feel dreadful about it. I'll tell her I'm sorry when I see her this evening, but that can't undo the nasty things I said.'

'Oh, come on, Grace. I can't believe it was all that bad.' Clara gave a pensive smile 'You couldn't be nasty if you tried, my dear. And rows happen in all families from time to time. I suppose it's because you've had so very few in

213

yours that it seems so much worse.'

'Yes, I'm sure that's true. We don't often fall out. Well, we haven't fallen out now, not really, but there's an atmosphere, if you know what I mean, and it's all my fault.'

'Come on, tell me.' Clara leaned across and patted Grace's hand with her own knobbly, prominently veined one. 'Tell me all about it.'

So Grace told her of Sarah's surprise announcement about the shop that was To Let in Gynn Square, her ideas for a business of her own and how Edwin and Sarah had gone, that very afternoon, to look over the premises. And about her, Grace's reaction to it all, her feeling that Sarah was letting them down in leaving Donnelly's, especially after all that her father had done for her.

'Mmm.' Clara nodded thoughtfully. 'I don't think your reaction was all that surprising. It is only a few months since Sarah took over the café. It's not unreasonable of you to assume that she would give it a bit longer before setting up on her own. I can see it must have been quite a shock for you, and for Edwin.'

'But that's not the point.' Grace shook her head in exasperation, but it was annoyance with herself rather than with Clara. 'I haven't been entirely honest with you. I haven't told you everything. I know only too well why I reacted the way I did. I'm jealous, you see, Mother-in-law. That's what I am – jealous.'

'Jealous?' Clara stared at her in surprise. 'Jealous of what? You've never been a jealous sort of person, my dear, I know that.' She shook her

214

head perplexedly. 'Whatever do you mean?'

Grace gave a serious smile. 'Then perhaps jealous is too strong a word. Envious, maybe. I'll try to explain. I helped Edwin at the shop, you know, all through the war, with the men being away and all that. And I quite enjoyed it. I felt I was helping the war effort and Edwin and I were able to spend much more time together, which we always like. But when the war ended my job ended too, of course. I thought I wouldn't mind. I was quite looking forward, in fact, to being at home again, to having more time to spend with my charities and organisations. But now ... quite frankly, I'm bored.'

'Bored?' Clara Donnelly's reaction showed in her voice and Grace began to feel a little guilty as she saw her mother-in-law's gimlet sharp eyes upon her. 'I should have thought you had too much to do, Grace, to ever feel bored.'

Grace sighed. 'Then perhaps I don't mean bored. No, I can see it's wrong of me to say I'm bored when Edwin does so much to make me happy. But I'm ... restless.' She put her hands to her head. 'Restless, that's what I am.' She gave a deep sigh again, letting her hands fall to her sides. 'And then when I heard Sarah, full of all these exciting plans for the future...' Grace's voice petered out.

She felt a certain relief now that she had unburdened herself. She had been busy, ever since she had relinquished her job helping Edwin, serving on committees of various charitable organisations. But she had found, to her amazement, that it was not enough, not after

215

she had been one of the world's workers. She had found herself missing the companionship at the shop, the excitement of the cut and thrust of the world of business – although Edwin had borne most of the burden of that – above all, the feeling that she was doing something of importance.

She looked at Clara now, somewhat apologetically. 'Can you understand what I'm trying to say? Does it make any sense at all?'

'Yes, of course it does, my dear.' To Grace's relief the slight look of rebuke in Clara's eyes had now given way to one of concern. 'I'm sure a lot of women must be feeling the same as you do. They have had a big part to play in running things – taking over the men's jobs in a lot of cases – while the war was on, and now they've got to get used to being subservient females again.'

Grace smiled ruefully. 'I doubt if women will ever see themselves as subservient again. And the funny thing is, it never used to matter two hoots to me. I had very little patience with the suffragettes and all the commotion they caused. I was always quite content to look up to Edwin as the superior male, the head of the household and the boss at the shop. He's always made all the decisions – he asks my advice as well, of course – but he usually has the last word and I've never wanted it to be any different. But now...'

'What exactly is it that you want now, Grace? Are you saying you want to go back and work at the shop?'

'Yes ... yes, I do want to go back.'

'And you've not discussed it with Edwin?'

'No I haven't, not yet. Do you know, it must be

the first time ever that I've failed to discuss something with my husband? You see, I don't want to go back and work as Edwin's helper, not any more. I couldn't anyway, now that the men are back in their old jobs. But I've got this crazy idea, Mother-in-law.' Grace leaned forward, her eyes shining with enthusiasm. 'I'd like to re-organise the whole of the first floor – you know, where they have the fashions and the materials.'

'I don't think it's crazy, Grace. Why should you think that it is? You're the owner's wife, when all's said and done. Surely that gives you some say in what goes on at the shop. And why haven't you told Edwin how you feel?'

'Because I'm sure he thinks I'm happy the way I am, running the home and attending meetings and doing "good works". He was glad of my assistance during the war, but I could tell that he was relieved when he got his male workforce back again and I could stay at home – where I belong,' Grace added with a wry grin.

'But the Fashion Department would be a woman's prerogative, surely?'

'Yes, but I doubt that Edwin would see it as mine. I don't think he's ever envisaged me as a career woman – that's the term they like to use. And I never wanted it, did I? I was always happy to be just Edwin's wife. And he's made me so happy. I don't want you to think that I'm not grateful.'

'And you've made him happy, too, Grace.' There was real warmth and compassion in Clara's glance. 'But maybe there's more to life than keeping house and serving on committees,

217

and if you want something more then I don't see why you shouldn't have it. As far as I'm concerned, when I married Edwin's father I was only too glad to be able to give up the daily grind, I can tell you. I was a common or garden little shop assistant, as you know, when William fell in love with me and married me. And I made jolly sure he did an' all, I can tell you!' A trace of Clara's working-class roots – which she had always striven hard to disguise and which weren't often apparent – showed in her intonation now. 'Yes, I was only too happy to stay at home amongst all the comforts that William provided for me, and to play Lady Bountiful at times.'

She gave a curt little nod at Grace's raised eyebrows. 'Oh aye, I know that that's what folk used to say about me and none too kindly neither. But I reckon I deserved it. I was a real stuck-up little madam when I first married William. But you live and learn, Grace, you live and learn...'

Clara stared unseeingly across the room for a few moments before she spoke again. 'I'm forgetting my manners today, right enough. I haven't even offered you a cup of tea yet. I'll ring for some and then you can tell me all about these ideas of yours.'

'When I started working at Donnelly's just after we came to Blackpool, it was in the Haberdashery Department,' said Grace a few moments later, as she and Clara sat balancing their Rockingham china cups and saucers on their laps.

Clara nodded. 'Yes, I well remember.'

'And I always enjoyed it so much there. I loved all the different fabrics – the colours and the

218

textures and designs, and helping the customers to match up their threads and trimmings and lace.'

'Yes, I remember William saying that you were invaluable there, my dear.'

Which no doubt annoyed you no end, thought Grace to herself, but that time, when Clara had been antagonistic towards her, was long gone. Now the older woman seemed only too ready to listen and advise.

'I've always been a competent sewer myself,' Grace continued. 'After Walter died – before I married Edwin – I took in sewing for a time, to help make ends meet. I haven't done any for ages, of course. I've been quite spoiled, being married to Edwin, with my pick of the choicest gowns in the Fashion Department, and my own dressmaker, as well, to run up anything I need.'

'And what's this idea you have now?' Clara prompted. 'I'm sure you don't want to go back into haberdashery, do you, selling pins and needles and reels of cotton?'

Grace smiled. 'No, I'm rather more ambitious than that. I've been reading the fashion magazines and the trade journals that Edwin gets and there are all sorts of new ideas coming into vogue now. Some of the big London stores are offering a dressmaking service that's a real boon to women who want something a little bit different, but who can't afford model clothes. Let me try to explain...

'There are always the readymade clothes, of course, the mass-produced ones, and these are much more readily available now, with factories

219

being modernised and with electricity being so widely used. And the clothes, too, are much easier to make nowadays. The loose-fitting dresses that women are wearing now are so easy to produce in a whole range of sizes. But not everyone wants readymade clothes. I've been reading that one of the London stores is offering three types of service to its customers. The most exclusive service is the Model Gown Salon – a very individual type of dressmaking, what they call *haute couture,* I believe, and, quite frankly, I can't see Donnelly's doing that. But as well as that they have a less expensive department, where the customer chooses a paper pattern and length of cloth from the Fabric Department, and then the garment is made up in the store's workroom, and the cost includes one fitting.

'And the next department offers what they call a "cut and fit" service. The customer chooses the pattern and material and then the workroom just cuts and fits the garment and tacks it together loosely for the customer to finish off herself at home.'

'It all sounds most ingenious, dear,' said Clara, when Grace paused to take a breath. 'And you think there would be a call for this sort of service at Donnelly's, do you?'

'I don't see why not. I think we could very well offer both types of service. We just need a few sewing machines and half a dozen or so good seamstresses. There must be lots of women who are looking for jobs. I know I would have been only too glad of someone to do the groundwork for me when I first started dressmaking. Some women are very nervous when it comes to cutting; that's the part you have to get right, or the garment's spoiled.'

'But what about the women who take in sewing for a living, like you used to do, Grace? The "little woman" on the corner of the street who is trying to make a few bob from it. Aren't you afraid that you might be taking the bread out of their mouths, in a manner of speaking?'

Grace looked serious for a moment. 'Yes...' she replied slowly. 'It had occurred to me, of course. But then you could say the same about the other things that Donnelly's sells. The ironmongery and the household goods and the clothes – everything, in fact. All these commodities are sold in smaller establishments all over Blackpool, and they're not going out of business, are they, even though I should imagine Donnelly's are sometimes quite a lot cheaper. I think there will always be a place for the small shopkeeper, and the home dressmaker, too. But, like Edwin has been telling me recently, we have got to move with the times.' Grace smiled. 'And he's only just beginning to wake up to the fact that we're almost into the nineteen twenties.'

'Well, I think it's a splendid idea of yours, Grace,' said Clara. 'And I wish you all the success in the world, I really do. But you won't get very far until you've told Edwin, will you? I'm sure he'll be only too ready to listen.'

'I'll talk to him as soon as there's an opportunity,' promised Grace. 'But today is Sarah's day. I'm longing to know how she's gone on at Gynn Square ... and to tell her that I really do approve, in spite of what I said. I hope she's not still annoyed with me.'

'Knowing Sarah, I'm sure she hates falling out as much as you do,' said Clara wisely. 'She'll be only too ready to forgive and forget. Bring her with you the next time you come, then I can listen to both your plans. And Grace – don't let it be too long, please.'

Grace saw the loneliness in her mother-in-law's eyes and knew, with a sudden stab of fear, that indeed, she mustn't leave it too long before she visited her again. For there was another look there, too; a farseeing look, one of resignation.

'Well, what do you think, Father? What do you honestly think?' asked Sarah as her father drove the Humber saloon along Dickson Road, heading for the town centre and home.

Neither of them had said much as Mr Butterworth had shown them over the premises. Sarah knew that it didn't do to be too enthusiastic or, on the other hand, too critical. She had tried to shut her eyes, as much as she was able, to the dilapidated state of the building – the obvious signs of woodworm in some of the woodwork, the peeling wallpaper, the mouse droppings and layers of grease – and to concentrate on the good points.

There was a large area on the ground floor which Sarah could see, in her mind's eye, as a confectioner's shop and café. The kitchen, also on the ground floor, was plenty large enough to work in, although the antiquated range would need to be replaced by a modern gas stove. There was a scullery opening off it with two sinks, a stone one and a wooden one for washing chinaware which was likely to chip; also a larder with marble slabs and slate shelves, a chopping block and meat hooks in the ceiling.

The first floor had obviously been used as living premises, but Sarah could imagine it, knocked through into one big room, as the restaurant of her dreams. She had grandiose schemes, but realised that it would be better to go steadily with Father, not to reveal too many of her ideas all at once, or he would say she was trying to run before she could walk.

'I think the place has potential,' said Edwin slowly, in answer to his daughter's question. 'The ground floor, certainly, although it will need a great deal of work doing to it. But it should be suitable for what you had in mind – a tearoom similar to the one at Donnelly's, I suppose?'

'Mmm, something like that,' replied Sarah cagily. 'Possibly a little shop as well, where I could sell cakes and jams and bottled preserves, that sort of thing.'

'All made by you, I suppose.' Sarah could hear the trace of amusement in her father's tone and she could imagine the twinkle in his eye, although he kept his glance firmly on the road ahead.

'Yes,' she answered confidently. 'I can make a few at a time, before I open, then I'll have a stock all ready.'

Edwin turned then, just briefly, and grinned at her, before giving his concentration once more to the road. 'I can see you've already got it planned, my dear. You're quite determined to take this property, aren't you, so it doesn't much matter what I say. But don't try to run before you can walk.' Sarah could have laughed at the way he had taken the words out of her mouth. 'One step at a time, eh? My main concern is that the premises are too big for you. You wouldn't need the first floor and the attic, surely? What about negotiating with Mr Butterworth for the ground floor only, hmm? And another point,' Edwin went on without waiting for her answer, 'Gynn Square is quite a long way from home. You're going to have to get up very early in the morning, aren't you?'

Sarah was silent for a moment. Father hadn't grasped the idea at all. What he was envisaging was a lock-up business, with his daughter coming home in the evenings, in exactly the same way as she did now. Whereas Sarah, her mind buzzing with a thousand and one ideas, could just see herself up there in the attic rooms with their splendid view of Gynn Square and the cliffs and the Irish Sea; retiring there after a fulfilling day's work in the first-floor restaurant and the ground-floor café and shop... But she knew that, like Father said, she must take one step at a time, both with her own plans and also about breaking them to her parents. She had been their 'little girl' for so long that they would find it hard, she knew, to adjust to the idea that she was now a grown-up woman with her own aspirations and ambitions – which didn't include staying at her home in Park Road.

'There's a good tram service,' she said evasively, 'and you know I'm an early riser. I've never found it hard to get up in a morning. And

I think it might be a good idea to rent the whole of the property,' she added bravely, 'for store rooms and so forth, you know.'

'Very well, dear. Just as you say. I know you have some grand schemes.' Sarah could hear the resignation in his voice and she reflected that he might not, after all, be too surprised when he heard the extent of her plans. Father was a very perceptive man. 'When were you thinking of opening?' he asked.

'By Christmas possibly, if I can get all the work done in time.'

'I don't see why not. It gives us – let me see – nearly five months. We'll get Sam Pickering's firm on to it right away, once we've sorted things out with Ernest Butterworth. I'll phone him tomorrow and tell him we've decided to go ahead.'

'Father, don't you think I had better do that?' Sarah's voice was quiet but firm. 'After all, it's going to be my business, isn't it?' She didn't add, not yours, but that was what was in her mind.

'Of course, Sarah. Of course. Whatever was I thinking about?' Edwin gave her a fond glance. 'I can't get used to you as a businesswoman, that's all. But I'm going to have to get used to it, I can see. Both with you, and your mother,' he added quietly.

'Mother? What d'you mean?' Sarah thought for a moment he was referring to Grace's fit of pique when she had first heard about the property to let, but it sounded as though he meant something else. 'What about Mother?' she repeated.

'Oh … I just have a feeling that she wants to go back to the store. I know she's restless – that

225

would be why she was so sharp with you, my dear – and she's forever asking me questions about the business and what's going on there. I'm only waiting now for her to tell me what it is she really wants. But there's something, I'm sure of it.' Edwin turned the car, somewhat cautiously, between the double gates that Grace had left open for him and into the driveway. He switched off the engine, then turned to look at Sarah, his hazel eyes serious. 'But that's between you and me.' He closed one eye in the suggestion of a wink. 'Don't let on I told you.'

'But how did you know, Father? I had no idea how she was feeling.'

'Because I know your mother so well. That's what happens when two people care for one another as much as we do. It's almost as if you can see into one another's minds. You'll find out that I'm right... Come on now, let's go and break the news to your mother. And don't worry, Sarah. She'll be delighted for you. I know she will.'

Sarah thought again, as she followed the tall figure of her father into the house, what a very admirable man he was, and how fond she was of him. She knew that when – and if – she ever got married, then it would have to be to someone with such sterling qualities as Edwin Donnelly possessed. When the next thought came, unbidden, into Sarah's mind, it took her by surprise: *that it would be someone not in the least like Zachary Gregson...*

Chapter 11

The creature was sitting on his bed, right there on the eiderdown. He could see its evil eyes glinting red in the faint light that filtered through the curtains, its nose twitching avidly for the scent of blood, its long tail snaking across the bed cover. And it was the largest one he had ever seen, as big as a cat, well-fed... As it leapt towards him, making for his eyes, Zachary screamed. He bounded from the bed and ran towards the door. He wrenched it open and fell headlong into the passage outside, colliding with a figure who was coming the other way. He felt a second scream issuing from his lips and knew that he was shuddering from head to toe, before he was aware of comforting arms around him and a calm voice telling him, 'Shhh... Steady on now. It's all right...'

Ivy Rathbone guessed what was the matter as soon as Zachary Gregson crashed into her, fleeing from his bedroom as though all the demons in hell were after him. She knew that he had served in France. It would be those damned trenches; the effect they had on the lads who had been there was a longlasting one that could not easily be brushed aside. Ivy knew because she had seen her brother, Jack, reacting in almost the selfsame way. He had suffered from nightmares for many months after returning to his home in Halifax. Nightmares and fits of depression and sudden, peculiar turns whenever there was a loud noise. According to her mother's letters Jack was gradually improving, after his return to the woollen mill and the recommencement of his friendship with his young lady, but she feared it might take a long time for him to make a complete recovery.

And it must be the same with Zachary Gregson, Ivy thought now, as she put her arms round his trembling form, although she would never have dreamed he was the sort of lad to suffer in this way. He had always struck her as a supercilious so and so; the way he nodded at the girls when they passed on the stairs, only condescending to speak when he felt inclined, and always with that sardonic curl to his lips. Which was the reason she had refused when he had asked her, quite out of the blue, if she would go out with him. Cheeky blighter, after he had practically ignored her for the last couple of months.

He was a good-looking lad, though, she had to admit that, with his gipsy-ish features, his black curly hair and deep brown eyes, so dark as to be almost black. But handsome is as handsome does, as her mother had often told her, and Ivy had felt not the slightest stirring of attraction for him. She felt sorry for him now, though.

'Are you feeling a little better?' she asked after a few moments, when his trembling had subsided. 'It was a nightmare, wasn't it?'

'Yes. I'm sorry – I've made a fool of myself.

Don't know what came over me.' Zachary's voice was just a mumble against the woollen material of her dressing-gown. He raised his head, looking at her shamefacedly. There was certainly no arrogance in his look now, only slowly subsiding fear and embarrassment. 'I'd best get back in there.' He gestured with his head towards the open bedroom door, but Ivy could tell as he did so that he was still fearful of what might be lurking in the deep shadows.

'No, I don't think that's a good idea. Not yet. I can see you've had a nasty fright.' Ivy patted his arm consolingly then rose to her feet, forcing Zachary to do the same. 'Let's go down to the kitchen and I'll make us a cup of tea. Your mother won't mind, will she?'

'No. She might still be down there herself. She's something of a night owl. I'm surprised she hasn't come running out to see what's up. She did once before. It's not the first time, you see.' Zachary gave Ivy a furtive look from beneath his long-lashed eyelids. 'These bad dreams – the doctor gave me a sleeping draught, but it doesn't seem to have done much good tonight.'

'A cup of tea then, that's the answer,' said Ivy, in a matter-of-fact voice. 'Come on, let's be having you. We can't stand here talking all night or else we'll have everybody wondering what's going on.' They had been speaking in hushed voices, but Ivy was conscious that there might be eavesdroppers behind the closed bedroom doors.

'I'd best get my dressing-gown then,' whispered Zachary, looking down somewhat embarrassedly at his blue striped pyjamas. With an apprehensive glance around him he dashed back into the bedroom, grabbed his woollen dressing-gown from behind the door and slithered his feet into his slippers. He closed the door firmly behind him as he came out again.

'What time is it?' Zachary asked, sounding perplexed, as they tiptoed down the first flight of stairs.

'It's about half-past twelve.'

'What were you doing then, wandering around the house after midnight?'

Ivy grinned. 'You don't ask a lady a question like that.'

'Oh, I see. Sorry, I wasn't thinking,' Zachary mumbled, but Ivy was relieved to see that he smiled, for the first time.

The kitchen was deserted; Hetty Gregson was not there after all, to Ivy's relief. She felt, somehow, that Zachary would not welcome the fussing of too many womenfolk just at this moment, but she hoped that a cup of tea would help to clear his mind and put him in the right mood for a restful sleep. Ivy bustled herself filling the kettle and putting it to boil on the gas ring. She hadn't been in this room before, but one kitchen was pretty much the same as another and Ivy had got used to all manner of cooking appliances in her journeyings up and down the country. She could see that, as well as the gas stove, Mrs Gregson also had a coal range with side ovens in the living room which adjoined the kitchen.

'For heaven's sake, go and sit yourself down,' she said to Zachary, who was hovering at her elbow. 'I can mange to make a cup of tea.'

'Thanks. The cups are on the dresser, tea in the caddy,' he muttered, looking ill-at-ease as men often did in a kitchen. Ivy guessed that his mother had spoiled him, waited on him hand and foot, no doubt. He sloped off into the living room and sat down in one of the shabby easy chairs at the side of the fire.

She joined him a few moments later, sitting in the chair opposite him. There were still a few glowing embers in the grate of the large black range; Ivy felt glad of their comforting warmth, for the night, though it was mid-August, had turned chilly. They sipped the tea from the willow-pattern cups, not speaking for several moments. Zachary still appeared edgy, which was, Ivy suspected, an unusual state of affairs for him. It was she who broke the silence.

'There's nothing like a cup of tea, is there?' A somewhat trite remark, she knew, but it would do as an ice-breaker. 'A cure for all ills. I don't know what we northerners would do without our cups of tea, do you?'

Zachary smiled and nodded, still rather abstractedly. 'It's very good of you ... to bother with me, I mean.' He stared down at the cup and saucer in his lap and Ivy could see that he was having a hard job, even now, to stop his hands from trembling. His knuckles were white as he grasped at the cup. 'Oh God! I feel such an idiot. Whatever must you think of me, showing myself up like this?' His voice rose in a crescendo of panic and Ivy could see the desperation in his eyes.

She rose to her feet and gently took the cup and saucer from him, placing it on the table, covered with a chenille cloth, to the side of him. 'Don't you start worrying about what I think, or what anyone else thinks, for that matter. What I think is that it's a damned disgrace that young men like you had to suffer the way you did, over in France. That's what it is, isn't it? It's still with you.'

Zachary nodded numbly, not even looking at her.

'I know, you see. I understand. I've seen it before. My brother is just the same as you are.'

'He is?' Zachary looked at her intently now. 'He was in France, like me?'

'Yes, for more than three years.'

'Poor devil! I was there for two and that was bad enough. And he's having nightmares, is he, your brother? Like I am?'

'Yes … but he's getting better now. My mother says he's starting to put it all behind him. It will improve, you know, Zachary.' She used his name for the first time and was pleased to see a glimmer of warmth and interest in his eyes now, instead of panic and fear. 'You will be able to forget, as time goes on. It will recede further and further back in your mind.'

'The doctor said I had to suppress these thoughts when they came into my mind, not to let them take control. "Push them away", he said, but it's easier said than done. It's not too bad during the day when I'm busy with all sorts of other things, but I can't control my mind at night. I can't control … the dreams.' Zachary's voice was husky with emotion and he shuddered again.

'Mmm, yes, I know. I know.' Ivy nodded slowly. 'Far be it from me to go against what the doctor says – I'm sure he thinks he's giving you the best advice – but I don't feel it can be doing you any good to suppress your thoughts. I don't mean that you should dwell on them, but ... have you ever talked about it to anyone?'

'You mean about ... what it was like ... over there?'

'Yes. Have you never told anyone? Tried to get it out of your system?'

'No. Who would I tell? I can't talk to Mam. I tried, once, when I'd been having a nightmare. She came in to see what was up with me and I tried to tell her. But I could see it was too upsetting for her. My father was killed out there, you see – well, my step-father he was, really – so it was all too much for her. And I'm not all that close to my sisters, our Nancy and Joyce. And I don't see Sarah any more,' he added, half to himself.

'Sarah?'

'She's my cousin. Well, she was a bit more than that at one time, but we decided it wasn't much use. I doubt if I could have talked to Sarah, anyroad. She's a very ... gentle sort of a girl. But perhaps you're right. Happen if I could talk about it, instead of bottling it all up, then it might begin to go away.'

Ivy made a sudden decision. 'Try talking to me,' she said.

'To you?'

'Yes, why not?' She gave a wry grin.

'Well ... I dunno. You're a lady, aren't you? There

are things I could never tell a lady.' Zachary's eyes clouded over for a moment as he stared into the fire. 'There were some things I saw over there ... I've seen tougher men than me retching at the sight of them. I couldn't tell you, Ivy.'

'Don't be deceived by my appearance, Zachary,' said Ivy quietly.

Zachary looked at her quizzically.

'By my blonde hair.' She patted at her short pale golden hair, 'and by the – er – wiggle in my walk.' She gave a little laugh. 'Most of it – my feminine guiles – are put on to appeal to the audience. Underneath it all I'm quite a tough lady. I've had to be. The eldest of six, I am, apart from our Jack – the one that was in the Army – who's a couple of years older than me.'

'And that's how old?'

'He's twenty-five, I'm twenty-three.'

'You're a year older than me.'

'Then imagine that you're talking to your old auntie,' said Ivy, smiling. 'I'm all ears, and I've a feeling that you're not going to feel right until you've a few things off your chest.'

Once Zachary started to talk it became much easier. He had had qualms about telling this fragile-looking girl of some of the fears and phobias that still haunted him, of the horrors that existed in the deep recesses of his mind. Ivy Rathbone looked delicate, almost ethereal; a pretty face with regular features on a long slim column of a neck and, topping it all, that pale dandelion clock of hair. But there was a look of astuteness in her dark feminine prettiness, her

234

charm which was, as she had said, mainly assumed to bewitch an audience.

The words tumbled from his lips in a neverending stream; it was as though, once he started, he couldn't stem their flow.

'It's the rats,' he said. 'That's what's still haunting me, even now. I can't get the bloody creatures out of my mind. Tonight, when I screamed, there was one sitting on my bed, at least I imagined it was. I've always been terrified of 'em, you see, and it was the one thing in the trenches that I couldn't abide. When I was a little lad I was even scared of mice; I know it sounds daft, but I was. Me mam used to set traps for them, but I'd never go anywhere near. I never got over my loathing for them, their long stringy tails and evil eyes.' Zachary gave a shudder. 'And these creatures in France, they were a hundred times bigger.

'The worst time was when I had to help with burial duty. We all had to take our turn, but it didn't come round all that often, thank God! They were there, in the rotting corpses; they ran out when we moved 'em. They'd made nests, some of 'em, in the ribcages...'

Zachary stopped as Ivy gave an involuntary intake of breath, putting her hand to her mouth. He could see that she had turned pale, paler than she already was, for she hadn't much colour to start with.

'I'm sorry,' he said gruffly, giving her an apologetic look. 'I know it's nasty. I did warn you.'

'It's loathsome,' said Ivy. 'It's beyond belief,

what you had to put up with. Thank God that it was the war to end all wars. That's what they say, don't they? Thank God it'll never happen again.' Her large brown eyes were misted with tears.

'I'm sorry if I upset you,' said Zachary. 'I'd better not go on. You don't want me to go on, do you?' he asked in a voice which, to his own ears, sounded unusually sympathetic.

'Yes, I do. I've heard some of it before, from my brother, although he didn't go into such ... detail.'

'I'm sorry,' mumbled Zachary again.

'There's no need to be. I've told you I'll listen and I will. Go on, Zachary. Talk it all out of your system, if that's what you want.'

'We shovelled the bodies into the shell-holes as fast as we could. The worst part was seeing the bodies of comrades, lads you'd fought alongside of; when you could recognise 'em, that was, 'cause a lot of the time you couldn't – the flesh had nearly all rotted away. We had to get their pay books out of their pockets – in good condition, most of 'em were, 'cause they were wrapped in oilcloth. There were photos in them, too – mothers and fathers, wives and sweethearts, children an' all, and sometimes a last will and testament. They tell me they didn't even need a witness for that. I never got round to making mine. Nothing to leave, you see.' He gave a self-conscious laugh.

'What happened to them?' asked Ivy quietly.

'The pay books? Oh, they were returned to brigade headquarters, and it was the job of an officer of the battalion to write to the parents or wives. Hundreds of 'em, they had to write. One of the officers told me that they tried to make them real letters of condolence – a bit personal, like – to say how sorry they were and that. And they always tried to make out that the poor devil had died instantly, even if he hadn't. But after they'd written so many, it wasn't to be wondered at if they turned out a bit stereotyped.'

'It wasn't always true, then, when they said the fellow had died instantly?'

'Was it hell! We could hear them sometimes, after there'd been a skirmish, the poor sods who had been left behind in no-man's-land, crying out with pain. The officers used to give 'em a dose of morphine sometimes, to relieve their suffering. Or if they were really bad – no hope cases – they were allowed to shoot 'em through the back of the head...'

'No! That's awful, it's obscene!'

'It's painless, I believe, Ivy. At least, so I've been told. Leastways it was better than writhing in agony, with not a cat in hell's chance of recovering. Aye, that's what it was over there – *hell*. Sheer hell on earth. Any one of our lads who's been out there will tell you the same.'

'It must have been like that for the enemy as well,' observed Ivy. 'I don't suppose any of them wanted a war any more than you did. Wasn't there some story about the British tommies and the Germans getting together, the first Christmas Eve of the war, singing carols and exchanging cigarettes and all that?'

'Mebbe. Whether it's true or not I don't know.' Zachary's voice sounded sceptical. 'I only know that I wouldn't want to give the time of day to any bloody German, not after that lot. I'd rather spit in his eye. Aye, it'll be a long time before some of us can forget, even though we are all supposed to be living in peace now.'

'And did it go on all the time, the shelling and fighting? It's hard for me to imagine, even now, with you describing it to me, just how dreadful it must have been.'

'No, not all the time. We had to sleep sometimes, and I reckon the enemy had to sleep an' all. The mornings could be quite peaceful. We used to stand there, staring across into no-man's-land, with our rifles at the ready – dawn was a good time for an attack, you see – and I've seen some beautiful sunrises. The sky all pink and red and gold, just like it is here in Blackpool, except that it's setting here, not rising. But I shall never feel the same about it again; it'll always remind me of that hell-hole.'

'Perhaps, in time,' said Ivy gently. 'All bad memories fade, Zachary.'

'Aye, no-man's-land,' Zachary went on, as though he hadn't heard her. 'It was hard to believe at times that it could be the scene of such carnage. Not when you watched the sunrise. And the wild flowers an' all. There were flowers growing there, in the fields that separated us from the Germans. I dunno what they were – I'm not much of a nature lover – but they were there all right. Poppies, blood-red poppies – I knew them – and buttercups and daisies and others as I didn't know the names of. You would hardly believe, would you, that flowers could grow in the middle of so much chaos.'

'Life goes on,' said Ivy simply. 'Even in the midst of death and destruction.' She looked across at Zachary who had fallen silent. 'Have you finished, Zachary? There's nothing else you want to tell me?'

Zachary shook his head. 'No ... no, that's it, I think.' He felt as though he were drained of energy, but he was surprised at how much clearer his mind felt now. 'Thanks for listening to me,' he said. 'I think you were right – it was what I needed. I only hope it hasn't been too much for you. You'll be the one having nightmares now.' He looked at Ivy in some concern. 'D'you think you'll be all right?'

'Of course I will. I'll have another cuppa, then I'll be off to bed.' Ivy lifted up the brown teapot, raising her eyebrows enquiringly. 'How about you?'

'No, no more for me, thanks.'

'Then I'll just drain the pot. Mustn't let good tea go to waste – that's what my mother always says.' She poured the last dregs of tea into her cup. 'But it might be a good idea if we talked of something more pleasant before we retire.' She smiled at him and Zachary noticed, as he had done when he saw her on the stage, how her wide lips parted to reveal a set of dainty white teeth. She really was a most attractive girl. 'The show,' she said now. 'Tell me how you liked the show.'

'How did you know I was there?'

'I saw you – quite near the front, weren't you?'

'Yes, but I didn't think you could see anything from up there.'

239

'Oh ... I saw you, all right. So what did you think of it?'

'I liked it fine,' replied Zachary. 'Especially The Tantalising Trio!' He rolled his eyes at her.

'Flattery'll get you nowhere,' she retorted. 'I don't believe you anyway. What did you really think of it?'

'I thought it was grand, honest. They're all good, aren't they, all the people that are staying here at Sunnyside. They all look so different when they get up there on the stage. I could hardly believe that the one they call Flo was the same person.'

'Yes, she really sparkles, doesn't she, our Florence, when she gets her finery on. I suppose it's the same with all of us. We take on different personalities when we get up there.'

'Mmm ... Must be hard for you to come down to earth again, to climb back into your own skin.'

'Oh no.' Ivy shook her head. 'Not for me, at any rate. I never lose sight of the real me. I've told you, what you see up there on the stage is just an act. I never confuse play-acting – singing and dancing – with reality.' She tapped at her blonde head with her forefinger. 'This is the real me – Ivy Rathbone – and I've got both feet firmly on the ground, I can assure you. They're not all like me, though. Some of them seem to live in a make-believe world all the time. It makes it hard to discover anything of the real person underneath.'

'Are you speaking of anyone in particular?'

Ivy gave a slight shrug. 'Not really. I'm just speaking generally. It wouldn't be the thing,

240

would it, to start criticising my fellow artistes.' Zachary sensed a touch of irony in the last two words and he began to wonder whether singing and dancing, even though she was so talented, was, to Ivy, just a way of earning a living. 'I'm certainly not talking about Sid and Flo,' she went on. 'The salt of the earth, those two. Real genuine, honest people, they are. That's why Ma was so keen on me doing it, because she knew Sid and Flo.'

'He's in charge of the company, then, is he?' asked Zachary.

'No – we're not really a company, as such, but people often think we are because we spend such a lot of time touring round together. We all have the same agent, you see, so we tend to get block-booked. That's what happened here, in Black-pool. And yes, I suppose Sid is our unofficial leader. He usually sorts out any problems for us.'

'How long have you been on the stage?'

'On the stage! I say, that sounds good, doesn't it, for a twopence-ha'penny act like ours?'

'It's not a twopence-ha'penny act,' said Zachary earnestly. 'I've told you – it's jolly good. How long have you been doing it?'

'Oh, only since the end of last year, just before the war finished. Sid's little lot were playing in Halifax, you see – that's his home and my ma's always known him – and there was a vacancy in the trio and he managed to pull a few strings. And that was that.' She spread her hands wide. 'At least it's a job and it helps to keep the wolf from the door.'

'But you must have wanted to do it, surely?

241

And you're very good, really you are, I'm not just saying it.'

'Oh yes, I've always enjoyed getting up on the stage and singing and reciting, at school concerts and chapel "dos" – all that sort of thing. Ma sent me to elocution lessons for a while, until it got too expensive when the younger kids came along.'

'Yes, I thought you talked posh. You've no trace of a Yorkshire accent, have you? I'd no idea where you came from, till you said.'

Ivy laughed. 'I don't know about posh. I suppose I've got into the habit of talking like this … although there's nowt wrong wi' 'avin' a Yorkshire accent, I can tell thi, lad! My mother wanted me to learn to speak nicely – "to talk proper", she called it – and I've always tried to do what Ma wants.'

'It was your mother's idea then, was it, for you to go on the stage?'

'Sort of. She thought it was a good opportunity for me, and I probably pretended that I was keener on the idea than I really was. At least there's a bit more room at home now I've gone and one less mouth to feed, and I try to send Ma as much as I can, when I've paid my way.'

'They're all still at home, are they, your brothers and sisters?'

'Yes – Jack and I are the eldest by quite a few years. The two of us have always been close. That's why I was glad I was at home when he came back from France. It was last March and I was "resting" for a week or two.' Ivy gave a little laugh. 'That's what stage folk call it when they really mean they're out of work. The Trio wasn't booked for a couple of weeks, so that's why I know so much about Jack's problems ... but we won't go into all that again.'

'No.' Zachary gave her a grateful look. 'What did you do before, Ivy?'

'Before I went on the stage? I worked in a grocer's shop, just round the corner from home.'

'You do enjoy it though, don't you? All the singing and dancing and everything? It seems such a pity if you don't.'

'Of course I do. It's good fun, and I've met a lot of people, made a lot of new friends since I started. But it's not the be all and end all of everything, that's what I meant.'

'Our Nancy's quite a nice singer,' said Zachary, somewhat condescendingly. 'She used to sing at chapel concerts, like you did, and now she's got herself a job down the Golden Mile, at a song-booth.'

'Yes, I've met Nancy. In fact we've got quite friendly. I've promised that I'll go and listen to her before we leave Blackpool. She's always asking me what it's like to be on the stage ... and I can't answer her, not properly. It's something you've got to learn about for yourself. You'll have heard her sing, haven't you, Zachary?'

'At the song-booth? No, I've not been down there.'

'Why ever not? She's your sister.'

Zachary shrugged. 'Dunno. I told you, I'm not all that close to my sisters.'

'No ... not all brothers are. I suppose Jack and I are an exception. Perhaps you'll come with me, then, to listen to Nancy sing, will you?'

Zachary's eyes lit up with pleasure. 'I'd like that. Yes, I will come. In fact, I was going to ask you, Ivy, if you would – er – reconsider. I asked you out once before, you remember?'

'Oh, that!' Ivy looked a trifle discomposed.

'And you said no.'

'I thought I didn't know you well enough, that was all.'

'And you do, now?'

'Oh yes, I think so.' Ivy's brown eyes glowed with an empathy that Zachary had not often seen in a young woman's look. Except for Sarah, but his thoughts at that moment were certainly not with Sarah. 'I think we might get on ... quite well,' said Ivy quietly.

'Sunday, then?'

'Yes, Sunday.' She was thoughtful for a moment. 'I was just trying to work out how many more Sundays there would be. We're here till the middle of September, so that makes it only about four.'

'Then we'd best make hay while the sun shines.'

'Let's just see how it goes, Zachary.'

He nodded soberly. 'And what happens when you finish here? A tour of the music halls?'

'Yes, we've a few bookings in the Lancashire inland towns – Blackburn, Burnley, Bury, Bolton – all the Bs. And then, possibly, a pantomime. I'm not sure yet.'

'But we'll keep in touch, won't we? You'll write to me?'

Ivy smiled in a warm-hearted way. 'Let's just see how it goes,' she said again.

But Zachary felt sure as he made his way up the stairs, his eyes on the back of her cherry-red dressing-gown, that Ivy Rathbone would be, indeed, just what the doctor had ordered!

'Good night, Zachary. Sleep well,' she whispered, as they paused on the landing by his bedroom door. She kissed his cheek fleetingly, then she was gone, leaving him staring in a bemused manner at her closed door. And he did sleep, much more peacefully than he had done since his return from France.

Chapter 12

'What did you think of her?' asked Ivy, as she and Sid walked back along the Golden Mile. The crowds had thinned considerably now, in this second week in September, and there was a definite nip in the air in the mornings and evenings. After their two performances at the pier on Saturday they would start packing up, and on the Monday they would be gone. 'Quite a nice little singer, isn't she? Didn't you think so?' Ivy persisted, when Sid didn't answer.

'Yes ... a nice little singer, "little" being the operative word,' said Sid Morris, otherwise Sidney Marchant. 'I don't mean the girl, you understand. It's her voice I'm talking about. Not exactly powerful, is it? You wouldn't be able to hear her from the other side of the promenade, would you?'

'No,' replied Ivy cautiously, 'but do you really want to? Hear her from the other side of the promenade, I mean. It's all very well having a resounding voice, but surely it's the *quality* that counts, rather than the volume. And I think Nancy Gregson's got quality. There's a real ... finesse there. I was quite surprised when I first heard her. She sounds almost like a professional, but she says she's never had a singing lesson in her life. But neither have I, for that matter,' Ivy added.

'No, but you've got a stage presence and you

know just how to get a song across,' added Sid. 'I agree that the girl has a lovely voice, very sweet and clear, but get her behind the footlights and I doubt if you'd hear her beyond the front stalls. And folks get shirty if they can't hear what they've paid good money for. You've never come across an ugly gallery crowd and I hope you never will, but it can be pretty frightening, I can tell you.'

'I shouldn't think it's something that's ever bothered you, Sid,' Ivy smiled. 'They can hear you all the way to South Pier when you're in full throttle.'

'Aye, that's as may be,' said Sid, a trifle edgily. 'So long as they can hear me on t'back row, that's all I'm bothered about.'

Ivy did hope that she hadn't offended him. Sid was inclined to be touchy whenever anyone mentioned the reverberating quality of his baritone voice. If Sid had any fault at all, it was a tendency to take himself too seriously. 'You'll be sorry to finish here, won't you?' Ivy said now. 'And Florence as well, I daresay. Those songs you both sing have gone down a treat with the Blackpool audiences,' she added placatingly, 'especially those patriotic ones at the end.'

'Aye, we've had a good season. I'm not complaining,' said Sid, his good humour quickly restored. 'And you've enjoyed it, haven't you, lass?' He beamed at her. 'Just the job, Blackpool, isn't it? Better than spending the summer amongst the mill chimneys, eh?'

'Yes,' agreed Ivy, although she was homesick at times, even for the smoky chimneys of Halifax.

'D'you think we're likely to be in Blackpool again next summer?'

'You're looking a long way ahead,' said Sid. 'Who can tell? It's a chancy business at the best of times. One minute the work's pouring in and the next you can be thrown back in the gutter. A lot can happen before next year, but no – it's doubtful that we'd be signed up on the North Pier again. One of the other theatres, possibly. We'll just have to wait and see. That is, if we're all still together next year. You're thinking of staying with us, then?'

'As far as I know,' replied Ivy. 'Thanks for coming with me to listen to Nancy. I promised her I'd go, then when I'd heard her once I thought it might be an idea to find out what you thought.'

'You've not said anything to her?'

'No, of course not. It was just an idea, something to bear in mind – if and when – you know.'

'And bear it in mind we will,' said Sid. 'It's certainly worth considering and she's a damned pretty girl. That ginger hair's a crowd-puller for a start. I'm sure I don't know why everyone asks my opinion though. It's got nowt to do with me, all the hiring and firing. It's up to Bert Aspinall, isn't it?'

'You've got a big say though, Sid, you know you have. Look how you wangled things to get me into the Trio.'

'That doesn't mean I'll always be able to do it. One of these days Bert Aspinall, our beloved agent, may well decide to split us all up, then where would we be, eh?'

'I'm not going anywhere without you and Flo,'

said Ivy loyally, 'and I know a few more that would say the same.'

'Aye, well, let's cross that bridge when we come to it and not before. And mum's the word as far as that little ginger-haired lass is concerned. She looks as though she's got quite enough stars in her eyes already without us planting any more there … especially when it might come to nothing.'

Ivy leaned against the railings by the North Pier, staring out to sea. The other two members of the Trio, Rose and Rita, had gone into the pavilion ahead of her and she was snatching a few moments' respite before the Saturday evening performances. The sun was glinting on the sea, setting a million golden coins winking and dancing. It was a sight Ivy had seen many, many times that summer. Earlier in the year she had sometimes stolen a few minutes between the two performances to emerge on to the pier and watch the spectacular display that was enacted, nightly, in the sky above Blackpool. It was a show that couldn't be equalled by anything on the stage, always supposing there was a visible sun to take part, which was by no means always the case. There was tonight, though, a fitting farewell to their last appearance on the stage of the Eastern Pavilion.

Blackpool was a grand place, Ivy mused, and she was so glad she had had the opportunity of spending some time here this summer. Previously, she had visited the place only once, on a day trip, and had returned home with an impression of milling crowds, Kiss Me Quick hats, bright pink rock, fish and chips ... and very little else. Now she knew differently. As Sid had said, Blackpool was 'just the job'. Where else could you watch the amazing sight of elephants walking, trunk to tail, across a deserted stretch of golden sand in the early morning? That is what Ivy had seen when she had risen from her bed and taken a stroll before breakfast one morning, and she had laughed out loud in delight at the spectacle of the performing pachyderms from the Tower Circus taking their daily constitutional.

Fish and chips and rock and crowds there were in plenty, but there was so much else besides. Three piers, a funfair to rival any in the world, electric trams to carry you almost the whole length of the promenade and thousand upon thousand of hotels and boarding houses. Blackpool was big and bold and brazen, but it was unashamed of its brashness, almost as though it were saying: 'Come on, enjoy yourselves, let your hair down! If you can't be happy here, then you don't deserve to be happy at all.'

But solitude could be found there, too, on empty expanses of beach at Norbreck or on the sand dunes at Squire's Gate. Ivy had sampled both sides of Blackpool – the noisy and the tranquil – in her outings with Zachary Gregson. She had been out with him only twice, apart from a short visit to the Golden Mile to hear his sister sing, but the time they had spent together had been filled to the brim with all kinds of experiences.

One experience, however, which Zachary had hankered after, Ivy had denied him. The first

Sunday they spent together they had travelled on a tram, southwards to Victoria Pier, then they had walked to the sand dunes which stretched from Squire's Gate to St Annes. It was a peaceful area, away from the hustle and bustle of the promenade and the laughing noisy crowds that milled round the Pleasure Beach; a popular place for a picnic and for those who desired a bit of solitude. They sat on the tussocky grass and picnicked from the tartan shopping bag which Zachary's mother had thoughtfully packed for them and which contained chicken sandwiches, meat pies, slab cake and bottled ginger beer.

'Mmm ... that was delicious,' said Ivy, gathering up the debris of their picnic – empty bottles, greaseproof paper and a tin box depicting the Coronation of George V and Mary – and stuffing them back into the bag. 'I couldn't eat another morsel. I wonder why food tastes so much better out of doors?'

'D'you reckon it does?' Zachary grinned at her. 'Even with the sand in the sandwiches? Don't you think it might have something to do with the company?'

'Maybe so.' Ivy smiled at him, but a trifle reservedly, as she brushed the crumbs from her skirt and fastened up the bag. She wasn't entirely certain of her ground, yet, with Zachary Gregson, not absolutely sure what made him tick. He was an odd lad in a lot of ways, although she had changed her original opinion of him, which had been that he was a supercilious so and so who thought he was God's gift to women. But when she had witnessed the terrified lad, cringing away from the pools of darkness in his room, and had realised how much he was suffering from nightmares and gruesome memories, there had awakened in her, not only sympathy with his plight, but a liking for him as well. She knew now that there was another side to him, that his disdainful manner was mainly a veneer; but she did fear, nevertheless, that Zachary was a young man who was used to getting most of his own way.

Hetty Gregson had spoiled him; that much was certain. Look how she had fussed around this morning when he had told her they were going out for the day, making sure that only the nicest pieces of chicken were put in the sandwiches and that they had more than enough to eat. Many a mother would have told him to fend for himself, but Hetty had seemed to consider it a privilege to be pandering to her son's slightest whim. Ivy had insisted on helping her with the preparation of the picnic while Zachary had sat in the adjoining living room reading the newspaper.

'I'm glad he's taking you out for the day,' Hetty whispered as they worked together at the pine table in the kitchen. 'He needs a bit of fresh company to bring him out of himself, help him to forget what he's been through. He's not the same lad at all since he came back from the war. Sometimes he's so moody and irritable I feel I hardly know him. And when I think what he used to be like when he was a little 'un...'

Ivy doubted if Zachary had ever been very much different. A flash of insight told her that he had been overindulged, even as a youngster, by his mother. But she nodded sympathetically now, saying that her brother, Jack, was just the same and how the war had changed him, too. 'I was telling Zachary that Jack has had some of the same problems,' she said. 'I think he was relieved to know that he was not on his own.'

'Yes ... I heard the commotion on the landing the other night,' said Hetty. She put a finger to her lips and motioned towards the living room. 'He didn't say anything about it, so I haven't let on that I know. He can be very funny, our Zachary, if he thinks folks are talking about him. But I'm glad you looked after him, dear. He certainly needs somebody ... and he doesn't always want me, I realise that.'

Ivy got the impression that Hetty Gregson, far from being a possessive mother-in-law, would be only too relieved if the right girl were to come along to take Zachary off her hands. Ivy pulled herself up short with a reminder that she hadn't even been out with him yet, but she felt that she had not been mistaken about the conspiratorial glance that his mother had given her.

And, so far, she was finding him very good company. She sat down on the grass again, letting the fine pale yellow sand trickle through her fingers. 'Nice and quiet here, isn't it? You wouldn't think you were in Blackpool at all. I haven't been down here before.'

'What do you usually do on a Sunday?' asked Zachary.

'Oh, this and that. Read, write letters, wash my hair ... And sometimes I go out with the other girls, a walk on the prom or window shopping or on the pier. Sunday's usually a dreary sort of a day when you're on tour, but you can't say that about Blackpool. There's always something to do here. And it's *so-oo* nice to have a free day, all to myself.'

In an impulsive gesture Ivy snatched off her close-fitting straw hat and threw it into the air. She caught it and placed it on top of the tartan bag and her hair, unconfined, shot out in springing curls all over her head. She leaned back against the prickly star grass, closing her eyes and giving a half-sigh of content. The sun shone from the cloudless sky like a benison upon her forehead and closed eyelids; she rested for a few moments in silence, rejoicing in the freedom of the day and the glory of the sunshine.

After a minute or two she was aware of Zachary at her side in the same half-sitting, half-lying position. She didn't open her eyes as she felt his arm come round her gently, then his fingers stroking her hair, her cheeks, her lips. That he should kiss her was inevitable; she was expecting it, longing for it, almost, for Ivy was not immune to the charms of Zachary Gregson. His lips when they came down on hers were soft and supple. She moved her own beneath them and found herself responding as his kisses increased in fervour. She opened her eyes then, to see his dark, dark eyes, almost black, gazing into her own. She kissed him back, unrestrainedly, stroking his black curls and the lobes of his ears, abandoning herself to the joy of the moment, for this was a very pleasurable experience.

But Ivy was a well-brought-up girl. She knew

what was right, and she knew that it most definitely was not right when she felt Zachary's hand upon her breast, then on her knee, feeling beneath her skirt.

'No! Stop it, Zachary!' She pushed his hand away and sat up straight. She felt, somehow, very disappointed that Zachary should behave in such a way. Perhaps this was the way he always behaved when he took a young lady out, but she had hoped that maybe he would be different with her. Or perhaps, because she was on the stage, he thought she was easy game. If so, she would have to put him right without delay. She was determined to make light of it, however, not to let her annoyance and disappointment spoil what had been, till then, a most enjoyable day. 'Kissing and cuddling's all very well, but nothing else, thank you very much, Mr Gregson,' she said pertly.

The half-aggressive, half-sulky look on his face changed, she was relieved to see, to one of wry amusement. He touched his forelock. 'Sorry, ma'am. Just as you say, ma'am.'

'I mean it, Zachary,' she said. 'I'm not … like that. Just because I'm on the stage it doesn't mean that I'm free with my favours.'

'I never thought that, not for one moment.'

'That's all right then.' She gave a curt nod. 'So long as you know.'

'I'm sorry,' he mumbled. 'Maybe I was a bit – er – previous. It's only the first time I've taken you out. Perhaps when we've been–'

'No! Not ever, Zachary.' Ivy had made up her mind, long ago, when the girl who lived next door to her in Halifax had 'got into trouble', that she would never bring such shame to her own parents. They had brought her up, not too strictly, as many parents did, but correctly and lovingly and Ivy was determined that when she got married it would be in a white dress – one that she was entitled to wear – in an atmosphere of rejoicing, not one of embarrassment and disgrace.

Zachary grinned at her. 'All right, if you say so.' But she could tell by the impudent gleam in his eye that he fully expected her to change her mind. But she wouldn't! 'Let's go to the Pleasure Beach then,' he said, 'I can't get up to any mischief there, and I don't suppose you've been, have you?'

Ivy hadn't, so they spent a happy couple of hours at the funfair, riding on the switchback railway and the Rainbow Wheel and gliding through the mysterious dark caverns of the River Caves in a shallow boat.

Their next outing was to hear Nancy sing, and the following Sunday they also spent together. This time, however, they were not favoured with the weather. It turned cold and drizzly, but they both found, somewhat to their surprise, that the inclement weather did little to dampen their enthusiasm for all that Blackpool had to offer … nor their growing liking for one another. They walked along the windswept cliffs, took refuge in a seafront café with other drenched holiday-makers, then, in a secluded corner of the lower promenade, Zachary drew Ivy into his arms for a few ardent kisses.

Now, leaning on the railings and watching the sun set, before her final performances, Ivy was trying to puzzle out just why she felt so attracted to Zachary, why she wanted to go on seeing him, when she had started by disliking him so much. There was no doubt that they enjoyed one another's company and, far from giving her the push when she spurned his amorous advances, he seemed all the more eager to be with her. It would be more difficult now, though. On Monday she and her fellow artistes would be leaving Blackpool, but she had promised to keep in touch with him. And they would still have most of Sunday to spend together, after she had finished her packing.

Ivy felt a surge of happiness at the thought of this as she made her way through the turnstile and into the pavilion. She was sorry that Zachary couldn't be here tonight; he was working, not coming home until the early hours. But after the final performance a bouquet of red roses, wrapped in cellophane, was handed to Ivy across the footlights, one of many floral tributes received by the ladies of the company.

'Please don't forget me,' it read. 'With love, Zachary.'

Ivy, as well as being thrilled and touched, was also astounded. Somehow she hadn't envisaged Zachary as the red rose type at all.

'Sarah dear, I've been thinking. I'm not at all happy about you living all on your own at the shop, especially up in that attic.' Grace put down the tapestry she was stitching – an exotic design of birds and flowers – on the cushion at the side of her and leaned forward slightly. Her brown eyes, almost a mirror-image of Sarah's own, were concerned.

As she looked back at her, Sarah couldn't help feeling a touch of annoyance that her mother should bring up this subject yet again. They had been over it so many times and Sarah had really thought that she had, at last, come to terms with it. She knew that her mother had long since got over her fit of resentment, if that was what it had been, at Sarah's decision to launch out on her own. Both her mother and father, in fact, had been wonderful in their support of her. They had listened to her plans as she gradually unfolded them and helped her with ideas for stock and furnishings and equipment; all the thousand and one little details which went with opening a business and which, Sarah had to admit, they both knew so much more about than she did. Her ideas about the living arrangements she had left till last, and it was only then that Sarah had run into some opposition.

'But where did you really expect me to live?' she had asked them, when at last she had plucked up courage to broach her ideas about the attic. 'Surely you didn't think I was going to stay on here and travel to Gynn Square every morning at the crack of dawn?'

'I rather think that's the impression you might have given,' said her father slowly, with a knowing look at her. 'I did suggest that it was a long way, and you said...'

'And I said that I didn't mind getting up early.

258

Yes, I know.' Sarah held up her hand in a gesture of defeat. 'I admit that I was finding it hard to tell you that I wanted to live on the premises, so I suppose I took the easy way out. I knew I'd have to tell you sometime though, and I can't honestly see what your objection is.' She looked first at Edwin, then at Grace, both gazing at her with such loving concern. 'I've got to leave home some time.'

'But you're so young, dear,' said her mother.

'I'm nearly twenty-two,' Sarah retorted. 'You can hardly say I'm still in the nursery. Plenty of girls of my age – those in service, for instance – have been living away from home for ten years or so.'

'It's not the same thing at all, dear,' said Grace. 'They've no choice, have they? Your father and I have been more fortunate than most with this world's goods – so much so that I feel quite guilty at times – and we want to make sure that you will be all right.'

'I think we might have been burying our heads in the sand to a certain extent, Grace,' Edwin said gently. 'Like Sarah says, it isn't reasonable for her to go on living here, is it, when her place of work will be at the other end of town? And we can't go on treating her like a child for ever, now can we?'

Sarah shot her father a grateful look and he closed one eye in a slow wink.

'But an attic!' said Grace. 'Won't it be cold up there? It's so near the prom. And lonely, too ... and what about the plumbing? Won't you need a bathroom?'

'We'll just have to make sure that it's as cosy as possible,' said Edwin. 'There are all sorts of new gas heaters and oil heaters on sale now. And I'm sure a reputable plumber would be able to install a bath up there as easy as winking. Sam Pickering'll know somebody who can do that.'

'But if you're so set on living there – and you certainly seem to be,' Grace persisted, 'then why not live on the first floor? I know it's in a dilapidated state at the moment, but it's obvious that that's where the previous tenants lived. It would be more comfortable surely?'

'I've already told you, Mother...' Sarah was trying not to sound impatient. 'That's going to be the restaurant ... eventually.' Sarah knew that her mother was not taking this part of her project seriously. A café and shop were all very well, but a restaurant! Grace hadn't actually said so, but Sarah got the impression that her mother thought it was an impossible pipe dream. 'Of course I know I can't do everything at once,' Sarah went on, 'but it's something to think about, for the future.'

Sarah knew, indeed, that her funds were not limitless and that the work that was already taking place would make a big hole in her savings. Samuel Pickering's firm – the building firm that had employed Albert Gregson until he went to the war, and still employed George Makepeace – was busy at work already, putting in new floorboards and joists and re-plastering walls and ceilings, in order that the premises would be habitable by mid-December. That was when Sarah planned to open her ground-floor shop and café, just in time for Christmas.

She had thought that her mother, as well as her father, had by now grown accustomed to the idea that she would be living there, so she was somewhat surprised at Grace mentioning it again. It was now October, only two months before the premises would be ready. Rather late in the day, surely, to still be harping on about it.

'Oh mother, do stop worrying,' she said now, trying not to sound irritable. Her mother, when all was said and done, always had her best interests at heart. Sarah's glance fell now on the exquisite tapestry that Grace had just laid down. She knew that it was to be made into a firescreen for her, Sarah, to take to her new home. Mother was so thoughtful in many ways. If only she didn't fuss so! 'I thought we'd had all this out ages ago. I thought you'd got used to the idea.'

'Not to you living alone,' said Grace. 'Now hold on a minute, hear me out,' she continued, raising her hand as Sarah cast an exasperated glance heavenwards. 'What would you think about having someone to share the place with you? Another girl?'

'It would depend on who it was, I suppose,' said Sarah. 'I know I can't manage to run the business on my own – the next thing I have to do is advertise for staff. But I hadn't really considered having anyone living there with me. I suppose I thought my assistants might live at home, especially if they came from the North Shore area. Why?' Sarah looked at her mother's eager face and thought she could see a hint of a secret there. 'Have you someone in mind?'

261

'As a matter of fact, I have,' Grace smiled. 'What would you say about your cousin, Joyce, coming to live with you?'

'Joyce?' Sarah's eyebrows shot up in surprise. 'Yes,' she said. 'I'd like that very much. But Joyce lives with Grandma Makepeace, doesn't she?'

'She won't be living there for much longer,' Grace replied. 'You see ... your grandmother is retiring.'

'Grandma retiring? Never!' Sarah could not have been more surprised had Grace announced that Grandma had gone to live in Timbuctoo.

Edwin, too, put down his newspaper with a sudden movement and cast a startled look at his wife over the top of his horn-rimmed spectacles. Until then he had been taking no part in the conversation – the daily news always engrossed him – and Sarah had thought that he wasn't listening. 'Old Martha retiring?' he said, then he added, as Sarah had done, 'Never!'

'Mother wouldn't thank you if she heard you calling her "old Martha",' said Grace, smiling, 'but that's one of the reasons, I suppose, for her coming to this decision. She is getting older, though she's never liked to admit it, until now.'

'How old is your mother, Grace?' asked Edwin.

'Oh, I'm not absolutely sure. She's always been very cagey about her age, like a lot of women of her generation. I'm forty-three, so I daresay she must be in her middle sixties. She's never seemed it, though, has she? She's always dashed around like a woman twenty years younger. Old Martha, indeed!'

'I didn't mean it disrespectfully, Grace, you

know that. It's more a term of endearment. I've always been very fond of your mother, and I think she is fond of me as well … now,' he added. Grace and Edwin exchanged one of their meaningful glances, and Sarah momentarily felt like an outsider. She found herself thinking, again, that when and if she married then it would have to be to someone who possessed the same steadfast qualities as Edwin Donnelly.

'But what's brought this on?' Sarah asked now. 'I can hardly believe it. How many times have we heard Gran say that she'll have to be carried out of that boarding house, feet first?'

Grace smiled. 'Possibly she's learning sense and she doesn't want that to happen any sooner than it should. The war took its toll of her, like it did with all of us and she's never seemed as sprightly as she was, not since Albert died. I know he was only her son-in-law, but Mother has always lived through our sorrows – Hetty's and mine – as though they were her own.'

'And I suppose Grandad George is getting tired as well,' said Sarah. 'It's a hard job for a man of his age, isn't it, working for a building firm.'

'Yes, that's what has made them come to a decision,' said Grace. 'He's worked for Pickering's for ages, long before he knew Mother, in fact. He was her lodger, you remember, and then they got fond of one another and got married. And I think he's a year or two older than she is, so it's high time he started taking things more easily.'

'It still takes some believing,' said Sarah, shaking her head. 'Grandma seems such a part of

263

Welcome Rest. I can't imagine her not being there. When did you find out?'

'Only this afternoon,' replied Grace. 'I called to see her, as I usually do when it's half-day closing at the shop, and she told me then. I gather they've only just made up their minds, so they haven't got very far with their plans as yet.'

'They're going to sell Welcome Rest then? And where do they intend to live? They won't be leaving Blackpool, will they?' Blackpool without Grandma and Grandad Makepeace was unthinkable to Sarah. They were as much a part of the place as Blackpool Tower.

'No, of course not,' said Grace. 'Could you see either of them stagnating away somewhere in the country? I couldn't. No, your gran will still be quite near to boss us all around. They're hoping to find a little terraced house not too far away, and the boarding house is going on the market in a few days, when they've contacted an estate agent.'

'Goodness! So soon?' said Edwin. 'Well, I must say your mother doesn't let the grass grow under her feet once she's made a decision. Like somebody else I know.' He glanced fondly at Sarah. 'You're a chip off the old block all right, young lady.'

Sarah smiled. 'If you think I take after Gran, then that suits me. And what does Joyce think about it?' she asked, turning to her mother. 'That's obviously why you mentioned her just now.'

'Ah … Joyce doesn't know about it yet,' said Grace. 'That was the thing that was worrying Mother the most; breaking it to Joyce that she no longer has a job, to put it bluntly. She's going to tell her tonight.'

'Or a home,' added Sarah thoughtfully.

'Oh, it's not as bad as that,' said Grace. 'The girl isn't going to be turned out on the streets. Joyce only went to live with her gran because it was more convenient with her working there. She'll just go back to living at her mother's again, across the road. She could work there too, I suppose, for our Hetty, but I couldn't help thinking that it might be rather a good idea if–'

'If she came to live with me and I found her a job as well,' said Sarah. She looked steadily at her mother for a moment before she grinned. 'Honestly, you're as bad as Grandma, you are really, for getting us all sorted out.'

Grace was looking a little worried. 'Don't you think it's a good idea? I wasn't trying to interfere...'

'Of course I do. I think it's a brilliant idea. You didn't mention it to her though, did you?'

'To Joyce? No, of course I didn't. I haven't seen Joyce, but the thought suddenly struck me when Mother was talking about her. I didn't even tell Mother what was in my mind, but I do know that Joyce is a good worker and you get on well with her, don't you, dear? Of course, any suggestion of a job would have to come from you, as though it was your idea.'

'Yes ... Joyce is grand,' said Sarah thoughtfully. 'Gran's often said that she can turn her hand to anything in the boarding house. I've been thinking that I shall need someone to help in the kitchen, a waitress for the café, and a shop assistant. I wonder where Joyce will fit in best?'

'You'll have to discuss it with her, dear,' said Grace. 'For all I know she may not even be interested.'

'I think she will,' said Sarah slowly. 'Yes, I'm quite sure she will. Mother, you're a genius. I'll go and see her tomorrow. And I know you'll be relieved, won't you, if she agrees to share the attic with me.'

'We both will,' said her father. 'We'll be happier to know that you're not on your own.'

Joyce was delighted, when Sarah saw her the following evening, at both her cousin's suggestions; that she should share the attic flat and that she should be employed at Sarah's new premises. 'When one door closes another door opens,' she said, shaking her head in wonderment. 'Gran said that to me only last night – you know how fond she is of trotting out words of wisdom – but I never thought another door would open for me so quickly.'

'I thought about you as soon as I knew Gran was retiring,' said Sarah, not letting on that it had been, in the first instance, her mother's idea. 'That is, if you haven't already got something else in mind.'

'How could I have?' said Joyce. 'Gran only sprang it on us yesterday, and what a shock it was, I can tell you. I don't mean that we're not pleased for her – we're all delighted that at last she's decided to take life a bit more easily – but it's something we never expected.'

'Yes, we were all surprised as well,' said Sarah.

266

'So you think it's a good idea, do you, coming to work for me? *With* me, I should say, rather than *for* me. I wouldn't want you to think I was lording it over you.'

Joyce smiled at her. 'I don't think you could ever do that, Sarah. Mam was suggesting that I should work for her, along with Nancy, and I suppose that's what I would have had to do. But you know our Nancy.' Joyce pulled her mouth down in a grimace. 'A little of her goes a long way and we'd probably end up tearing one another's hair out if we had to work together. We're better when we don't have to see one another all the time, although I've moved back here, you know, now that the season's come to an end.'

'Yes, the stage people have gone, haven't they, the ones that were on at the North Pier.'

'Yes, several weeks ago, and our Nancy has been moping around like a wet week ever since.'

'Why? What's the matter with her?'

Joyce's grey eyes opened wide in a candid state. 'Can't you guess? She's in love ... or thinks she is. Shhh, I can hear her coming.' Joyce lifted a cautionary finger. 'Don't let on.'

Nancy seemed surprised, but nevertheless pleased, to see her cousin. 'Hello, stranger,' she said, flopping down on the cretonne-covered armchair opposite Joyce and Sarah, who were sitting on the couch. 'To what do we owe this honour?' Her green eyes twinkled mischievously. 'You'll get lost, you know, if you wander too far from the posh part of Blackpool.'

'Give over, Nancy.' Sarah smiled good-humouredly. She knew her cousin too well to

267

take any notice of her gibes. 'I'm sorry I haven't been round for a while, but I've been very busy, as you can imagine. I'm hoping to open the shop and café before Christmas.'

'You're still at Donnelly's, though, aren't you?' asked Nancy.

'For the moment, yes, but I'm finishing at the end of this month. Father thought that would be a good idea; it will give me time to see to things at Gynn Square and get my stock ready for the opening. Actually, that's why I'm here.' Sarah looked at Joyce and they exchanged a knowing smile. 'I've come to offer Joyce a job.'

'Have you indeed? Jolly good.' There was no trace of resentment in Nancy's voice. 'What's she going to be? Head cook and bottle washer? Or is she going to be the scullery maid, washing the greasy pans and scrubbing the potatoes?'

Sarah laughed. 'I was just going to get round to that before you came in. I shall need a shop assistant, a waitress for the café, and someone to help me with the cooking ... to begin with. I'll have to walk before I can run, as Gran would say.' She turned to Joyce. 'So I was wondering if we could do the cooking and the waiting-on between us, until we see how it goes. What do you think?'

'Suits me. I'll fit in wherever I can. There's bound to be a bit of trial and error at the start, isn't there, until you get the business going. I do admire you, Sarah, for having the guts to do it.' Joyce's clear grey eyes were a shade anxious. 'Don't you feel worried at all?'

'If I stop to think about it, yes, I suppose I do,' said Sarah. 'But I'm determined to make a go of it and before very long I won't have time to stop and think. I'll just have to get on with the job. I think Mother was right, though, about me having someone to live there with me. I thought she was making a silly fuss at first, but now I can see what she means. It'll be good to have somebody there, for company and to talk things over with.'

'And to moan to when things go wrong,' said Joyce. 'Not that they will,' she added hastily.

'They may well at first.' Sarah gave a wry grin. 'Thanks for saying yes, anyway, Joyce. It'll be grand to have you there with me.'

'Is my little sister going to live with you an' all?' said Nancy. 'Goody! I can have the bedroom all to myself again. You couldn't find a job for me as well, could you?' Nancy turned her roguish green eyes upon Sarah. 'I can cook and clean and wait on tables. I could even sing for you. I tell you what, Sarah, you could have those afternoon tea dances, like they do at the Palace, and I could be the vocalist.'

Sarah laughed, hoping that her cousin was joking. She was joking about the dances, that was certain, but about the job as well? Sarah was inclined to agree with Joyce that a little of Nancy would go a long way. Of the two girls she had always been the more friendly with Nancy, possibly because she was the one nearer to her own age. Nancy was now nineteen whereas Joyce was only seventeen. But to work with and live with in the somewhat confined area of the attic rooms, Sarah could see that the calm and level-headed Joyce would be a much more agreeable prospect than the volatile Nancy.

'Whatever would Aunt Hetty say if I were to pinch her best worker?' said Sarah, trying to laugh it off. 'I don't know what she'll have to say about me stealing Joyce from under her nose.'

'She'll be glad to get rid of her,' said Nancy, pulling a face at her sister. 'I was only kidding about the job, Sarah – you know me.' She gave an impudent grin. 'I had you worried for a moment, though, didn't I? No … I'm all right here – till something better comes along – and I've still got my singing job with Barney.'

'Oh yes. How's it going?' asked Sarah. 'The visitors have all gone now, haven't they?'

'Yes, but a lot of the song-booths stay open all year. We're not as busy, of course, but we still get folks coming in for a sing-song and we do quite a good trade with amateur operatic companies. Barney's hoping we can stay open … and so am I.' Nancy looked dejected for a moment. 'Still, we've got to look on the bright side. That's what Barney's always saying.' She turned to Joyce. 'Where's Mam? Over at Gran's, I suppose?'

'Yes, she's gone over for her nightly chat,' replied Joyce. 'She won't be able to do that for much longer. It'll seem strange, won't it, when Gran's no longer over the road.' There was the sound of the front door opening and closing and footsteps along the passage before the living-room door opened. 'Speak of the devil,' said Joyce. 'She's here now. You're back early Mam.'

'Yes, the estate agent's just called to see your gran and granddad, so I thought I'd best make myself scarce.' Hetty Gregson smiled warmly at Sarah. 'Hello there, Sarah love. Nice to see you.

270

And what were you all saying about me, eh?' She pulled out a dining chair from under the table and sat down on it somewhat heavily. She leaned her elbows on the brown chenille table-cover. 'Come on, spill the beans. You're talking secrets, I can see.'

'It's my doing, Aunt Hetty,' said Sarah, smiling affectionately at her aunt. She was her mother's sister, but as unlike Grace as it was possible to be, both in looks and in temperament. Just as the comfortable clutter of her aunt's living room bore no resemblance to the elegant drawing room where the Donnelly family spent their leisure hours. 'I came to ask Joyce something, you see.'

Hetty listened, all the while nodding approvingly, as Sarah unfolded her plans. Aunt Hetty seemed to age a little more every time she saw her, thought Sarah. Her auburn hair, once the self-same colour as Nancy's, was now sprinkled with as much grey as ginger, her cheeks were beginning to sag a little and there were tell-tale lines around her eyes and mouth. But her green eyes were as lively and sparkling as ever, responding with enthusiasm to Sarah's plans.

'Well, I think that's a wonderful idea,' she said. 'I do wish you the best of luck, Sarah, but if anybody can make a go of it, then you certainly will. And to get Joyce off our hands as well!' She grinned at her daughter. 'I was wondering what we were going to do with her. Your gran will be relieved. She was worried sick about "throwing Joyce on the scrap heap", as she put it. You'll go across and see her, won't you, dear, before you go home?'

'Yes, Aunt Hetty; I'll go and tell her my plans. Grandma and Grandad have both been so interested in what I'm doing, and Grandad has been working at the shop, of course, with Pickerings doing the alterations.'

'And how's your mother?' asked Hetty. 'It's a good while since I saw our Grace, to speak to, that is. I caught a glimpse of her in Donnelly's the other day, but she didn't see me. She was busy with a client – looking very efficient, she was, tape measure round her neck and all that. I expect she's busy, isn't she, with her new schemes an' all.'

'Yes, Mother's very well, thank you,' replied Sarah. 'And busy too. She's thrilled to bits with her new dressmaking service, and Father seems delighted at the way it's all going. It's only in its early stages, but they seem to think it'll do well.'

'Yes, I must pop into Donnelly's meself and get measured up,' said Hetty. 'It's ages since I had a new frock, and our Grace always seems to know what suits me best.'

Sarah glanced at the maroon marocain fabric straining across her aunt's ample bosom and heavy thighs and she thought solicitously that Aunt Hetty, indeed, could do with a new dress. Sarah doubted, though, whether the loose tunic styles, so fashionable now, would be flattering to Hetty's large proportions, whereas they might have been designed for the slender, willowy Grace. But, as Aunt Hetty said, her mother would know just what would be suitable. It was part of Grace's new job to give advice and she had always been a genius with a needle and thread. Now, though, she wasn't actually making the garments herself, but supervising the four seamstresses that Donnelly's now employed.

'Yes, you do that, Aunt Hetty,' Sarah said. 'Mother will be pleased to see you.'

Hetty rose to her feet, motioning to Nancy. 'Come on, let's go and make a cup of tea and leave these two to have a natter. I'm sure they'll have a lot to discuss.'

Sarah and Joyce looked at one another as the other two went into the adjoining kitchen and there was a moment's silence before they both laughed. 'I don't think there is much more to discuss at the moment,' said Sarah. 'I've just about said it all. But perhaps when I've finished at the shop – at Father's shop, I mean – we can get together again?' Joyce nodded her approval. 'That's fine then.' Sarah gave a satisfied nod. 'Nancy seems in quite good spirits,' she went on, lowering her voice. 'I thought you said she was down in the dumps since the stage people left?'

'She's putting on a good face while you're here,' said Joyce. 'You should see her sometimes, honestly!'

'You said she was in love,' Sarah whispered. 'Could it be that tap dancer, what was he called? Clive Conway?'

'That's the one,' said Joyce, glancing apprehensively towards the kitchen door, but the sound of the whistling kettle and the rattle of cups and saucers was drowning their voices. 'You noticed then, did you?'

'Yes. When I went with her to the show, I thought she was … interested. Did she get

273

friendly with him, then?'

Joyce shook her head. 'I don't think he's even noticed her. That's the trouble.' Joyce, far from poking fun at her lovelorn sister, looked really sorry and Sarah immediately felt the same. After all, she knew what it felt like as well.

'Oh dear! Poor Nancy,' she said, still whispering. 'Never mind, I expect she'll get over it. It isn't as though she's actually been out with him, is it?' Sarah found her thoughts flying to Zachary, the only member of the family who wasn't there that evening. She had been relieved when Joyce said he was on a late shift. It was so much worse, surely, to lose someone when you thought they had returned your love.

'She's not the only one in the doldrums,' Joyce went on. 'Our Zachary's like a bear with a sore head an' all since that lot went. Didn't you know?' she said, in answer to Sarah's surprised look. 'That Ivy Rathbone, one of the Trio. He got friendly with her and he's writing to her. At least she's writing to him – there's letters arriving every few days, Mam says, but whether he's replying or not we don't know. He's lovesick, at any rate.'

'No, I didn't know,' said Sarah in a small voice.

'I thought our Nancy would have told you. She usually tells you everything, doesn't she?' Joyce looked concernedly at her cousin, then put her hand to her mouth. 'Oh I say, I'm sorry. You don't still mind, do you? I thought–'

'Of course I don't mind,' said Sarah with forced brightness. 'Whatever gave you that idea?'

Chapter 13

Sarah stood back, her arms folded and her head on one side, surveying with pleasure the interior of the Gynn Square shop and café, now ready to open the following day. It was not a large place – just half a dozen tables which would each seat four, and a little shop at the far end, but Sarah, for the moment, was well-satisfied. She had realised her dreams; she was about to open up in a business of her own.

The plate-glass windows were now sparkling, both inside and out, with repeated cleanings; the exterior paintwork, green and cream – the same colours as Blackpool's famous trams – gleamed with newness, and over the door there was a sign in curly writing, *Sarah's Café*.

The naming of the establishment had caused some animated discussion in the family circle, but Sarah had stuck to her guns. It was simple and said all that she wanted it to say. She had refuted her mother's argument that it was a shop as well as a café, saying that anyone looking through the window could see that for themselves at a glance. Indeed, there had been several inquisitive folk peering through the windows already. Sarah and Joyce, busy inside, had watched them and had exchanged gleeful smiles.

Sarah, at this moment, was scarcely able to contain her excitement, although it was tempered with a touch of trepidation when she thought about the morrow. Her father's tentative suggestion for the name – Sarah Donnelly, High-Class Confectioner – she had politely but firmly declined as well. Donnelly's, to most Blackpool folk, was the well-known store in the centre of the town; both for her own sake and for her father's she wanted there to be no connection between the two places, no suggestion of rivalry, or on the other hand, of cashing in on her family name.

'You're sure you don't mind me setting up in opposition?' she had asked Edwin more than once, jokingly, but wanting to make sure that he had no reservations.

'Good heavens, no! Why should I?' he had replied. 'It's far enough away – a good mile and a half, I should say – and you'll soon build up your own clientèle in the North Shore area. I'm only too grateful to you, my dear, for setting Donnelly's Tearoom on its feet the way you have done. I'm sure it will continue to go from strength to strength, even without you there to run it. And your own business will be a huge success as well. I know it will.'

He had looked at her seriously for a moment. 'Don't be too disappointed if it's a little slow to start with. Tearoom business always slackens off in the winter when the visitors have gone. Well, you know that yourself, don't you? We've found that every year, but you should do a roaring trade come the summer.'

'There are the housewives in the meantime, Father,' Sarah had pointed out optimistically. 'Women doing their shopping. I'm hoping they'll

276

pop in for a cup of tea or coffee, and then, once they're in, they'll hardly be able to refuse my tempting merchandise, now will they?'

North Shore was a rapidly developing area. There were several high-class hotels on the seafront, as well as hundreds of boarding houses in the streets near the prom, and private houses, too, being built further inland. There were various small shops along Warbreck Road – butchers, grocers, greengrocers, ironmongers; there was another confectioners, too, Sarah had noticed to her slight dismay – but not another café anywhere near. Besides, Sarah intended her produce to be a rival to anything in the vicinity.

She couldn't help a satisfied smile creeping over her face as she looked at the tempting merchandise arrayed in rows on the shelves behind the long mahogany counter. Mouthwatering jams and marmalades; bottled fruits – blackcurrants, gooseberries, plums and apricots – glistening in transparent syrup; savoury produce, too – deep yellow chutney, silver-skinned onions, pickled beetroot and cabbage of a deep red; all these had been made by Sarah, with Joyce's assistance, in the weeks leading up to the opening. Mrs Jolly's kitchen had never seen such activity and the cook herself had been only too happy to help the two girls when she wasn't occupied in cooking for the Donnelly family. There were jars of mincemeat, too, and plum puddings in basins and rich dark fruit cakes, for it would be Christmas in another couple of weeks.

Not all the produce was home-made though.

There was a variety of Peek Frean's and Huntley & Palmer's biscuits displayed in glass boxes at the front of the counter. On the shelves were packets of India and China tea, boxes of chocolates and sweets, specially packaged for Christmas, and tin boxes, in silver and blue, of the famous Harrogate toffee. Edwin had managed to procure special orders of these items for Sarah; in fact she wondered what she would have done without her father's help and expertise. Now, though, it was time to let go of the reins and to launch out on her own.

One thing Sarah had decided *not* to do, for she felt it to be beyond her capabilities at the moment, was to bake her own bread for the sandwiches in the café. Instead, the bread was to be delivered each day from a bakery and flour merchant's in the centre of Blackpool, a well-established business which delivered to many of the hotels and boarding houses, including her Aunt Hetty's. Sarah intended to concentrate on the luxury items of confectionery to be served in the café and sold from behind the counter; Madeira, sultana and seed cakes, iced 'fancies', almond tarts, Eccles cakes, scones, coconut pyramids ... all the cakes which she had seen both her gran and Mrs Jolly baking over the years and which she would now try to reproduce. These, of course, would have to be baked fresh each day and Sarah could foresee some very early risings for herself and Joyce – 6 a.m. or possibly earlier, but she refused to be daunted by the thought. She was young and strong and full of enthusiasm and, if she was any judge, Joyce was her equal both in ability and in eagerness to get on with the job.

Also to be delivered each day were the cooked and potted meats they would require for the sandwiches, and sausages for the sausage rolls. There was an adequate larder with a marble slab for keeping things cool – it was doubtful, in any event, that they would go off in the cold winter weather – but Sarah was determined to take no chances. Everything was to be fresh each day and of the very highest quality.

Joyce, who had been busy in the kitchen, joined her a few moments later. 'It all looks grand, doesn't it?' she said, nodding appreciatively at the rows of gleaming bottles and jars. 'Every bit as good as that big shop in London – what do they call it? – Fortnum and Mason's.'

Sarah laughed. 'At a fraction of the price, too, I should think. Still, you know what our gran always says; "the proof of the pudding is in the eating". Very apt in this case. Now all we have to do is wait for tomorrow and see what happens.'

The shop was due to open at nine o'clock, but the two girls had been busy for hours and hours before that, baking their first batches of scones, cakes and mince pies, the latter a timely reminder, to anyone who might be in any doubt, that Christmas was on its way. Sarah hoped that a luscious mince pie, made with golden-brown pastry and oozing with fruity mincemeat, would go down a treat with a cup of tea or coffee.

'*Come and sample Sarah's delicious mince pies,*' the advert in the local *Gazette* had proclaimed for the last few evenings. *'This new establishment occupies a very advantageous position in Gynn Square, near to the seafront, and comprises a small shop and an elegant tearoom. The shop is well-stocked with high-class confectionery, made by Sarah herself, plus a wide range of tempting delicacies. Come and see for yourselves. You will not be disappointed. Opening 9 a.m. Monday, December 8th, 1919.'*

'Let's hope they won't be disappointed,' Sarah had said. She couldn't help feeling that the advert was somewhat extravagant in its claims, smacking very much of blowing her own trumpet, something she was always loath to do, but her father had deemed it necessary.

'If you won't advertise yourself, then no one else will, my dear,' he had told her. 'It's all part and parcel of business and we have to do it, like it or not. You have to sell yourself, Sarah. Let folks know that what the other confectioners can do, you can do better.' This was something that Edwin had often needed to be reminded of, Sarah knew, in his own line of business. Selling himself did not come easily to the modest Edwin Donnelly either.

Sarah and Joyce were ready and waiting at nine o'clock in their bottle-green skirts, cream long-sleeved blouses and matching cream aprons and mobcaps. Dressed in a similar uniform was Doris, the fifteen-year-old girl whom Sarah had employed to work behind the counter and to do odd jobs as and when they arose. The two cousins between them were to be responsible for the baking and for serving in the café; and though the responsibility for the overall management lay in

Sarah's hands, she wanted there to be no distinction between herself and the young women she employed. In Sarah's eyes they were all working together as a team.

Now the batches of newly-baked cakes and pastries lay, row upon row, in their wooden trays upon the shop counter and on the pine tables in the kitchen at the rear, just waiting for someone to come and buy them. As nine o'clock approached Sarah felt as though she could hardly breathe for the tightness in her throat and the tangled knot of nerves at the pit of her stomach. She was beginning to wonder if, after all, it had been worth it... Then, at ten minutes past nine, the door opened and a middle-aged woman entered. Never had there been a more welcome sound to Sarah than the jangling of the doorbell. She motioned to Doris to step forward and help the lady; after all, it was Doris who was to be the shop assistant.

The young girl, distinctly nervous, cleared her throat. 'Good morning, madam. Can I help you?'

'Aye, you can that, lass. I'd like half a dozen of your mince pies. Let's see if they're all that they're cracked up to be.' The woman had obviously read the advertisement and now her eyes scanned the shelves behind the counter. 'Mmm ... Christmas puddings an' all, I see. I'll take one of your small ones, while I'm here.'

'Certainly, madam.' Doris smiled charmingly at the woman and Sarah could see already that the girl would be quite an asset. She had a winning way with her which should work wonders with the customers.

Sarah and Joyce looked at one another, exchanging conspiratorial smiles and Sarah felt the tightness in her stomach starting to ease a little. It was all beginning. They were in business!

Sarah was now her own boss and every jangle of the doorbell and ting of the cash drawer spoke to her not only of customers coming to buy her goods, but of money in her pocket. For she had found, to her consternation, that the money in her bank account – some left to her by her Grandad Donnelly and some carefully saved, week by week – had dwindled alarmingly. There was still a little left, to be sure, but with two wages to pay each week, plus the rent on the premises and day-to-day living expenses to be met, Sarah was finding out, for the first time in her life, what it was like to have to count every penny. She knew that, if the worst came to the worst, her father would not see her in difficulties, but Sarah was determined, if at all possible, to go it alone.

During the first week things had got off to a somewhat slow start. There had not been the immediate rush that she, optimistically, had hoped for, and when she balanced the books on the first Saturday night she found that she had hardly broken even. The following Monday was the start of the last full week before Christmas and it was then that business really began to pick up.

Sarah had always loved Christmas, ever since she was a little girl and this year the excited anticipation which always led up to the day itself seemed to be heightened. For Sarah had her own part to play in the frenzied preparations that were going on all over the town. Model housewives, like her Grandma Makepeace, had, of course, made their Christmas puddings, cakes and mincemeat months before. But there were others, less serious-minded, who left things until the last minute. And yet another group – and how thankful Sarah was to be for these improvident housewives – who actually resorted to shop-bought produce! All week there was a constant flow of such women – young women, in the main – buying puddings, cakes and mince pies. No sooner had Sarah and Joyce made a batch of mince pies than they were gone; and by the Thursday evening all the puddings and cakes in stock had gone as well. The two cousins burned the midnight oil baking fresh supplies. It wouldn't have to matter that, ideally, such rich fruity mixtures should mature for several weeks. The heedless housewives didn't seem to mind – if indeed they knew that the produce had been baked in a hurry – so why should Sarah worry? She was selling her goods and making a profit and Sarah's Café, as Christmas approached, was being patronised more and more.

The rush continued until Christmas Eve and when the door finally closed behind the last customer at seven o'clock Sarah breathed a long sigh of thankfulness; partly because she was dead beat, but mainly because she knew that this week had been a resounding success. She couldn't have wished for more.

'Off you go home now,' she said to Doris. 'Joyce

and I will do the rest of the clearing away. You've already worked more than an hour longer than you're supposed to.' She pushed a gaily-wrapped package into the girl's hands. 'A Happy Christmas to you and thank you for everything. You've worked like a Trojan. Now go and enjoy yourself and we'll see you on Monday.'

The girl, pink-cheeked with delight, ran off to her home a few streets away and Sarah and Joyce stared round at the piles of washing-up still to be done, and that was after Doris had already done a vast amount.

'Never mind,' said Joyce, cheerful as ever. 'We'll soon tackle this lot. It's clean muck, as my mam would say. Only cups and saucers and plates – no greasy pans and dishes, thank goodness.'

'All the same, it's a daunting sight,' said Sarah. 'I tell you what, Joyce,' she went on, as she plunged her hands into the sink of soapy water while her cousin stood by with a pot towel at the ready, 'we could do with one of those newfangled washing-up machines. A Polliwashup, I think it's called.'

'What's that when it's at home?' asked Joyce. She looked dubious.

'I've seen it advertised in Mother's *Good Housekeeping* magazine,' said Sarah. 'You put in hot soapy water and then turn a handle and it does all the work for you. Without breakages, so it says.'

'You'd have to wipe the pots afterwards, though, surely?'

'Apparently not. After you've put in the rinsing water you just leave them to drain. Of course it costs a bob or two, as Gran would say.'

'I know what else Gran would say,' said Joyce, laughing. 'She'd say we were blooming lazy! How many times has she said that if washing up is all you have to worry about, then you have no worries at all.'

Sarah smiled. 'Times change. We're in the twentieth century now. Goodness knows how many new things'll be invented as time goes by, and you can be sure I'll take advantage of them here when I can afford them. I've already got my Hoover cleaner and my new gas stove.'

'I'm glad you decided to keep the coal range as well, though,' said Joyce. 'We certainly need it with all the baking we're doing. Mam and Gran have both hung on to theirs, haven't they? I know Gran wouldn't be without it.'

'She'll have to manage without it when they move to their new place,' Sarah observed. 'She's already complaining that the kitchen isn't big enough to swing a cat round. They're moving next month, aren't they?'

'Yes, the new people are taking over the second week in January,' said Joyce. 'It'll seem strange not to have Gran and Grandad across the road from Mam's. Still, they won't be far away. It's a grand little house they've got, just off Talbot Road, plenty big enough for the two of them.'

'Mmm ... I can't help wondering how Gran will take to it, though,' said Sarah. 'After cooking for twenty or more people she'll find it a big change just having herself and George to see to.'

'There's only the two of them during the winter,' Joyce pointed out. 'I expect she'll adjust,

and Grandad George intends to take her out and
about as much as he can. She says herself that
there are parts of Blackpool she still hasn't seen,
even though she's lived here for donkey's years;
she's always been too busy to go gadding about,
as she calls it.'

Joyce shook out the pot towel and straightened
it, then hung it on the drying rack which was
suspended from the ceiling. 'There,' she said.
'We've finished all the washing up while we've
been talking, never mind your Polly ... whatever
it is. There's nowt wrong with a good pair of
hands.'

'You're getting to sound more and more like
Gran every day,' said Sarah, smiling. 'Thanks for
everything, Joyce. I don't know what I'd have
done without you.' She looked at her cousin's red
face and shiny nose and at her straight brown hair
protruding untidily from beneath her mobcap,
wondering if she, too, looked as dishevelled as
this.

As if aware of her scrutinising glance, Joyce
gave a grin. 'Yes, I can tell what you're thinking.
I must look like the wreck of the *Hesperus*.' She
peered into the small fly-blown mirror which was
propped up on a shelf on the dresser. 'Gosh, yes!
What a sight I look.' She snatched off her cap and
hastily straightened her hair. 'Still, it isn't
everybody who can sail through the day looking
as immaculate as you do.' Joyce took off her
apron, then carefully folded it with her cap and
put them both into her holdall. 'We won't be
needing these for a day or two, will we? I'll take
them home and give them a wash and iron, then

I'll be all spick and span for Monday.'

Sarah smiled at her warmly. She had grown even fonder of her cousin during the last few weeks while they had been working so closely together. She hadn't known Joyce all that well before – it was Nancy with whom she had always been more friendly – but now she was realising the sterling qualities of the younger sister. 'I wasn't thinking that you looked a mess at all,' she said, in a white lie. 'I was thinking that you looked tired. I am, I can tell you, so I know you must be as well. Let's just make sure that everything's shipshape here, then we'd better be making tracks for home, both of us. You know how they worry if we're later than they expect.'

The house in Park Road where Grace and Edwin lived was still 'home' to Sarah, even though she now had her own attic domain and had settled in there nicely with Joyce. She was to spend the Christmas period with her parents, returning to Gynn Square on Sunday night in order to be ready for the re-opening of the premises on Monday. Joyce, too, would be at home at the Sunnyside boarding house with her mother, and Nancy and Zachary.

'See you on Boxing Day, then,' said Joyce, as they closed the shop door behind them and began to walk towards the tramstop. It was a clear bright evening, but piercingly cold, and the change in temperature after the warmth of the café made them catch their breath. 'Isn't it nice to see the lights again after four years of darkness?' Joyce remarked, pointing to the Christmas trees sparkling in a few windows along

Warbreck Road. It was the second Christmas since the war, but people still made the remark. 'I love Christmas, don't you?'

One or two of the small shops were still open, catching the last of the trade. 'Open all hours,' was a well-known slogan in the outskirts of many northern towns, Blackpool amongst them; and now the street-lamps and the lights in shops fell upon piles of apples and oranges and nuts, cheap tin toys and books and boxes of crackers, all festooned with gaily coloured paper streamers.

'Yes, they always say Christmas is for the children,' replied Sarah, 'but I never seem to have got over the thrill of it. Yes – I'll see you on Boxing Day, Joyce, for the family shindig.' They grinned knowingly at one another. 'Look, here's our tram.'

Joyce alighted near North Station while Sarah rode further on to the centre of Blackpool. Boxing Day, as always, was to be a gathering of the clans; the Donnellys and the Gregsons together with Grandma and Grandad Makepeace, at Gran's boarding house. It would be the last time, because next year the grandparents would be in their much smaller terraced house. Sarah had told Joyce that she was looking forward to Christmas, and she was, but her enthusiasm this year was modified by the prospect of seeing Zachary again, with all the family around. As the lurching Dreadnought tram clanged its way into Blackpool, Sarah was thinking that she would be glad when it was all over, when she could return on Sunday night to her eyrie up in the rooftops and to the job that

288

she was finding so fulfilling.

It was during the second week in January that Sarah had an unexpected visitor at the café. She was surprised, soon after lunch – or dinner, as it was usually called in the north – to see her father walk into the café and, leaning on his arm, her Grandma Donnelly.

Sarah dashed forward. 'Gran, how lovely to see you!' She kissed her grandmother on her paper-thin cheek, remarkably free from wrinkles, but gaunt, so very gaunt, Sarah thought with a tinge of alarm. 'What a nice surprise. And you as well, Father. Come along in – there's a table in the corner that will be out of the draught. Come and sit down and I'll get you a cup of coffee. No ... I think you'd prefer tea, wouldn't you?' Sarah was falling over herself in her anxiety to make her grandmother welcome. She knew that the old lady very rarely paid such visits and that when she did, she was used to getting preferential treatment.

'Not for me, my dear.' Edwin raised his hand. 'I've a business appointment, so I'll just leave Mother here for a while and call back for her later. I think she wants to have a chat with you ... if you can spare the time.'

'Of course I can,' said Sarah, delighted. 'We might get a rush on in the middle of the afternoon, but it's always pretty quiet at this time of day. Anyway, Gran's a special visitor. I can always make time for her.'

'I told you I'd come if it kept fine, didn't I?' said Clara Donnelly, using a northern saying that

Sarah had heard her other grandmother use as well. 'And here I am.' She eased herself stiffly into the bentwood chair that Sarah had pulled out for her while Sarah placed her walking stick in the nearby umbrella stand. 'I promised when I saw you on Christmas Day that I'd pay you a visit before long. I bet you didn't believe me, did you?' She smiled affectionately at Sarah and her pale blue eyes lit up with warmth, making such a difference to her aristocratic, somewhat haughty, countenance. When she had first got to know her, as a little child, Sarah had been overawed by her august presence; now she was very fond of the old lady.

'I know you don't get out very much, Gran,' she said, 'but I knew you'd come sometime.'

'Aye, this damned rheumatism's the bane of my life, it is that.' Clara Donnelly sighed. 'When I think how I used to dash about like a two-year-old... Never mind, old age comes to everybody, I suppose, and I've had a good innings. I've been out and about a bit more since our Edwin started running me around in that there Humber of his. So I told him he could bring me here today. He's a grand lad, my Edwin, the pick of the bunch... Now, lass, what are you going to offer me? I've not long had my lunch, but I reckon I could manage a little something or other.'

Sarah smiled. 'I think you prefer tea to coffee, don't you, Gran? And what about a nice buttered scone with jam?'

Clara Donnelly pursed her lips. 'Too ordinary. I can have scones anytime.' She peered towards the counter where a variety of cakes was displayed on glass stands. 'I'll have one of them cream cakes with chocolate on. The gooier the better, but don't forget the serviette to wipe my sticky fingers, will you?'

'So how's it going then?' asked Clara, a little while later, after she had tucked into the cake with relish and pronounced it the best she had tasted for a long time. 'This business of yours, coming up to expectations, is it?'

'Yes, I think so, Gran. It's early days yet, but I'm quite pleased at the way things are going. We're showing a small profit – only a very small one, mind you – but I'm sure things will improve when the season gets under way and the visitors start coming.'

'Well, if you're anything like your father, and his father before him, then you'll do all right,' said Clara. 'A fine businessman, my husband was.' She lifted the rose-patterned china cup to her lips and drank the last drops of tea. 'I'll have another cup if there's one in that pot, please, lass.'

As Sarah obeyed her grandmother's somewhat autocratic demand she was thinking to herself that, in reality, none of either Edwin nor William Donnelly's blood ran in her veins. But she knew that Clara had long regarded her, Sarah, as one of the Donnelly family even though the name was only hers by adoption.

'And what about the restaurant?' Clara went on. 'You could do with opening up in time for the season, I can tell you. If you don't you'll be missing a gold mine.'

'How did you know about that?' Sarah looked

291

at Clara in some surprise. She was sure she hadn't said anything about it to her grandmother. Her grandiose schemes had been pushed to the back of her mind for the moment as her funds had run out.

'Oh … our Edwin told me,' replied Clara. 'And I think it's a grand idea. How about it, then?'

Sarah smiled ruefully. 'Grand idea it might be … a bit too grand. No, that'll have to wait until some time in the future. A year or two, maybe. By that time I might be able to manage it.'

'Short of cash?' Clara was nothing if not forthright.

'You could say that, but I think I've enough on my plate at the moment.' Sarah's reply was evasive. Not for one moment did she want her grandmother to think that she was hinting. Clara Donnelly was a wealthy woman, but never once had Sarah thought of taking advantage of this.

Clara stooped down without speaking and picked up her capacious handbag from the floor. Her knobbly fingers fumbled with the clasp and Sarah felt a stab of pity as she watched her, but she knew better than to offer to help. Her grandmother was very independent. Clara rooted in the depths of the bag, but not for long because she obviously knew what she was looking for. She drew out a rectangular slip of paper and handed it to Sarah. 'Here you are, lass. Take it and say nowt. This should help.'

Sarah stared in disbelief at the paper in her hands. It was a bank cheque, made payable to herself, for … £300!

'What's this for?' she stuttered, although she

did, of course, know.

'It's for you, lass, for that restaurant of yours. You can do with it, can't you?'

'Yes ... yes, of course I can. But this is a fortune, Gran. I can't possibly take all this ... or anything, for that matter.'

Clara gave a wry grin. 'A fortune it may be, but I can afford it, I can assure you. My William left me comfortably off and I haven't spent much since he went. And I can't see that I'll be spending much more now, not at my time of life.'

'Don't say that, Gran.'

'Now don't you start softsoaping me, telling me that I'm still a young woman, like some of 'em try to do. I know I'm not, and you've too much sense to go pretending that you think I am. Do you know how old I am, Sarah?'

'I don't, Gran, not really.'

'Well, I'm seventy-eight. No spring chicken, you see. And I know that my time's nearly up. I've already had a lot more than my allotted three score years and ten.'

'Don't say that, Gran,' said Sarah, for the second time. 'Look at Queen Victoria. She lived till she was well into her eighties.'

'This is Clara Donnelly we're talking about, not Queen Victoria,' replied the old woman tartly. 'We can't all be pampered like Royalty, although I must admit I didn't do too badly myself once I'd met William. I can sympathise with the old girl in one respect, and that's over being left a widow woman. She couldn't have missed her Albert any more than I miss my William. It's not much of a life without him...' Clara's eyes grew

293

misty for a moment as she stared into space, but when she looked back at Sarah they had recovered much of their former shrewdness.

'Well, are you going to take it or aren't you?' she said sharply. 'You'll make an old woman very happy if you do,' she went on, more gently. 'And I'm hoping I'll live long enough to see it put to good use.'

'Yes, thank you very much,' said Sarah, simply. She knew that it would hurt Clara if she refused and that she would be a fool to let her pride stand in her way when her grandmother wanted so much to help. Her grandmother... But that, surely, was a difficulty, wasn't it? And if Clara's other grandchildren were to find out ... 'I really can't thank you enough,' Sarah went on. 'It's been so unexpected. I never thought–' She was silent for a moment, before she added, very quietly, 'It isn't as if you were my real–'

Clara silenced her immediately with an upraised hand and a sharp retort. 'Don't say that! Don't ever say that. I know full well what you were going to say, lass. That I'm not your real grandmother.' Clara Donnelly shook her head, a trifle sadly. 'No, maybe I'm not, not as far as the blood in our veins goes. But in every other way – I'm talking about affection and trust and friendship – you've been a real granddaughter to me. I couldn't have had a better one.' Her eyes glistened a little as she smiled at Sarah. 'I've been real fond of you ever since Grace first brought you to see me, a little mite of two or three you were then.'

Sarah nodded. 'I remember ... just. I was a bit

overawed, I think. I'd never been in such a posh house before.'

'Nor had I, till I married into the Donnelly family,' said Clara. 'There was a world of difference between their way of living and what I'd been used to on Marton Moss. That's one of the reasons I want to do some good with my brass now, while I'm still here. I believe in spreading the wealth around a bit.'

'Socialist leanings, eh, Gran?' said Sarah, teasing a little.

'No, I wouldn't go so far as to say that. I've always been a Tory – not that us women have had much chance to vote so far, have we? – and I can't see as I'll ever be any different. But I want to see my money put to good use.'

'You can rest assured there,' said Sarah, her eyes shining with pleasure and excitement. 'I had such plans, but I thought I'd have to shelve them. Now I can get on with them right away. We can get Pickering's firm in again and I can start thinking about colour schemes and furniture and menus...'

'Aye, don't forget the food,' said Clara. 'That's the most important.'

Sarah impulsively kissed her grandmother on both cheeks. 'Thanks again, Gran. I don't know what else to say, except thank you.'

'I told you to say nothing,' said Clara, getting a little flustered. She patted at her lips and cheeks with her serviette. 'You're the pick of the bunch,' she went on as Sarah sat down again. 'Just like our Edwin is. I've two more sons, Giles and Charles – of course you know that, don't you, although I don't suppose you see any more of them than I do. And quite a few grandchildren an' all.' Sarah noticed with a quiet amusement how often her grandmother lapsed into the Lancashire idiom. She had done so much more frequently since she got older, as though it no longer mattered to keep up the pretence that she was something she wasn't. 'Aye, there's five more of 'em besides you,' Clara went on, 'and I've got a great-grandchild now, but I'm lucky if I see them more than twice a year. I saw most of 'em at Christmas – their usual courtesy calls – but they couldn't wait, all of 'em, to get back to their posh friends and their gay social whirl.'

Sarah reflected that she and her parents hadn't seen her father's relations at all last Christmas. She could count on the fingers of one hand the number of times she had seen Edwin's brothers since he and her mother were married. So much for sibling affection, she thought. Maybe the whole concept was overrated; maybe she wasn't so unlucky, after all, to be the only one. She had an idea that Giles and Charles, a lawyer and an estate agent respectively, considered their brother Edwin, the owner of a seaside store, to be hopelessly provincial.

'There'll be something for all of them,' said Clara now. 'That's only fair, but the rest of 'em'll have to wait till I'm pushing the daisies up.'

Sarah felt a pang of sorrow as she heard her grandmother utter the words, half in jest, but with an underlying resignation. She couldn't bear to think of a time when Clara would not be there. And she thought how very lucky she had been with her grandparents, as well as her parents. George Makepeace, too, was not a real grandfather. She had two surrogate grandparents – three before William Donnelly died – but all of them had shown her such genuine love and concern. No girl could have been more fortunate.'

'And here's our Edwin,' said Clara as the doorbell jangled. 'Time for me to be making tracks. And you'd better get on with what you're supposed to be doing, my girl. That poor cousin of yours looks as though she's rushed off her feet.'

Sarah noticed with some surprise that there were now several people in the café, a few of them still waiting to be served. And there was Joyce, red-faced and unusually flustered, dashing about with a laden tray whilst she was sitting here talking. 'Good gracious!' she said, leaping to her feet. 'I'd never noticed. Whatever will Joyce think of me?' But she knew her amiable cousin would forgive her, especially when she heard the stupendous news.

'Yes, get on with the good work now,' said Clara, rising stiffly to her feet. 'Our Edwin'll see to me. Pass me my stick, lad. And pick my bag up off the floor, then we'll be on our way. You don't want to stop for a cuppa, do you? I doubt if Sarah's time to serve you, anyroad.'

'No, Mother,' said Edwin, with a twinkle in his eye. 'I'd better get back to the shop now, when I've seen you safely home. You've finished your business, I gather, the pair of you?'

His astute nod told Sarah that he already knew

of his mother's plans and that he approved wholeheartedly. Sarah knew that a great deal of hard work lay ahead of her, but she felt more than equal to the challenge.

Chapter 14

It was also during the second week in January that Zachary Gregson sat in the red plush seat of a Manchester theatre, watching Ivy Rathbone performing as Dandini in the pantomime *Cinderella*. The Alhambra was only a small provincial theatre in the suburbs, a few miles from the city centre, not to be compared with the Palace or the Opera House in the heart of Manchester, but Ivy had been delighted to get a booking there and Zachary was as pleased as Punch, now, to be watching her.

He was already thinking of her as 'his girl' and he hoped that tonight, after the performance, he would make that true in a very real sense. She was still holding out on him, but Zachary was confident enough of his charms to feel sure that she would succumb, sooner rather than later. Not that there had been much opportunity for the pair of them of late. Since Ivy had left Blackpool in September Zachary had seen her only twice, when she had been appearing with the Trio at variety theatres in Preston and Blackburn. He had managed to swap his shifts on the railway so that they coincided with Ivy's engagements but, even so, they had been fleeting visits; there had been barely time for a quick conversation and a kiss and a cuddle before he had to be on his way back again.

They had corresponded regularly, however. Zachary had been surprised at how quickly Ivy had replied to his letters and now he was pleased to note that she wrote more often than he did; he had to admit that he had never been much of a scholar and didn't really know what to say in letters. He found himself looking forward more and more to the missives which arrived twice weekly from Ivy; neat round writing on the blue notepaper she always used filled with anecdotes and witticisms, as lively as Ivy herself.

Zachary had taken a day's leave that was owing to him and had booked in overnight at a small commercial hotel near to the theatre and near to where he knew Ivy was staying. It wouldn't be very convenient, he knew, for him to go to her place – she was still sharing with the other two members of the Trio – but with a bit of luck he might be able to persuade her to go back with him to his digs. From what he could see of the casual way the place was run there would be no questions asked.

His seat was in the front stalls and from there Zachary had an excellent view of the stage and of Ivy's wide smile and magnificent legs, which was really all he had come to see. She had seemed delighted, out of all proportion, Zachary had thought, to procure this part of Dandini, especially as she had led him to believe, when she was appearing in Blackpool, that it was 'just a job' to her. The other two members of the Trio, Rose and Rita, were also in the show, acting as broker's men, parts normally taken by male actors, but in a pantomime it was a case of 'anything goes'. There was certainly nothing masculine about that pair with their tight jerkins and very short breeches; just as it was obvious that Dandini, the second principal boy, was most definitely not a boy!

Zachary found himself wondering, as he watched her on the stage, whence had come the tradition that the pantomime dames – the Ugly Sisters in this case – were played by men and the principal boys were played by women. Ivy in her fishnet tights and slim-fitting tunic, with a saucy three-cornered hat on her head, was a sight for sore eyes. He felt very proud that she, of the three girls, had won the most important part, while the other two were merely make-weights. Of course they couldn't hold a candle to Ivy for looks and personality, or for the quality of their performance.

She was getting ready to sing now, with the second principal girl, a dainty little thing who scarcely came up to her shoulder.

'If you were the only girl in the world, and I were the only boy...' they sang, gazing into one another's eyes. Zachary suddenly felt quite jealous of this insignificant little thing who was claiming his Ivy's attention. Although he knew it was only play-acting. He was even more determined to make sure that she was his girl; he was convinced at that moment that Ivy Rathbone was, indeed, the 'only girl in the world' for him.

He was not normally given to flights of fancy nor was he easily swayed by emotion, but he was finding himself singularly moved by this performance of *Cinderella*. He knew that it was, in reality, a rather third-rate production. Some of the costumes were tatty, the scenery could do with a fresh coat of paint and Cinderella and Prince Charming had difficulty in reaching the high notes, but Zachary felt himself, to his amazement, transported back to his childhood, caught up in the magic of it all. *Cinderella*, of all pantomimes, was a perennial favourite, and Zachary recalled seeing a performance of it at the Grand Theatre in Blackpool with his sisters, Nancy and Joyce and, as always, his cousin Sarah. The girls had oohed and aahed at the transformation scene – the glittering coach and the real live ponies on the stage – and here they were again tonight. Zachary felt a surge of nostalgia and a feeling of happiness and contentment as he watched, a feeling that was still with him as he sat with Ivy later that evening, in a little pub near the theatre.

He thought she looked enchanting tonight. She was suitably dressed for the winter weather. The brown fur collar of her coat – an exact match to the deep brown of her eyes – was turned up against the cold, framing her lovely face. Her cloche hat was pulled down over her ears, but it was unable to completely confine her springy blonde hair which peeped out alluringly at each side of her face. Zachary felt an unusual tenderness as he looked at her, a strange feeling for him and one he had very rarely experienced before. He had been fond of Sarah – very fond – but he had known nothing like the surge of affection that engulfed him now, a feeling which he was discovering, to his amazement, was not entirely founded upon lust. He suspected that he might be falling in love with this girl.

'What did you think of the show?' she asked, when he had ordered their drinks, a pint of bitter for himself and a port and lemon for Ivy. 'It's good, isn't it?'

'It was grand. You were marvellous,' he told her. 'I was that proud of you, Ivy. You could knock spots of any of 'em, even Cinderella and Prince Charming. They can't sing as well as you, either of them. How come you're not the principal instead of only the second in line? I reckon you were the best by far.'

'You couldn't be just a teeny bit prejudiced?' said Ivy, smiling. 'No, I admit they're not up to Drury Lane standard, either of them, but they've both been around a lot longer than I have so it stands to reason that they'll get the best parts. No one's heard of me, 'specially with me being just one of a trio. And I've got Sid to thank for this. He persuaded Bert Aspinall – that's our agent – to try and get this part for me and the broker's men for the other girls.'

'Yes … what about Sid and Flo?' asked Zachary. 'I thought you lot always stayed together. I was expecting to see them in the show an' all.'

'Ah, that's rather a sore point with Sid and Flo, I'm afraid,' Ivy told him. 'They would have loved the parts of Baron Hardup and the Fairy Godmother, but it wasn't to be. Bert wasn't quick enough off the mark and, as you see, some other artistes got the parts. Not nearly as good, to my mind,' she added loyally, 'but that's showbusiness for you.'

'So where are Sid and Flo then?' asked Zachary.

'Resting. Sid is pretty fed up about it, I can tell you. He feels that Bert Aspinall hasn't been pulling all the stops out lately, not by any means. In fact...' Ivy leaned forward in a confidential manner '...there are great plans afoot. Can you keep a secret?'

Zachary grinned at her enthusiasm although he was not all that interested in these tales of stage folk; all he wanted was to get Ivy on her own. 'Try me,' he said.

Ivy glanced round uneasily. 'You never know who might be listening,' she said, keeping her voice low. 'Lots of them use this place.' Zachary looked round as well, but it didn't seem to him as though anyone was taking any notice of himself and Ivy. They were all very engrossed in their own affairs, many of them talking and laughing loudly.

It was, as Ivy had already told him, typical of the small pubs to be found near to any stage door. There were signed photographs of stage artistes on the walls. He recognised Marie Lloyd, Nellie Wallace and the comedian, Harry Tate, and he wondered if these famous personalities had actually appeared on the stage of the nearby Alhambra or if they were merely there for prestige. He recognised, too, some of the people leaning on the bar. The chap in the long overcoat with the shaggy fur collar that nearly reached the ground was Baron Hardup, the one who had, according to Ivy, got the role coveted by Sid. And the lean-faced, miserable-looking chap with him was Buttons; he looked as though he would be a

304

loser both on and off the stage.

'Sid's thinking of branching out on his own, you see,' Ivy was saying. 'He's thinking of sacking Bert Aspinall, the agent, and being his own manager; and what he really wants is for the rest of us to join him, to form our own company. There's him and Flo, of course; then there's the three of us – myself, Rose and Rita; Clive Conway, the tap-dancer...' Ivy was counting them off on her fingers, 'Charlie Chinn, the comedian; Albertino, the juggler – you know, Albert Smith; and Marvin the magician and Maria. All the ones, in fact, who stayed at your place last year.'

'Sounds fascinating,' said Zachary, not very convincingly. He was getting a little bored with all this stage talk and could feel his eyes beginning to glaze over. He blinked them rapidly to keep awake. He certainly mustn't nod off now. There was so much that he wanted to achieve tonight, but it was little wonder if he was tired. He had been up since 5 a.m. and had done his early shift on the railway before dashing over here to Manchester. Tomorrow, though, was all his own, a day's precious leave to be spent, he hoped, with his Ivy.

'And when's it going to come off, this company you're talking about?' he asked, trying to show at least a little enthusiasm.

'Soon, we hope,' said Ivy eagerly. 'In time for the summer season at any rate. Sid's contacted all the others and they all seem keen to give it a try. Then he can go ahead and try to get us a good booking.'

'Blackpool?' asked Zachary, raising his eyebrows.

'I doubt it,' said Ivy. 'It wouldn't be advisable to

spend two years running in the same resort.'

'Why not?' asked Zachary. 'I remember when I was a kid the same Pierrot troupe used to perform on the sands year after year. I knew the gags so well I could say them with 'em.'

Ivy laughed. 'It'll be a bit better than a Pierrot troupe, I hope, and I think Sid wants us to get known in other places as well as Blackpool. It's not the only seaside resort in England, you know.'

'Tis to me.' Zachary grinned at her.

Ivy poked out her tongue at him. 'Well, I must admit we'll probably stay in the north, if Sid can come up with something worthwhile. Our type of show might not go down too well in the south. But there's something else I haven't told you yet, and you really must keep this a secret, Zachary.' Ivy's brown eyes were alight with enthusiasm. 'Rita, the little one of the Trio – you know, the dark-haired one – she's getting married in the spring and we've got to get somebody to replace her. Her future husband doesn't want her to carry on with her stage career.'

'Can't say I blame him,' said Zachary, wondering where all this was leading and not terribly interested either.

'Well, I thought...' Ivy's eyes opened wide '...I thought we could ask Nancy to join us.'

'*Nancy?*' Zachary didn't need to feign an interest now. 'D'you mean *our* Nancy?'

'Yes, why not? She's a good little singer and a lovely-looking girl, and I think she'd jump at the chance.'

'Don't know what Mam would say, though.

She's not twenty-one yet, in fact she'll only be twenty this coming spring. She always says she's just as old as the year.'

'I can't see that your mother would raise any objections,' said Ivy. 'She was on the stage herself, wasn't she?'

'Yes, but it was only a part-time thing, singing in a local tavern, similar to what our Nancy's doing now at the song-booth. I don't know what she'd have to say about Nancy joining a company, touring around and all that.'

'Well, it's early days yet,' said Ivy with a slight shrug, 'and there's nothing definite been decided. But I thought I'd let you know what was in the air. And your mother wouldn't need to lose any sleep about Nancy. When Sid's around he rules us with a rod of iron. There's no getting up to mischief when Sid's there, and that's a fact. Now, you won't go telling your Nancy, will you?'

'Would I be likely to?' said Zachary, somewhat scornfully. He wasn't in the habit of talking a great deal to either of his sisters.

'It might all come to nothing,' said Ivy, 'but if not then I think she'd be great as part of our trio.'

'Sid's not here at the moment, is he?' said Zachary, changing the subject. 'So who's going to see that you stick to the straight and narrow tonight, eh?'

'I can look after myself,' said Ivy, looking at him levelly. 'I don't need a keeper.'

'Glad to hear it,' replied Zachary. He reached across the table and covered her small hand with his own, squeezing her fingers tightly and rubbing his thumb across her palm.

'I never do anything Sid wouldn't approve of,' Ivy went on, her eyes narrowing slightly.

There's always to be a first time, thought Zachary, abruptly letting go of her hand. He pushed back his round stool and stood up. 'Come on. We've sat here talking long enough. We can't talk properly, anyroad, not with you looking over your shoulder all the time and whispering.'

The cold air met them as the doors swung open and Ivy shivered, drawing herself closely inside her fur-trimmed coat. Zachary put a protective arm around her. 'Don't worry, love. You won't be cold for long, I'll see to that. Now, where's it to be? Your place or mine?'

She looked at him appraisingly. 'Rose and Rita are at my digs. They usually go straight back there after the show. Besides, the landlady doesn't approve of–'

'All right, I get the message. My place then,' said Zachary, propelling her firmly across the road and round the next corner. To his surprise Ivy didn't demur though she gave him a shrewd glance from beneath her dark-lashed eyelids.

Ivy knew only too well what she was letting herself in for, going back to Zachary's digs but, as she had already told him, she felt that she was quite capable of looking after herself. Besides, they couldn't spend the rest of the evening in the pub, it was too cold to be wandering the streets or seeking seclusion in back alleys and doorways, and she wanted to be alone with Zachary almost as much, she suspected, as he wanted to be alone with her. She was growing very fond of him, possibly too fond for her own good and, for the life of her, she couldn't imagine why it was that she had fallen for him in such a big way. She knew that he could be moody and difficult and he didn't always treat his mother as kindly as he should. A bad sign, this, surely; wasn't it always said that you should take careful note of how a lad treated his mother, especially if you wanted to be his wife? Not that Ivy had looked so far ahead, but she was certainly more attracted to him than she had been to any young man before. At his best he was good company, amusing, generous with his money and, when the time came, Ivy felt sure that he would be an ardent and skilful lover.

But that time was not now, not yet. Ivy didn't approve of the fast goings-on of some – though by no means all – of her fellow artistes. At this moment, though, hurrying through the dark and chilly Manchester streets, she was aware of how very much she was looking forward to feeling Zachary's arms around her again and his lips upon hers, to know that they would be undisturbed for an hour or two, until she felt it was time for her to return to her own lodgings. There had been very little opportunity whilst she was in Blackpool for them to be really alone. Ivy would never have abused Hetty Gregson's hospitality by going into Zachary's room or inviting him into hers – an impossible situation anyway, sharing, as she did, with three other girls – and since she had been touring these last three months she had seen him only twice.

Their letters, however, had fanned the flame of their friendship. His simple sentences had said little of import, but Ivy had felt herself drawing closer to the strange enigma that was Zachary Gregson. But as for more intimate embraces, those would have to wait, as far as Ivy was concerned, until there was some sort of understanding between them. And when that would be she didn't know, for Ivy was, to her surprise and in spite of her best intentions, getting more and more involved in this stage career into which she had somehow stumbled.

Zachary's room, on the first floor of the tall narrow commercial hotel, was typical of many that Ivy had seen, even in her limited experience of touring. The wallpaper was a nondescript mottled fawn with one or two damp patches near the ceiling, the carpet square was worn thin in the area near to the bed, the mahogany chest of drawers and wardrobe looked as though they could do with a good polishing and the jug and basin which stood upon the marble wash-stand were crazed with age. The room was not dirty, just cheerless and impersonal, and the huge Victorian engraving of ragged children in a London street which hung over the bed only served to add to the general gloominess.

Ivy tried to keep her eyes away from the bed as she sat down on the easy chair. Not a particularly easy one, however; the upholstery was stiff and unyielding, stuffed with horsehair which was oozing from a tear in the cushion. Zachary put a few coins in a slot and held a match to the gas fire. Ivy was glad of its instant warmth. She was beginning to feel a little nervous, wondering what she was doing here; she didn't make a habit of going into young men's bedrooms.

'Take your coat off and make yourself comfortable,' said Zachary, 'and I'll go and get us a drink from the bar downstairs. What would you like?'

'I'd really prefer a cup of tea,' said Ivy hesitantly. 'If it's possible...'

'Don't see why not. I'll have one as well. I reckon I've had enough beer. I'll go and find out.' Zachary was back in a few moments. 'They're bringing it up for us. Room service an' all – can't be bad.'

Ivy smiled uncertainly at him, wondering why her normal self-confidence was fast disappearing. The arrival of the tea in thick earthenware cups provided a welcome distraction and they chatted of inconsequential matters; Zachary's job, the sameness of the Lancashire mill towns where Ivy had performed recently, Christmas with their respective families. But Ivy felt ill-at-ease and, from the guarded look in Zachary's eyes, she guessed that he felt the same.

'How's your brother?' he asked, when she mentioned her family in Halifax. 'Jack, was he called? The one that was in France. No more – er – problems?'

'Nightmares, you mean? No, Jack's fine now. He's just got engaged to Elsie, the girl he's been going with for ages, and he seems to have put it all behind him. How about you?'

'Oh, I'm fine an' all,' said Zachary dismissively. 'It's a lot better. The dreams don't trouble me now ... not much. Of course I haven't got something to take my mind off it all the time, like

311

your brother. Or somebody, I should say.' He looked across at Ivy from where he was sitting on the edge of the bed, his eyes softening as he regarded her. 'I do miss you, you know, Ivy,' he said. 'I reckon nothing to you gadding about all over the country.' He patted the eiderdown at the side of him, a dingy fawn and brown patterned thing, as nondescript as the rest of the room. 'Come here... Come and sit with me.'

Ivy placed her thick white cup and saucer on the chest of drawers and sat down next to Zachary. Her legs were trembling a little, but as soon as she felt his arms around her she relaxed, wondering why she had felt so uneasy. It was only Zachary, the frightened lad that she had comforted all those months ago. She was very fond of him. She wanted him to kiss her, she wanted it so badly. He had kissed her many times before and he had always stopped when she had given the sign. There was no reason to suppose he would not do so this time.

She didn't resist when he pushed her back against the lumpy flock pillow, kissing her ardently, demandingly. She responded to him in a way she had never done before, opening her mouth beneath his, feeling his tongue probing between her teeth, wrapping itself sensuously around her own. And it was all so nice, so pleasurable. Ivy was aware of the secret hidden places in her body being awakened, opening up to him...

She still didn't resist when he unfastened the buttons of her blouse and pushed it back off her shoulders, then unhooked the rigid camisole top, freeing her breasts from the restricting garment. Then she felt Zachary's lips upon them, his face buried in the hollow between them. She ran her fingers through his black wiry hair, pressing him even closer to her.

It was when she felt the hardness of his body against hers, pressing upon that very intimate place, that Ivy came to her senses. But not before Zachary had lifted her skirt, pulling at her undergarments, all the while kissing her and repeating her name. What on earth was she doing? What was she thinking of, allowing him to take such liberties? She had let him do much, much more than she had ever intended. She grabbed hold of his shoulders and pushed him away. 'That's enough, Zachary. I'm sorry ... I can't.'

'What d'you mean, you can't?' She was unprepared for the look of anger in his eyes as he once more put his hands amongst her under-clothes, tugging at them, whilst she struggled to keep them in place. 'It's a bit late now to start saying no. Not when you've let me get this far.' He bent his head to kiss her again, a kiss that this time was devoid of any feeling save lust.

Ivy pulled her mouth away from his, feeling the roughness of his chin grazing her cheek. 'No, I can't. We mustn't. I've told you before that I won't do it. It's not right.'

Zachary pushed her away from him with such force that she almost tumbled off the narrow bed. 'It's not right, eh? I'll tell you what's bloody well not right. It's not right to lead a fellow on the way you've done and then say no. There's a name for girls like you. D'you know what it is? D'you know, eh?' Zachary took hold of her shoulders, shaking her roughly, forcing her to look into his eyes.

Ivy numbly shook her head, feeling the tears well up behind her eyelids. She blinked rapidly; she very rarely cried and didn't want to do so now. 'I'm sorry,' she said in a small voice. 'I didn't mean to lead you on. I know it was my fault.' For she was realising now what a fool she had been, how lucky she was that Zachary hadn't forced her to surrender to him completely. There was the threat, even now, that he would do so, but she felt that the dangerous moment had passed. The angry look was receding from his eyes to be replaced by one of puzzlement and of frustration.

Zachary let go of her shoulders then, so suddenly that she fell back against the upraised pillow, banging her head on the brass bed rail. He sighed, a long shuddering sigh. 'Then for God's sake don't do it again. Not if you know what's good for you. I'm warning you, I won't let you off so lightly next time.'

'No ... I'm sorry,' said Ivy again, although she was not altogether sure why she should be apologising. 'I can't let you, though,' she went on. 'It wouldn't be right, you see, unless we were ... I know some girls would – that they do – but not me. I'm sorry.' She turned her back on him then, hooking up her camisole and fastening her blouse, finding that her hands were shaking.

His next words took her completely by surprise. 'Then marry me, Ivy.'

'*What?*' She turned quickly. 'What did you say?'

'You heard what I said. Marry me.'

'Don't be silly, Zachary. We can't get married.'

'Oh, why not? Who says we can't?'

'We just can't! I've got my job, and I'll be all over the place more than likely, and–'

'Give it up then.'

'What?'

'Give it up. This … this prancing about on the stage.' Zachary waved his hands in the air. 'Give it up and marry me.'

'No! Why should I?'

'Because I want you to. Because you told me, ages ago, that you weren't very keen on it all anyway. That it was just a job.'

Ivy looked at him steadily, relieved that his anger had subsided, but not quite believing that he had asked her to marry him. Her answer surprised herself. 'I've changed my mind,' she said slowly.

'What d'you mean?'

'I've changed my mind about being on the stage. It's not just a job any more. It's what I really want to do. I'm enjoying it … very much. And I don't want to give it up.' As Ivy heard the enthusiasm in her own voice she realised she was only putting into words the thoughts that had been forming in her mind for the last few months.

'You won't marry me, then?'

'I don't know, Zachary.' Ivy shook her head perplexedly. 'Give me time. I've told you … I want to go on singing and dancing. I like it: I'm good at it. But I want to go on seeing you as well, when we can.' Ivy knew that this was true. Zachary had frightened her badly, but he had calmed down now and she knew that, in spite of all his faults, she didn't want to lose him. 'Can't we just … see how it goes?'

Zachary shrugged. 'Suppose so. Looks as though I'll have to.' His full lips turned down to a pout. 'What's brought all this on, anyroad? Why d'you suddenly want to be Marie Lloyd or summat?'

Ivy smiled. 'I don't know that I'm aiming so high. But I've enjoyed being Dandini. It's given me a chance to do something on my own, without the rest of the Trio.'

'You'll still be with them, though, if Sid forms that company you were on about,' argued Zachary.

'Yes, I know. But he wants us all to do more solo work. And there might be sketches and all sorts of things to do if we have our own company…'

As they talked about it for the next half hour or so Ivy realised afresh what she had long suspected, that Zachary didn't like playing second fiddle to anything or anybody. She was surprised, therefore, when at last he walked her back to her lodgings, that he was still saying that he wanted their friendship to continue. He wanted her to get engaged to him … quite soon.

Zachary wondered, as he tumbled into bed after what seemed like endless meanderings through the dark silent streets, why on earth he had let the wretched girl get the better of him. It would have served her damned well right if he'd ripped the clothes off her and taken her there and then. She'd been asking for it, for God's sake, almost begging for it, and then for her to turn all prim and prudish on him – well, it was a wonder he hadn't knocked her senseless. That's what he'd felt like doing.

But Zachary knew, as he lay in the darkness of the strange hotel bedroom, that with Ivy Rathbone he had met his match. If it had been any other girl he would have forced himself upon her or, if that had failed, he would most certainly have sent her packing. Ivy though ... he knew that he was more than halfway to falling in love with Ivy, if, indeed, he hadn't done so already. All the feelings of tenderness that he had experienced earlier that evening, when he watched her performing as Dandini and, later, in the cosy warmth of the public house, resurged now. Zachary knew that it wasn't just her looks that attracted him. He admired her spirit, her wit, her vivacity, her ability to stand up for herself and what she wanted. And he would make her want him if it was the last thing he did. In the end she would be pleading with him to make love to her.

When he had asked her to marry him Zachary had shocked even himself, but he knew, deep down, that it was what he wanted. A girl like Ivy Rathbone was what he had always wanted ... needed, in fact. And it seemed that with Ivy the only way to get her was to marry her. Or at least, *to promise to do so...*

Chapter 15

There had been no indication that the second week in March 1920, was going to turn out to be so calamitous – or so momentous – for Sarah, but troubles very seldom announce their arrival, they just creep up on one, unexpected and uninvited. Things had been going very smoothly at Sarah's Café; too smoothly, Sarah thought afterwards, looking back on the events of that awful week. There were bound to be gremlins at work sooner or later to remind her that it wasn't wise to rest on one's laurels.

There had been a steady flow of regular customers throughout the first two months of the year, both in the shop and the café, residents of the North Shore area where Sarah's homemade produce was already making a name for itself. The books invariably showed a credit, albeit a modest one, at the end of each week, and Sarah was expecting great things when the season started. The three of them, Sarah, Joyce and the young assistant, Doris, enjoyed a harmonious relationship; never had Sarah had to offer even the mildest rebuke to either of her staff, even if it had been in her nature to do so.

Samuel Pickering's firm had moved in again, thanks to the welcome monetary gift from Clara Donnelly, and work was now progressing satisfactorily, converting the first-floor rooms into a restaurant. Sarah hoped that this would be ready to open by early summer and already her mind was leaping ahead, trying to think of original ideas to get the place off to a flying start.

There was little time for leisure, but when the day's work was finished Sarah was only too happy to retreat to her snug little nest – which was how she thought of it – up in the eaves above Gynn Square. And Joyce was an ideal companion, good-natured and unflappable, always ready to fall in with Sarah's plans, although Sarah invariably consulted her cousin, down to the smallest detail, about any ideas she might have.

Their attic apartment was not magnificent by any means, but it was homely and comfortable and not once had Sarah found herself looking back to the luxury – and the pampering – she had enjoyed in her home on Park Road. She had not moved any of her bedroom furniture from there, guessing that it might upset her parents were she to do so. Instead, she and Joyce had hunted round the salerooms and secondhand shops for bargains for their two rooms. For that was all they had; a shared bedroom and a living room, and the tiniest bathroom imaginable where the plumber had, miraculously, managed to install a simple white bath, wash basin and lavatory. The ceiling above the bath sloped at an alarming angle so that you had to bend almost double to dry yourself, after making sure, of course, that you didn't give your head a nasty bang by inadvertently standing at your full height.

They had all the essentials for the main rooms and that was all that mattered to them. In the bedroom there were two single beds with wooden headboards, a dressing table and a large shared wardrobe, all of which had been stripped down and repainted in a bright primrose yellow, with the willing help of Grandad Makepeace. Floral patterned curtains of a toning yellow hung at the window and the polished wooden floor was partially covered with strips of carpet made into makeshift rugs. The bare boards were chilly to the feet on a winter's morning, but instant heat was provided by a Valor oil-heater which stood at the side of the room.

A similar heater was used in the living room, for neither of these attic rooms had fireplaces. Sarah's mother had thought at first that her daughter was quite mad to even consider living in the attic when the first-floor rooms were so obviously intended to be the living quarters. But Sarah had known from the beginning that the first floor was destined for more important things and now, with work on the restaurant going on apace, she felt that her optimism had been vindicated. The living room was sparsely furnished. There was an old oak sideboard, more to their grandmother's taste than that of Sarah and Joyce, with its high mirrored back and elaborate carvings of fruit and flowers. It was, however, all they could afford and they had lovingly restored its patina with an application of both wax polish and elbow grease. Along one wall were wooden shelves, erected in his spare time by George Makepeace, in his role of grandfather, not as employee of Pickerings. These were filled with books and ornaments – mainly Sarah's – and sewing baskets and knitting bags which belonged to Joyce.

An elegant standard lamp – Sarah's choice and the only really luxurious article in the room – stood in a corner. The whole of the premises were, to Sarah's relief, wired for electricity, but this was an 'Aladdin' paraffin lamp. Its glowing incandescent light was clearer and yet more intimate, Sarah thought, than the harsh gleam of an electric light bulb. The bright orange shade, diffusing the radiance, and the brass three-legged stand, toned well with the rest of the room.

There were a couple of easy chairs and a matching sofa; matching because Grace had skilfully transformed their shabbiness into comparative splendour with loose covers; these were of gaily patterned chintz in a design of ferns and leaves, brown, orange and gold, the colours of autumn. Curtains of the identical material – purchased at cost from the furnishing department at Donnelly's – hung at the windows. They were low windows, touching the floor, and you had to kneel to look out of them because of the sloping roof.

Sarah loved the view from them. To the right was the old whitewashed building, the Gynn Inn, and ahead, not more than twenty yards away, you could see the start of the elegant cliff gardens with their tidy lawns and steps topped by stone urns, all surrounded by jagged 'pseudo' rocks of white granite. A lot of the landscape in Blackpool was artificial, like these rocks. Even the cliffs that began just north of the Gynn, stretching as far as Bispham, were manmade; huge concrete boulders which, to Sarah's mind, looked nothing like cliffs; but they were all part of the brash allure which was Blackpool and which attracted visitors in their thousands every summer. And beyond the cliff gardens was the sea. It frequently looked grey and forbidding, not often the sparkling blue of oceans depicted in stories and pictures, but Sarah considered it an added bonus to be able to view it from her very own windows. She thought that Park Road, where she had lived before, was too far from the sea which was, after all, one of the chief delights of living in Blackpool.

Not that there was much time for either of the cousins to stare out of the windows. They were both too busy, but each of them thought that they were more contented than they had been in the whole of their lives.

Sarah realised halfway through Monday morning that the premises were abnormally quiet. Not as far as customers were concerned – there had been the usual slow trickle which was all that they expected on a Monday – but their work in the kitchen and café was always done to the accompaniment of bumps and bangs and the occasional shout from the first-floor rooms. Sounds that were absent this morning. Pickering's firm hadn't arrived and Sarah was just beginning to wonder why when the phone rang.

It was Samuel Pickering, the owner of the firm, and this in itself was unusual. Like George Makepeace, who had recently retired, Samuel himself was thinking of handing over the reins before long and he was gradually doing less and less actual work.

'Sorry, luv. I'm afraid we're held up for a while

now. Material's not come through, you see.' Samuel Pickering's gruff Lancashire voice sounded regretful, but not, Sarah thought, all that much so. After all, he didn't have a restaurant to open in a couple of months' time.

'What exactly are you waiting for, Mr Pickering?' Sarah asked politely. 'And how long do you think it will be?'

'It's that oak panelling, luv. You know, that you wanted for the walls. I did tell you it 'ud be simpler just to replaster and paper it, but you insisted–'

'I insisted because it's what I wanted,' said Sarah firmly. 'I still want it. How long will it be?' she repeated.

'Well, I don't rightly know. It's hard to say.' Sarah could just see Samuel scratching his head. 'They promised me faithfully we'd have it by now, but you know how it is.' No, I don't, thought Sarah, getting more exasperated by the minute. 'Now they're telling me it could be six weeks … or more,' said Samuel, the last two words barely audible.

'Six weeks – or even more?' Sarah's usual gentle voice rose both in volume and in pitch, so much so that a couple of women in the back corner of the café stared in her direction. 'Six weeks?' she said again, more quietly this time, turning the other way so that the women couldn't lipread her words. 'That's a very long time. I don't think we can wait so long. That would take us to…' she counted in her head '… the end of April, possibly the beginning of May, and then it would all have to be assembled. I was hoping to open for Whit week. Yes, maybe it could be done, just about.'

'Whit week? End of May?' She heard Samuel Pickering give a low whistle. 'Out of the question, luv.'

'But surely, Mr Pickering,' Sarah argued, 'when the panelling arrives it's only a simple matter to put it on the walls. It wouldn't take more than a week or two, surely?'

'I wouldn't like to promise.' Samuel sounded evasive. 'It isn't so much a question of when it arrives as *if* it arrives. They say six weeks, but ... I'd better be honest with you.' She heard him sigh. 'I reckon it could be a damned sight longer.'

'Oh dear! This is most annoying.' Sarah couldn't remember when she had felt so aggravated; then she reminded herself that it was hardly Mr Pickering's fault. He was trying to be fair with her and he had rung her up in person to tell her. And he was one of the most reputable businessmen in Blackpool; everyone said so. He couldn't be held responsible if his suppliers let him down. She said as much to him now. 'I'm sorry. I know it isn't your fault. The job's finished, isn't it, apart from the panelling?'

'Aye, as near as damn it. If you take my advice you'll forget all about the fancy work. Just get a decorator in to finish it off, that's if you don't want to wait.'

'I don't know. I really don't know.' Sarah had set her heart on an elegant restaurant, and oak-panelled walls had been one of the main features she had had in mind.

'Well, let me know by the end of the week, then I can cancel the order if needs be,' said Samuel.

'I've sent the lads somewhere else today, seeing that they've nowt to do at your place. Sorry an' all that.'

Sarah replaced the phone with rather more force than was necessary. 'Did you hear that?' she said to Joyce, who had been hovering nearby.

'I got the gist of it,' Joyce replied. 'I thought something was up when the workmen hadn't arrived. The oak panelling, is it?'

Sarah nodded. 'I'd really set my heart on it, and yet I want the restaurant to be ready for Whit week. Oh Joyce, I don't know what to do.'

'Well, you know what Gran always says. "Don't spoil the ship for a ha'porth of tar".' Joyce smiled consolingly at her cousin. 'And it would be a heck of a rush, you know, for us to open the restaurant in May. It's well into March already.'

'Trust you to look on the bright side,' said Sarah. She smiled affectionately at her cousin. 'At least I've got till the end of the week to think about it.'

It was about midnight when Sarah awoke with a violent pain in her stomach. She only just made it to the bathroom; then she lay shivering in her narrow bed, wondering whether it was worth the effort to go down to the kitchen to make a warm drink and refill her hot water bottle. She really did feel ghastly.

In a few moments Joyce, too, was awake with a similar complaint. The two girls stared at one another, an hour or so later, across the space between the two beds.

'Are you thinking what I'm thinking?' said Joyce.

'I might be,' said Sarah.

'Sausage rolls?'

Sarah nodded. 'Yes, sausage rolls. Oh lor,' she added in a whisper. 'Just think what that might mean. Oh no…'

'Don't let's meet trouble,' said Joyce. 'It might not be. At least I'm feeling a bit easier now, are you?'

'Mmm … a bit.'

'I tell you what, I'll go down and make us both a hot drink and put a drop of brandy in it. Mam swears by brandy for a tummy upset.'

'We'll both go.' Sarah swung her feet out of bed, feeling for her furry slippers. 'That kitchen's a spooky place at night.'

It was certainly not an ideal situation, living two floors above the kitchen. Sarah and Joyce, for convenience, ate their meals in the kitchen adjoining the café and shop and usually took it in turns to go down and make an evening cup of tea or cocoa.

'I know what we could do with,' said Sarah, as they sat at the kitchen table, their hands cupped round the comforting warmth of the earthenware mugs which they used when they were on their own. 'One of those electric kettles. We could plug it in upstairs then it would save us the bother of trailing down here every time we want a cup of tea. We're still short of a lot of the necessities, aren't we? Still, perhaps in time…'

'I don't know about a necessity,' said Joyce. 'I'd call an electric kettle a luxury. My man hasn't got one and Gran certainly wouldn't hear of it. She says they're downright dangerous anyway, and that it's asking for trouble having water anywhere near anything electric.'

'Oh well, you know Gran.' Sarah smiled weakly. She was still feeling far from well, all shaky and shivery, and was finding it hard to stop her hands from trembling. She took another sip of the strong tea, well-laced with brandy, feeling its fieriness trickle down to her stomach. 'Gran's hardly moved into the twentieth century yet. And I must admit my mother has very little electricity in the house, apart from the lighting, of course. She swears by gas… How are you feeling, Joyce?'

'A bit better. I think this brandy's done the trick. How about you?'

'I daresay I'll live.' Sarah could feel her eyelids pricking with tiredness. Maybe sleep would prove to be the best cure of all. 'Come on, let's get back upstairs and into bed. We've still a few hours before we have to be up again.'

'Ugh! Don't remind me,' said Joyce. They both glanced at the wooden clock on the dresser, loudly ticking the night away. It was twenty minutes past two. 'Another three and a half hours if we're lucky. I hope Doris is all right.'

'So do I,' said Sarah with feeling, as they made their way back up the creaking stairs in the darkness. 'She did eat quite a lot of them, didn't she?'

'Don't let's meet trouble,' said Joyce, for the second time, but her tone was not entirely convincing.

At half-past eight the same morning the cousins knew that their fears were not groundless. It was Doris's mother, Mrs Jackson, who came into the

327

shop, not the fifteen-year-old assistant.

'Our Doris has been taken bad,' she informed them. 'Been up all night, she has. In fact I've just been round to get the doctor to her. From the look of her I doubt if she'll be in for a few days. I thought I'd best let you know, Miss Donnelly.'

'Thank you, Mrs Jackson. I do hope she'll soon recover. It's very good of you to come and tell us.' Sarah's voice was feeble and she could feel beads of perspiration breaking out on her forehead. She put up her hand to wipe them away, at the same time glancing nervously at her cousin.

'Least I could do,' said Mrs Jackson. 'You've been real good to that lass of mine. Always talking about you, she is. It's "Miss Donnelly this and Miss Donnelly that" all the time.' She stopped and looked anxiously at Sarah. 'I say, luv, you don't look so dusty yerself, if you don't mind me saying so.' She glanced at Joyce. 'Nor you neither, Miss. Oh crikey! Don't say you two's got it an' all. Have you…?'

'Yes, I'm afraid so,' said Sarah quietly. 'My cousin and I were both ill during the night, but we think we'll be all right now, don't we, Joyce?' Joyce nodded in agreement. 'We probably look rather tired because we lost some sleep and we've been up since six o'clock.'

Sarah was well aware that she was sounding much braver than she felt. The truth was that it had been sheer purgatory this morning, dragging herself out of bed, seeing to the coal range, making the pastry and batter for the first batches of pies and cakes. Sarah's fragile stomach was still resisting any suggestion of food and she was sure that Joyce felt the same; but her cousin, like Sarah, was not one to give in easily. 'We'll be all right,' she told Mrs Jackson again.

'Well, you don't look it,' replied that lady, not very tactfully. 'D'you reckon it's summat you've eaten? Our Doris mentioned something about sausage rolls. She says she had a few before she came home.'

Sarah gave a deep sigh. 'Yes, she did.' Doris, indeed, had consumed five at least of the wretched things, saying that it would save her the trouble of getting her tea ready when she got home. There had been a surfeit of sausage rolls towards the end of the day and Sarah had suggested that the three of them should eat them up at their teatime breaks. She never liked there to be any food left over at the end of the day, certainly not anything perishable, preferring to make fresh supplies each morning. But it was beginning to look as though the sausagemeat had already been past its best when it was delivered. 'I'm sorry, Mrs Jackson,' said Sarah now. 'If it was the sausage rolls – or anything that she ate here – I'm very sorry.'

'No need to apologise, Miss Donnelly. As sure as I'm standing here I'm sure it wasn't your fault. Doris is always telling me how your kitchen's as clean as a new pin. "You could eat off the floor, Mam," she says. No, you've no need to go blaming yourself. Perhaps you should have a word with your butcher, though, whoever he is. I only hope there won't be any nasty repercussions for you. You know what I mean – some of the folks round here can be very quick to take umbrage.'

Oh, do shut up, woman, Sarah thought to herself, for Mrs Jackson was giving voice to her worst fears. An epidemic of food poisoning, traced back to Sarah's Café, hundreds ill, dying...

'Still, I doubt if any of 'em were as greedy as our Doris,' Mrs Jackson went on. 'She loves her food, does Doris. How many did she eat, did you say?'

'I think it might have been ... six,' replied Sarah weakly.

'Six bloomin' sausage rolls! Then she deserves to be ill.' Mrs Jackson tutted. 'No, I shouldn't say that. The lass really has had a nasty turn, but the doctor'll soon get her right, I'm sure of that. I hope it's that new 'un that comes to her. I hear he's quite a marvel. It's going to be hard for you, Miss Donnelly, trying to carry on when you're not feeling well. Listen...' She leaned her elbows on the counter. 'How would it be if I were to come in a bit later on and give you a hand? I could clear away and wash up. Not cooking, though – I'm not much good at all that fancy stuff.'

'That would be wonderful, Mrs Jackson,' said Sarah warmly. Any help for the next day or two would be more than welcome. 'You don't happen to know of anyone who could act as a shop assistant, do you? Until Doris is well again, I mean.'

Mrs Jackson frowned. 'Let me see... There's young Maisie as lives next door to me. I know she's worked in a shop, but she hasn't got a regular job at the moment. She's just helping her ma with the little 'uns. There's a big family of 'em and I daresay they'd be glad of the extra bob or two.'

Sarah agreed that she would give the girl a try.

'Young Maisie' came in later that morning and it was obvious at a glance that this girl would certainly not be another Doris, but Sarah thought philosophically that it was any port in a storm. Her hair was lank and greasy, with traces of dandruff on her collar, her hands were rough and red, though this was hardly the girl's fault if she had to spend most of her life in the kitchen, and she seemed to be troubled by a permanent sniff. She was uncommunicative, too, a great contrast to Doris who loved to exchange pleasantries with the customers and make them feel at ease. Apart from the odd 'Ta very much,' and 'Morning,' Sarah hardly heard her utter a word.

But she had other, more pressing, matter on her mind than a surly shop assistant who, at all events, would only be with them for a few days. Several customers had been in to complain about the sausage rolls. There were lurid tales of husbands who had been up all night, children who were still vomiting and had to be kept off school, and one irate man threatened to 'have the law' on her. He was a ruddy-faced fellow with arms on him like ham shanks and Sarah felt herself flinching away from both his menacing presence and his beery breath. His wife, so he said, thought that her last moment had come, but that hadn't prevented him, thought Sarah, from calling at the pub on the way to tell her so.

'Tek no notice of him, Miss,' said Maisie as he departed, speaking more now than she had done all morning. 'He'll do nowt about it. He's all mouth and trousers, that one. He lives down our street and he's forever fallin' out wi' t'neighbours. You'll hear no more from him, mark my words.'

'Thank you, Maisie,' said Sarah gratefully. 'I only hope you're right.' All she had been able to do all morning was to apologise, to say that she would make sure it didn't happen again, that she would, if needs be, change her butcher.

'But how can I be sure?' she said to Joyce, blinking away the tears that she could feel at the back of her eyes. 'They tasted all right, didn't they? How can I possibly know? And how do all those people know it was our sausage rolls?'

'They're just guessing,' said Joyce, 'and as it happens I suppose they're right. But you can't ever know for sure that your food's fresh. It's one of the bugbears of owning a café, or a boarding house, come to that. I know Mam and Gran have both had scares of this sort now and again. You can't do anything, not until they invent a way of keeping food fresh for a long time. I believe they've already got something in America that can do that.'

Sarah shook her head pessimistically. She wasn't much interested in what they did in America; it was a very long way away and it didn't help her much at the moment. 'We'll have lost some customers,' she said. 'We're sure to have done.'

'Never mind,' said Joyce. 'You win some, you lose some. I'm sure all shopkeepers would tell you the same, and it's the first setback we've had, isn't it?' Sarah nodded. 'Well, there you are then.' Joyce nodded decidedly. 'Now, shall I make us a cup of tea? There's a lull at the moment. Perhaps you could manage a sandwich, as well. I know I could. My stomach's beginning to think my throat's cut.'

Sarah smiled. 'Thanks, Joyce. You're a great comfort to me, you are really. I don't know what I'd do without you. Perhaps Doris will be back sooner than we expect. You and I seem to be recovering quite quickly.' She cast a surreptitious look at Maisie who was leaning against the counter examining her nails; they were, Sarah had noticed, none too clean.

'Let's hope so.' Joyce grinned. 'I'll make Maisie a cup of tea, along with us, try to make her feel at home.'

But Sarah was doomed to disappointment. When Mrs Jackson came in later in the day she explained that Doris was not only suffering from a severe gastric attack, but was also having trouble with 'the usual'. 'Very bad it is sometimes,' her mother confided in a whisper. 'Lays her low for a day or two.' But Doris would try, her mother told Sarah, to get back by Saturday if she could, always their busiest day.

Four days, thought Sarah, counting on her fingers and wondering how she could possibly put up with Maisie for so long. At the end of the day, when the cash drawer was two shillings short, Sarah decided at first that her reckoning must be at fault. Mathematics was not her strongest point and, though she tried to keep a check on sales, it was sometimes difficult with the many different items that were sold. Also, she was very tired. But when it happened again the next day – two shillings and sixpence this time – Sarah knew that her suspicions were correct.

She had deliberately done her cashing up early that day and she tackled Maisie just as the girl was putting on her coat, ready to go home. Her denials at first were indignant. 'It weren't me, Miss! I never, honest to God, I never.' Eventually, though, under Sarah's steady glance, she broke down, confessing that she never thought they'd notice, that her mam had four little 'uns at home, that her father spent most of his time – and his money – at the pub, that they sometimes didn't know where the next meal was coming from... 'And you won't get the police to me, will you, Miss?'

Sarah assured her that she wouldn't, that she didn't need to give the money back, but that she would not be needing her services the next day. That would be Thursday, so for two days, until Doris returned on Saturday, Sarah and Joyce would have to manage on their own.

'Oh dear, I'm not sure that I can cope with all this,' said Sarah that evening, collapsing inelegantly into an easy chair. 'Sacking people, telling people off ... it's not me.' She had had quite an altercation with the butcher, having been persuaded by her father that it wasn't worth the risk and that she must find another supplier. 'Why did I ever want to own a café? And to think that I'm actually going to open a restaurant as well. I must be mad! I just hope nothing else goes wrong.'

She spoke too soon, because when they went down to the kitchen later that evening to make a drink they startled a mouse sitting on the corner of the dresser. It immediately scampered off to its hole, thought where that was they had no idea. Sarah screamed. She detested the creatures; it was something that she had secretly dreaded since opening the café, knowing it was more than likely that one would appear sooner or later. It was up to Joyce, who did not have the same irrational fear of them, to set the trap and get rid of the evidence the next morning.

And it was the following day that the lavatory refused to flush and they had to call a plumber. Sarah found herself laughing hysterically. 'I suppose it has been working overtime,' she said, 'and at least we've got the one in the backyard.'

'And chamber pots,' added Joyce, grinning. 'Don't worry, I'm quite used to 'em, working in a boarding house, although neither Mam nor Gran would have them in the bedrooms, except in an emergency. They said it wasn't seemly, young girls like me having to empty them.'

'Well, it's an emergency now, all right,' said Sarah. 'What a week it's been! I would never have believed all this could happen in a week.'

'It never rains but it pours,' said Joyce.

'I suppose that's what Gran says?' Sarah gave a wry smile.

'How did you guess? And one of these days you'll look back on it all and laugh,' added Joyce. 'That's something else she says.'

'I wouldn't be too sure,' sighed her cousin. 'I certainly don't feel like laughing at the moment.

At least Doris is back tomorrow so we'll have an extra pair of hands. And I must admit we still seem to be quite busy, in spite of everything.'

'Do be careful, Miss Donnelly,' said Doris, just after the shop had closed on Saturday. She turned from the sink, watching Sarah carry an overladen tray into the kitchen. 'You've got too much on there. You shouldn't be doing that anyway. It's my job and I know you're not feeling well.'

'Nonsense,' said Sarah, trying to smile, although she was feeling very tired, much more so than she normally felt at the end of a week; but then it had been quite a week. 'You should know by now that we all pull together here. We don't have special jobs. Besides, you're washing up, aren't you? How many pairs of hands do you think you've got? We're glad to have you back,' Sarah went on, as she and Joyce, who had been drying the pots, started to unload the tray. 'You must take care as well. You're still looking a bit peaky.'

'Oh, I'm fine now,' said Doris cheerfully. 'As right as rain. That new doctor worked wonders for me. Have you seen him, Miss Donnelly? He's a bit of all right, I can tell you!'

Sarah shook her head listlessly. 'No ... no, I haven't.' She was finding it difficult to concentrate and as she lifted her hand to tuck a stray piece of hair into her mobcap she realised that her forehead was wet with perspiration, although she felt quite chilly. Her head was aching a little, too; obviously the stomach upset earlier in the week, plus the past events, had all taken their toll of her. Just one more sinkful of pots, then she would be

336

able to have a rest.

Sarah knew very well that she had overloaded the tray again. Doris had just warned her about it, but she was anxious to get finished. Perhaps it was too heavy, perhaps she had suddenly gone dizzy, perhaps the floor was slippery. Sarah was never to know what had happened when she suddenly lost her footing and crashed to the ground. Her leg twisted beneath her and her head banged against the corner of the dresser with a sickening thud. Joyce and Doris stared in horror at the unconscious form of their friend and at the broken crockery scattered far and wide across the concrete floor.

Chapter 16

When Sarah opened her eyes it was to see a pair of kindly, yet grave, grey eyes regarding her anxiously. She thought for one moment that it was her father, then, as she gradually came to she realised that, of course, it wasn't. Edwin Donnelly's eyes, though often filled with the same gentle concern, were hazel, not grey; and Edwin's hair was golden-brown, now flecked with silver, not the deep glossy brown of this man's ... whoever he was. There was a similarity, though, in the lines of the face; the lean, almost gaunt features, the wide, well-shaped lips and the deep clefts leading outwards from nose to chin. And the laughter lines, creasing round his eyes and mouth, as he smiled at her now ... whoever he was.

'You gave us all a fright,' he said, 'but you're going to be all right.'

'I'm sorry,' Sarah began, trying to sit up, but finding herself restrained by a firm hand on her shoulder. 'I don't know who...' She frowned, shaking her head confusedly, realising then that her head was laid on her pillow, that she was in her own bed up in her attic room.

'I'm Dr Duncan,' the man said. 'Alexander Duncan. Your friend came to fetch me because you had a fall. But you mustn't worry, you're going to be all right,' he said again.

'What … what have I done?' Sarah could feel that her right leg was bandaged and she tried to glance down at it. She felt dizzy, though, when she raised her head.

'You've sprained your ankle, Miss Donnelly. It is Miss, isn't it?' Sarah gave a brief nod and at this the doctor's enquiring glance relaxed a little. 'Quite a nasty sprain. You'll no' be walking on it for quite a wee while.' Sarah could detect a faint Scottish burr in the doctor's voice, a pleasing sound which brought to her mind a picture of heather-clad hills and granite towns, although she had never been to Scotland.

'And of course the bump on your head hasn'a helped.' He put his hand in front of her face, holding up two fingers. 'Now, Miss Donnelly,' he said, moving his hand across her field of vision. 'Tell me – how many fingers can you see?'

'Two,' Sarah replied.

'Good … good. There should be no problems there, but I'll check again tomorrow, just to be on the safe side.' He smiled at her again and patted her arm. 'Just you have a wee rest, Miss Donnelly, and don't worry about a thing. I've left you some tablets – you might have a slight headache – and I'll be back to see you again in the morning.'

A sudden thought struck Sarah. 'Are you the new doctor I've been hearing about? Doris mentioned you.'

'Ah-ha, I suppose I must be.' Alexander Duncan grinned. 'I'm quite new. I've been here about six months, but I guess I'll still be the new doctor when I've been here six years. I'm with Dr Mason. Yes, I was called in to see Miss Jackson earlier this week. You and your friends are making sure I'm no' short of work.' His grey eyes twinkled appealingly and Sarah had the most extraordinary feeling; a fluttering in her stomach, but not at all like the discomfort she had known earlier in the week. This was a delicious, exciting feeling, and a glow of warmth which spread right through her. 'See you tomorrow, Miss Donnelly.' The doctor nodded and smiled, then he was gone.

Sarah heard him talking to Joyce, who had obviously been hovering in the living room, then the sound of his footsteps going down the stairs. The doctor was right; her head did hurt and her ankle, too; she could feel the throbbing pain beneath the tight bandage. But Sarah was strangely unconcerned about the pain and all her other worries, too. All the dreadful things that had happened this last week seemed to have flown out of the window. All she could think about was the look in Dr Duncan's serene grey eyes and how much she was looking forward to seeing him again tomorrow. It was incredible – unbelievable – that it could happen so quickly, but Sarah knew that it had. She had fallen in love.

Joyce came dashing in now, followed very quickly by Doris. She came over to her cousin and kissed her cheek, something that Sarah could not remember her ever doing before. 'Goodness, you didn't half give us a fright!' said Joyce. 'Didn't she, Doris? I was scared out of my wits, I can tell you, when I saw you lying there, all still and pale. I thought for one awful moment that you'd gone.'

Sarah knew that she must have looked bad for

340

her normally level-headed cousin to be talking like this.

'Doris dashed round for Dr Duncan – he's only a few streets away, you know – and he was here in no time. Wonderful, he was, Sarah. He knew just what to do. We thought you might have broken your leg, as it was twisted round at such a funny angle, but he says there's nothing broken; it's just a bad sprain. He put some smelly stuff on it, embrocation, I think they call it, and bandaged it up. And all the while you were lying there as still as could be. You put the wind up us, you did that.'

'Did he … he had to take my stocking off, then?'

'Of course he did, you daft pie-can. He's a doctor, isn't he? And then he carried you up here, as if you were as light as a feather.'

'He carried me?'

'Well, how d'you think you got here, for heaven's sake? You couldn't walk, and it looks as though you won't be walking for quite some time, too. He says you've to rest, especially with having that bump on your head as well. So you'll have to do as you're told, think on!'

Sarah nodded and smiled serenely. It was amazing how calm she felt, as though all her cares had gone, and the fact that she had to stay put while there was a shop and café to run worried her not a scrap. 'I know you two can cope,' she said, 'although you'll have to get in some extra help. You can't possibly manage on your own.'

'Let me worry about that.' Joyce sat on the edge of the bed and put her hand on Sarah's arm. 'I'm sure I'll be able to find somebody; anyway, as I've

341

said, it's my problem. I don't want you to worry about a thing. Just concentrate on getting better.'

Joyce would be surprised if she knew how little she was worrying, thought Sarah, and how detached she felt. She did realise, however, that Doris was still here and goodness knows what time it must be. The girl should have gone home ages ago. 'What time is it?' asked Sarah now.

Joyce glanced at Sarah's prettily enamelled boudoir clock which sat on the dressing table. 'It's half-past seven, but it doesn't matter, does it? The shop's shut all day tomorrow and our time's our own.'

'Half-past seven! Good grief!' Sarah looked at Doris who so far hadn't said a word; very unusual, this, as the girl was normally such a chatterbox. She was still hovering in the doorway, regarding Sarah with soulful eyes. 'Doris, you must get off home right away,' Sarah told her. 'Your mother will be wondering where on earth you are.'

'It's all right, Miss Donnelly. She'll not bother, 'specially when she knows why I'm late. I couldn't go with you in a state like this, could I?' Sarah was surprised to see tears in the girl's blue eyes and her usually cheerful red face creased with concern. 'Eeh, I'm that glad you've opened your eyes, Miss.' Doris gave a sniff, hastily wiping her hand across her nose and cheek. 'I've never felt so worried in all me life, not even when me mam was bad with pneumonia.'

Sarah felt touched by Doris's anxiety, although she had been aware that there was a touch of hero-worship in the girl's attitude towards her. 'Well, you don't need to worry any more,' she

342

said. 'I'll be as right as rain in a day or two.'

'Yes, I'm sure you will, 'specially with that nice Dr Duncan looking after you.' Doris gave an impish grin, adding slyly, 'I told you he was a bit of all right, didn't I? Lovely, isn't he?'

Sarah felt a smile tugging at the corners of her mouth; she had to be careful, in fact, that her face didn't break out in a radiant beam. 'Yes,' she said, trying to sound noncommittal. 'He seems very nice...'

Later that night, after her parents had been to see her – Joyce had insisted on phoning them and telling them what had happened – and after she had eaten the light supper that Joyce prepared for her, Sarah tried to give herself a good talking to. She lay in her narrow bed, listening to Joyce's gentle snores. The poor lass had gone to sleep as soon as her head touched the pillow, tired out with her solicitude on her cousin's behalf, and Sarah thought again how fortunate she was in having such a good friend and partner at the café. The events of the past week – the non-appearance of the joiners, the food poisoning scare, Maisie's dishonesty, the mouse, the non-flushing lavatory – Sarah could now view them all rationally for what they were, just pinpricks of troubles, such as any café-owner might reasonably expect. It was just that they had all come at once, catapulting against one another like skittles in a row, taking her by surprise because, until then, everything had been going so smoothly. Problems were all part and parcel of running a business and Sarah knew that she would have to get used to them.

She knew too that she should be trying to go to

sleep, that it was all part of the healing process, but she felt as wide-awake as if it were the middle of the day. Her mind was a maelstrom of jostling thoughts, but the most intrusive one was of a pair of clear grey eyes looking earnestly into her own. And this was the chief reason why Sarah was trying to rebuke herself. She knew that she was an intelligent, normally sensible girl; and sensible girls didn't fall in love in a split-second, 'at first sight', as they said in romantic stories. This was real life that she was living in, not the pages of a book, and Sarah tried to tell herself that it just wasn't possible. Don't be ridiculous, she lectured herself. You've only just met him, you don't even know him. You're confusing love with gratitude. Obviously you're grateful to him because he was so kind and you were feeling vulnerable. You might have imagined yourself in love with any man who came along at that moment, who was as concerned as he was. When you see him again in the morning you will realise how foolish you are… And to even imagine that he might feel the same way about you, good gracious girl, you must be out of your mind!

But as Sarah turned sideways and closed her eyes she could still see him there at the forefront of her mind. Alexander Duncan, with his glossy dark brown hair, his firm jawline and clearly cut features, the compassionate look in his luminous grey eyes. Her head was aching and her ankle was hurting, but the pain was overshadowed by the happiness which was flowing through her whole body. Sleep came at last: deep dreamless, and refreshing.

When, next morning at ten o'clock, Dr Duncan called to see her again, Sarah knew beyond all doubt that she had not imagined any of it. And, what was more, unless she was very much mistaken, Alexander Duncan felt just the same as she did.

Alex Duncan had known instantly, when Sarah Donnelly opened her lovely brown eyes and looked at him, that he was going to marry this girl. He wondered afterwards how he could have known so suddenly, how one could fall in love in an instant, and he tried to tell himself, later that night, not to be so foolish. But when he saw her again the next morning his feelings were just the same. He knew that he loved her and that, come what may, he was going to make her his wife. There would be obstacles, he knew, but none that he was unable to overcome.

He had left his problems far behind him in Scotland, six months ago, and he knew that he had done all that it was humanly possible to do. Now it was only a matter of time… He had made a fresh start down here in the north of England where no one knew him. His references from Dr McCallum, his previous partner in Melrose, had been very good, for he had been well thought of in the Border town.

There had been a slight setback, of course, over that business with the gipsy woman. She had threatened to sue him, to blacken his name all over the Scottish lowlands, when her little son had died. But it hadn't been Alex's fault at all. The woman had tried to cure the child with her own gipsy remedies; it had been her husband, who, in the end, had called the doctor. But it had been too late ... much too late. Dr McCallum had understood that. So, it seemed, had the rest of Alex's patients, for there had been very little falling off in the number of people waiting to see him in the surgery. But mud tended to stick. One never knew when the incident might be revived in folks' minds, and the people in that area were somewhat insular in their outlook. This was one of the reasons why Alex had been so glad to get away. And he had had no regrets. He got on very well with Dr Mason, his partner here in Blackpool. Alex had grown to love both the seaside town and its people during the few months he had been here and he was determined never to look back. Especially now that he had met this lovely girl, such a girl, as he had always dreamed of meeting some day.

He knew that he mustn't rush her, he must take things nice and steadily. He had, after all, only just met her and he was supposed to be visiting her in a purely professional capacity. He learned from her cousin, Joyce, who ushered him up and down the stairs, that Sarah – for this was how he thought of her now, not as Miss Donnelly – was, in fact, the daughter of Edwin Donnelly who owned the large store in the centre of Blackpool. Joyce informed him that Sarah's parents had wanted her to go back with them, to their home on Park Road, to recuperate after the accident, but Sarah had refused point-blank, insisting that she must be at the shop to keep her eye on things and that she knew Joyce would look after her admirably.

'My gran's going to come in each day,' Joyce explained to Alex, 'until Sarah's better, that is. She's recently retired from her boarding house and time's hanging a bit heavy for her, so she jumped at the chance to come and help out at the café.'

'Good ... good. Sounds like a great idea.' Alex smiled at the girl's cheerful enthusiasm. Sarah was certainly in good hands with this competent wee lassie looking after her. 'Your cousin should be up and about in a few days,' he told Joyce. 'I foresee no problems. She needs to rest her ankle, but it should be all right, provided she doesn't try to walk on it for a day or two. And there are no repercussions from the bump on her head, I'm glad to say. She still has a slight headache – that's only to be expected – but there's no sign of any concussion. Just make sure that she takes her tablets and that she doesn't go dancing the Highland Fling. I'll be back in a day or two, Miss Gregson, to see how she's progressing.'

Alex knew that his next visit was not absolutely necessary, that if it had been any other patient he would most likely not have bothered. There were no complications and doctors were very busy people. But this wasn't any other patient; this was Sarah Donnelly, whom Fate had wonderfully, miraculously thrown into his path and Alex knew that he had to go on seeing her.

'My, my, aren't you the lucky one?' said Joyce, re-entering the bedroom after the doctor had gone. 'A handsome young doctor dancing attention on you, to say nothing of your poor weary cousin

347

waiting on you hand and foot.' She straightened the covers on Sarah's bed and picked up an empty glass from the small table at the side. 'Now, can I get you anything? A cup of tea or coffee – a magazine to read?'

'No thanks, love. I've got a book here that I'm trying to read, although my head hurts a bit. And after that lovely bacon sandwich you made me I couldn't eat another thing for ages. I really am so grateful to you, Joyce. I don't know what on earth I'd do without you – and it's not the first time I've said that, is it? You certainly must be weary, like you just said.'

''Course I'm not,' said Joyce. 'I was only joking. Besides, Gran'll be here this afternoon to help me to get organised for tomorrow.'

'You're all very good to me. I'm being such a nuisance. Fancy the doctor calling again. That was really thoughtful of him.'

'He said that he would.'

'Yes, but to come on a Sunday when it's supposed to be his day off … I think that was very considerate. Do you think he is young, Joyce?'

'What?'

'The doctor. You just said "the handsome young doctor". I agree that he's handsome – he looks a bit like Father – but d'you think he's young?'

'Oh, I don't know.' Joyce pursed her lips. 'Youngish … mid-thirties, perhaps. Why?'

'Oh, nothing. I just wondered, that's all.' Sarah could feel a smile coming on again and she tried to suppress it. She was aware that Joyce was giving her an odd look so she glanced down, fixing her eyes on the bright yellow bed cover. She placed her hand on the book that lay there. 'I think I'll try and read for a while. I know you must have loads to do so don't feel that you have to stay and chat to me. And Joyce…' Sarah looked up again, her features quite composed now. 'I'll make it up to you, you know, for all this extra work you're doing. There'll be a good bonus for you, and an increase in your wage each week as well.'

'Oh, forget it.' Joyce shook her head embarrassedly. 'We'll talk about it some time, when you're feeling better. But d'you know what I've been thinking? It's perhaps just as well that Pickerings let you down with the wood panelling. You might not have felt like dashing around and trying to open the restaurant in May.'

'Mmm … you're right, Joyce. I'd thought the same thing myself,' said Sarah. It wasn't strictly true. Her plans for the restaurant, which had been all-important to her at one time, had hardly entered her head since she had the accident. It was amazing how little it all seemed to matter now. It wasn't that she had lost interest in her business. She knew that when she was on her feet again she would be as keen as ever to make a go of things, but for now, another consuming matter was filling her mind.

She turned back to her book, an old favourite, chosen at random from the row of leather-bound classics she had brought from home – *Rob Roy* by Sir Walter Scott. But could it be purely at random that she had chosen this book, Sarah wondered – a story of one of the Border chieftains, set in the rugged Highlands of Scotland.

Alexander Duncan called to see her a couple of days later, as he had promised. But she couldn't help feeling disappointed when the next visit, on the Friday, was made by the senior partner, Dr Mason. By this time Sarah was out of bed and hobbling around the attic rooms although she had not yet been downstairs. Dr Mason pronounced that she was doing very nicely and that she could venture downstairs, so long as someone was with her to watch that she didn't fall. And provided she took care and didn't go dashing madly around, she could start helping out at the café again on Monday. Dr Duncan, he explained, was very busy and had asked him if he would call.

Sarah's disappointment grew at this news. Could she, after all, have been mistaken? She wondered. Surely not; at their last meeting they had chatted like old friends. He had commented on the book she was reading. Sir Walter Scott was one of his favourites too, he had said, and he had gone on to tell her about Melrose, the town where he had lived previously, which was in the heart of the Border country. He had seemed pleased to see her, very reluctant to leave, in fact. Surely it couldn't be all an illusion, something she had dreamed up because he was kind and considerate and was possessed of skilful healing hands? She was very quiet for the whole of Saturday, trying hard to hide the let-down feeling which was threatening to engulf her. It was a good job that Saturday was the most hectic day of the week at the café, and so Joyce and Doris and her grandmother were too busy to notice her preoccupation.

It was all the more amazing, therefore, when he turned up on the Saturday evening. Doris and Martha Makepeace had both returned home by this time and the two cousins were taking their ease, listening to a record of songs from *The Maid of the Mountains* on Sarah's gramophone. There was a side entrance to the upstairs premises which was used by visitors when the shop and café were closed, but the knock on the living-room door startled them both; they were not expecting any callers.

'Dr Duncan! How nice to see you. You're very late, though,' said Joyce, as she opened the door. 'I thought you'd have finished your calls ages ago.'

Sarah jumped to her feet, forgetting for the moment her lame ankle, then winced as a sudden pain shot up her leg. 'Er … this is not a business call,' she heard the doctor say as she hobbled towards the door. 'Good evening, Miss Donnelly.' His eyes lit up as he saw her. 'Now, do take care, won't you? You shouldn't be prancing around for a wee while yet.' He smiled at her, removing his soft brown trilby hat. 'I – er – I was wondering if…' He glanced at Joyce now. 'This seems an awful cheek, but I wonder if I could have a word with Miss Donnelly … in private?'

He was passing his hat from one hand to the other as he spoke, in a nervous manner, an unusual state of affairs for the normally self-possessed doctor.

'Of course you can.' Joyce grinned at him, taking his hat and placing it on the sideboard, and immediately he seemed more at ease. 'I'll make myself scarce. I tell you what, I'll pop down and make us all a cup of tea while you have a chat with Sarah. Go on in, Doctor, and make yourself at home.'

Sarah hadn't spoken at all yet. Feeling rather self-conscious she went over to the gramophone in the corner of the room, lifting the arm and putting a stop to the music. 'Oh lor...' she said, under her breath, as her trembling hand faltered slightly and the needle scratched across the surface of the record. Calm down, you idiot, she thought, feeling very cross with herself.

When she turned round the doctor was sitting in one of the easy chairs and she sat down opposite him. 'It's nice to see you, Doctor,' she began. 'I wasn't expecting–'

'Sarah,' he said quietly. It was the first time he had used her name, then there was silence for several seconds as they regarded one another. And Sarah knew then that she definitely hadn't misread the signs.

'You don't mind me calling you Sarah do you? Because that's how I think of you, how I've thought of you ever since we met.' Slowly Sarah shook her head. 'I asked Dr Mason to call yesterday because it wasn't ... it isn't possible for me to go on visiting you, Sarah, in a professional role. Do you know what I'm trying to say?'

'Yes, I think I do. You mean that you–'

'I mean that I want to go on seeing you not as a patient, but as a friend. As more than a friend, I hope – much more. Would you come out with me, please, Sarah? Next week? Please say that you will.'

'I would love to,' said Sarah softly. 'Thank you for asking me. Doctor…' She hesitated. No, that didn't sound right at all. She knew that his name was Alexander, but that, surely, was rather a mouthful.

'I'm usually called Alex,' he said now, his grey eyes warm as he smiled at her. 'Or Alec, but I think I prefer Alex.'

'So do I.' She smiled back at him feeling that her heart would burst with happiness. 'I'd love to come out with you, Alex.'

Their friendship developed rapidly and when, a month after their first meeting, Alex asked Sarah if she would marry him, she said yes without a moment's hesitation. Her parents, Grace in particular, advised her to be cautious.

'You've known him such a short time, dear,' her mother said. Sarah was making her customary Wednesday-afternoon call at her former home, it being 'half-day closing' for the Blackpool shops. Grace was alone as Edwin was still occupied with office work at the store. 'Are you sure? Are you very, very sure that you want to marry him?'

'Very, very sure, Mother,' Sarah answered with a quiet smile She had never felt more sure of anything in her life, or more confident that Alex was the one and only man for her. She half-anticipated her mother's next remark.

'But you were – forgive me for mentioning it, dear – you were very sure about Zachary, weren't you?'

'You never really liked him though, Mother.'

'That is not the point. You loved him, didn't

you? Or thought that you did. You were heartbroken when he let you down. Oh yes, I know you told us that it was mutual, but I realised that it was he who had changed his mind, and I know how much he hurt you.'

'It's all a long time ago,' said Sarah. 'Yes, I loved Zachary. I still do, in a way, but I've realised now that it's a different kind of love.'

She would have found it hard to explain exactly to her mother about her feelings for Zachary, her realisation that her love for him had been founded on a deep family affection brought about chiefly by propinquity. They had been thrown together as youngsters, they were much of an age and Sarah had had little opportunity to meet other young men. It was hardly surprising, therefore, that she had imagined herself to be in love with her handsome cousin. No – not imagined it: she *had* loved him. She was still very fond of him, but her affection for him could not be compared with the deep love that she felt for Alex. Nor with the trust that she knew she could place in him. Looking back, Sarah acknowledged that she had never been able to trust Zachary Gregson entirely.

'I trust Alex,' she said now. 'I know that he will never let me down. Please be happy for me, Mother. You do like him, don't you, you and Father?'

'Of course we do, dear. You know that we do. We both think he's a splendid young man in every way and we can see that he makes you happy, which is the most important thing. But we just want you to be very sure. It all seems such a rush. There's so much to think about. Where will you live? And what about the café, and the restaurant you were planning?'

'Still planning, Mother. Nothing has changed. There was a setback with the building materials, as you know, but we hope to be able to open the restaurant by August Bank Holiday weekend.'

'And Alex has no objection to you going on working, after you are married?'

'Of course not. We're in the 1920s now, you know. Lots of women are carrying on with their careers these days instead of just staying at home. You're working, aren't you – and enjoying it as well.'

'Yes, I know I am, dear, but it's rather different for me, isn't it?' Grace hesitated, looking a trifle embarrassed. 'I've had my family and I know that I'm not going to have any more. As it happens, I only ever had you, but that's another story. What I'm trying to say is–'

'I know what you're trying to say, Mother,' Sarah said, coming to her rescue. Grace had never found it easy to speak of intimate matters. Sarah, too, felt that certain things were better not discussed too openly. Private and personal matters should not be bandied around in the way that she knew some modern young women did today. 'You're wondering what will happen if we start a family? Well, we'll just have to meet that problem when it arises, won't we?'

'Problem? Surely it wouldn't be a problem dear, having a family? Doesn't Alex want to have children?'

'I'm sure he does,' said Sarah, realising it was

something they hadn't yet discussed. As her mother said, she had known him only a comparatively short time and there were still a few gaps in Sarah's knowledge of Alex. 'I wasn't meaning a problem in that sense,' she went on. 'Of course we will have a family, but give us time. I'm still quite young.'

'Nearly twenty-three dear – not all that young. I was a couple of years younger when you were born. And Alex is ... how old? I know he's a few years older than you are.'

'He's thirty-three, ten years older than me. But I do see your point. We shouldn't wait too long. The business is going well though, and Alex is quite agreeable that I should keep on with it. I've got Joyce and Doris there and they're two in a million, I can assure you. And I shall have to employ several more staff in August. So there'll be plenty of people to carry on the good work, should I be ... otherwise engaged.'

Sarah smiled at her mother, feeling the deep warmth and assurance she always felt when she thought of her relationship with Alex. A purely chaste one as yet, apart from the passionate kisses and embraces that they frequently exchanged. Sarah knew that Alex would not seek to consummate their relationship until after they were married, but she looked forward to her wedding night with not a trace of fear.

'And when is the wedding to be?' asked Grace. 'Before you open the restaurant? It's going to be very hectic for you.'

'No, we had thought of October,' replied Sarah. 'Blackpool will be quieter by then. There won't

356

be so many people milling round the church.'

'St John's, you mean?'

'Yes,' said Sarah. 'I'd like to get married at St John's.' But this was something else she hadn't discussed with Alex. There hadn't been much opportunity! It was only a few days since he had asked her to marry him; then he had insisted on behaving conventionally and had gone to ask Edwin if he could marry his daughter, before she started, officially, to wear his engagement ring. Sarah looked down at her ring now, a cluster of nine small diamonds in a platinum setting. She was getting used to the feel of it on her finger and was loath to take it off, even for jobs like making pastry or washing up.

'Yes, St John's is a perfect setting for a wedding,' said Grace happily. 'Oh, isn't it all exciting? I shall have such fun, won't I, planning the dresses for you and the bridesmaids. You will let me, won't you? You'll make use of Donnelly's exclusive dressmaking service?'

'Who else would I ask?' said Sarah, laughing. She was pleased to see that her mother, after her initial reservations, was now ready to throw herself wholeheartedly into the wedding plans. 'I'll be only too delighted for you to take charge of that. But we'd better wait until I've discussed it with Alex.'

'Of course, dear. And where are you going to live?' Grace went on excitedly.

'We'll be looking for a small house in the War- breck Road area,' replied Sarah. At the moment Alex had comfortable rooms at the home of Dr Mason, from where the surgery was run, but he and Sarah wanted their own place, not too far from both the surgery and the café, but somewhere where they could be completely alone. She looked round now at the Donnelly's elegant drawing room. 'It won't be anything like as grand as this, of course.'

'Who wants grandeur?' said Grace. 'If you're happy then that's all that matters, and I know that I'd have been happy anywhere with your father, even in a little terraced cottage. All this…' she waved her hand casually at the furnishings '…has been a bonus. A very pleasant one, I must admit, but I could have managed quite well without it all.'

Grace leaned forward, her eyes glowing with affection as she looked intently at her daughter. 'Be happy, Sarah. I know that Alex is a good man, and all I want is for you to be happy with him. I know it was all rather sudden, but I can't really blame you for that, can I?' Grace gave an enigmatic little smile. 'Your father and I fell in love at first sight, just like you did.'

'You mean … Edwin?'

'Of course I mean Edwin! I tend to forget at times, as I know you do, that he's really your stepfather.'

'But you didn't get married straight away?' Sarah knew that, in between, there had been Walter Clayton, her real father, but she didn't know the full story and doubted that she ever would.

'No…' said Grace slowly. 'There were certain complications, but it all turned out for the best in the end. And we've been very happy.'

'As I know we will be,' said Sarah calmly. 'I've

felt – just right, somehow, with Alex ever since I first met him. I know he's the right man for me.' She paused, then went on reflectively: 'D'you know, he reminds me such a lot of Father. Don't you think so, Mother? Not so much his looks, although they're both tall and slim...'

'And handsome,' Grace smiled.

'Yes ... and that, too. But it's his manner as well. Alex is gentle and kind and considerate, and yet he can be quite forceful. All the characteristics I've always admired in Father.'

'Yes, and if he makes you only half as happy as Edwin has made me, then you'll be a fortunate young woman,' said Grace seriously. 'I've no doubts now, after talking to you. I'm so pleased that things have worked out so well for you, darling. You deserve all the happiness in the world.'

Alex gave in, though somewhat reluctantly, to Sarah's desire for a church wedding with what he termed 'all the trimmings'.

'Hmm.' He pursed his lips and looked thoughtful when Sarah broached the subject that same evening. They had been for a stroll along the prom and had ended up, as they usually did, at Alex's lodgings. 'I'd thought more along the lines of a quiet wedding,' he said. 'Just the two of us – and a few of your relations, of course. After all, it's our concern, isn't it, yours and mine? Not something to be shared with the whole of Blackpool.'

'You don't mean...? You hadn't been thinking of a registry office wedding, had you, Alex?'

Sarah was quite horrified and must have sounded so as well, because Alex looked at her in some dismay.

'Well – yes – I suppose I had,' he admitted. 'I can't see that it would make much difference. We'd still be married, darling. But if it means so much to you, then we'll be married in church.' He put his arm round her, drawing her close to him and kissed her cheek. 'All I want is for you to be happy, my love.' Words that were almost an echo, Sarah thought, of what her mother had said that very afternoon. *I only want you to be happy …* And Sarah was happy, happier than she had ever been in her life, but she wanted Alex to be in complete agreement with her about something that was so important. She thought that he looked a little disturbed.

'What is it, Alex?' she asked. 'Is it because I have quite a few relations and you don't have any? Are you worried that there will be lots of people on the bride's side of the church and very few on yours?'

Alex chuckled. 'I've always thought that was an odd way of doing things. As if it mattered two hoots where anybody sits.'

'It's just tradition, love.'

'Aye, so it is, and we have to go along with tradition. No, it's no' that that's bothering me. Why should it? You've every right to fill the church with your folk if that's what you want. And they're grand folk, Sarah, they are indeed. I'd be proud of them if they were my relations, to be sure I would.'

Alex had met Sarah's grandparents and her

360

Aunt Hetty and her cousins, including Zachary; that had been, to Sarah's relief, only a brief meeting as Zachary had been departing for work. Alex had declared himself to be charmed by them all. He seemed to set a great store by relations, probably because he had very few of his own. He was, he had told Sarah, an only child of somewhat elderly parents who had both died while he was in medical school. His only close relative was an old uncle, a curmudgeonly sort of fellow, Alex declared, who lived near Edinburgh, and who seemed to like to keep himself to himself. Alex had been to see him before he left Scotland to take up his new post, but, as he told Sarah, he might just as well have not bothered, so uninterested did his Uncle Andrew seem.

'It's no' your relations that I'm concerned about,' Alex went on. 'It's the church. This business of asking God's blessing...' he said, as although he were weighing every word. 'I'm no' sure about God, you see.'

'You're not sure that you believe in God, you mean?' asked Sarah, trying not to sound too alarmed.

God had been a part of Sarah's life ever since she could remember. A benevolent father figure was her image of Him; she had learned of Him in Sunday School and at church and had never thought to question her childlike belief. She knew that her relations, between them, represented quite a few different denominations. Her father, Edwin, had once been a Catholic, but had what they called 'lapsed' since he married her mother. Now both Grace and Edwin attended the Church

361

of England, Grace more regularly than her husband, and it was this church, St John's, that Sarah had been encouraged to attend ever since she was small. Her grandmother, Clara Donnelly, unlike her son, was still a staunch Catholic, attending Mass every Sunday, whilst Sarah's maternal grandmother, Martha Makepeace, was just as resolute a Methodist. But Sarah believed that it was the same God they all worshipped, albeit in different ways. It had come as rather a shock to her to discover that this man, whom she loved so much, might not believe in God at all.

She was relieved when he answered her with: 'I'd like to believe. I went to Sunday School when I was a wee lad, just like you did. Och aye, my father was a stern old Presbyterian and my mother had to toe the line along with him. If they weren't there at the kirk, twice every Sunday, then there had to be a good reason for it.'

'And you went with them?'

'Aye, most of the time. I'd no choice until I left home, then I started thinking for myself.'

'Maybe that's why you turned against God,' said Sarah gently. 'Because you were forced to go to church so much as a child.'

'I wouldna' say I've turned against Him exactly,' replied Alex. 'It's just that I'm no' sure. I saw so much when I was in France that made me doubt. How a God of Love could allow such suffering, such inhumanity...'

'But that's the point, surely, Alex,' Sarah argued. 'It's man's inhumanity: he is to blame, not God.'

'But why does He allow it? If He's an all-powerful God, and that's what they try to tell us...'

'He's given us free will, to do as we please. And we often choose to please ourselves and not Him.'

Alex smiled affectionately at her, but a trifle sadly. 'It's a very facile argument, my love. Yes, I know it's what we are taught, but I find it hard to accept. When I think of some of the sights that I saw in that hospital...'

Sarah knew that Alex had worked in a hospital near to the Front Line. He had not been a pacifist, although the whole idea of war had been abhorrent to him; but he had been relieved when he was able to make good use of his skills to help the injured and dying, rather than taking part in armed combat.

Alex shook his head rapidly as if to clear his mind of gruesome thoughts. 'We'll no' argue about it, darling. You go ahead and plan your church wedding. October we said, didn't we?' He counted on his fingers. 'Six months. We should have found a nice wee place by then and it will give us plenty of time to make all the arrangements. Six months...' He turned to look at her, his grey eyes full of love and a quiet longing. He cupped her face between his hands. 'Oh, my darling, sometimes I feel as though I can't wait six days, never mind six months, to make sure you're mine. I love you so much.'

As his lips met hers, gently at first, then increasing in ardour, Sarah thought again how happy she was. She had never known such happiness. 'I love you too, Alex,' she murmured.

'So very much.'

'You know what, darling?' He released her then, leaning back against the cushions of the settee as he gently traced the outline of her face with his forefinger. 'If there *is* a God, then I am so thankful to Him for giving you to me.'

Joyce was delighted when, later that night, Sarah asked her if she would be her bridesmaid. She had been thrilled, right from the start, by her cousin's blossoming friendship with the doctor. Quite often she tactfully made sure that they had the attic living room to themselves. She would go into the bedroom to read or sew, or sometimes she went out for the evening with Doris, with whom she had become quite friendly.

'I'm thrilled to bits,' she said. 'I was hoping you'd ask me, but I didn't know what sort of a "do" you'd be having.'

'A church "do",' said Sarah, smiling. 'We've been talking about it tonight. And I'll ask Nancy too, of course. D'you think she'd like to be a bridesmaid?'

'I'm sure she would. Neither of us have ever been bridesmaids before.'

'I'll go round and see her tomorrow night. Will you come with me, Joyce?'

Joyce nodded. 'Yes, why not? It's ages since I saw my big sister.'

Nancy smiled when she heard her cousin's request, an odd little secret smile. 'I might...' she said.

'Don't strain yourself, will you?' said Joyce, sounding unusually sharp. 'Can't you see what an honour it is? Why, I was over the moon when Sarah asked me.'

'But again, I might not,' said Nancy. 'And you don't need to get so shirty with me either, our Joyce!' She scowled at her sister before turning to Sarah. 'Thanks for asking me. I appreciate it, really I do. And I'm ever so thrilled about you and that lovely doctor. But I think I'll have to say no. You see, I might not be here.'

Nancy stood up then and removed an envelope from behind a pot of multi-coloured spills on the mantelpiece. She took out a sheet of notepaper and waved it at Sarah and Joyce. 'Just look at this...'

Chapter 17

The letter from Sid Morris, otherwise known as Sidney Marchant, inviting Nancy to join his newly-formed concert party, was greeted with mixed feelings at Sunnyside. Nancy, of course, was ecstatic.

'Fancy him asking me!' she said, reading over and over again the part where he was asking her if she would like to be one of The Tantalising Trio, along with Ivy and Rose. Rita, the third member, was getting married in a few weeks' time and would be giving up her stage career. 'Ivy, Rose and Nancy,' she said excitedly, clutching the letter tightly to her chest and, at the same time, glancing at her reflection in the mirror above the mantelpiece; at her dancing green eyes, her curly auburn hair and – she had to admit it – her pretty heart-shaped face. Though she were to say it herself, she knew she had all the attributes necessary to embark upon a stage career; the face and figure, the personality and a pleasant tuneful voice.

'Ivy, Rose and Nancy,' she said again, dreamily, turning to look at her mother. 'That's what we'll be billed as, instead of Ivy, Rose and Rita. It has a ring to it, don't you think so, Mam?'

'Yes, happen it has,' said Hetty flatly. 'Don't start getting your hopes up too high though, our Nancy. You're not going to tell me that Sid

366

Morris has asked you to join his concert party, just like that, without an audition or anything.'

'He's heard me sing at Barney's,' replied Nancy. 'He and Ivy came to listen to me when they were at the North Pier and he told me I sang very nicely. He must have remembered. What's up, Mam? You don't look too pleased. In fact you look proper disgruntled. I thought you'd've been glad for me.'

Hetty sighed. 'I'm trying to be glad, love, but there's such a lot to think about. I can't quite take it in. Like I've just said, I can't believe he'd just engage you without an audition, or seeing how you fit in and all that.'

'Oh, there's a trial period,' said Nancy airily. 'They've a few inland town bookings for the next few weeks, then they've got a summer season at Scarborough. Rita's getting married in May, so he wants me to ease myself in, gently like, and then if it works out he says I can be in the show in Scarborough. Here, read the letter, then you can see for yourself.'

Nancy sat down by the table, idly playing with the bobbles on the fringe of the chenille cloth, trying to contain her impatience while her mother perused the letter. She knew that one thing she must try to do was to keep her temper and not fly off the handle if her mother seemed less than keen at the idea. She remembered the set-to they had had when she first wanted to go and sing for Barney, but her mam had agreed in the end. It was best to try a bit of 'soft-soaping' with Mam.

'Aye, it sounds all right,' said Hetty at last, though still very noncommittally. 'It can be a tough life though, Nancy. It's not all beer and skittles, you know. It can be bloomin' hard work and I don't want you dashing off with stars in your eyes and then coming down to earth with a wallop. I know you, love.' Her mother looked at her with affectionate concern. 'I know how you're up one minute and down the next, like a yo-yo on a string, and if ever there was a job with highs and lows then it's the stage. I just want you to be careful, love. To think, before you dash into anything.'

'I know what I'm doing, Mam,' said Nancy quietly. 'I have thought. I've thought for some time that I'd like to go on the stage, properly, I mean.'

'It'll be vastly different singing on a real stage than it is singing at Barney's,' Hetty went on. 'You haven't had all that much experience, have you, love?'

'I'm doing fine,' said Nancy. 'Barney says I am. I'm much more confident now than I was when I started. I must take after you, Mam,' she went on, smiling beguilingly at her mother. 'Gran's told me what a sensation you were at that Tilda's Tavern, with all those Gilbert and Sullivan songs you used to sing. I'm sure you must be thrilled, really, that I'm following in your footsteps.'

'I don't know about a sensation.' Hetty gave a wry grin, but Nancy could tell that she was pleased. 'I sang quite nicely and I was quite confident, after the first time or two, but I was never away from home, like you're thinking of being… And flattery'll get you nowhere, my lass, so just think on. I know only too well what your

368

game is, but I've already made up my mind. You can go – I know I'll have no peace if I don't say yes – but you'll have to behave yourself. Promise me, now?'

Nancy got up and put her arms round her mother, something she didn't do all that often. Hetty, like her own mother, was not much of a one for spontaneous hugs and kisses except in moments of extreme crisis or rejoicing. 'Oh, thank you, thank you, Mam,' said Nancy. 'I knew you'd say yes. And of course I'll behave myself. What d'you mean, anyway?' Her green eyes opened wide in surprise.

'What do I mean? If you don't know, and I can't believe that you don't, then I reckon you'll soon find out.' Hetty's voice held a cautionary tone. 'Just keep yourself to yourself, that's what I mean. I can tell you straight, our Nancy, if Sid Morris and Flo weren't in charge of this little lot, then I wouldn't be letting you go at all. But I know Sid and Flo and I can trust them to keep their eyes on you. I know what he was like with the young lasses when they were staying here. He wouldn't have no carrying on, and that's the way it should be.'

'He says he's writing to you as well, Mam.'

'Yes, I've just read that and I appreciate it, too. And Ivy Rathbone's there an' all, so I suppose that's another good reason for letting you go. She's a grand lass, and I only hope our Zachary sees sense before long and settles down with her.'

'I think he would, Mam. I think it's Ivy that doesn't want to get engaged just yet.'

'Hmm... You're lucky that you're in his

confidence,' said Hetty tartly. 'He tells me nowt, but then I'm only his mother.'

Nancy was silent for a moment, not liking to admit that Zachary hadn't told her anything at all; he didn't confide in her or Joyce any more than he did in his mother. She had taken a crafty peek at a letter he had left lying around. She had read only a line or two, then had felt guilty and pushed it back into the envelope, but not before she had gathered that Zachary had 'popped the question', but Ivy thought it would be better to wait a while. 'Oh, he just happened to mention something about it,' she said casually. 'Yes, it'll be nice to see Ivy again. I got on well with her.'

'You're a caution though, you are really,' said Hetty now, shaking her head reproachfully at her daughter. 'You've not given a thought to how I'm going to manage here without you, now have you? The season'll be upon us before we can say "Jack Robinson", and I can't very well ask our Joyce to come back. She's as happy as Larry with that job she's got at Sarah's place.'

''Course I've thought about it, Mam,' replied Nancy. 'You've got the two girls from Burnley starting in May, haven't you? And I'm sure Gran would come in and give you a hand if you're stuck.'

'My mother is supposed to be retired,' said Hetty. 'Although I must admit she's not taking to it all that well. She jumped at the chance to help Sarah out when she had her accident. Yes … it's a thought, and there are always folk looking for boarding-house work in Blackpool. I daresay I'll manage.'

'Of course you will, Mam,' said Nancy brightly. 'You always do.'

'It's all right for you to say that when you're swanning off and leaving me,' said Hetty, with mock disapproval. 'It won't be long either, will it? I must say, Sid hasn't given you much time to make up your mind.' She glanced at the letter again. 'He wants you to join them in Halifax – that's Ivy's home town, isn't it? – the second week in May, that's if you decide you'd like to take up his offer. Good gracious, that's only about three weeks away. And what's Barney going to say about it all, I wonder?'

'I should think he'll be tickled pink for me, Mam,' said Nancy. 'After all, he's the one that gave me my start, isn't he?' She stood up then, giving a satisfied little smile as she looked again at her reflection in the mirror, patting her auburn curls and rearranging the collar of her dress.

Hetty couldn't help laughing to herself as she watched her daughter prinking and preening in front of the mirror. When, a moment or two later Nancy went out to start her work in the bedrooms – Hetty had to admit that the lass was a good worker when she set her mind to it – her mother sat on at the table, her chin cupped in her hands, deep in thought. Nancy was for all the world just like she, Hetty, had been at the same age; not only in looks, but in personality as well. She was bent on having her own way, given to highs and lows of temperament and, it had to be admitted, was just a teeny bit selfish. Hetty had behaved in such a manner with her own mother, insisting that she must have the chance to sing at Tilda's Tavern; which was the main reason why Hetty was not opposing her daughter now. She had tried to oppose her at first, over that job at Barney's. That had worked out all right in the end, so Hetty decided that it would be best to let the girl have her head. To make her own mistakes, if needs be, though that was a difficult thing for any mother to do, to stand by and see your child dashing headlong into trouble. There shouldn't *be* any trouble, though, Hetty tried to console herself, not with Sid Morris at the helm. He would make sure that her headstrong daughter didn't go doing anything foolish. He kept a tight rein on all the young lasses who worked with him.

You're a fine one to talk anyway, Hetty Gregson, Hetty admonished herself. Didn't you find yourself pregnant when you were not quite twenty – younger than Nancy is now – and having to get married to Reuben Loveday? No, we didn't 'have to' get married, Hetty reminded herself, with a pang of bittersweet anguish that always returned whenever she thought about her beloved Reuben. They would have got married in any event. She had given herself to Reuben, willingly, un-reservedly, knowing full well what she was doing, because she had loved him so much. Hetty had been fully cognisant of the facts of life even though she hadn't learned them from her mother. Both she and Grace, before coming to Blackpool, had worked in a weaving shed in Burnley with lots of other lasses and you couldn't do that without ending up knowing what was what.

And that, Hetty mused, was possibly one big difference between herself and her elder daughter. Hetty was not at all sure that Nancy, for all her show of self-confidence and bravado, did know a great deal about the ways of the world … the ways of men, was what Hetty really meant. 'What d'you mean?' Nancy had said to her mother a few moments ago, seemingly in all innocence. Hetty found it hard to believe that any girl of twenty could be so guileless, but maybe Nancy was? Nancy hadn't mixed with crowds of girls in the way that she and Grace had done; her life since she left school had been spent mainly in the boarding house. Neither had she known many young men. They had all been in the Army until a couple of years ago and since then she had not had a steady boyfriend. She had, now and again, gone out for the evening with one or another of the lads who had stayed at Sunnyside; on the whole, though, she had seemed to concentrate on her job at the song-booth, and her jaunts out were usually with her sister or her cousin.

Hetty hoped that her daughter knew what was what, but one thing was sure; she, Hetty, couldn't tell her. It must be one of the hardest things in the world, Hetty thought, to explain to your daughter about what went on between a man and a woman. Martha, for all her northern bluntness and her matter-of-fact manner, had found such things difficult and had never explained them to her daughters, not in so many words. And now that she was in the same position, Hetty was finding it equally impossible; she was pretty sure that her sister, Grace, would agree with her, too.

Maybe a time would come, years hence, when there would be complete frankness between mothers and daughters about 'certain matters' but, as far as Hetty was concerned, the time was not now. It might be the 1920s, but there were things that one just couldn't talk about. Hetty only hoped that her daughter knew enough about it all to behave sensibly.

Barney Bellamy was delighted at Nancy's news, as she had predicted, but at the same time he was sorry to be losing her. The song-booth on the Golden Mile employed two girl vocalists who split the week between them, but only Nancy had stayed the course. She had been singing at Barney's for almost a year now, whilst there had been a succession of girls doing the other shift. Nancy knew that she had gained in confidence and she was grateful to Barney for all that he had taught her. She had never had a proper singing lesson in her life – neither had Barney – but thanks to him, she now knew much more about breath control and rhythm and expression, and about how to hold an audience in the palm of your hand by the use of a pregnant pause. A sudden silence in music, Barney had told her, could be just as eloquent as the most melodious harmony or counterpoint – words which had been unknown to her before, but which now, thanks to Barney, she was beginning to understand.

But her voice was still somewhat lacking in power and vibrancy, and she could tell that this bothered Barney just a little. 'You'll have to sing up you know, my love,' he told her, his prominent blue eyes opening wide. 'Sing up and sing out. Let them hear you in the back row. There's a world of difference between singing for the crowds here and singing in a theatre.' Something that her mother had only recently pointed out to her. 'They get restless if they can't hear you.'

'Why, don't you think they'll be able to hear me?' asked Nancy. She knew that she was no Marie Lloyd, or, on a more serious note, Dame Nellie Melba. She had bought a record of the famous Australian soprano to play on her recently acquired wind-up gramophone, and had marvelled at the strength of the woman's voice, at her crystal clear – though almost ear-splitting – tones. Never in a thousand years, Nancy had thought, would she be able to sing like that; it was a wonder the glass vase on the mantelpiece hadn't shattered at the force of it. Not that Dame Nellie was really to Nancy's taste; she preferred music-hall songs or the revues and musical-comedy numbers that were now all the rage.

'D'you think I don't sing loud enough?' she asked Barney now, a little apprehensively. It was something that had never worried her unduly and Barney had seldom mentioned it before, except in a casual, half-joking manner. 'I daresay they'll use microphones, anyway.'

'Oh, you don't want to depend on those things,' said Barney. 'If you get too near they distort your voice, and they crackle and whistle and konk out more often than not. The best music hall acts never needed microphones. No, I'm sure you'll be fine, my love, just fine. You'll be singing with another couple of girls, won't you, harmonising

375

with them? I'm sure you'll be a knock-out in Scarborough. I only wish I could come to see you.'

Nancy wished that he could come, too. During the past year she had grown very fond of Barney, not in the adulatory way in which she had at first regarded him, but more as a friend and a mentor. The act that he put on to attract an audience – the brashness, the coquetry and the innuendoes – were just a veneer. Nancy knew that underneath it all Barney was a very genuine sort of man; a very ordinary man, really, with a wife and family, some of them grown-up now, whom he was trying to support the best way he could. He had certainly made the song-booth a going concern. It was popular with both visitors and residents, and Nancy knew that she would miss the happy times she had had there.

'I wish you all the luck in the world,' Barney said, kissing her on both cheeks as he said goodbye to her. 'Now, write to us, won't you? And when you're as famous as Vesta Tilley, don't be thinking you're too grand to come and see us.'

'As if I would.' Nancy could feel tears pricking at her eyelids and she began to wonder, for the first time, what on earth she was doing. She loved it here on the Golden Mile amongst the sideshows and cockle and mussel stalls and the comic hats. She felt sure that Scarborough wouldn't compare with it at all. But she knew she had to take her chance. She owed it to herself.

'Don't do anything I wouldn't do!' said Barney now, rolling his blue eyes expressively, a mannerism that was typically Barney and one that Nancy had come to know so very well.

'That gives me plenty of scope!' she replied, right on cue; an obvious remark, but the one that Barney was expecting. That was how things were at the song-booth, simple and predictable, not the least bit subtle. You always knew where you were with Barney, and Nancy was aware that she would miss him more than she could say.

And now, a couple of months later, here she was in Scarborough, already into the third week of the *Summer Follies of 1920* at the Arcadia Theatre. It had all been tremendously exciting, and Nancy, looking back on the way she had felt just before she left Blackpool – the apprehension and the second thoughts that had threatened to overwhelm her and about which she couldn't tell anyone, certainly not Mam – wondered why she had ever felt afraid. Of course there was always that initial nervousness when you stepped on to the stage at each performance; but her fellow artistes had told her that that was quite natural. Without that feeling of the nerves fluttering in the pit of your stomach and the adrenalin racing through your blood you wouldn't be able to perform at all, they told her.

Nancy had been eased into the company very gently, as Sid had promised she would be. She had worked along with Rita, the girl she was replacing, at first, to learn the songs and simple dance routines. She had found no difficulty, even though she couldn't read a note of music, in harmonising with the other two members of the Trio. Ivy sang the soprano line, the melody, Rose the lower notes and she, Nancy, fitted herself in somewhere between the two of them. It was quite easy, she found, once you knew how and she was grateful for the guidance that Barney had given her. They had had bookings at a few Yorkshire towns before opening at Scarborough and Nancy had made her début on the stage of the Empire in Huddersfield. What grand-sounding names all these theatres had – Empire, Hippodrome, Palace, Alhambra – when, in reality, they were often poky little places hidden away down a side street.

The Arcadia in Scarborough was, however, quite an impressive-looking place, a one-storeyed white-painted building with a balcony surrounding a flat roof, from which flew flags of all nations. It was on the South Bay, on the stretch of promenade which reminded Nancy very much of Blackpool. Here were the amusement arcades, the shops selling rock and souvenirs and comic postcards and, across the road on the side nearest the sea, the stalls which sold cockles and mussels, crabs, lobsters and shrimps and all sorts of fish which were unloaded in the nearby harbour. But there, the resemblance to Blackpool ended. Nancy tried to remain biased in favour of her home town, but she had to admit that, in many ways, Scarborough was just as captivating and it did have many features that Blackpool lacked.

The harbour was a fascinating place and Nancy loved to watch the local boats, as well as those from Cornwall, Lowestoft and the east coast of Scotland – even some from Scandinavia – landing their catches. Dripping fish carts, passing through the streets of the town to the railway station, added a touch of local colour – and smell – to the resort. Scarborough folk were proud of their harbour, which had been a centre of commerce, so they boasted, since the tenth century when the Danish fishermen traded there. For Scarborough had a history which stretched back over the centuries, something which Blackpool couldn't claim. The castle up on the hill high above the town had been there since Norman times, and opposite the harbour was the house where, it was reputed, Richard III had stayed in 1484. Then there was the magnificent Spa Bridge, the marine drive linking the two bays, and beautiful wooded gardens stretching down to the sea. In all, it was a lovely picturesque town and Nancy had completely fallen in love with the place.

'And when I told them,
How wonderful you are…'

She sang to herself as she climbed the steep slope leading up from the harbour to the castle. She had spent a pleasant afternoon on her own, mooching around the shops on Newborough and Westborough, and she was now returning to her digs near the Market Hall for a quick snack before the evening performances.

'They didn't believe me,
They didn't believe me…'

This was one of the numbers that the Trio sang in the second half of the show, a slow seductive

379

song which lent itself to syrupy-sweet harmonies and suggestive glances at the audience. For this act, a selection of the songs of Jerome Kern, the three girls wore their evening attire; identical dresses, but in three contrasting pastel colours – pink, yellow and green. Nancy wore the green one, a very delicate apple green, which went well with her green eyes and auburn hair. It was a sleeveless satin dress with a low scooped neckline, straight hip-length bodice and a dark green velvet cummerbund above a mid-calf-length flounced skirt. At the hipline was a corsage of silk flowers and her shoes were of dark green satin with narrow cross straps, pointed toes and low louis heels. Nancy thought it was the loveliest thing she had ever worn and she did so wish that the folks back home could see her in all her finery. She knew she looked nice in it; Clive Conway's appreciative glances as she stood in the wings had told her so, and this was the reason why Nancy sang to herself so joyfully. He had invited her to have tea with him tomorrow afternoon at a little café near the Grand Hotel, but before that, he said, he would like to take some photographs of her, posing at appropriate vantage points, with his new box camera.

Nancy could hardly wait for tomorrow to come and had to keep pinching herself to make sure that she hadn't dreamt it. She had admired Clive Conway ever since she had seen him on the stage at the North Pier in Blackpool. His flashing feet and dazzling smile had captivated her, but in those days, when she was just the landlady's daughter, he hadn't taken much notice of her. He had remembered her, though. 'Nice to have you with us, Nancy,' he had said, the very day that she joined the company. 'How's Blackpool these days? And how's your mother?'

They had chatted together a few times since the Scarborough season started and had sometimes walked back, apart from the rest of the company, to their digs. All the ten members of Sid's troupe were staying at the same place, a comfortable boarding house run by a woman who, like Hetty, specialised in taking in 'pros'. Sid had made all the arrangements about the rooms; the women were on the first floor and, as far away as possible, the men were up in the attic.

'And never the twain shall meet,' Ivy had said laughingly to Nancy. 'Dear old Sid. He's determined that we girls'll hang on to our virtue. He's right, though. He wants to run a respectable troupe and I admire him for it. He feels he's got a responsibility to look after girls like us who are away from home.'

'Yes,' said Nancy. 'That's the only reason Mam would let me come, because she knew Sid would look after me.'

It wasn't possible, however, for Sid to look after his charges all the time, as Nancy knew full well. She was aware that Maria, the assistant to Mervin the Magician, often sneaked into the room that she shared with the Trio very late at night; there was one night when Nancy was sure she hadn't returned at all. Her name wasn't really Maria, of course, she was Edna Halliwell from Barnsley, but she, of all the 'Marias' that there had been, had lasted the longest. This was her second season with Mervin, so maybe Sid turned a blind eye to whatever was going on between the pair of them. She was thirty if she was a day anyway, quite old enough to look after herself.

Nancy had noticed Sid's eagle eye upon her as she chatted with Clive, but he hadn't remarked upon it. After all, there could be no harm in talking, nor in taking tea with him and posing for photographs. Unable to keep her elation to herself, Nancy had confided in Ivy about her date with Clive. Ivy had warned her to be careful.

'Why? What do I have to be careful about?' asked Nancy in all innocence. 'I think he's really nice. He's been proper friendly with me since I joined the company.'

'Yes … Clive's all right, I suppose,' Ivy said, sounding somewhat guarded. 'A bit full of himself, but I don't suppose you can blame him for that. He's a jolly good dancer – I've never seen a better one – and I daresay he knows he'd be hard to replace. Just watch him though, Nancy love. He's a bit of a one for the ladies.'

'Why? What d'you know about him?' Nancy thought that Ivy was being unfair. 'I've never seen him flirting or anything like that. He's always very well-mannered and respectful.'

'Just watch your step, that's all,' Ivy replied and would not be drawn any further. Nancy wondered if her friend was feeling a bit peeved – jealous, maybe – because she was so far away from Zachary. She was sure to be missing him, even though she had declined to become engaged. Nancy had to admit that her brother was a goodlooking lad and she supposed he could be quite charming when he wanted to be.

She paused, out of breath, at the top of the steep slope. It was a long way round, but it was the way she often chose to go back to the digs because of the superb view from the road leading to the castle. She looked down through the trees, bursting with early summer greenness, over the slated rooftops to the splendid vista of South Bay; golden sand, sparkling sea, the Grand Hotel, the Spa Bridge and, just visible at the lower level, the Arcadia Theatre where she would be performing again that evening. She made her way down again past the twelfth-century parish church of St Mary, pausing for a moment to look at Anne Brontë's grave.

Poor lass, she thought, as she read the inscription. *Daughter of the Rev P Brontë... She died aged 28, May 28th, 1840.* Fancy coming on holiday to Scarborough and then dying! But even thoughts of poor Anne Brontë couldn't sadden Nancy on this glorious June afternoon. There were the two performances to look forward to tonight, when she knew that Clive would be watching her from the wings – he had taken to doing that recently – then tomorrow ... tomorrow was the day when, for the first time, she would have him all to herself.

They played to a capacity audience the second house that evening and they knew even before the curtain went up that it was going to be a good night. There was something about the whole atmosphere of the place that made you certain that everything would go well. The audience was one which was just waiting to be entertained, to laugh and clap, to shed a tear, maybe, and to join in the choruses of the songs. When the Trio sang their selection of seaside songs in their saucy bathing costumes they could feel the whole house warming to them, tapping their feet and humming and clapping, then joining with abandon in the choruses.

'… *It wasn't the girl I saw you with at Brighton, Who, who, who's your lady friend?'*

Looking back on it afterwards, Nancy was to remember that night as the high-spot of her time in Scarborough. Everything was going well for her. She was happy, she was gaining in confidence – never had she felt more at home with an audience – and she was on the brink of falling in love. It had seemed as though nothing could possibly go wrong.

'That's a very fetching costume you wear for the seaside scene,' Clive remarked the following afternoon. 'Now, what I'd really like to do is to take some photographs of you wearing that.'
Nancy was pleased and flattered. She knew that the costume suited her; all the same, she wasn't sure that she would have the nerve to pose in it, the way she had just been doing in her summer dress, striped blazer and straw boater. Clive had taken dozens of shots of her – by the harbour, on the Spa Bridge, in front of the theatre – and now they were sitting companionably at a small table for two in a very posh little café that Clive had found, drinking tea from egg-shell china cups

384

and eating scones with jam and cream.

'Don't be daft!' she giggled at Clive. 'We wouldn't half attract a crowd if I was to go posing in that thing. I'd most likely get arrested!' The blue and white striped bathing costume, with the sailor collar and the very short gathered knickers, was all very well for cavorting about on stage or for swimming in, but not for parading about on the promenade.

'Don't talk silly.' Clive smiled back at her, showing a set of dazzling white teeth. His startlingly blue eyes opened wide. 'You can't think I was suggesting that you should wear your bathing costume in the middle of Scarborough? You'd stop the traffic all right. No … I'd have to take some indoor shots, back at the boarding house.'

'With that, d'you mean?' Nancy nodded towards the square black box which he had put on the floor at the side of his chair. 'You can't take pictures inside, can you? It 'ud be too dark.'

'Ah, but you don't know what else I've got, do you?' said Clive teasingly. 'I've got another camera, you see. A much more complicated affair than this one. I only bought it recently and I'm still learning how to use it. D'you think you might come and pose for me, Nancy?'

'I might,' said Nancy. A sudden thought struck her. 'Where is it, your camera, I mean? Where d'you want to take these photographs?'

'In my room, of course. Where else?'

'In your bedroom?' Nancy was horrified at the suggestion. 'But we can't! Sid doesn't allow it. You know how strict he is about things like that.

He'd go mad if he thought I was in your room.'

'But Sid doesn't need to know, does he?'

Nancy shook her head. 'No, it's not right. I can't. Besides, what about Albert? You share a room with Albert, don't you?' Nancy knew that Albert Smith, alias Albertino, the Wonder Juggler, was Clive's room-mate.

'Albert isn't always there. He has relatives in Scarborough – didn't you know? – and he's often away visiting them.' Clive looked at her soberly then, his blue eyes no longer amused or teasing. He reached across the table and took hold of her hand. 'Nancy,' he said quietly. 'I'm not asking you to do anything wrong. Only to come and pose for a few photographs for me, like you've been doing this afternoon. That's not so very dreadful, is it? And if it makes you feel any better, then why don't you tell Sid exactly what you're going to do? I'm sure he would say it was all right.'

'No, I wouldn't like to say anything to Sid,' said Nancy.

'You're probably right.' Clive's answer came a shade too fast and Nancy thought she could see a flicker of relief in his eyes. 'It might be best to say nothing to Sid. But don't decide now. Just think about it, eh? Will you do that, Nancy?'

'All right.' Nancy nodded her agreement and they didn't talk about it any more just then. They went on to talk about themselves, mainly, Nancy had to admit to herself, about Clive. She learned that he was twenty-eight and that he had been 'treading the boards' since he was eighteen. The war had interrupted his career, but he had been

386

one of the lucky ones and had returned unscathed.

'It was a great night last night, wasn't it?' Nancy said eagerly. 'Didn't you feel it, Clive, how the audience was really with us?'

'Yes, and it was so unexpected, too,' agreed Clive. 'Thursday night, the middle of the week. You'd expect it to be quiet. It can be as dead as the grave sometimes. But I think there were a lot of parties in – social clubs, Women's Institute outings, that sort of thing. It makes a big difference when people are set on enjoying themselves. An audience can make or break you. You'll find that out before you're much older.'

'Mmm.' Nancy nodded happily. Oh, she was enjoying herself. Clive was a lovely man and she was beginning to convince herself that there could be no harm whatsoever in doing what he asked. After all, it was all part of her career. She owed it to herself, didn't she, to have some classy photographs that she could show to her friends and relations, send off to her fans – didn't all artistes do that? – and even show to agents. Nancy's thoughts were running off at a tangent.

By the time they arrived back at the boarding house she was very sure. 'Yes, Clive,' she said, as they walked up the stairs to her first-floor room. 'I've been thinking about what you asked me and – yes – I'd like to do it.'

'Good girl.' He smiled at her, so very charmingly, then his blue eyes twinkled as he said in a soft voice, 'Having me on a bit, weren't you? I'm sure it's not the first time you've been in a man's room, is it, a pretty girl like you?'

'Ah … that would be telling, wouldn't it?' She

387

fluttered her eyelashes at him in the provocative way she had recently learned from watching Ivy and Rose, the way they used their charms to captivate an audience. 'It might be … or it might not be. When did you have in mind?' she asked, keeping her voice low. They were outside her bedroom door and she wasn't sure which of her colleagues might be on the other side.

'Oh, Sunday afternoon, I think,' said Clive casually. 'Sunday's usually a dead sort of a day, and I know Albert'll be out. About three o'clock suit you? It's Room 15, by the way.'

'That'll be lovely,' said Nancy. 'I'll look forward to it.'

'Don't forget your costume,' Clive reminded her. 'Bring it home from the theatre. Bring your other stuff as well, if you like. That short frilly thing you wear for the opening number.'

'Mmm, I might.' Nancy knew that she looked stunning in the short can-can skirt and fishnet tights. 'Yes, I think I will.'

Clive leaned forward then and took hold of her shoulders. Very gently he kissed her on the lips, a tender fleeting kiss, but Nancy felt a tingle of warmth right through her body. 'You're lovely, Nancy,' he said in a whisper. 'Sunday then? Don't forget.' Then, as if it were an afterthought, 'Oh … don't go telling the others, will you? Ivy and Rose might be jealous.'

''Course I won't,' said Nancy. 'It'll be our secret.'

She felt a bit mean, and deceitful, too, when Sunday afternoon came and, instead of accompanying

388

Ivy and Rose on their proposed walk round the headland, she said that she wanted to stay behind and do a few odd jobs.

'I've loads of letters to write,' she said, 'and some mending to do, and I want to wash my hair.'

The two girls didn't argue and when she was left to herself Nancy began to feel doubtful. Sid wouldn't like it, she knew; he trusted her and she was letting him down. But what harm could there be, the other voice inside her said, in posing for a few photographs? That was all Clive wanted. Ivy wouldn't approve either. She would warn Nancy to 'watch her step', as she had done the other day. As if Ivy had any room to talk! Nancy knew that Ivy and Zachary had spent a lot of time alone together, and if Nancy knew her brother they wouldn't be just talking, either, or just kissing. Nancy felt sure they would be doing … whatever it was that a man and a woman did when they were alone together. Because the truth of the matter was that Nancy was not altogether sure what it was that they did do. She had never been able to find out what this thing was that only married people were supposed to do, but that other couples sometimes indulged in. She knew of one or two girls who had 'had to get married', and that was always spoken of in hushed tones. She knew that it was something to do with the private part of you 'down there', the part where you could get such funny feelings when a boy kissed you. Nancy had been kissed a few times and had found it very pleasurable.

She also knew that her brother, Zachary, was made differently from her and Joyce. She had

389

caught a glimpse of him once, ages ago, when they were all little, when he was getting undressed, but Mam had always been very strict about them keeping themselves to themselves. But what exactly you had to do – she'd heard it called making love – Nancy wasn't sure. There had never been anyone that she could ask; she certainly could never have asked her mother.

Perhaps Clive would kiss her again today. She hoped that he would, although she knew that what he really wanted to do was to take her photograph. He might, though. She felt all tingly at the thought of it. Before she could deliberate any more she snatched up the bag containing her clothes and darted up the stairs. She was to wonder, afterwards, why she hadn't changed into her costume before going into Clive's room.

The camera, a complicated affair on a tripod, stood by the window and Nancy noticed that the curtains were closed. 'The darker it is the better,' Clive said, as he saw her glancing in that direction. 'I've just been getting everything ready. You're not ready thought, are you, Nancy? I thought you would have had your costume on.'

Nancy felt a bit foolish. 'I didn't know who I might meet on the stairs,' she said, shuffling her feet self-consciously. 'I'll get ready now, shall I?'

'Righty-ho then. I'll not look.' Clive grinned at her, pretending to cover his eyes with his hands.

Nancy was in a quandary. Oh heck! What on earth was she going to do? If she acted all shy and coy she would look silly, and she was sure that Clive would have no time for silly little girls. Besides, he had been touring around for ages; he was sure to have seen girls in their underwear before, and her underwear was a great deal less revealing than that tantalising little skirt and tights that she wore on stage. 'Oh, it's all right,' she said, giving a nervous giggle, but at the same time trying to look him straight in the eye. She smiled at him. 'I don't mind you looking. Shan't be a jiffy.'

She did turn her back on him though, and with trembling fingers she undid the buttons down the front of her cotton dress. She stepped out of it, put it on a chair at the side of her and reached into her bag for her bathing costume. She took it out, then turned to look at Clive. 'This one first, d'you think?'

'I think so,' he said, his voice sounding a little husky, 'but I think it can wait for a few moments, don't you?'

He was beside her then, his hands upon her bare shoulders, his eyes looking into hers. Very gently, just like he had done the time before, he leaned forward and kissed her on the lips. 'Come on, Nancy. Come and sit down.' He patted the chintz eiderdown on one of the single beds. 'I think we've time for a little chat before I begin to ... take photographs.'

Once they had sat down, Nancy knew that the last thing Clive wanted to do was chat. He kissed her properly then, but it was very nice and she responded eagerly to him, enjoying the warmth of his lips upon hers and the feel of his hands caressing her shoulders and back. There was no harm in kissing, she told herself. But she was not so sure when she felt his tongue probing into her mouth. That was very unexpected and she didn't know that she liked it. Was that one of the things you had to do, she wondered? Nor did she think he ought to be touching her breasts. He had pushed back the straps of her art silk camisole – she had made sure she was wearing her nicest underwear – and now she was beginning to feel afraid. And she still didn't understand.

Suddenly he stood up and Nancy watched with slowly dawning horror as he unfastened the buttons of his trousers and stepped out of them, then out of the white cotton garment he wore underneath. Then, in a moment of blinding comprehension, at last she understood. She had known that men were different, but when she caught sight of ... *that* ... the sign of his manhood, enlarged and erect, and realised what it was he intended to do, then she was terrified. That ... *thing* was to go inside her!

'No – no!' she cried, sitting up and pulling her camisole back on to her shoulders. 'Don't, Clive. Please don't. I don't want to–'

'It's too late for that now.' Clive's voice was huskier than ever. He pushed her back against the pillow, then, pulling aside the wide legs of her French knickers, he forced himself upon her, inside her. Nancy opened her mouth to scream, but no scream would come and any sound she might have made was stifled by Clive's mouth upon hers. His rough chin grazed her tender skin and the kissing was no longer pleasant. And all the time he was thrusting away inside her; Nancy thought she would die with the agony of it. She bit at his lips and, raising her back, she tried to throw him off her, but it was no use. She gave in then and suffered what it was he had to do. Fortunately it didn't last long, not more than a minute or two, but it seemed like hours. At last he gave a long shuddering sigh and rolled away from her.

It was then that Nancy screamed. She opened her mouth and let it all out, all the misery and fright and hurt, and acute disappointment, too, for she had been looking forward to this afternoon.

'Shut up, you silly little fool!' Clive turned savagely and slapped her face. She felt his knuckles bruising the corner of her mouth. 'D'you want the whole house to hear?'

She couldn't answer him. She just stared at him, her mouth trembling and tears beginning to ooze from under her eyelids, unable to speak.

He hung his head then and, slightly to his credit, he did try to apologise. 'I'm sorry I hurt you, Nancy,' he said. 'I didn't mean to, but you wanted it, didn't you?'

She shook her head numbly.

'At first you did. I could have sworn you did.'

Nancy just went on staring at him.

'Oh, my God!' Clive put his head in his hands. 'What a bloody mess. What a goddamned bloody fool I am.' He looked at her, his eyes no longer warm or teasing; he looked almost as afraid as she was. 'You'd better go. And for God's sake don't say anything. There'll be all hell to pay if you do.'

Nancy snatched up her bag, then her costume and dress from the chair and stumbled towards the door.

'Put your frock on, you bloody little fool,' Clive called after her, but Nancy paid no heed. Luckily there was no one on the stairs or on either landing as she fled to the safety of her room.

It was there that Ivy and Rose found her an hour later, still huddled in a pathetic heap on her bed. She hadn't even had the strength to wash away the evidence of her nightmarish encounter with Clive Conway.

'Oh, dear God in heaven! Whatever has happened?' said Ivy in horror. But as she looked at her friend's bruised mouth and her half-clad, dishevelled appearance she guessed straight away. 'Was it Clive?'

Nancy nodded, then at last she found her voice. 'Oh Ivy, it was awful! He said he wanted to take some photographs of me, and then he made me. I didn't want to.'

'You don't mean that he…?' said Ivy slowly. She glanced down at her friend's underwear and the telltale traces of blood there told her that the worst had happened. 'Oh no, not that,' she breathed. 'I tried to warn you, love. I did tell you.'

'I didn't understand,' said Nancy tearfully. 'I'd no idea. Oh Ivy, whatever am I going to do?'

'You're going to get dressed and have a nice wash,' said Rose, who so far hadn't said a word. 'What's done can't be undone, but you'll be all right. We'll take care of you. Come on now, lovey. We'll go along to the bathroom and see if there's some nice hot water and you can have a good clean up, then we'll say no more about it, eh? Eeh, men are bastards, and that's a fact.' Rose was a forthright Lancashire lass, not so genteel in manner as Ivy, but the three of them, though very different, got on well together.

'And I'm going to see Sid.' Ivy was making for the door.

'No! Oh please, Ivy, no,' begged Nancy. 'Clive said I wasn't to say anything.'

'Did he indeed?' said Ivy grimly. 'I'll bet he did! But he's not going to treat a friend of mine like that and get away with it. No, Nancy, it's no use you arguing. Sid will have to know.'

Sid Morris caught up with Clive later that evening when the young man returned from the pub where he had been drowning his sorrows.

He didn't waste any words. 'You! Pack your bags this minute and go,' he shouted. 'I won't have this sort of behaviour in any company of mine.'

'Aw, some on, have a heart,' said Clive, looking at Sid with bleary eyes. He'd had a skinful, something he didn't often do, and his head was pounding like a sledgehammer. And it was all because of that blasted girl. 'You can't mean that. She was asking for it, the little tart. Taking her clothes off in front of me, fluttering her eyelashes. You can't go blaming me.'

'Don't you dare say that! Nancy Gregson's a respectable young lady.'

'Respectable my arse!'

'And I won't have language like that neither,' Sid roared. 'You'll pack your bags and clear off, this minute.'

'You can't fire me like that, not without any notice.'

'I can and I will. And if you dare complain I'll blacken your name with every theatre in the north of England.' Sid reached for his wallet, peeled off several notes and thrust them at Clive. 'Here – there's a fortnight's wages and that's more than you damn well deserve. Now, get out!'

Clive knew that he had no choice. He knew, too, that it shouldn't be difficult to get another job. But it was all so unfair, and all because of that stupid little cow, Nancy Gregson. He could have sworn that he'd been right about her, that she was a hot little piece who wanted it just as much as he did. All that 'Oh no, we can't!' nonsense he had thought was part of her act, her way of getting him going. He had had his eye on her ever since he had first seen her in Blackpool, but the time had not been ripe then, not with her mother, fat old Hetty, keeping her eye on them all the time.

He hadn't intended to go so far though, not at first. Just a bit of a kiss and a cuddle – more, if she was willing – and he really had wanted to take some photographs. But to see her standing there, as bold as brass, in that seductive pink underwear, those frilly knickers just inviting him... He'd had the shock of his life when he'd found out she was a virgin.

He'd get even with her, though. Clive thrust his belongings into his battered suitcase, swearing all the while under his breath. He'd get even with that bloody little madam if it was the last thing he did.

Chapter 18

The Gynn Restaurant, as it was quite simply called, opened in time for the August Bank Holiday weekend.

'*You are already acquainted with Sarah's café,*' read the advertisement in the *Evening Gazette*. '*Now you are invited to come and sample the delights of the new Gynn Restaurant on the first floor of this well-known establishment. The dining room is elegantly furnished with every regard for the comfort and convenience of customers and is under the personal supervision of the proprietor, Miss Sarah Donnelly. Luncheons served daily from Monday to Saturday. Bookings taken for family parties, weddings, funerals, etc. This new venture is worthy of your patronage.*'

To Sarah's consternation, all the money which Clara Donnelly had given her, and more besides, had been swallowed up already in the new fittings and fixtures, but as she looked round at the stylish surroundings she had to admit that it was worth every penny; provided that the customers came, of course, but she had every confidence that they would. The oak panelling which had caused such problems had at last arrived and been installed, and was well worth the wait. It added that touch of refinement which Sarah felt was so important – a touch which, sadly, was lacking in some of Blackpool's other eating places. She had continued with the green and cream colour scheme – Blackpool's own colours – in the restaurant as well as in the café downstairs. Green velvet curtains hung at the windows and the small tables were covered with cream damask tablecloths. The two waitresses whom Sarah had employed were to wear the same uniform as the original staff; a dark green skirt with a cream blouse, frilly apron and mobcap.

A nice finishing touch to the restaurant were the enlarged sepia photographs of Victorian Blackpool which hung at intervals along the oak panelling. The Tower, now twenty-six years old; the Big Wheel, still going strong; the three piers; Talbot Square; Uncle Tom's Cabin; the scenes all as they had looked when Sarah's mother and her Aunt Hetty had first come to Blackpool – not all that long ago, Sarah supposed, in the general scheme of things.

'You should really wear an afternoon dress, Sarah,' her mother had counselled her, 'so that you'll look different from the other staff. Something elegant – what they used to call a tea-gown. Will you let me design one for you, dear?'

But Sarah had insisted that she was just one of the team and would continue to dress in exactly the same way as the others. She had also employed two extra kitchen staff to assist with the cooking, cleaning and washing up. It would be hard work for all of them, herself included, there was no doubt about that; therefore she had also invested in one or two labour-saving devices.

A large refrigerator now stood in the pantry. Sarah had learned her lesson with that dreadful episode of the sausage rolls and she was determined that such a thing would never happen again. The refrigerator was, in reality, a large ice-chest. A huge block of ice wrapped in clean sacking was placed in a metal-lined cavity at the top of the chest and food was placed either on top of the ice or on perforated shelves in the cupboards beneath. The chest was well-insulated, but the block of ice did eventually melt and had to be replaced. There had been one or two floods at first until they got used to it; now, Sarah had to remember to place a bowl under the tap and drain off as much water as possible. It was rather a messy business, but it did at least ensure that the food was kept fresh. Sarah had heard that a refrigerator run by electricity had been invented in America – everything seemed to happen first in America – but nothing like that, as yet, was on sale in England.

Another innovation was the installation of a lift, not for people, though, but for plates and dishes. It worked by a pulley system from the ground-floor kitchen to the restaurant and was to save the waitresses carrying heavily laden trays up and down the stairs.

'You mustn't go working yourself to death,' Grace had warned Sarah more than once. Sarah knew that her mother was concerned for her, but the thought of hard work didn't worry her; she felt that her feet had wings these days. 'Start with something simple at first,' Grace urged, 'until you see how things are going. Then you can be more adventurous later if you like.'

Sarah could see that what her mother said

made sense. Her first restaurant menu consisted of vegetable soup, a choice of either Lancashire hot-pot made with the best lamb chops, or freshly caught cod served with chips, followed by apple or damson tart. A simple meal designed to satisfy hearty appetites; such was the tradition in the north of England and Sarah knew that she wouldn't go far wrong if she stuck to this idea.

She had been aware that some of her friends and relations were dubious. Martha Makepeace, though she had been all in favour of the original shop and café, had had slight reservations about a restaurant. 'Folks have their dinners at home,' she said. The midday meal was still 'dinner' to most people in Blackpool. 'It's all very well having a bit of a snack – a cup of tea and a cake, like – but d'you think folks'll pay good money for summat they can cook for themselves at home?'

'We'll have to wait and see, Gran,' replied Sarah. 'I'm hoping some women might, if their husbands are at work all day and they want to treat themselves. You've said yourself that the folk in North Shore aren't short of a bit of brass. But it's the visitors I'm aiming at really, and the people who come for the day.'

'Aye, so long as your prices aren't sky-high you might do all right wi' t'day-trippers,' said Martha. 'Visitors have "all found" though, don't they, same as I used to do – bed and full board. They'll not be wanting a midday dinner.'

'Some of the larger hotels, like the Imperial and the Savoy, are doing just bed, breakfast and evening meal now,' Sarah told her, 'so I'm hoping their clients might come along to the Gynn in the middle of the day. Anyway, we can but try.'

'You're right, lass,' said Martha. 'You don't get anywhere if you don't try, and you're a trier if ever there was one. You deserve to do well if anybody does.'

The place got off to a good start and when a couple of weeks had passed it was clear that it was going to be a success. Sarah's café and shop had already proved popular, the food-poisoning scare having hardly affected the sales at all, and people were equally willing to give the restaurant a try. The prices were reasonable, the food tempting and wholesome, and Sarah Donnelly herself was a very popular young woman; especially so when it became known that she was soon going to marry a handsome young doctor, that nice Dr Duncan. Now, that was a real love match if ever there was one, people told one another; what a delightful young couple they were.

Plans for the early October wedding, to be held at St John's Church, were now going on apace. Grace was in her seventh heaven planning dresses for the bride and bridesmaids. Joyce – and Doris, to that young person's delight – were to be Sarah's attendants as Nancy was otherwise occupied with her stage career. It was hoped, however, that she would be able to attend the wedding as the Scarborough season was due to finish in the middle of September.

Alex and Sarah had found a small terraced house which was to their liking near to both the café and the surgery. The opening of the restaurant, exciting though it had been, was eclipsed in Sarah's mind by her delight in their new home-to-be. Most of their spare time was spent there, decorating it in readiness for them to live there after their marriage.

'Where shall we go for our honeymoon, darling?' Alex asked, about a month before the wedding, as they were busy painting the kitchen walls with pale green emulsion. 'Is there anywhere you fancy particularly? We can jump into the motorcar and then the world's our oyster – well, Britain at any rate. I've no desire to go further afield, have you?' Alex had recently bought a motorcar, a Morris Cowley saloon, and he was like a child with a new toy.

'What about Scotland?' asked Sarah. 'I've never been north of the border, and I'd love to see the places that you–'

'No! Not Scotland.' Alex's hand, holding the paintbrush, swung round quickly, splattering the paint in an arc across the room. 'Anywhere but Scotland.' His face held a closed look and Sarah could tell from his tone that he would brook no argument. But as he became aware of Sarah's puzzled expression his grim countenance softened a little. She was relieved when he smiled at her and she could see once again the familiar warmth and love in his eyes. 'Somewhere different, please, my love,' he said. 'After all, you wouldn't want to spend your honeymoon in Blackpool, now would you? And it's the same; it wouldna be much of a change for me.'

'Very well, Alex. It's all right with me,' said Sarah, though she still felt a little bewildered by his reaction. 'I hope you'll take me some time, though. I'd like to see the places that Sir Walter

Scott wrote about, as well as your birthplace. You know, for someone who's an exiled Scotsman, you don't talk about it very much, do you?'

Alex smiled. 'Och, I think you'd find that a lot of Scotsmen are like me, if they were to tell the truth. These singers, for instance, who are forever warbling about their ain folk and their wee hame amidst the heather, if they were honest I think they'd say that they no' want to return. I'm very happy here, my darling. You know that, don't you? Blissfully, unbelievably happy… Here, you've got a paint splash on the end of your nose.' He drew out a handkerchief and wiped it off, then very gently kissed the tip of her nose, her eyes, her mouth. There was no more painting done for several minutes… But Sarah remained puzzled by the incident.

In the end they settled on the Yorkshire Dales, which Alex said was very much like Scotland though not quite so rugged. They would book in at a hotel in Skipton for the first night, then drive wherever their fancy took them.

Nancy sat next to her mother in St John's Church, listening to the resounding tone of the organ and waiting for the bride to arrive. She had been pleased that the Scarborough season had finished in good time for her to be here, although she was relieved not to be acting as a bridesmaid, which had been Sarah's original intention for her. No, Nancy was glad today to be taking a back seat, as it were, and viewing the proceedings as one of the guests.

She had travelled from Yorkshire a few days ago

403

with Ivy who, as Zachary's young lady, had also been invited to the wedding. They were both staying at Sunnyside, but Ivy would soon be going to Halifax to spend some time with her family, whilst Nancy was spending a few weeks in Blackpool before the next engagement of the company, which was in Oldham. Then there would be Rochdale, Burnley, Nelson, Colne – several of the Lancashire cotton towns – before they opened for the pantomime season at a theatre in Manchester, where Sid had managed to procure parts for most of the troupe. Nancy knew that it was doubtful, though, if she would still be with them by then.

Hetty, at Nancy's side, seemed fidgety and somewhat ill-at-ease, fiddling with her handbag and gloves, taking them off then putting them on again and continually turning round to see who was coming in next. But it was quite an event for her mother, Nancy thought; she didn't often get out these days, continually working, as she did, in the boarding house. Nancy was pleased to see that her mother had indulged in a new outfit for the occasion; a mid-calf-length coat of cream wool flannel, very smart and slimming for Hetty's ample figure, but one that she could readily wear again. From Donnelly's exclusive fashion department, Nancy guessed, together with the dark green velvet turban hat and the green tunic style silk dress which she wore underneath. She was pleased to see her mother looking so smart for once.

'All right, Mam?' she asked, as Hetty dropped her gloves for the second time and bent beneath the pew to retrieve them.

'Yes, I'm all right, dear. Just a bit hot and bothered, you know.' Hetty's round face was pink and there were beads of perspiration on her nose and forehead. Nancy thought that her mother was rather young for it to be 'her age', although she wasn't exactly sure about such matters.

Nancy smiled encouragingly at her now. She hadn't realised how much she had missed her until she saw her again. 'You look lovely, Mam,' she whispered. 'A real bobby-dazzler, just as nice as anyone here.'

Hetty nodded, obviously gratified. 'Thanks, love. Are you all right?' she asked, with a slightly anxious look at her daughter.

''Course I am. Why shouldn't I be?' Nancy looked away then, further along the row. Zachary caught sight of her and winked, giving an impudent grin. He was very bright and breezy at the moment, unlike the often awkward, moody person that Nancy remembered, no doubt because he'd got his lady love with him again. Nancy hoped that Ivy would agree to marry him soon, for all their sakes. She knew that it must be hard for Mam putting up with him at times. She remembered how she had, at one time, been peeved because he was so obviously Hetty's favourite, making herself and Joyce feel very undervalued. Nancy no longer felt that this was the case; she was appreciating her mother's affection more than ever at the moment.

They were all there today, at the 'bride's side' of the church. Old Clara Donnelly, looking very frail, together with her two elder sons and their families, relations whom, Nancy knew, her Uncle Edwin's family didn't often see. They were here in full force though, for the wedding. There were Grandma and Grandad Makepeace, occupying the pew in front of Nancy and her family, and, behind them, friends of Sarah's from her own café and from the tearoom at Donnelly's where she had worked previously. This side of the church was quite full, whereas the bridegroom's side was very sparsely occupied. Just a few colleagues of the doctor, and several patients, too, who had wandered in, uninvited, to watch the wedding. At the front were Alex Duncan and his friend and colleague, John Mason, who was acting as his best man. They both looked very smart in their morning suits and as Alex turned round, anxiously awaiting the arrival of his bride, Nancy thought again what a very handsome man he was. Not only handsome, he was kind and loving, too. On the few occasions when she had seen him and Sarah together Nancy had been very much aware of how he adored her cousin. Oh, she did so hope that Sarah would be happy, that everything would be all right for her; that 'that' would not be too awful...

Nancy's recurring thought, which she always tried so hard to stifle, was threatening her again and she was glad when her Aunt Grace entered the church, taking her mind away from it. Grace was elegance personified in a dark red crepe-georgette dress with finely ruched decoration at the hipline and at the cuffs of the long tapering sleeves. Her red straw hat with a deep crown, trimmed with a large matching ostrich feather, added the final touch of distinction. There was an appreciative murmur, 'The bride's mother,' as she walked, calm and dignified, to her place in the front pew. Not so dignified, however, that she didn't turn to smile radiantly at her family; her mother and step-father, her sister, niece and nephew. Aunt Grace is lovely, Nancy thought, and her daughter was so much like her in every way.

And now, of course, it was time for the arrival of the bride. The congregation stood as the deep notes of the organ changed to Wagner's *Bridal March*, from 'Lohengrin', that piece of music the simple tune of which almost asked to have incongruous words put to it. Nancy tried not to think of the silly words now as she watched her cousin walking down the aisle on the arm of Edwin Donnelly.

Sarah was the most beautiful bride you could ever wish to see, thought Nancy, feeling tears springing to her eyes. Her dress was not merely pretty, nor was it at all fussy. It was, like Grace's, the epitome of elegance; heavy white silk brocade, bordered with bands of white and gold embroidery, flowing into a short train. Her veil was of fine silk chiffon kept in place with a headdress of tiny silk flowers. The golden roses she carried in her bouquet toned exactly with the dresses of the bridesmaids. Joyce and Doris both looked unusually attractive in their ankle-length, pale golden brocade dresses which were, like Sarah's, striking in their simplicity. Neither of the girls would have suited being attired like a 'fairy on a Christmas tree', as Joyce had remarked to her sister. Nancy noticed, the tears still in her eyes, the look of love that was exchanged by the bride and groom, and then the service began.

'Dearly beloved brethren, we are gathered together in the sight of God and in the face of this congregation to join together this man and this woman in holy matrimony...' It was an honourable estate, intoned the vicar, and was not to be undertaken lightly or wantonly, 'like brute beasts that have no understanding...'

As Nancy listened to these words they impinged themselves upon her mind, and immediately she found herself, in memory, back in that awful bedroom; that fateful camera looming in the background, her clothes in disarray, the lumpy eiderdown rucked up beneath her, and Clive Conway relentlessly thrusting himself into her virginal body. 'Brute beasts', the vicar had said; that was what Clive had been – a brute beast with no understanding; no love or understanding whatsoever. And as the marriage service progressed Nancy felt more and more sorry for Sarah. Did the girl know what she was letting herself in for? But with someone as good and kind as Alex undoubtedly was, it couldn't be like that, could it? No, Nancy knew that Alex was as unlike Clive as it was possible to be. There was bound to be the same pain though, surely, that feeling of being torn apart and that same sense of violation, as though your body were being invaded and didn't belong to you any more. Nancy had vowed to herself that never, as long as she lived, would she marry; never again would she subject herself to such treatment by

408

any man.

She gave an involuntary shudder and she saw her mother glance questioningly at her. She tried to smile back reassuringly, then she made herself concentrate on the lovely part of the service. The bridal couple exchanging their vows, Alex slipping the ring on Sarah's finger, the singing of 'O Perfect Love'. And afterwards, outside the church, the red carpet and the joyous peal of bells and the sentimental Saturday-afternoon shoppers stopping to stare. Then, at the reception at the Imperial Hotel, Sarah and Alex cutting the cake, listening to the toasts and good wishes and, throughout it all, looking so blissfully happy together.

Nancy was not normally a praying sort of person; she didn't often go to church now, but during the wedding service she had found herself praying that God would look after Sarah and keep her happy. And when Sarah changed into her pretty pink going away outfit and stepped into the little Morris Cowley motorcar with Alex, Nancy said a simple prayer again. *'Please God, let her go on being happy ... and help her tonight, please God.'*

Sarah threw her wedding bouquet high in the air, as tradition demanded, and a crowd of young women, Sarah's friends and work-mates, surged forward to catch it. There was general laughter when it fell into the arms of Doris from the café. That young woman blushed a deep pink. 'Eeh no, not me,' she was heard to say. It was unlikely, indeed, that she would be the next to be married, but it was just a bit of fun and not meant to be taken seriously.

Nancy, however, had not been taking any chances and hadn't rushed forward in the mêlée. No, marriage was not for her, not in a thousand years. But now that the wedding was over she knew that she couldn't keep her awful secret to herself any longer. So far she hadn't told anyone and, strangely enough, no one in the company seemed to have suspected anything. But it wouldn't be long before it became obvious. Nancy knew that she would have to confide in someone, and who else should it be but her mother?

Nancy may have been ignorant of some of the facts of life – she had learned the hard way about the mysterious happenings that took place between a man and a woman – but she had enough common sense to know that when a girl hadn't had a period for more than three months then there was a very obvious reason for it. She had tried to ignore the signs at first, telling herself that it couldn't possibly be so, not when it had only happened once. She had tried to erase all memories of that horrific encounter from her mind. Clive Conway had gone, to her immense relief; and after she had got over the initial shock of her experience, which had kept her trembling and frightened in her room for the rest of the day, Nancy had tried manfully to pull herself together. 'The show must go on' was an adage she had heard many times, even in the short time she had been with the company, and Nancy was determined to be a real trouper, one who didn't let circumstances get the better of her. Sid and

Flo had been kindness itself, not uttering one word of recrimination, and it was because of this that Nancy knew she mustn't let them down. She was back on stage the next day, though still rather shaken, and the good sense and comradeship of her colleagues had helped her to get back to normal.

There were a few rumours flying around the company about the absence of the talented male dancer. Some put two and two together; all knew better than to ask Sid the real reason. And in a few days' time, after the rest of the company had improvised with a certain amount of 'filling in' and lengthening of their acts, a replacement was found for him. Toni Tarrant was slim and dark with lean Italianate looks, as unlike Clive as could be; a private sort of person, aloof and shy, until he got on-stage, when his feet took over and made him come alive. It was obvious before long that Clive Conway would not be missed at all.

Yes, he had gone for good ... but he could not be forgotten, for Nancy knew after a few weeks had passed that she was pregnant. She had known vaguely about morning sickness, but apart from a slight queasiness when she awoke she hadn't suffered unduly from this. In fact, it had been quite easy all along to hide her condition from her room-mates. But as she stood in front of the mirror in her attic bedroom the morning after Sarah's wedding, she knew that she could hide it no longer, nor did she want to. It would be a relief to confide in someone at last. She smoothed her tunic-style dress over her stomach, pulling it close to her figure. Yes, there was a slight bulge there now, although these straight-up-and-down dresses that most women were wearing at the moment were ideal for disguising the early stages. Nancy took a deep breath. She would tell her mother just as soon as they had finished their breakfast.

Hetty's immediate reaction, when she heard Nancy's staggering news, was one of disbelief, then horror, then anger, all following swiftly one upon the other. She had felt like leaning across the table and slapping her daughter's face. *'You silly little fool!'* she had wanted to cry, and what mother wouldn't have felt the same? But then, in a flash, Hetty remembered a similar occasion, some twenty-three years ago. It had been a breakfast-time then in Welcome Rest, the boarding house across the road, and a daughter telling her mother the selfsame news; herself, Hetty, telling Martha that she was to have Reuben Loveday's child. Her mother, she recalled, had not been surprised; she had already guessed.

Hetty, however, had not had any idea about Nancy's condition, but now, with gradually dawning realisation, things were beginning to fall into place. Nancy's obvious joy at being home; Hetty hadn't expected the girl to be so overwhelmingly pleased to see everyone again, and she had been very surprised at Nancy's desire to spend time with her, Hetty; her unwillingness, though, to talk about the company and her future plans; her withdrawn manner at the wedding yesterday – that had been very unlike the normally gregarious Nancy. Yes, Hetty now wondered why on earth she hadn't guessed what

412

was the matter. And how could she, in any honesty, be cross with the lass, she who had once been in the same predicament herself? Hetty knew she must try to treat her daughter with the same loving concern and forbearance that her own mother had shown to her.

'Good gracious!' Hetty said, after a few seconds had passed. After all, what else could she say? 'That's a bit of a shock, Nancy, I must admit,' she went on, trying to keep her voice calm. 'I'd no idea that you even had a boyfriend. Who is he? I suppose it's someone that you've met...'

'I haven't, Mam.' Nancy's voice was flat, emotionless.

'What d'you mean, you haven't?' Hetty gave a slight frown. 'You haven't what?'

'I haven't got a boyfriend. I didn't... It wasn't... Oh Mam, it was awful!' Nancy's cup rolled across the table, spilling tea all over the checked tablecloth, as she put her head down on her folded arms and wept and wept. 'Oh, Mam ... Mam. It was terrible. I never meant to... He forced me, he made me do it. And I never knew it would be like that.'

Hetty stared for a moment, horrified, at the paroxysm of weeping that was shaking Nancy's shoulders, at the tears streaming down her grief-stricken face. This was much worse than she had thought. Dear God, the girl must have been... She got up from her chair and, moving round to the other side of the table, she began to stroke her daughter's auburn hair which lay in tangled curls at the nape of her neck. 'Come on now, lovey. Stop crying. It's all right now, your mam's

413

here. I'll take care of you.' She sat down next to her and placed her arm round her shoulders, holding her close, trying to give her what comfort she could.

In a few moments Nancy's sobs grew fainter. Then they ceased altogether and she turned a tragic face to her mother. 'Oh Mam, it was awful,' she said again in a whisper. 'Why didn't anybody tell me it would be like that?'

'Who was it?' asked Hetty gently. 'You've got to tell me, love … please.'

'Clive Conway,' said Nancy dispiritedly. 'You remember him, Mam.'

'Yes, of course I do,' said Hetty, bringing to mind the flashy young tap-dancer whom she had never cared for. He had thought he was *it* all right, had that one. But she would have thought that Nancy would have had more sense than to trust a fellow like that. The young swine! Hetty's protective instincts rose to the fore at the thought of him with his hands upon her daughter. She'd like to murder him, to tear him limb from limb. 'But what happened, love?' she prompted. 'You must have been going about with him, for him to–' She was aware that she mustn't pry too much.

'Not really, Mam. I'd been out with him once, then he said he wanted to take some photographs of me, in his room. I thought he was real nice, Mam.' Nancy's lovely green eyes, one of her best features, so often sparkling with merriment, were now bewildered and lacklustre.

Oh dear! Hetty sighed inwardly. Nancy really had been much more naïve than she had supposed. Fancy being taken in by an old trick like that. But it was no use scolding her now and it did seem as though the poor girl wasn't to blame in any way. 'And where is he now?' asked Hetty. 'He's not still with the company, is he?'

'No, Sid sent him packing as soon as he knew. Sid's been wonderful, Mam. You mustn't go blaming him. He does try to keep his eye on us all. I know I was just stupid...'

'Never mind, love. It can't be helped. We'll just have to make the best of it.' Hetty knew that her words were inadequate; platitudes, in fact, such as were always uttered in a crisis like this. The enormity of the situation was just beginning to dawn on her. What the hell were they to do? The lass was pregnant, but unlike herself in the same situation, there was no possibility of her getting married. 'But why didn't you tell me before?' she asked, 'about what happened. Why didn't Sid tell me? You're my daughter, love, and you were a long way from home. He could have let me know.'

Nancy shook her head. 'There'd have been no point, Mam. Sid was very upset and he did want to write to you, but I told him he mustn't. I was all right, you see, once I'd got over it.' Hetty was relieved to see that Nancy was talking more rationally now, appearing to take the whole thing in her stride, if that were possible. 'You know what they say, don't you, Mam?' She tried to smile. 'The show must go on.'

Hetty smiled back, though sadly. 'You're a brave lass,' she said, 'and you mustn't worry about a thing.' After all, there was nothing else

415

for it, was there, but to let things take their natural course? The lass would have to go through with it, have her baby, and be damned to what anyone might think – and then they'd just have to take a day at a time. And through it all she, Hetty, would be there to stand by her. 'I'll look after you, don't worry,' she said. 'You're at home now, where you should be. I daresay Sid knows you're not going back, doesn't he? You'll likely have told him.'

'I haven't told a soul, Mam, except you,' said Nancy. 'And of course I'm going back. We've an engagement next week and a few more before Christmas. And then there's the pantomime.'

'What are you talking about, you silly girl?' Hetty raised her voice for the first time. 'Engagements … pantomime indeed! You'll be in no fit state… When is it due, anyway? How … how far are you?'

'It was June,' said Nancy, a trifle sullenly. 'More than three months, I suppose. It'll be … the middle of March, something like that. But I've *got* to go back, Mam! For a few weeks, anyroad, until…' Nancy glanced down reluctantly at her figure. At the moment she didn't show.

'All right then, we'll see,' said Hetty, relenting. At least it was good to see that the girl had some spirit and she seemed to be in the best of health. 'But you're coming along with me to the doctor's, this very day, and you'll have to take notice of what he says. You will, won't you, there's a good lass? I suppose you might manage for…' Hetty did a quick calculation '…another month or so.'

416

'Thanks Mam,' said Nancy. 'I'll have to go through with it, I know that. But I love being on the stage and I don't want to–' She stopped suddenly, staring down at the tablecloth. Mechanically she reached out and set the upturned cup back on its saucer. When she looked back at her mother her eyes were again full of the puzzlement that Hetty had noticed before. 'Mam,' she said. 'Why didn't you tell me?'

'Tell you what, love?' said Hetty, although she thought she knew.

'About ... *that*. About what it was like. Being married. Well, not married, but you know what I mean. I never imagined it could be so awful.'

'Nancy ... Nancy, love. You've had a bad experience. All that you went through ... it has nothing to do with marriage.' Hetty was not finding it easy to talk of such matters, but she knew she had to try. 'I've been married twice, as you know,' she went on, somewhat embarrassedly, 'and I can assure you that it was never like ... what happened to you. Never, not once. When two people love one another, then it can be a very ... lovely thing that they do together.' She stopped, feeling a flush stain her cheeks. 'You'll find out one day, Nancy, I can assure you.'

But Nancy was shaking her head. 'No, never, Mam. I shall never get married.'

Hetty smiled. 'You say that now. But you will. One day ... you will.' But as she said it the thought struck her that Nancy, before long, would have a child. Would anyone want her, then? 'You'll fall in love and get married,' she went on, trying to sound convincing.

Nancy was silent, and when she spoke again her mother was surprised, and touched, too, at the concern in her voice. 'D'you think Sarah'll be all right?' she said. 'I'm so worried about Sarah. I keep thinking about her and Alex and–'

Hetty almost laughed, but it wasn't a laughing matter, not any of it. 'Then I shouldn't worry any more,' she soothed, 'because I never saw two people more in love than Sarah and that young doctor. Believe me, Nancy, your cousin will be all right.'

Sarah Duncan, as she sat beside her husband in the motorcar, heading northwards from Bolton Abbey along the banks of the River Wharfe, was very much all right. She was filled with a sense of wonderment, as though it were all a beautiful, impossible dream. Her wedding night had been real enough; herself and Alex in that olde-worlde hotel in Skipton. If she were honest, it had all been something of a surprise to Sarah. Quite a pleasant surprise, though, once she had got over the initial shock, and she was sure that things could only get better. Alex was such a considerate person, tender and gentle and anxious to please her, to ensure that she should enjoy their lovemaking just as much as he did. This morning, though, this golden, sun-dappled, crisp October morning, there was a dreamlike quality about it; Sarah was fearful that she would wake up and it would all disappear.

They had breakfasted on homely Yorkshire produce – bacon, eggs, sausages, mushrooms, tomatoes and fried bread, served with strong tea and followed by toast from a crusty loaf smothered in butter and orange marmalade. A feast such as Sarah hadn't enjoyed in years; her breakfast, more often than not, was a slice of bread or a bowl of cereal. Then they had set off in the motorcar, heading east to Bolton Abbey. Sarah had been enchanted by her first view of the twelfth-century priory ruins, in their setting of lush green meadows and wooded hills, beside the gently flowing river.

This was the first of many, many breathtaking scenes that Sarah was to see in that memorable week. This area of Yorkshire, lonely and in previous times inaccessible, was where the Norman barons had built their castles and the church its religious houses. As well as Bolton Abbey she was to see the abbeys of Fountains, Rievaulx and Jervaulx; Castle Howard, the palatial home of the Carlisle family, viewed from a distance across the Vale of York; the awesome limestone splendour of Wharfedale and Wensleydale with their sleepy greystone villages and bustling market towns; Aysgarth Falls, cascading in a series of foamy, white-capped waterfalls for half a mile along the River Ure; the secluded, rugged grandeur of Swaledale, now painted in the glowing tints of autumn, leading to the starkness of the Buttertubs Pass... Sights and impressions, too numerous to recall them all when she looked back, crowding one upon the other as day followed golden day, in that magical, memorable week.

The roads were quiet, almost free from traffic, save for a rumbling hay-cart or tractor, or a herd

419

of cows being driven to the barn for milking. It seemed at times as though she and Alex were the only two inhabitants of this wonderful world. When the week ended, Sarah returned from her honeymoon far more deeply in love with her husband, if that were possible, than she had been before.

Chapter 19

Hetty paced up and down the living room, trying to shut her ears to the screams emanating at regular intervals from the room on the first floor but, at the same time, listening frantically for a different sound, the first infant cry which would signify that it was all over. All over ... and yet all just beginning. Hetty prayed, as she had done so many times over the past few months, just a simple prayer that all would be well.

The midwife had assured her that everything was going as well as could be expected and that there should be no complications, but it was likely to be a long labour. Nancy's waters had broken at about six o'clock in the morning; now it was late afternoon and she still hadn't given birth. And a 'dry' labour was always worse; or so Hetty had frequently been told by women of her mother's generation, but whether or not it was an old wives' tale she wasn't sure. At all events, Nancy certainly wasn't parting with her burden soundlessly, Hetty thought, as another ear-piercing scream broke into the silence. But then she had never expected her to; that wouldn't be Nancy. She was bound to make a bit of a fuss, but her mother hoped that the pain would soon be forgotten when she held the new baby in her arms. Hetty had found it to be so each time she had given birth; but then, she was not Nancy and these circumstances were very different. No husband, no home of her own, except the one that her mother would willingly and lovingly provide for her until such time as ... well, they would just have to wait and see what happened.

Nancy had worked with Sid's company until the end of November. Her mother wondered how on earth she had done it, parading on the stage in all those revealing costumes, but her pregnancy had not become obvious until the last couple of months. From the look of her it promised to be a small baby; but small or not, it still had to be parted with, thought Hetty ruefully. And it was no picnic, giving birth, let anyone try to tell her any different. She hadn't warned Nancy about the agony to come. That was something that every woman had to experience for herself; there was no point in frightening her to death unnecessarily. It was a pity, though, that she hadn't had the courage to warn her daughter about other matters, then none of this might have happened... Hetty shook her head dismissively. It was futile to think of such things now. What was done couldn't be undone. She hoped, though, that Nancy's attitude would change, that she would begin to face up to the situation she was in.

Hetty had been relieved that never once had Nancy mentioned trying to get rid of the child, a risky business, not even to be considered in Hetty's opinion, although she knew that some poor women resorted to it. Whether Nancy had ever had such thoughts, Hetty didn't know, but she certainly hadn't voiced them to her mother.

She had returned to the company, full of beans, after the doctor had pronounced her fit and well – but undoubtedly pregnant – and when she came home some six weeks later she had still appeared bright and breezy; quite the old Nancy. But, as the weeks passed – Christmas, New Year and onwards into1921 – she showed no interest whatsoever in the coming child. Hetty and Martha, and Joyce, too, were all busy knitting little garments, white, blue or yellow, which would 'do for either', but not so with Nancy. She read magazines, she played gramophone records; it had to be admitted that she did her share in the house, too, and she went for walks on the promenade. She didn't seek to disguise her condition, nor did she appear to be ashamed of it; she just ignored it.

But all that would change – of course it would, Hetty told herself – at her first glimpse of that little baby … whatever it was. For no one had dared to ask Nancy the familiar question, did she want a boy or a girl? Hetty would have been delighted to hear her make the age-old reply that she didn't care, 'so long as it was all right'. But the truth of the matter was that Nancy didn't seem to care at all.

Hetty stopped her pacing to poke at the fire, separating the glowing coals, then she switched on the electric light and drew the curtains. The days were lengthening nicely now, the third week in March, but the grey dusk was beginning to creep over the rooftops and Hetty was glad of a little light and warmth in the room. She glanced at the wooden clock on the mantelpiece. Quarter past six and she hadn't even thought about making herself some tea. She wouldn't be able to eat a thing, not until it was all over. Fortunately she had no people in this week, no 'pros' for once and it was too soon as yet for the spring visitors. Zachary was on late shift and had gone out in the middle of the afternoon so she had the house to herself. And it was now beginning to get on her nerves. She missed having her mother and George across the road. Martha, it was true, did still come round quite often for a chat and a cuppa – time was hanging heavy for her in her retirement – but today she and George had gone to visit Alice and Henry in their home at Layton. Martha would be here tomorrow though, no doubt about that, when she heard the news about her first great-grandchild. Alice as well, more than likely, Albert's mother, the other great grandmother. There would, surely, be some news by tomorrow. Hetty felt a wave of panic beginning to seize her. It had been such a long, long time. She grasped hold of the edge of the mantelpiece to steady herself. *'Please, please God, let it be soon…'*

And then she heard it, faint but unmistakable; the cry of an infant. She crept out of the living room and stood at the bottom of the stairs, ears strained to catch every sound. Yes, there it was again, and from what she could hear it seemed as though it was a healthy child, right enough; it was certainly crying lustily. She felt tears of thankfulness come into her eyes and she breathed a heartfelt prayer: *'Thank God. Oh thank You, God, for letting it arrive safely.'* It … this was her first

424

grandchild and she didn't know yet what 'it' was. She bounded up the stairs, then, stopping by the door of Number 4 bedroom where all the activity was taking place, she deferentially knocked. This, after all, was the midwife's domain, and such women were sticklers for protocol; it wouldn't do to offend Mrs Ackroyd even if it were Hetty's own house.

She entered at the call of, 'Come in, Mrs Gregson, we're just about ready,' and her eyes went immediately to the bed in the centre of the room where Nancy was lying with her eyes closed, sweating and dishevelled, her auburn hair lying in damp untidy curls on her forehead and neck.

'My poor baby,' whispered Hetty, feeling such a surge of affection for her elder daughter as she had never felt before. She went over to the bed and laid her hand on the girl's clammy brow. 'Never mind, my pet, it's all over now and you've got your little baby.'

Nancy opened her eyes, but very apathetically and gave a ghost of a smile. 'Hello, Mam,' she said in a murmur, then closed her eyes again.

It was only then that Hetty turned to the midwife. 'And what is it, Mrs Ackroyd?' she asked, at the same time answering her own question as she watched the woman gently wiping away the mucus from the tiny red face. It was a boy.

'A bonny boy, aren't you, my pet?' Mrs Ackroyd held up the infant who resembled nothing more than a skinned rabbit at that moment; but to his grandmother's eyes and to the eyes of the woman who had just delivered him he was, indeed, bonny. 'There's nowt wrong with this little bairn,' Mrs Ackroyd said softly, smiling at Hetty, as she wrapped him in a piece of soft blanket. 'He's strong and healthy. A grand baby if ever I saw one.' She walked across to the bed. 'Come on now, Nancy. Sit up, there's a good lass. Here's your little lad. Give him a cuddle. That's what he wants now.'

Nancy half-raised herself against the pillows, looking down at the bundle in the midwife's arms. Then, to her mother's horror, she turned her head away, slumping down again beneath the blankets. 'No,' she said. 'I can't. I don't want to.'

Hetty, as well as being horrified at her daughter's reaction, was dreadfully embarrassed. Whatever would Mrs Ackroyd think? She gave the woman a pleading, half-apologetic look as she saw her shrug and then carry the child over to the window. 'I'm terribly sorry,' she said in a whisper, as she followed her across the room. 'I can't think why she's behaving like this. Whatever must you think of her?'

'I don't think anything,' said Mrs Ackroyd calmly. 'Believe me, Mrs Gregson, I've seen it all before. She'll come round.' She gave a curt nod. 'Here, Grandma, you have a hold of him.'

Hetty sat in a low chair by the window and Mrs Ackroyd placed the baby in her arms. Very gently Hetty pulled away the blanket that enveloped the child, looking down in wonder at the tiny red face, the eyes screwed up tightly against the light so that it was impossible to see what colour they were. Blue, no doubt – weren't all newborn babies' eyes blue? – but perhaps they might turn green later, like her own and Nancy's. She remembered then, with a stab of unease, that his eyes were blue, a startling brilliant blue – him, Clive Conway, this child's father. He had Nancy's hair though, bless him, unmistakably ginger tendrils clinging wetly to his scalp, over that tender part where she could see the pulse of life throbbing.

She looked at the tiny arms and legs and the little round protruding stomach, all covered with faint purplish mottles – a sign of good health, so she believed – marvelling that such a small infant could be so perfectly formed in every detail. So it must have been with her own three children, but she had forgotten … she had forgotten. The realisation that each birth is in itself a minor miracle resurged as she gazed at her grandchild. A miracle … and Nancy, the naughty girl, wouldn't even look at him. 'Never mind, my pet,' she said to the child, feeling love such as she had never known before flowing through her, 'if your mam doesn't want you, then there's someone here who does. I'll have you … I'll take care of you, my little lamb.'

As quickly as the thought formed Hetty tried to banish it. What on earth was she thinking about? This was Nancy's child, and Nancy would come round; of course she would. She turned to the midwife, at the same time motioning with her head to the prone figure on the bed. 'Is it usual?' she whispered. 'I mean, for her not to want…'

'Not all that unusual,' Mrs Ackroyd replied in a whisper, looking sideways at Nancy, who appeared to be asleep. 'Like I've said, I've seen it all in my time. She's had a bad time, a long labour. No complications, thank God, and she didn't need any stitches, which is a blessing. But it was hard for her, especially as she wouldn't help herself very much, and it might take her a while to forget. And then ... she's on her own, of course, poor lass. It's bound to affect her. But she'll come round, Mrs Gregson, don't worry about that. She'll have to, 'cos that little mite'll be wanting his dinner afore long. And that's summat that no one else can do for him.'

But Nancy did not come round. As the long day lengthened into evening she was persuaded, at last, to hold the child in her arms, but when it came to feeding him, holding him to her breast and letting him take her milk she flatly refused.

'No ... *no!* Take him away!' she cried, pulling her nightgown tightly around her and refusing to cooperate. 'I can't ... I won't. It's horrible!' And there was nothing that her mother or Mrs Ackroyd could do to make her change her mind.

Hetty was at her wits' end as she watched her daughter turn her head into the pillow, giving way to a fit of frenzied sobbing. She felt like shaking and slapping her, but that would doubtless only make things worse. She had always known that Nancy was highly strung, but never before had she seen her in such a hysterical state as this. She was afraid that to be angry with her might only serve to send her right over the edge.

'I'll go and boil some milk,' she said in a low voice to Mrs Ackroyd, 'and I've got a feeding bottle somewhere. Is that all right?'

'It'll have to be,' said the midwife grimly. 'Milk

428

and boiled water at first, Mrs Gregson. He'll not be all that hungry till tomorrow, then we'll have to get one of them patent mixtures from the chemist. But let's hope that by tomorrow she's more herself.'

But when Martha Makepeace called the next morning, summoned by a message from Zachary, who had gone round to tell his grandmother the news, it was to find Hetty sitting at the fireside cradling her new grandson in her arms.

'What's up?' said Martha, looking in puzzlement at the bottle in Hetty's hand. 'Can't the lass feed him? There's nowt wrong with her, is there?'

Hetty looked resignedly at her mother. 'It's not so much a question of can't, Mam, as won't. She won't feed him and that's that. And we can't let the little chap starve, now can we?' Her voice softened and her expression, too, as she looked down again at the hungry mouth closing eagerly and noisily around the rubber teat that seemed far too big for him.

'Eeh! The naughty little madam! She wants a good smacking,' said Martha; and Hetty almost laughed at what she might have known would be her mother's reaction.

'It wouldn't do any good, Mam,' she said calmly, still looking at the child and not at Martha. 'It's no use being cross with her. We'll just have to give her time. I'm sure that's all she needs … time.'

'What about her milk?' asked Martha. 'She'll have to get rid of it, or else she'll be ill. I remember when I had you two I was awash with it.'

'The doctor's here now,' replied Hetty. 'He'll no doubt give her something to stop it. Perhaps if she doesn't start to feed it'll not flow so much. And she's adamant she won't do it.'

'I don't know,' said Martha, shaking her head. 'It's a pretty kettle of fish.' She looked concernedly at her daughter. 'You looking after a bairn again at your time of life, our Hetty. It's to be hoped that lass shapes herself before long. You can't be doing with sleepless nights and all that carry-on, not with a houseful of visitors to see to. Anyroad, let's have a look at him.' Martha bent over the child in Hetty's arms. 'Let's have a look at my first great-grandchild. Just imagine that! Great-grandchild!' She chuckled slightly as the child grasped hold of her outstretched finger, clinging to it tightly. 'Well then, you are a bonny lad, aren't you? Tch, tch, tch, you are that! And what are they going to call you?'

'We haven't got round to that yet, Mam,' said Hetty. 'It'll be up to our Nancy.'

'Aye, you'll have to get him registered afore long,' said Martha. 'And christened an' all. I don't reckon they're properly here, not till they've been received into God's family. Eeh, Hetty lass, let's hope she sees sense, or else you're going to have a devil of a job ahead of you.'

'What else can I do, Mam?' said Hetty simply. 'I'm her mother, aren't I? And this little un's grandmother. And if I don't look after him then no one else will.' As Hetty looked at the child he suddenly opened his eyes, a cloudy greyish blue they were, gazing unfocusedly into her face; and she knew then that there was nothing that she wanted more than to bring up this little one as her own.

He was christened Joseph at a simple service at the Methodist Church in North Shore, four weeks later. By that time Nancy had come round sufficiently to nurse him now and again, to push him out in his pram and – very occasionally – to change his nappy. But it was, Hetty thought, almost as though she were his big sister and not his mother. Sometimes she appeared quite fond of him, after a fashion, smiling at him when he gave a satisfied gurgle on finishing his bottle or peeping into his pram to see if he had gone to sleep. Hetty often left the pram in the tiny garden at the front of Sunnyside, where he could have the benefit of the sunshine and fresh air. But Nancy appeared detached, aloof from him; never did she coo at him or talk the little nonsenses that were all part of nurturing a baby. It was Hetty who did that, who was continually cuddling the little fellow and telling him how much she loved him. It was Hetty, too, who prepared his bottles, who awoke in the night to feed him, who changed him and bathed him and brought up his wind … with Nancy, now and again, lending a hand.

After a few weeks it was almost as though little Joseph were her own child, and Hetty found that the spontaneous actions of motherhood had returned to her just as though it were only yesterday that she had been nursing a baby. More so, in fact, for she couldn't remember ever having had so much joy looking after her own three.

There was nothing new in the idea of a mother looking after a daughter's illegitimate baby,

431

sometimes passing it off as her own. There was that Mrs Bennett down the street, for instance; she was a case in point. She was fifty if she was a day, and there she was, pushing the ten-month-old child around in his pram, referring to him as her 'little afterthought'; but everyone knew that he belonged to Dora, her fifteen-year-old daughter who was generally reckoned to be 'only eleven pence in the shilling'. A sad case, Hetty always thought, but at least Mrs Bennett had stood by her daughter. There were other girls whom Hetty knew of who had been sent into homes for unmarried mothers and then forced to have their babies adopted. And Hetty's mother, Martha, even knew of a lass in Burnley who had been put into an asylum, the 'loony bin', and just because she had conceived a child outside of marriage.

For her part, Hetty hadn't consciously sought to claim this child as her own; it had just happened, brought about by Nancy's indifference and her own consuming feeling for the baby which was increasing day by day. She didn't deny that he belonged to Nancy; many people, indeed, knew that this was the truth but, tactfully, they chose to ignore it. But there were others, holidaymakers and people she met when she was out shopping, who assumed that the child was Hetty's own; and – well – she didn't disillusion them; it was up to them to think what they liked.

It had been Nancy, though, who had chosen the child's name, and that was as it should be. When Nancy had been asked, a few days after the birth, what he was to be called, she had said

432

without hesitation, 'Joseph. I've always liked that name, and that's what he's going to be. Joseph Gregson.'

He had had the statutory godparents; Zachary, who although he didn't show much interest was, after all, the child's uncle, and Joyce, who was thrilled at her role of aunt and godmother, carrying the baby into church in the new shawl which Hetty had crocheted for him. And Nancy had also invited Sarah and her new husband to 'stand' for the baby. She had always been fond of Sarah, and Alex Duncan was fast becoming a very popular member of the family. So it had been a happy enough little christening party that congregated at Sunnyside after the church service; and if any of them noticed that it was Hetty, rather than Nancy, who was seeing to the child's welfare then no one made any comment.

When Nancy started hinting, around the middle of May, about the summer season that Sid's company would soon be beginning in Morecambe, Hetty was only too happy to suggest that the girl should go and join them. It was quite obviously what she was hankering after; besides, Hetty was sick to death of her mooning around the house, doing some desultory cleaning or washing up when she felt inclined – which wasn't often – or disappearing for hours at a time. Hetty knew that she often went down to Sarah's Café – Joyce had told her mother so – where she was inclined to be a nuisance when they were busy, as they usually were. And Hetty had also heard that she frequented the Golden Mile and Barney's song-booth, although Barney had not offered to give her back her old job; he had a new vocalist, apparently, who seemed to be quite a crowd-puller. Hetty wasn't sure whether Sid had suggested that Nancy should return to the Trio, but it transpired that her replacement had proved unsuitable, and when Nancy hinted that she might return he had been delighted at the proposal – or so Nancy said.

At all events, Hetty was glad to see the back of her when she departed from North Station at the beginning of June; full of glee she was, with a cheery wave and a beaming smile, even a kiss for the baby and a promise that she would see him soon and that he must 'be a good boy for Grandma'. Hetty, though she was undeniably relieved at her departure, at the same time felt guilty that she should feel this way about her own daughter – glad to see her leaving so that she could have the child all to herself. There was no doubt about it, though, it would be hard work – damned hard work – she thought, as she pushed the high black pram back to Sunnyside. But she would cope; like her mother before her, Hetty had never been afraid of hard work and she would manage, somehow. And this little lad, asleep now in the pram, would make it all worthwhile.

She had heard other grandmothers say that having grandchildren was like having a second chance, 'the pleasure without the pain', she had heard someone say. But to Hetty it was more than that; it was like beginning again, making up for what she had lost. For she had to admit to herself now that Zachary had turned out to be a bitter disappointment to her, and that was something she never thought she would say. And Nancy, too; all that she seemed to be concerned about was herself. Joyce was all right, of course. Good old Joyce, sensible and reliable, but very ... ordinary, just like her father had been. Hetty immediately castigated herself for such unworthy thoughts. Albert had been a good husband – very good indeed – and Joyce was a daughter she should be proud of. But it was wonderful to have this chance to start again with young Joseph, just when she had begun to think that it was too late for anything.

Her mother thought that she was crazy and told her so too. Martha called round, as she often did, soon after Hetty returned from the station.

'So she's gone then, has she, the young madam?' said Martha, following Hetty into the kitchen where the meat and potato pie, simmering in the oven, had to be checked to ensure that it would be ready for the return of the visitors at one o'clock. She watched as Hetty took out the huge enamel dish, removed the lid and prodded a fork into the potatoes. 'By heck, our Hetty, that looks good,' she commented. 'I couldn't have made it any better meself.'

Hetty grinned. 'You're welcome to stay and have some, Mam. Yes, as you were saying, Nancy's gone. I know you don't approve, but she's gone and that's all there is to it. We've said many times over all this, that what's done can't be undone, and we've just got to get on with it now and make the best of a bad job. Although, when you look at our little Joseph, can you honestly believe that it's a bad job, Mam?'

'That's as may be, Hetty,' replied Martha. 'I know he's a grand little lad, but that's not the point. It's her, Nancy, that should be seeing to the bairn – making the best of it, as you say – not you. Just look at all this...' She waved her hands at the pots draining by the sink, the earthenware bowl containing flour and lard to be made into pastry for the top of the pie, a pile of apples waiting to be peeled. 'Here you are, trying to make a meal for hungry visitors, then you've got that lot from the Palace Varieties, and your Zachary, and on top of it all, a newborn baby to see to. It's too much, our Hetty.'

'Hardly newborn, Mam. He's nearly two and a half months now, and he's coming on a treat. You should have seen the stuff he put away this morning, the greedy little chap. He'll be ready for solids before long, I can see.'

'Don't change the subject, Hetty. It's too much and you know it. Don't you?' Martha looked searchingly at her daughter and Hetty was forced to nod in agreement.

'Yes ... it's hard work, Mam, I won't deny it. But I'm not complaining. Like I've said to you before, what else can I do? If I don't look after him no one else will. I know you don't like what our Nancy's doing, but I've got to think of her as well. She's had a rough time – it wasn't her fault, you know – and I was really worried about what would happen to her if I didn't agree to her going back. I think she'd've gone potty. She was nearly driving me potty, I can tell you. At least she'll be happy now, doing what she wants to do.'

'We can't all do just what we want to do in this life,' said Martha grimly. 'You know that as well as anyone does, our Hetty.' She smiled sympathetically at her daughter. 'And I do understand what you're doing and why you're doing it. I just think it's too much for you, that's all.'

'I'm all right, Mam,' Hetty insisted. 'I've got those two lasses from Blackburn helping out for the season, and I can't say that Zachary is much trouble. He's in a good mood, for once, now that he's finally got engaged to Ivy. But I hardly ever see him – he's always out. And it'll be one less now our Nancy's gone. She was supposed to be helping, but I must admit that she's done precious little lately.'

'Well, here's somebody who's going to help.' Martha nodded decidedly. 'I've made up my mind, Hetty. I've been thinking about it for a while… I'm going to stay and have some of that meat and potato pie, but before that I'm going to help to get it ready. And not just today; I'm going to come in every day and do whatever wants doing.' She took off her black coat now and reached for the flowered cross-over apron that was hanging on the back door. She put her arms into it and fastened it determinedly. 'So there you are and I want no arguments neither.'

'I shan't argue, Mam,' said Hetty quietly, knowing that it was no use to do so. It was, in fact, what she had been hoping her mother would say, but she hadn't liked to suggest it. Martha was, after all, supposed to be retired, although she had been helping her daughter out

437

now and again when she was particularly busy. 'Thank you very much. I'm very grateful.' Hetty could feel some of her burden lifting already. In spite of her protestations she had been worried as to how she would manage. 'What about George, though?' she asked. 'Won't he mind? I thought the idea was that you were going to go out more, the pair of you, now he's retired.'

Martha chuckled. 'I'm lucky if I can get him off that there bowling green. That's where he is today – there's a tournament on so I'll not see hide nor hair of him till tonight. No, he'll be only too relieved that I've got summat proper to do again. It'll be grand to get back into harness. Now ... those apples want peeling, I suppose? Apple Charlotte, is it, for pudding? And you'll want this crust making for t'pie.' Martha rolled up her sleeves. 'Come on, lass. Let's get stuck in.'

A couple of miles away Martha's eldest grand-daughter was also getting 'stuck in' to the task of peeling apples in readiness for the fruit pies to be served in the restaurant at lunchtime. It was really a job for one of the kitchen girls, and so they often reminded Mrs Duncan. She was a wonderful person to work for – everybody said so – and there was nothing that she wouldn't turn her hand to, to help out in an emergency and to ensure that everything was running smoothly.

As for Sarah, she had never been happier, both at work and at home. One very slight shadow marring her happiness was that Alex was away at the moment, in Scotland. She had seen the look of consternation cross his face as he opened the

438

letter at the breakfast table a few days ago.

'It's my uncle,' he had told her. 'You know, Uncle Andrew in Edinburgh. He's ... he's died, my dear. Och, I've been expecting it,' he went on, at Sarah's gasp of sympathy. 'You remember ... I was up there earlier this year, sorting out his affairs.'

'Yes, of course I remember,' said Sarah, recalling that Alex had been away for a few days in March, summoned by a sudden letter from his uncle's solicitor. 'So ... you'll have to go and make the funeral arrangements?'

'Something like that.' Alex nodded distractedly. 'I daresay most of it will be taken care of, but I'll have to be there. He was my mother's brother, and as far as I know I'm the only close relative. There's no money though. Well, very little.' He had smiled ruefully. 'I told you he was an old recluse. He's leaving it nearly all to charity, or so he warned me.'

'So what does it matter?' Sarah said. 'We don't need any more money, do we, darling? We're very happy just as we are, aren't we?'

'Blissfully happy, my darling.' Alex's grey eyes as he smiled at her had seemed to Sarah to be more loving than ever.

'But I'm sorry about your uncle,' she went on. 'Poor old man. He seems to have been such a lonely old soul. Let me come with you, Alex.'

'No!' His over-quick response startled her. Then, 'No ... best not to, darling,' he said, more calmly, seeing her look of surprise. 'You never knew him, and it'll all be rather depressing. Besides, you've the business to see to, haven't you? And I'll be back just as soon as I can manage it, you can be sure of that. I shall miss you too much, my darling, to stay away for long.'

His ardent kiss as he departed for the surgery that morning affirmed his words; but Sarah found herself thinking, after he had gone, that they had had to manage without her at the café when she had been away on her honeymoon last October. And the two of them were hoping to have a holiday in September when the seasonal rush was over; the staff at the Gynn Restaurant would no doubt manage perfectly well then, without their commander-in-chief.

She was missing Alex so much, Sarah thought now, as she sliced the apples and placed them on top of the pastry. He had been gone for two days, only two days but the place seemed so lonely without him. She wondered, as she frequently did, how she had ever existed before she met Alex... But that was all that she had been doing before, just existing. Now she was living, really and truly living life to the full, now that she had Alex to share it with her. And he would be back with her tomorrow. Only one more day to wait, and their reunion would be all the more rapturous because they had been apart. A glowing smile lit up Sarah's face at the thought of it.

Chapter 20

Zachary leaned against the promenade railings, gazing out at the grey sea. Grey sea, grey sky, and a grey murkiness inside his mind, a feeling of despondency that he couldn't shake off. He was standing in almost the selfsame spot, when he came to think of it, where he had stood with Sarah, that night when he had told her that it was all over between them. And how he had cursed himself since for being such a damned fool as to send packing a lovely girl like his cousin. Especially now, when he had to watch her with that doctor chap, smiling up at him with those big trusting eyes, and him, Alex Duncan, caring for her so attentively.

'What a lovely couple they make.' 'Aren't they happy together?' 'That's a marriage made in heaven if ever there was one.' These were the sort of fatuous remarks Zachary had to listen to from his, and Sarah's, relations. And he had to admit that it seemed to be true. Sarah and Alex had been married for – how long was it? – nearly eighteen months now, and they always looked blissfully happy, as though they couldn't bear to be apart for even a minute. And to think that she had acted so hurt when Zachary had told her that there wasn't much point in them going on seeing one another. Well, she hadn't been upset for long, that's all he could say; she had soon forgotten all about him.

Zachary was forced to remind himself that he, too, had been quite quick in replacing Sarah in his affections. He had met Ivy Rathbone later that year ... and what a merry dance that one had been leading him ever since. She, more so than Sarah, was the cause of his present dejection. More than two years it was – almost two and a half – since he had first taken her out, and she was still shilly-shallying around, refusing to give him a definite answer as to when she would marry him. He reached in his pocket for his packet of Wills Woodbines, then, cupping his hand round the flame to protect it from the slight sea breeze, he lit a cigarette. He inhaled deeply, then blew out a ring of smoke, watching it evaporate in the still air. Still for Blackpool, that was; there was only the gentlest breath of wind from the sea on this March afternoon, a month usually noted for high tides and raging winds. It could, however, just be the still before the storm. It wasn't often that many days passed before the coast was again battered by equinoctial gales. He took a few more deep puffs, then tapped the long column of ash against the green-painted railing. That was better; there was nothing like a fag to calm you down, and he certainly needed something with that blasted girl playing fast and loose with him.

No ... Zachary knew he must be fair. He was the one that was playing fast and loose. It wasn't likely that Ivy was playing around with other fellows, whereas he ... well, he'd had a few girls while Ivy was away on this singing and dancing

442

lark. But what the hell was a chap supposed to do? He wasn't a monk, for God's sake, and Ivy, even when she was around, wouldn't give him everything he wanted. She was wearing his engagement ring, however, which he supposed was a step in the right direction. They had been engaged since last summer, just before Ivy started the season at Morecambe. It was only a small ring, a tiny solitaire diamond, not like that huge thing that Alex Duncan had bought for Sarah, but it was all that he could afford. At least it was a promise that she would marry him ... sometime. It was always 'sometime' with Ivy. 'Let's wait until the pantomime season is over,' or, 'Sid's managed to get us a fortnight in Manchester ... or Leeds ... or Birmingham.' Now it was, 'We'll think about it when I've finished the Blackpool season.' For that was one ray of hope in a dismal scene. Sid's company had managed to get a booking for the North Pier in Blackpool for the summer season of 1922, the place where they had been appearing when Zachary first met Ivy; but then, of course, they hadn't been Sid's company, just a group of people who generally appeared on the same bill. They would be staying at Sunnyside again, all the lot of them, so maybe when he got Ivy on his home ground he would be able to make her see reason.

Zachary was anxious to be married. He had never dreamed, at one time, that he would ever feel like this, but now he couldn't wait to get away from that blasted boarding house. He knew only too well that he could leave if he wanted to. He could get digs somewhere or even a one-room flat; there were plenty to let in Blackpool, especially out of season. But if he did that, Zachary knew that it might be a question of jumping out of the frying pan into the fire. A landlady might not see to his needs as well as his mother did – for all her faults; and if he took a flat, well, he'd have to get his own meals then, wouldn't he? Blow that for a game, thought Zachary. Cooking and all that nonsense was no job for a man. No, it would be far better if he could persuade Ivy to name the day, then they could set up home together. She could give up all this stage nonsense and settle down and look after him. Just like Sarah was looking after that Alex fellow.

Zachary was fed up to the back teeth of the boarding house and it was mainly because of the baby, young Joseph. He would never have believed that a kid could cause so much upheaval or take up so much of his mother's time and attention. Everywhere you looked there were signs of the child's predominance; nappies drying in front of the fire, bottles standing on the mantelpiece and sideboard, toy cars and teddy bears cluttering up the chair where he wanted to sit, and his mother dashing about like somebody demented, making sure that 'our little Joseph' had everything he wanted. Anybody 'ud think she was his mother and not his grandmother, thought Zachary, and indeed, many people thought that she was. Nancy had opted out of her responsibilities very nicely, swanning off with Sid's touring company at the first chance she got;

and on the rare occasions when she came home she took very little notice of the child, or he of her. His mother though – she was besotted with the kid. It was Zachary's opinion that she was making a rod for her own back; it couldn't do any good to spoil a child in the way that his mother was spoiling young Joseph.

He was a bonny little lad, though, there was no doubt about that. He had inherited Nancy's – and Hetty's – auburn hair, and his big blue eyes – a legacy from his father, Zachary supposed – seemed to have a very knowing look when he fixed them upon you.

'That one's been on earth before,' he had heard his Grandma Makepeace say. Zachary didn't think that she really meant that; it would, after all, be contrary to all her Methodist indoctrination to believe that the child could have lived before in a previous existence. What she meant was that he had a very mature look about him for so young an infant; he certainly seemed to understand what everyone said and to take an interest in all that was going on around him. And little Joseph already had his favourites among his doting relations. He and Hetty, of course, were inseparable, forever trotting around the house together hand in hand, now that he had started to walk.

'At eleven months, would you believe?' Hetty boasted to everyone. 'He's going to be a sharp one and no mistake is this little lad.'

Grandma Makepeace seemed to idolise him too, always dangling him on her knee and singing daft songs to him. Whereas he, Zachary, was completely left out of all this infant adoration that was going on at Sunnyside. The child, after fixing him with his solemn blue gaze, would then completely ignore him. And as far as Zachary was concerned the lack of interest was mutual. He had very little time for Joseph, just as Joseph had all too clearly shown him that he had very little time for his uncle.

Be hanged to the lot of them, thought Zachary moodily, puffing away at his cigarette and staring out at the grey landscape. Why should I care? I don't see all that much of 'em, thank goodness, and I shall see even less of 'em before long if I have my way... He had taken to working overtime on the railway whenever he could; and last week, on one of his visits to the Imperial Cinema, he had struck up an acquaintance with a pretty little usherette who worked there. He had already taken her for a drink, and then on to the lower promenade, where she had proved herself to be very accommodating – far more so than Ivy had ever been. He was seeing her again tonight, after the second house finished. He was on early shift tomorrow and should really be getting his sleep, but Zachary hadn't had so much of that just lately. For sleep only brought bad dreams, or at least the fear of them. There had been a recurrence of his nightmares recently ... and that was all his mother's fault, Zachary thought savagely now, grinding the stub of his cigarette against the railing then throwing it out to sea. He lit another one, thinking of that incident last December which had caused it all to start up again. Damn her to hell and back, her and her blasted 'pros'.

'Zachary,' she had said, all apologetic-like, 'I'm going to have to ask you to move up to the attic again, just for a couple of weeks. I've got quite a lot of theatre folk coming in just before Christmas. They're all on at the Palace Varieties and I've been very lucky to get them.' Lucky for some, Zachary had thought, looking at his mother's face, already pink-cheeked with excitement at the thought of it all. He had been enjoying the comparative luxury of his first-floor room, but he might have known that it wouldn't be for long. It was always a question of, 'You don't mind, do you, Zachary?' when someone more important than he was came along.

That was just what his mother had said then. 'You don't mind, do you, Zachary? I can't very well ask them to sleep in the attic, can I?' Zachary recalled that Ivy and her cronies had slept in the attic when they had stayed at Sunnyside, though in a much larger room than the one he was being asked to occupy. If it hadn't been for that attic room he might never have got friendly with Ivy. But he didn't mention this now; he just shrugged and said, 'Suits me. I'll move my stuff out tonight.' There was no point in arguing. It wasn't the first time and it certainly wouldn't be the last that Zachary would have to play second fiddle to a bunch of pros.

But he had been unprepared for the person who was occupying his room. He had gone back to the first floor, realising that he had left his best pair of boots at the back of the wardrobe, and there had been his mother, as bold as brass,

447

holding open the door and ushering the fellow into the room – his room, for God's sake! She had looked a little startled on seeing him, as well she might, and her introduction had been somewhat hesitant. 'Oh er, Zachary, this is the gentleman who's in your ... who's going to be in this room. Mr Muller, this is my son, Zachary.'

Zachary had stared in disbelief at the young man who was smiling at him so politely; at his short blond hair and blue eyes, his stiff bull-neck and squarish shoulders, and when he saw him give a brief nod of greeting and click his heels together, then he was in no doubt at all. The fellow was a German, a bloody Kraut, and his mother had the audacity to let him sleep in his, Zachary's, room. Not caring how rude he might seem, Zachary had pushed past him into the room, grabbed his boots, and without speaking to either of them, had fled up the stairs back to the attic. His mother's voice, hushed but still audible, had followed him.

'Mr Muller, I must apologise. My son ... he was ... the war...'

And the German's guttural reply: 'I understand, Mrs Gregson. My people ... we are used to it. There are memories, always the memories...'

Too damned right there are, Zachary had thought. He had believed that he was free from the ghastly memories, but that night, after the inevitable row with his mother, the horrific dreams had started again.

'Zachary, how could you?' she had chided him. 'I didn't know where to put myself, I was that embarrassed. And Mr Muller is such a nice polite young man.'

'He's a German, Mam,' Zachary retorted. 'A bloody German. How d'you expect me to feel, for heaven's sake? I gave two years of my life, fighting such as him.'

'And your father gave his life,' Hetty replied quietly. Zachary had no answer to that, not even a reminder that Albert Gregson was not his father. He just scowled and stared down at the carpet while his mother went on in a reasonable voice, too reasonable to Zachary's thinking: 'We can't live in the past. We've got to go on and build some kind of a future. Don't you think that I remember Albert every day of my life and wish to God that he was still here? But he isn't, and being rude to a nice young man won't bring him back. Johann Muller can't help being a German.'

'No, but you can help inviting him into our house,' Zachary stormed. 'I'm fed up with it, I can tell you, Mam. My home's not my own any more. First it was our Nancy's kid ruling the roost. You've never had time for anybody since he came along. And now it's damned Germans cluttering up the place.'

'If you don't like it you know what you can do,' his mother replied, much more calmly than she would have done at one time. There had been a time when she would have moved heaven and earth to make sure that all was well with Zachary. 'You can find yourself some lodgings, like you're always telling me you'll do.' And she had walked away into the kitchen without another word.

That night the nightmare had returned; the mud, the rats, the faces of his dead comrades and, punctuating it all, the smiling face of the blond-haired, blue-eyed German who was occupying his room. The dreams that followed on subsequent nights were not quite as bad as that first time; but Zachary found himself spending less and less time in his bed and more and more working or going out on the town in an endeavour to forget. And now he knew that the lack of sleep was inevitably taking its toll. Maybe that was why he was so dispirited, why all his problems seemed to be crowding in upon him – simply because he was tired. He enumerated them now in his mind. His jealousy of Alex Duncan; his frustration with Ivy – and the guilt, too, which came in its wake, because he knew he was not being true to her; his deteriorating relationship with his mother – since that episode with the German it had gone from bad to worse. And there was never anyone to talk to. Polly, the usherette, was only good for a laugh and for a bit of 'you know what'. But Ivy would be here again in another couple of months, when the Blackpool season started. Zachary tried to comfort himself with that thought, and at the same time decided to pay a second visit to the doctor. Maybe another bottle of that sleeping draught would help to ease his muddled mind.

Zachary stared again at the foam-capped waves pounding against the sea wall, then at the distant horizon, grey sea meeting grey sky in an almost indiscernible line. There was a limitless quality to the ocean which could, if you let it, help to put your own problems into perspective.

It was at that moment that Zachary became

aware of someone staring at him. He turned his head and found himself looking into the dark eyes of a tall, shabbily dressed, black-haired woman. She was gazing at him with a look of recognition in her eyes, although he was sure that he had never seen her before. Her stare was hypnotic and he found that he couldn't look away. She moved a few steps nearer to him, a smile lighting up her angular features.

'Reuben...' she breathed, putting her hand on his arm.

It was more than twenty years since Drusilla Murray, formerly Loveday, had lived in Blackpool. She had always promised herself that one day she would return, but until now the time had not been ripe. At first, of course, after that horrific incident with her cousin, she had not wanted to go near the place, not ever again. All she had wanted was to put as much distance as possible between herself and that little cottage on Marton Moss, and the sight of her cousin, her beloved Reuben, lying dead on the floor, his sightless eyes staring up at her. It hadn't been her fault, not her fault at all that he had tripped over the hearthrug and cracked his head against the steel fender. They had quarrelled bitterly, angrily ... but that had been the fault of that scheming, treacherous Hetty, the young minx who had stolen her Reuben away from her...

...And given him a child. That had hurt Drusilla, right down to the depths of her soul she had felt that hurt, and she had determined that one day she would get even with the girl whom she had come to detest with every fibre of her being. Even when, many years later, Drusilla had given birth to her own child, the anguish inside her had not been entirely eased. He had been a comfort and a blessing, of course, her dear little Matthew. She had hardly been able to believe, at times, that this had happened to her at last. And then for him to be taken from her so cruelly, all because of the carelessness of an incompetent doctor, it had been almost too much for her to bear; for a time she had nearly gone out of her mind. She had certainly lost her faith in God, or O' Del, as the gipsies called him. It was a long time since Drusilla had believed in a God of any kind.

She had never lost her bitterness against the woman whom she believed had been the start of all her troubles. Hetty Turnbull, she had been called, all those years ago when she had paid a visit to Drusilla's fortune-telling booth. 'Henrietta', Reuben had called her, dwelling on her name with such tenderness in his tone. Henrietta … Turnbull. Never had Drusilla been able to think of the girl as a Loveday. She was not worthy of the name; she had never been worthy of such a fine young man as Reuben Loveday had been.

Drusilla had fled back to the gipsy encampment on that fateful day in the spring of 1898, flung a few belongings into a bag and then had taken to her heels and run. She hadn't known where she was going, nor had she cared very much; she had just known that she had to get as far away from Blackpool as possible, away from the police who would pounce on her and throw her into prison and then hang her, for causing the death of her cousin. Fruitless it would be to say that it hadn't been her fault; she had been there, hadn't she? And he had died and they would put the blame on her. Much as she had loved her cousin and, for a brief time, had felt that she wanted to die herself, the urge for self-preservation had been strong in Drusilla. And so she had disappeared, never knowing the outcome of the inquest, never sought after or even missed very much by the gipsy community, for Drusilla had never been popular.

After living rough for a week or so, heading northwards, she had fallen in with another group of gipsies near the town of Appleby in Westmorland. There had been few questions asked; members of the tribe were invariably made welcome and so she had thrown in her lot with them. In 1908, she had met Jock Murray. Jock had not been a gipsy, but a master carpenter with his own small business. Drusilla was surprised to find herself attracted to such an unlikely person. She had been old for marriage, thirty-four, and Jock, at thirty-eight, a seemingly confirmed bachelor. But he had fallen in love with the handsome and bewitching young woman who had told his fortune. He had only been coerced into the fortune-telling booth for a lark, but once in there had lost his heart and – so his friends had thought – his reason.

His courtship of Drusilla, amongst the wooded valleys of the River Tweed, where the gipsies had set up camp for the summer, was relentless. And at last she had said yes, seeing in this man something she had never thought she would want – the means of a settled existence, a respite from the unpredictable, insecure life she had been living for the last ten years or so. For, since leaving Blackpool, Drusilla had never really felt that she 'belonged'. She had adjusted as well as she could – all Romanies were well-used to settling into new surroundings – but she had missed Reuben with an intensity that frightened her. And she had missed her other relatives, too, more than she had imagined she would; and more, it seemed, than they had missed her, for they had never tried to seek her out … to her relief, but also to her dismay. But now that she had met Jock, she was wanted, and it was good to be wanted, to be desired.

She married Jock Murray in the autumn of that year in a simple service at the church in Melrose. There was to be no 'jumping over the brush' for Jock. His Presbyterian principles were firm and he wanted to be sure that this young woman was really and truly wedded to him.

They were both overjoyed when, in the autumn of the following year, their son was born, and they called him Matthew. He was an appealing little lad who had inherited his father's sandy hair and blue eyes, rather than his mother's swarthy looks. Drusilla felt maternal instincts that she had never known she possessed swelling inside her and she had loved this little child as she had never loved anyone in her life before … save one.

Young Matthew was, however, the cause of the first serious disagreements between husband and wife. Jock Murray became impatient at Drusilla's

insistence on treating the boy's infant ailments –
feverishness, sickness, running nose and the like
– with old gipsy remedies; the herbs and plants
and lotions that had been used by her family for
generations and, so Drusilla averred, never been
found wanting.

It was in the month of January, 1914, when
Matthew was four years old, that he was taken ill
with what seemed to be a common cold. Jock was
working away for a few days, as he occasionally
did, on a joinery job at Hawick, some fifteen
miles distant. The weather was bad with blizzards
and high snow-drifts, and rather than make the
journey home through the treacherous country
roads, Jock had stayed for a few nights with some
cousins who lived in the town. When he did
eventually return home, four days later, it was to
find his son ill in bed with what was obviously a
high temperature. He stormed off into the
deepening twilight and returned with the local
doctor.

But, alas, it was too late. Matthew died the next
morning; he had actually drawn his last breath
whilst the doctor was there, paying his promised
visit. And for that Drusilla had never forgiven
him. She had pushed aside in her mind the fact
that she didn't believe in doctors anyway; what
use was a doctor, she asked herself, if he couldn't
prevent a young child from dying? She had heard
the mutterings between the doctor and her
husband.

'Too late...'

'I wasna here, you understand...'

'If I'd been called sooner...'

And the hatred had festered deep inside her. There had to be someone to take the blame, and it wasn't going to be her, the child's mother, who had loved him to distraction. She had never forgiven that doctor for failing to save her son. His name was Dr Alexander Duncan.

Things were never the same after that between Drusilla and Jock. For a while she retreated within herself, seeing no one, going nowhere, and when in August that year war was declared and Jock went off to join the Army she was relieved to see him go. Like so many thousands more, he had not returned.

It was then that memories from the past – not the recent past, but the past of more than twenty years ago – started to haunt Drusilla. They had always been there at the back of her mind, but now they were predominant. She knew that she had to return to Blackpool, to where it had all happened. She wasn't sure why, but she felt compelled to seek out Henrietta, to discover what had happened to the woman, to wreak, if possible, some sort of revenge…

She had left her little home in Melrose; it would still be there for her when she wanted to return, if ever, and had made the train journey south to Blackpool. She had found a one-room flat in a street off Dickson Road, for she had an idea that it was somewhere in that area that Hetty's mother had had her boarding house, although it was doubtful that she would still be there … or Hetty either, but Drusilla was determined to find out. It hadn't been difficult to find a job, two jobs, in fact, which would provide her with the money she needed for her food and lodgings. One was with a firm of solicitors, two hours' cleaning each morning, and the other was at a café near Talbot Square, washing up after the dinnertime rush.

She was on her way there, the second week of her stay in Blackpool, when she caught sight of a familiar figure leaning against the promenade railings. She had crossed the tramtrack to walk on the sea side of the prom as she was half an hour early, and what a stroke of luck it had been that she had done so, or she might never have seen him.

Drusilla stopped in her tracks and gave a gasp of astonishment. *Reuben...!* It couldn't be, and yet it was. She was sure it was... The same black wavy hair, curling untidily over his coat collar; he was bare-headed as Reuben so often used to be. The same profile, the long patrician nose, the swarthy skin. And, when he turned to glance in her direction, as though suddenly aware of her scrutiny, the same deep brown eyes, but looking at her with no sense of recognition. It was him though. It was her Reuben, come back to her after all this time.

She took a few steps towards him and laid her hand on his arm. 'Reuben...' she breathed.

Chapter 21

'I'm sorry,' said Zachary. 'I think you've made a mistake. I'm not–'

'You're not Reuben?' The woman was looking at him strangely, making shivers run up and down his spine. 'What's your name, then?' she asked abruptly, letting go of his arm, but still fixing him with those dark, fathomless eyes.

'I'm called Zachary,' he faltered. 'Zachary Gregson.'

'Zachary.' The woman's eyes left his for a moment, seeming to go out of focus as she stared at a point behind him. 'Yes … I'm sure that was the chavi's name. Zachary.'

Chavi… Something stirred in the recesses of Zachary's mind. That was an old gipsy word, meaning child, one that he had heard long, long ago. And this woman, from her appearance, was surely a gipsy. You couldn't tell from her clothing; she was dressed conservatively enough, though rather shabbily, with her drooping black coat with the shaggy imitation-fur collar and round felt hat. But that didn't entirely cover her black hair, streaked here and there with silver, that strayed over her brow and round the collar of her coat; and there was no mistaking her olive skin and her black eyes; eyes which were very like his own, thought Zachary now, as realisation began to dawn. He had probably been aware, subconsciously, from the moment she uttered the name, that this person was connected with his gipsy father, but only now did the full comprehension take hold of him. She had mistaken him for his father. He had sometimes been told how much he resembled him, chiefly by his mother, but there were few now who would remember Reuben Loveday.

'My father was called Reuben,' he said now, 'but I never knew him. He died a long time ago, when I was only a baby. Are you– Did you know him?'

A smile lit up the woman's lean features, making her look almost attractive. Zachary could see that, in her time, she must have been handsome, but now her face was deeply scored with lines, ravaged by the years which he guessed had not been kind to her. Her eyes had taken on a look of normality now, Zachary was relieved to see. It was the strangeness in them, a farseeing look yet with a hint of wildness, that had been unnerving him. 'Yes, I knew Reuben,' she said softly, nodding all the while. 'Reuben Loveday. He was my cousin. I'm Drusilla Loveday.'

Her eyes stared past him again, unseeingly for a moment, then she looked back at him. 'I'm Drusilla Murray now, have been for fourteen years or so, but I'll always be Drusilla Loveday in my mind. So you're Zachary...' She scrutinised him keenly. 'Well, well, well. Just fancy meeting up with you again, after all these years. I used to come and see you when you were only a tiny chavi, in your little house on Marton Moss. You and Reuben ... and your mother.'

459

The woman's eyes narrowed, though only very slightly, as she spoke the last two words, but Zachary noticed it. 'You knew my mother, then?' he asked, wondering why he had never heard tell of this cousin of his father's, a sort of aunt to him, he supposed, who seemed to know so much about them all.

'Yes, I knew Henrietta,' said the woman. 'Of course I knew her. She came to my booth to have her fortune told ... and then she married Reuben. I was at their wedding, then I was there soon after you were born. I told you, I used to come and see you ... but you don't remember me, hmmm?'

'No, I'm sorry I don't,' confessed Zachary.

'No, you wouldn't. How could you? You were only a little mite when ... the last time I saw them.'

'I haven't heard my mother speak of you,' said Zachary, growing more and more puzzled. There was a mystery here, something he didn't understand. 'Did you lose touch with them? You must have done if you haven't seen them since I was a baby. Didn't you know my father was dead?'

'Oh yes ... I knew that Reuben had died.'

'But when you saw me, you thought that I was...'

Drusilla nodded, quite sanely. 'Memory can play tricks at times. Of course I knew you couldn't be him but when I saw you standing there it took me back more than twenty years. You're very like him, you know ... Zachary. The spitting image of him.'

'So I've been told. My mother's often said that.'

Zachary looked curiously at his new acquaintance. He was determined to get to the bottom of this conundrum. Where had the woman been all these years? Why had he never heard of her? And did she live here now? 'Did you live in Blackpool then, at that time?' he asked.

'Yes, I lived at the camp-site at Squire's Gate,' said the woman. 'They've gone and built a big fairground there now, I see.' Zachary nodded. That figured. His mother had told him how his father had used to live there, before they got married.

'Then I moved away, soon after Reuben died.' Drusilla's voice was guarded now and Zachary sensed a flicker of unease, just for a second or two, in her dark eyes. He was beginning to guess that his father had meant a lot to this woman; possibly she hadn't wanted to stay in the town where she had known him, where memories were strong. But he was only surmising. He carried on listening to her story, but he had an idea that she was only telling him the barest facts.

He learned that she had lived in the Scottish lowlands for several years, married to a man who had not been a gipsy. Now that he had died she had decided to return to her old haunts. She had always liked Blackpool, she said wistfully.

'And there's nothing to keep me up in Scotland,' she told Zachary. 'Not now. I lost my son as well, you see. He was only four, my Matthew.'

'You mean that he … he…?'

'Aye, he died, poor little lad. It's a long time ago now, must be eight years or so, but I still think of him. I always will, I know that, but there're no memories of him down here, not in Blackpool. That's why I came. One of the reasons, anyway.'

'Oh dear. That's very sad. It must have been dreadful for you.' Zachary looked down, shuffling his feet and not wanting to look the woman in the face. He was unused to listening to tales of woe and not very skilled in the art of proffering sympathy. He knew that his was certainly not a shoulder to cry on. Expressions of grief only served to embarrass him.

But the woman seemed to have pulled herself together. 'Aye, it was dreadful,' she said. 'I thought I'd die myself, for a time. But life goes on, lad. It has to.' She looked at him keenly again. 'You're so like him.'

Zachary shook his head, a trifle impatiently. 'So you're down in Blackpool for a holiday, are you?' he asked.

'No, not exactly. I'm working – I've got a couple of cleaning jobs. I've got to keep the wolf from the door. I might stay ... or I might not. I don't know. It just ... depends.'

She didn't say on what, and Zachary noticed an enigmatic little smile and a trace of malice in her eyes. He felt uneasy, not for the first time since he had met Drusilla Murray. 'So you're living here?' he prompted. 'In digs?'

She told him that she had a room on Banks Street. 'That's not far from where you live, is it?' She gave him an enquiring glance. 'At least, I think your mother used to live in this area, didn't she, before she was married. It's all a long time ago, of course.'

'A long time, yes, but she's still in the same

place,' said Zachary. 'Well, as near as makes no difference. I daresay when you knew her she would be living at Welcome Rest – that was my gran's place, across the road. My mother runs Sunnyside now, at the top of Lord Street, near North Station. It belonged to my other grandma, then my mam and dad took it over, and now that Dad's gone...'

'Your dad?' Drusilla Murray looked puzzled.

'My stepfather,' Zachary explained. 'Albert Gregson. I said I was called Gregson, didn't I? Albert was killed at Ypres.'

'Your mother ... she got married again then?'

'Yes, when I was about three, I think. I've got two sisters.'

Drusilla's eyes again took on that faraway, mysterious look that unnerved Zachary so much. 'But of course. I told her she would. A fair young man ... I told her.'

'Pardon?' Zachary gave a frown.

'Your stepfather – was he a fair young man?' Drusilla's eyes were boring into him.

'Fair hair, you mean? Yes, I suppose so. He had fairish hair. Why?'

'Your mother came to see me and I told her fortune. I said she'd marry a fair young man ... but that there'd be a lot of trouble before that. And I was right, you see. Drusilla Loveday was always right.'

'You were a fortune-teller?'

'I was indeed, lad. As well-known in my own small way as old Sarah Boswell. I used to set up my booth on the sands near South Pier – Central Pier, I believe they're calling it now.'

'On the Golden Mile, you mean?'

'No, on the sands, lad. I told you.' Drusilla frowned, a little impatiently. 'We were all on the sands in those days – fortune-tellers, oyster-sellers, sideshows, all the lot of 'em – till the Corporation got uppity and moved us all off. Anyway, your mother, Henrietta, came to see me. That was how I first met her. She was with her sister – Grace, wasn't that her name?'

'My Aunt Grace – yes, that's right,' said Zachary, startled that this woman seemed to know so much about them all.

'A nice young thing she was. A bit shy, not much like her sister.' Again Drusilla's eyes narrowed and she was silent for a moment. Then, 'What about Grace?' she asked. 'She's still in Blackpool, is she?'

'Yes, Aunt Grace is still here.' Zachary smiled. 'She did very well for herself, my aunt. She married Edwin Donnelly – you know, the owner of the big store in Bank Hey Street. You must have seen it.'

'Donnelly's? Yes, of course I have.' Drusilla made a *moue* with her mouth as though impressed. 'And he's Grace's husband? Well, well, well, just fancy that.'

'They've got a daughter, Sarah,' Zachary went on. He still felt compelled to say her name at times. He knew that he might be rubbing salt into the wound by so doing, but he liked to speak of her. 'My cousin … she has a café at Gynn Square. "Sarah's Café", they call it. My sister works for her.' He didn't mention Alex Duncan. He didn't want to talk about him. It was none of this woman's business anyway. Zachary wasn't altogether sure why he had told her as much as he had, except that she was so compelling; she seemed to be drawing the information out of him in spite of himself.

'Well, well, well,' she said again. 'You live and learn, you do indeed. It's been lovely talking to you … Zachary. I can't get over meeting you like this. It's Fate, that's what it is. I've always been a great believer in Fate. But I'll have to get a move on or I'll be late for my job. I mustn't risk getting the sack.' She put a hand on his arm. 'I'll see you again, I daresay, now we're living so near to one another.'

'Maybe. Yes … perhaps you will.' Zachary felt a chill run through him, though he wasn't sure why. She was just a harmless old woman, surely. A lonely old woman who had been glad of a chat. 'I'll tell my mother I've seen you, shall I?' But as soon as he said the words he felt that this would not be a good idea, and Drusilla Murray seemed to be of the same opinion.

'No, I shouldn't do that, lad,' she said. 'Henrietta and I … we didn't get on to well. Best to leave things as they are. She can get on with her life, and I'll get on with mine.'

'But you might bump into her, living so near.'

'I might, lad. I might, indeed,' Drusilla answered. 'But we'll let Fate decide that for us, shall we?' She put a finger to her lips. 'No … best to keep quiet, eh? Our little secret. But I'm glad to have met you. Goodbye, for now … Zachary.'

'Goodbye.' Zachary watched as she turned and walked away, and he kept on watching as her tall

465

dark figure crossed the tramtrack and made its way towards Talbot Square. What an extraordinary meeting that had been ... and what an odd, old woman. Zachary knew that he shouldn't really be thinking of her as old. She was possibly a year or two older than his mother, but even so, she was probably not yet fifty. She seemed old, though; her face was lined, her eyes age-old with the wisdom and sorrow that the years had brought to her. Obviously she had not had an easy life and Zachary felt sorry for her; an unusual feeling for him, but he also knew, instinctively, that he didn't like her.

He knew, too, that he ought to tell his mother of this meeting, despite Drusilla's protestations that he mustn't. He should warn her ... but warn her of what? he asked himself. He was being fanciful. Drusilla Murray was just a harmless, middle-aged woman, albeit a strange one. Zachary wouldn't easily forget that wildness that he had seen, once or twice, come into her eyes – and it might be better, as she said, to leave things to chance. After all, why should he tell his mother anything? He stubbed yet another cigarette out against the promenade railing, the resentful thoughts again taking pre-eminence in his mind. It wasn't often that he talked with his mother these days; she was always too busy, wrapped up in her blessed pros and in that blooming kid, Joseph. Well, if that was the way she wanted it, why should he bother to confide in her? Let her get on with her life, he thought bitterly, echoing in his mind the words that Drusilla had uttered, and he would get on with his own.

Drusilla hovered near the top of the back entry on the opposite side of the road from Sunnyside. It was some fifty yards distant, but she could see quite clearly from here without being visible herself. She was used to living and moving by stealth and she had no fear of Henrietta espying her. The woman was blissfully unaware of her presence, though she had been watching her for several weeks now. It was amazing how easy it had been to dog Henrietta's movements, once she had found out the whereabouts of the boarding house, thanks to that fortuitous meeting with the lad.

Drusilla had had a shock at her first sight of her enemy, for that was how she thought of her; an enemy to be vanquished. Surely that fat blowsy woman emerging from the door of the Lord Street boarding house couldn't be Hetty? Henrietta, the 'Girl with the Sparkling Eyes'; that was how she had been billed when she had sung at that tavern on the central promenade; when Reuben had watched and been captivated by her, witless young fool that he was. No one would fall for her now, that was certain, Drusilla thought gleefully, watching the portly figure almost waddle along the street, her shopping basket over her arm, her feet – obviously giving her some trouble, to judge by her halting gait – encased in heavy black lace-up shoes, more suited to a woman of sixty. Drusilla had recognised her, though. There was no mistaking that springing auburn hair, now liberally sprinkled with grey, that refused to be confined by her close-fitting hat, nor her fresh-complexioned face. Drusilla had to admit that the woman was still bonny, though she guessed that her green eyes, once her most appealing feature, would by now have lost some of their sparkle. But she was just an ordinary middle-aged woman, such as one would pass in the street without noticing, and Drusilla was glad, so very glad, that the passing years had taken away her rival's allure.

But she had had an even greater shock the next time she set eyes on Hetty, for this time the woman was pushing a pram. This had been an accident sighting and Drusilla, spying her adversary on the other side of Dickson Road, had quickly turned away, ostensibly to look at a display of souvenirs in a shop window. Hetty had stopped at a grocer's shop, left the pram by the doorway, and gone inside. Very daringly Drusilla crossed the road and, as nonchalantly as she could, walked past the grocer's shop. Hetty stood at the counter; Drusilla could make out her stout figure in the shadows, her back turned to the door. Drusilla paused by the perambulator, one eye still on Hetty – it was more than likely she would suddenly turn round – and took a look at the child.

What she saw made her give an involuntary gasp of astonishment. The child sitting up in the pram might even be her own Matthew come back to her, he was so much like him. Drusilla was sure that the infant was a boy; it was often difficult to tell at that age – she guessed him to be about twelve months old – but he was wearing a blue bonnet and a blue knitted jacket. The hair that protruded from the bonnet was sandy, just as Matthew's had been, and his eyes were blue with the same uncompromising stare; he was staring at Drusilla now. Then Hetty had half-turned and Drusilla had walked quickly away, very shaken and puzzled. He had a look of Matthew, yes, but then she had seen many babies since her precious boy had died who had reminded her too forcibly of him. But he also had an unmistakable look of her, of Hetty Turnbull; the same gingery hair and round face; not the eyes, though, but they might well be inherited from the father. But hadn't Zachary told her that his stepfather had been killed at Ypres? Then whose child was this? Zachary had made no mention of any child, but this one obviously belonged to Henrietta.

Drusilla had grown more vigilant then. She gave up her job at the café near Talbot Square so that she could keep a closer watch on the household at Sunnyside. The money she earned from her cleaning job at the solicitor's was sufficient for her needs, and there were things that were more important than money. Things such as revenge and retribution. There would have to be a day of reckoning for Hetty Turnbull. Drusilla wasn't sure how she would bring it about, but the woman would get her come-uppance one of these days, or her name wasn't Drusilla Loveday. She had tried once, more than twenty years ago ... and failed. And because of that her beloved Reuben had been taken from her instead. But she wouldn't fail this time. She might not be able to bring about her death. Even

Drusilla, deranged as she was becoming, could see that that might prove impossible, but she would hit her where it hurt most. And, from watching her movements, Drusilla knew that the one sure way to harm Henrietta was through the child.

Her resentment and bitterness at the hand that Fate had dealt out to her had grown as she observed the routine of the family at Sunnyside. She didn't always watch from the same place. Drusilla was cunning; she shifted her vantage points so as not to become conspicuous and she was sure that no one had noticed her. Her envy and hatred had assumed uncontrollable proportions as she had seen how tenderly and lovingly Hetty cared for this child. Why should she have a child – the fat, blowsy, good-for-nothing trollop – when all that Drusilla had ever cared about had been taken away from her? For that was what Hetty Turnbull was – a trollop, a whore. That was what she had been all those years ago when she had stolen Reuben. She had led him along and seduced him, so that he hadn't known whether he was on his head or his heels. Hadn't they had to get married because the child was coming? The child that was Zachary. And even now, it seemed she was still up to her old tricks, for there was no sign of any husband.

There was an old woman there a lot of the time, the grandma, no doubt, that Zachary had spoken of, Hetty's mother. Drusilla thought she recognised her from the time of the wedding, all those years ago. And Zachary, the lad who was the very incarnation of her darling Reuben; she sometimes saw him departing for work or returning and she gathered that he was employed on the railway. Then there was her, Henrietta, and the child. It was her custom to put him out in his pram every afternoon, weather permitting, at about two o'clock, in the tiny garden at the front of Sunnyside, no doubt for his after-dinner nap. At that time of day it was the 'sunny side' of the street, although the black hood was drawn up to keep the harmful rays from his fair complexion.

He was there on this May afternoon as Drusilla hung about in the back entry in the shadow of the high brick wall. By this time she had discovered that the child was not Henrietta's, as she had assumed, but her grandson, although many, she had been told, thought it to be Hetty's own child. She had done some surreptitious questioning at the grocer's where she knew Hetty did her shopping. Not too openly, so as to arouse suspicion, but it was amazing what you could find out by keeping your eyes and ears open. It made no difference to Drusilla that the child was, in fact, a grandchild. It was clear that Hetty doted on him and it was time now that she got what was coming to her...

Drusilla stepped out of the shadows of the back entry into Lord Street. She glanced around her, but not too furtively. She felt bold, confident that what she was doing was right. She had had these feelings of boldness quite a lot recently, when she felt that she could conquer the world, overthrow all her enemies with one fell swoop... But her vengefulness now was centred on one person, the grandmother of the little boy who was sleeping in

471

his pram across the road. Lord Street was quiet, as these North Shore streets behind the station often were at this time of day. There were quite a few visitors in the town in this second week in May, but not as many as there would be in a few weeks' time; by then the place would be bursting at the seams with them. Such visitors as there were would, in the early afternoon, be taking their ease on the beach or promenade or browsing round the town-centre shops.

Drusilla walked quickly across the road. There were a few people at the far end of the street, the Pleasant Street end, but they were too far away to see what she was doing. The iron gate of Sunnyside was open and Drusilla walked fearlessly up the path. Not a sign of life, at least none that she could see, behind the neat lace curtains; only the child asleep in his pram beneath the bay window. Drusilla let down the brake, cringing a little as it gave a squeak, then turned the high black pram around. It felt heavy and cumbersome, but she would soon get used to it; she was well-accustomed to handling a pram.

She wheeled it down the path, out of the gate and along the street. Once she had turned right into Queen Street it would be plain sailing. It was only a little way along Dickson Road to Banks Street, then she would be safely home. Home with her lovely boy who had, miraculously, been given back to her.

Zachary gave a start as he turned the corner away from North Station into Queen Street. Surely that was that peculiar old woman coming towards him, the woman he had spoken to in March who had said she was his father's cousin. Zachary had caught sight of her a couple of times since then, but not to speak to. He wasn't sure that he would want to speak to her again. One time she had been at the other side of the street, but when Zachary looked again she had vanished. And another time he was sure he had seen her loitering in a back entry near his house. Again, though, when he had got near, she had disappeared. He hadn't worried unduly and had tried to dismiss her in his mind as a bit of a barmpot. When he had talked to her he had got the impression that she was a few bricks short of a load, although a lot of the time she had spoken to him quite rationally. He had believed her story at any rate, about being related to him. The tale was too incredible to be anything but true; how else would she have known all those things about them all? But he had quickly pushed her to the back of his mind. He had other more pressing matters to think of. And he had never told his mother of the meeting.

Now, though, Zachary felt the hairs on the back of his neck begin to prickle and the sense of unease that the woman had aroused in him coming to the fore. The woman was pushing a pram ... and unless he was very much mistaken it was their Joseph's pram. What the hell was going on? He strode purposefully towards her, and as he approached her he saw that she had recognised him. He watched the expression on her face change to one of dismay, fear ... then panic. She tried to turn the pram round, to escape across the road, but Zachary was too quick for her. In a few strides he was at her side. He put his hand on the pram-handle, pulling it back from the kerb. There was a coal-cart coming, pulled by a big shire horse, but he knew she hadn't even seen it.

'What the hell d'you think you're doing with our kid?' he yelled. 'What are you playing at?' He cast a quick glance downwards. Yes, it was Joseph's pram all right. That was his woolly blanket with the bunny rabbit appliquéd on it, and he could just see the child's gingery hair emerging from the huddle of covers.

'Your mother said I could.' Zachary could tell that the woman was saying the first thing that came into her head. She was looking at him brazenly, but was obviously agitated. 'She said I could take him for a walk.'

'You're a liar!' he shouted. 'My mother wouldn't trust our Joseph with somebody she doesn't know. And why did you try to run away, eh, if my mam said it was all right? Answer me that!'

'I didn't … and she does know me. Your mother's known me for years.'

'You told me not to tell her you were here.'

'I changed my mind. I called to see her and she said–' Zachary could see that she was panicking now, groping wildly in her mind for something to say. 'She said … "Take the baby out for a walk, Drusilla. It's only right you should get to know him. He's your … your great-nephew."'

'Great nephew, my Aunt Fanny! You're a bloody liar! Our Joseph's nothing to do with you at all. He's our Nancy's kid, and she was Albert's daughter, not… You're talking a load of rubbish!'

'I'm not! I'm not! He's mine, I tell you.' Drusilla was almost screaming. 'When I saw him there, asleep in his pram, I knew it was my Matthew come back to me. And this time I'm not going to let him go.' She bent over the pram, rearranging the blankets lovingly. 'You're my little chavi, aren't you?' she cooed. 'My precious little boy come back to me.'

Zachary was really worried now. Good grief! The woman was as mad as a hatter, completely pots for rags. His impulse was to grab hold of her and push her away from the pram, but something told him that he must try to behave calmly or he might make the situation even worse.

'Come along, Drusilla,' he said, putting his hand on her arm. 'You know that's not true, don't you? This is Joseph, not Matthew. He's called Joseph Gregson and he belongs to my sister. My mother's looking after him for her, and I'm going to take him back to her, right now. Yes, I am,' he said, as she tightened her hold on the pram, 'so let go of the handle … please. Or I shall have to get the police.'

The words were spoken calmly. Much more so than he was feeling, but there was no mistaking the effect that the last two words had on the woman. 'No … you mustn't!' she yelled. 'Not the police. They've been waiting to catch up with me all these years. Don't tell them. Promise me you won't tell them!'

'All right then, I won't tell them. Not if you do as I say.' Zachary shook his head bemusedly. What the hell was the woman ranting on about? 'Just go away from here,' he said, speaking quietly and deliberately, as one would do to a child. 'Go right away, and don't let me see you round here again … or I might have to tell them.' So that was why she had been skulking in the back entry, he thought now. She'd been waiting for her chance. He shuddered at the thought of what might have happened if he hadn't come round the corner at that moment. 'If you know what's good for you, you'll get right away from Blackpool,' he went on. 'Why don't you do that, Drusilla? Go back to Scotland, eh? There's nothing for you here. You know that, don't you?' Zachary was surprising himself at how rationally he could talk to the woman when his instinct was to shake the life out of her.

She regarded him sullenly, without speaking, her dark eyes full of venom … and yet clouded with disappointment. It was almost in him to feel sorry for her, if he didn't dislike and fear her so much.

It was at that moment that the child woke up. He began to stir amongst the heap of blankets, his head poking out, then his bottom making a hill of them as he struggled into a sitting position. He stared in bewilderment at the strange woman leaning over his pram, and Zachary could see his lip beginning to tremble. Then his big blue eyes moved from Drusilla to Zachary. He regarded him for a moment, still puzzled, then gradually recognition dawned. His chubby face broke into a beaming smile, revealing the two tiny teeth on the lower gum which had recently broken through. 'Zac…' he said, reaching out his plump fist.

'Hello, young Jo,' said Zachary softly, feeling unusually moved.

Drusilla gave a strangled cry and turned away from the pram and the child. She didn't say another word as she hurried away, head down, in the direction of Dickson Road. She didn't even stop at the kerb and Zachary heard an angry shout, 'Watch where you're going, you silly fool!' as a cyclist swerved to avoid her.

Zachary shouted too, 'Drusilla, be careful!' But she had gone.

He turned back to Joseph, who was now fully awake and playing with the string of coloured beads that were stretched across his pram. 'Well, I don't know; this is a right carry-on, isn't it, young Jo? We'd best get you home before your gran finds out you've gone. There'll be all hell let loose if she does, and no mistake.'

He pushed the pram towards Lord Street, feeling a little self-conscious. He was still very worked up about what happened. It was a miracle that he'd been able to keep his hands off the woman. Never had he felt more like murdering anyone, not even during the war, he thought with a stab of surprise. And he was surprised, too, at his feeling of attachment – tenderness, almost – towards the child in front of him who was now grinning at him so gleefully. But as he turned the corner he could see that he was too late. There was his mother, dashing up and down outside the house like somebody demented; his gran too, and the woman next door. Oh hell! What on earth was he going to say? He couldn't tell his mam what had really happened. She'd go berserk. Zachary's brain began to work overtime as he feverishly searched around for something to say to her. He'd just have to behave as casually as possible.

Hetty spied him then, and from about forty yards away he could hear her cry of relief. 'He's here! Oh, thank God – he's here.' She dashed towards Zachary and the child in the pram and immediately, without waiting for an explanation, began to berate him. 'Zachary, what on earth d'you think you're playing at? I've been out of my mind. What in heaven's name were you thinking of, going off with our Joseph like that? I thought he'd been kidnapped. I thought–'

'Now calm down, Mam,' said Zachary, knowing full well he was taking the blame for something he hadn't done, but not minding very much. 'He's quite all right, you can see he is. He was awake when I came home – sitting up and laughing, he was – and I wanted some fags from the shop, so I took him with me.' He turned to the child. 'You've been as right as rain with your Uncle Zachary, haven't you, Jo?'

His mother was looking at him strangely, as well she might. He could tell, too, that she was still angry. 'You silly young fool!' she said. 'Why didn't you have the sense to come and tell me? Of all the stupid...'

'I never thought, Mam.'

'No, that's the trouble with you, Zachary Gregson, you never think at all – only about yourself – and there's me nearly having a heart attack with worry.' Hetty gave a deep sigh and put her hand to her chest. 'My heart's going twenty to the dozen. Don't you ever do that again!' Two vivid red spots burned on her cheeks and her plump face was pink all over and perspiring with her agitation. 'First time I've ever known you take any notice of the lad, anyroad. You're a funny-ossity all right, our Zachary,' she added, more calmly.

She turned then to little Joseph, who was observing them all with his knowing stare. 'Well, I'm certainly glad you're safe, my little lamb.' She ruffled his ginger curls and gently touched the tip of his nose. 'Perhaps your Uncle Zachary'll pay a bit more attention to you now. D'you think he will?'

Zachary tutted impatiently.

'Never mind. All's well that ends well,' said Martha Makepeace, joining in for the first time. She gave Zachary a reproachful look. 'You really should think what you're doing, lad. You had your mother frightened out of her wits. Taking him for cigarettes, indeed.'

'All right, all right. Let it drop, can't you?' said Zachary, casting his grandmother a baleful glance. 'You've had your say, both of you. Now, for God's sake, give it a rest.' He turned quickly and stormed off up the street towards Sunnyside, leaving them both staring after him in bewilderment.

He bounded up the three flights of stairs and into his room; the attic room again, now that the summer season was starting. He flung himself on the bed and was still for a few moments, hands linked behind his head, staring up at the ceiling. He was in a right fix now, wasn't he? In the dog-house good and proper, and all for something that wasn't his fault. Still, it didn't make much difference; he was always in lumber with his mother for something or other and this was only one more instance.

Zachary sat up then, removing his dirty boots from the counterpane – another thing that would rile his mam, were she to see them. He took his cigarettes from his pocket – he hadn't needed to go to the shop for any as he had said; he already had a full packet – and thoughtfully tapped one on the side of the box before lighting it. He was wondering if he ought to tell his mother the truth... He thought about this for a moment, then shook his head; but it was Hetty's feelings that he was considering this time, not his own peevishness. No ... his mother would be devastated if she knew that Joseph had been abducted. Not as much as she would have been if Zachary hadn't rescued him, but there was no need for her to know about that. She didn't need to know about any of it. If Zachary was any judge, Drusilla wouldn't be showing her face around here again; the mention of the police had really put the wind up her for some reason. He just hoped that she would take herself back to Scotland. It was a mystery what she was doing here anyway. No doubt the sight of the child had reminded her of her own lad. It was a pity, of course, very tragic, but Zachary had his own family to consider.

He could perhaps mention to his mother, casual-like, when she had calmed down a bit, that it might be better if she didn't leave Joseph's pram outside quite so much ... although he was sure that she would be more vigilant in future. It had given her a turn, sure enough, when she thought he'd gone.

He was a bonny little lad, young Jo, Zachary pondered as he puffed away at his cigarette. Bright an' all, bright as a button. The thought gave him an unexpected surge of pleasure.

Chapter 22

Drusilla shambled northwards along Dickson Road, staring at the ground and muttering to herself. A few passers-by gave her curious looks, but she paid no heed to them. She didn't turn down Banks Street to her home – not that she could call it a home, but it was the only one she possessed at the moment – but kept on walking. She had to get away, right away from here, for the moment, at least. After all, that lad Zachary might tell the police. He'd promised that he wouldn't, but Drusilla wasn't sure that she could trust him.

'You can't trust any of 'em,' she muttered, almost colliding with a lamp-post. She righted herself, then carried on with her faltering walk. 'Thought it was Reuben at first,' she mumbled, 'but it wasn't. He would never have said those things to me, not my Reuben.'

'Hey, missus, you should take more water with it,' shouted a cloth-capped man with whom she had just come into collision. 'Get yerself off home before you cause an accident.'

She heard him well enough, but she didn't answer him, neither to apologise nor to tell him that she was not drunk. She, Drusilla Loveday, had never been drunk in her life. She'd been strictly brought up, she had. Her parents had always discouraged her from drinking alcohol.

O'Bengh's brew – the devil's brew – her father had called it. He'd been as strict as any Presbyterian, had her father, and then she'd gone and married another one that didn't approve of drinking either. Not that Drusilla had ever wanted to drink wine or spirits. She didn't need their stimulus. There was quite enough in her natural make-up to inflame her passions...

They'd thought she was a wild one, her relations and friends, and they'd tried to restrain her; but no one had ever been able to subdue Drusilla Loveday, save one. Reuben was not that one, strangely enough; it had been the fellow she had married, Jock Murray, who had seemed to know how to tame her. She'd behaved decorously enough with him, most of the time, until her beloved Matthew had been taken from her. It was then that she had had a relapse, a return to her former frenzied behaviour; the way she had behaved when her parents died ... and that other time, in the cottage on Marton Moss, when Reuben had come back and found her there.

'I didn't mean it, Reuben. I didn't mean to hurt you,' she mumbled, earning herself some more odd looks from passers-by. She stared back at them boldly now. Why were they looking at her like that, as if she were crazy or something? She had suddenly returned to her senses, as was usually the way when she had one of her funny turns. 'S'pose I must have been talking to myself,' she said under her breath. 'Watch it, Drusilla, or they'll be coming to cart you away.' She gave an hysterical laugh which came out much louder than she expected, and a woman who was approaching stopped and looked in a shop window rather than pass close to her.

At times Drusilla was confused as to where she was, or even what year it was. Sometimes it seemed to her as though she were back in the Blackpool of more than twenty-five years ago, the time when Reuben and his parents had come to be with her after her mother and father died. She had fallen in love with her handsome cousin and had believed that he was the one and only man for her ... but that was before Hetty Turnbull came on the scene. It was seeing that lad that had done it, that lad Zachary, who was the living image of him. That was what had brought it all back to her.

Her mind seemed clearer for that moment and she glanced at the street sign on the brick wall next to her. She had wandered quite a way, almost a mile from North Station, and she was now on Warbreck Road. She knew that this road led to Gynn Square. Yes, she could see the whitewashed building of the old Gynn Inn ahead of her. Gynn Square ... something struck a chord in her brain. She had heard something about Gynn Square recently, hadn't she? Something that Reuben – no, Zachary – had told her. Drusilla frowned. Now ... what was it? She stopped in her tracks, thinking hard. Then she had it. 'My cousin has a café there,' he had said. 'Sarah's Café...' And Sarah, from what Zachary had told her, was the daughter of Edwin Donnelly, the owner of the big store, and of Grace, the girl who had come to her fortunetelling booth all those years ago ... with her sister. Drusilla knew that she would have to keep her distance from that woman, Henrietta Turnbull, for the moment, or Zachary might carry out his threat. But there could be no harm in having a little look at the café and at Sarah Donnelly, Grace's daughter. Drusilla had never had anything against Grace – a shy, very sweet girl, she had seemed; she and that other one had been as different as chalk and cheese – but it was the same family, wasn't it? – the family that had caused her such anguish. Drusilla couldn't, at that moment, have explained her motives, even to herself. She just knew that she couldn't keep away from the Turnbull family.

Drusilla paused on the corner opposite the Gynn Inn, quite taken aback at what she saw. The girl had obviously done well for herself just as her mother had, from all accounts, by marrying the Donnelly fellow. *Sarah's Café* read the inscription over the door, but Drusilla could see that it was much more than a corner café. Through the plate-glass window she could see small tables covered with crisp cream cloths, and customers, mostly women, partaking of tea in delicate china cups and daintily cut sandwiches, tempting cakes and pastries. At the back was a mahogany counter and a goodly array of produce; it seemed as though it was a shop as well as a café. And a restaurant too, Drusilla noted, as she stood there taking it all in. There was a notice on the door which said that three-course meals were served each lunchtime in the first-floor restaurant and, glancing upwards, Drusilla could see green velvet curtains hanging at the windows, and oak-panelled walls. That had all cost a pretty penny, she didn't doubt. The lass had certainly landed on her feet. It was all right for some, Drusilla thought, feelings of malice and envy coming to the fore; feelings which were totally unjustified, if she stopped to think, for she had enjoyed quite a reasonable standard of living herself with Jock Murray, the master carpenter. They had owned their own little house and, since he died, Drusilla had been much better off than a lot of widows were. It was her own choice that she dressed so shabbily. The Drusilla of twenty years ago would never have looked so down-at-heel, but there no longer seemed much point in bothering to dress up these days.

She glanced at the small notice above the door. *Proprietress, Sarah Duncan,* it read. Duncan… The girl must be married, although Zachary hadn't said so. And at the sight of the name, another chord sounded in Drusilla's brain. The name was familiar to her – for a reason she wanted to forget. But it was a common enough surname, Drusilla thought, as she pushed the memory away. There was another notice in the window, and this Drusilla read with interest. *Wanted, a cleaning lady, two hours each afternoon. Please apply within.* Her eyes began to gleam and a faint smile curved her lips. Why not? That 'ud teach 'em, wouldn't it? She'd be right there, working for one of them, and no one would ever know. It wasn't likely that Henrietta ever came up here – she was too busy with her boarding house and her baby, but Drusilla might hear something about her if she was working for her niece. And Grace Turnbull, or Donnelly or whatever her name was, most likely wouldn't recognise Drusilla after all this time, if she ever came to the café. Nobody ever took any notice of a cleaning lady anyway.

Nice of the girl to ask for a cleaning 'lady' though, thought Drusilla as she pushed open the door. It was better than saying 'charwoman'. It never occurred to her at all that she might not get the job, and it seemed, indeed, that luck was with her. Or Fate ... yes, it was most definitely Fate, she thought afterwards when the job was hers. And she was to be even more convinced of this later...

The pleasant fresh-faced girl had gone into the kitchen at the rear when Drusilla had asked if she might speak with Mrs Duncan; and when she returned with the proprietress Drusilla had had to stifle a gasp of astonishment, for the young woman in front of her was the very image of Grace Turnbull as she had been twenty-five years ago. The same dark curly hair, atop of which was a cream mobcap, the same delicate features and friendly smile and warm brown eyes. You couldn't help but like Grace – in spite of her being who she was, Drusilla had never disliked her – and it was the same with her daughter. Sarah Duncan was the sort of young woman to whom people instinctively took a liking. She seemed more self-confident, however, than her mother had been as a girl; she would need to be, thought Drusilla, being in charge of a thriving business at such a young age.

She interviewed Drusilla – or talked with her, rather than interviewed her – very competently and offered her the job there and then. She was to start the following Monday. Drusilla hadn't given her usual name. She said that she was Mrs Murray – no harm in that – and that her first name was Pearl. It was in fact her second name, but she hardly ever used it. You couldn't be too careful.

Drusilla's job was to clean the restaurant in the mid-afternoon, after all the customers had eaten their lunches and departed, and the downstairs kitchen, too; all the baking and cooking had been finished by that time and didn't start again until six o'clock the next morning. The girl called Doris, and Joyce – who, Drusilla gathered, was Zachary's sister and Hetty's daughter though she didn't look much like either of them – popped in and out making cups of tea or coffee for the late-afternoon customers in the café, but they didn't pay much attention to Drusilla; they just left her to get on with her work. That wasn't to say that they were unfriendly or stand-offish. Drusilla found all the staff, including Mrs Duncan, very pleasant and amiable. It was a nice place to work and there was a happy atmosphere; it was Drusilla who preferred to keep herself to herself, not getting involved in long conversations with anyone or joining in the cheerful banter that went on between the waitresses. She just got on with what she had to do, quietly and capably, all the while watching and listening … and waiting, though she wasn't sure just what it was she was waiting for.

She didn't hear or see much of importance

during the first day or two. She deduced that Joyce – Henrietta's daughter – lived in the attic rooms upstairs with Doris, the young fresh-faced assistant, whilst Mrs Duncan and her husband lived a few streets away. Drusilla didn't know what the husband did for a living and she hadn't asked – she didn't want to appear nosey – but it was obviously nothing to do with his wife's business because he wasn't in evidence there. She imagined in her own mind that he might be a solicitor, or at least a clerk, certainly someone with a posh sort of job; Sarah Duncan was a refined young lady. But thoughts of Sarah's husband were soon forgotten for on the Wednesday afternoon she set eyes on Grace Turnbull again.

Grace Donnelly as she was now, of course. It was twenty-five years or more since Drusilla had seen her, but she recognised her instantly. Whether she would really have identified her, had she not known that this was Sarah Duncan's mother, she wasn't sure. But she did know, and she also knew that the years had been kind to the woman, more so than to her sister ... and more so than to Drusilla herself.

Grace seated herself at a small table in the café whilst her daughter and her niece, Joyce, fussed around her as though she were Queen Mary. And Drusilla noticed that Grace seemed to accept it as her due. Feelings of resentment stirred in the gipsy again as she kept her eyes and ears on the little group, at the same time getting on with her work. It had been quite late in the afternoon, about half past four, when Grace had arrived and Drusilla had been just about to start sweeping and dusting the café; this was her last job of the day, but one she could only do if there were no customers there.

'Oh … Mrs Murray, do carry on,' Sarah said, smiling at her sweetly, as she saw her with her duster and carpet-sweeper at the ready. 'We'll sit in the corner over there, then we won't be in your way. I don't suppose there will be any more customers in now. Thank you, Mrs Murray.'

The last words were spoken dismissively. There was no attempt to explain that this latecomer was her mother, or to introduce the two of them. Whoever heard of introducing the cleaning woman to your mother, anyway? Especially when the mother was someone as prestigious as Grace Donnelly now seemed to be. But it suited Drusilla. She had no wish to make the woman's acquaintance and risk being recognised; it suited her purpose to keep well in the background, though close enough to hear and see what was going on.

That dress must have cost a bob or two to start with, to say nothing of the stylish cream leather shoes with matching handbag and the cloche hat with the two huge feather pom-poms on the side. The hat that Grace was wearing was an exact match to her dress, a lilac striped silk affair with full bishop sleeves gathered into a velvet band at the cuff. What they called an afternoon dress, Drusilla thought with a derisive sniff; folks like herself could only afford one dress for all times of day, be it morning, afternoon or evening. Drusilla knew quite a lot about fashion though. There had been a time, especially in the early years of her marriage when Jock had been earning good money, when she had liked to dress herself up. Not any more though; there was no point in it.

Grace Donnelly was quite a fashion model. It seemed that she was in charge of the fashion department at her husband's store – Drusilla had heard tell of this, from one or two sources, before she actually set eyes on the woman – and she was here today because Wednesday was half-day closing at the shop. So it was in most of the Blackpool shops, but Sarah's Café, operating as a café and restaurant more than as a shop, didn't abide by the same rules. Here the staff took an afternoon off in their turns.

'So I thought I'd come and take a look at you, darling,' Grace was saying in her melodious voice, and in Drusilla's hearing. Hmmm … she'd got rid of her Lancashire accent all right, Drusilla thought. Proper 'bay windows' she was talking now. She'd have to, of course, being married to a nob like Edwin Donnelly.

'I thought you might have brought Aunt Hetty with you,' Drusilla overheard Sarah say, and at this her ears pricked up even more.

'Our Hetty? That'll be the day...' Grace laughed. 'It's not for want of asking though, I might tell you. I'm always asking her if she'll go to places with me, but you should know your Aunt Hetty by now. You can't drag her away from that boarding house in the summer, especially since she started taking the theatre folk. And she's got Joseph now, of course.' She turned to Joyce. 'Well, you know what your mother's like, don't you, dear? She thrives on hard work, like our own mother did.'

Joyce nodded. 'She's certainly very busy, Aunt Grace. I worry about her at times, but it's been better for her since Gran's been coming round to help. Speaking of theatre folk, you know our Nancy'll be here again soon, don't you? They've got a booking at North Pier.'

'Yes, I believe I did know that, dear. When does the show start?'

'First week in June, I think. Nancy'll be here next week, though. They'll be having a week of rehearsals, I suppose, before the show opens.'

'Who's Nancy? thought Drusilla, her ears out on stalks as she carefully dusted each of the bentwood chairs at the nearby tables. She was being very bold, going as close as she dared, but at the same time keeping her head averted from Grace Donnelly.

So this Nancy they were talking about must be the mother of the baby that Drusilla had seen … had taken care of, so very briefly. This incident had been pushed aside, momentarily, in Drusilla's muddled mind as she eavesdropped on the little family group. *Nancy* … maybe that was the one she should be concentrating on. The girl had no right to give birth to a lovely boy like Joseph and then go away and leave him in the charge of a trollop like Hetty Turnbull. But it sounded as though she might be something of a trollop herself. A wave of bitterness and a desire for revenge took a fresh hold of Drusilla, concentrating themselves now upon Nancy, a young woman she had never even seen. Perhaps that was the reason she had been sent to work at Sarah's Café; for by now Drusilla was convinced that it was Nemesis that had put her in this place.

Her confused mind remained fixed upon the unknown Nancy ... until the following week, when she set eyes on the person to whom the hand of Fate had undoubtedly led her.

'Who's that?' asked Grace, nodding towards the tall dark woman who was just disappearing into the kitchen at the rear of the café.

'It's our new cleaning lady,' said Sarah. 'She started on Monday.'

'Yes, I can see that, dear. But who is she? What is her name?'

'Mrs Murray.'

'Do you know her first name?'

'She said she was called Pearl,' replied Sarah, looking at her mother in some surprise. 'Why, Mother?'

'Oh ... nothing, dear,' said Grace. 'She reminded me of somebody, that's all. But of course it couldn't be...'

'Who?'

'Oh, just somebody I knew a long time ago. But I've told you, it couldn't be. That wasn't her name, anyway. No matter.' Grace smiled at her daughter. 'It's just something that came into my mind.'

'She's a good worker, that Mrs Murray,' put in Joyce. 'A lot better than some of them we've had, Sarah.'

'Yes, I must agree with you.' Sarah nodded. 'She gets on with the job without a lot of fuss and that's what we want. She doesn't waste her time standing around chatting, which is what some of them have done. The last lady we had, I'm sure she only came so she could have a good old chinwag with the rest of the staff.'

'So you sacked her, did you, dear?'

'No, Mother.' Sarah gave a rueful smile. 'I'm not very good at that. Luckily it was her decision to leave. I don't think she needed the money ... but I'm sure Mrs Murray does.'

'I like the way you always refer to them as ladies,' said Grace.

'So they are, Mother. They're people, just the same as we are, and they're entitled to all the courtesies. It's just that some of us have been a bit more fortunate than others. I know I have.' Sarah's eyes went out of focus for a moment and her face held a dreamy look. 'Sometimes I can't believe how lucky I am.'

Grace was to remember those words of her daughter's a couple of weeks later.

The following week, Grace was surprised when Nancy breezed into Donnelly's Department Store. There was no other word for it. She was like a fresh spring breeze in her dashing outfit of green striped linen blazer, the petersham ribbon on her straw boater and the cotton tie of her V-necked dress just matching the sparkling green of her eyes.

'Hello, Aunt Grace. Lovely to see you again!' She greeted her aunt warmly, kissing her on both cheeks. It must be a habit learned from the stage folk, Grace thought with fond amusement. She had always got on well with Nancy, seeing in her so much of Hetty at the same age. 'Hard at work I see,' Nancy went on, fingering the tape measure which hung round her aunt's neck. 'As a matter of fact, that's what I've come to see you about, Aunt Grace. I wondered if you might do a little job for me. That's not the only reason I've come, of course,' she added hastily. 'I wanted to see you again, all of you. I thought I'd pop up and call on our Joyce and Sarah later this afternoon.'

Grace laughed and gave her niece an affectionate shove. 'Get along with you! You don't need to weigh your words with me, young lady. I might have known you'd want something. You're your mother all over again, do you know that? She always knew how to get round me – and your grandmother, as well – with a bit of sweet-talking. And you're just like her. Now, what is it you're wanting?'

Nancy sat on the small gilded chair that Grace pulled out for her and her aunt sat opposite whilst they chatted. Donnelly's was quiet at this time of day, it being just on lunchtime. The store didn't close between the hours of one and two as a lot of the town-centre shops did; this wouldn't have been feasible as the refreshment room, which Sarah had once run, served midday snacks, but this was always the quietest time of day in the other departments. Nancy explained that she wanted two new dresses for the summer season show. One was to be loosely cut, she told her aunt, with a low waist and a fringed hemline.

'One that will swivel around me when I dance – you know the sort of thing,' she said, waving her hands in the air expressively. 'And perhaps it could be decorated with glass beads. They'd dazzle in the lights, wouldn't they? And I shall wear a long bead necklace with it. We're going to dance the Black Bottom you see, in one of the scenes, and the Charleston.'

'Yes, I think I know just what you mean,' said Grace, her eyes twinkling at her niece. 'The sort of thing the Flappers are wearing.'

'That's it!' said Nancy delightedly. 'You know all the new words then, Aunt Grace?' She sounded impressed.

'Oh, I've had to keep up with all the new trends, now I'm more or less in charge of the whole show here. It's surprising how much I've learned.' Grace looked as she spoke at the display that surrounded them. Bales of cloth, some rolled up, others draped artistically over stands, in a variety of materials; tweeds, soft woollens, silks, satins and muslins, a myriad of dazzling colours, textures and designs. Some were brilliantly eye-catching; bright emerald green, acid yellow, royal blue – colours which fashionable women were wearing nowadays in the aftermath of the drab, austere days of the war. Others were more delicate; subtle shades of lavender, pink and pale blue, such as Grace had favoured when she was younger, although she had, of late, gone in for bolder, brighter colours in an attempt to keep up with the dictates of fashion. Always, though, she had loved materials in all their colours and textures; ever since she had worked in the weaving shed of the Burnley cotton mill, and later as a junior assistant in this very store, this very department.

'How's it going, Aunt Grace, your new dress-making department?' asked Nancy. 'Not that it's so very new now, is it? You must have been doing it for a couple of years … but then I've been away.'

'Yes, it's more than two years now,' said Grace. 'And I'm pleased to say it's all going very well. It was rather a leap in the dark, but it was something I badly wanted to try, and Edwin had faith in me. He always has,' she couldn't help adding, though she knew it sounded a trifle smug. 'Yes, women seem to like the idea of choosing their own material and pattern and then having it made up in our workroom. The other idea that I had – the "cut and fit" – never really got off the ground. The customers didn't seem to like the idea of finishing the garments off themselves. They like us to do all the work for them – those that can afford it, that is – and I can't say I blame them. Of course we're very good. We've four seamstresses working for us in the back room over there.' She pointed to the rear of the store where an area was partitioned off. 'I do most of the fitting myself, and advising, when it's needed. Clients like those little individual touches. A bit like *haute couture* but a good deal cheaper.' Grace laughed. 'Folks in Blackpool like value for their money.

'Now, you say you want a Flappers-style dress? I think we might have something in the readymade department that would do – we have some quite exclusive things there, you know, dear – and we could always add one or two finishing

497

touches to make it really unique. I tell you what, Nancy. Let's go up to the tearoom and have a spot of lunch then you can tell me exactly what you have in mind...'

During the simple meal of egg and cress sandwiches and freshly brewed coffee, the conversation drifted away from fashion to the family.

'And how's your little boy?' asked Grace. 'I daresay he would be pleased to see his mummy again, wouldn't he?'

Nancy gave a frown, but it was one of puzzlement rather than annoyance. 'I think so. I think he remembered me... He calls me Nan.' She smiled ruefully. 'Of course he would, wouldn't he? He's just beginning to talk and I suppose it's only natural he'll call my mother Mam.'

'Don't be afraid to get to know him, Nancy,' said Grace, who never hesitated to speak her mind. She had watched her sister with the little boy and wasn't altogether happy with what she saw. Unless she was very much mistaken, there was going to be some heartache there before much longer, but for whom, Grace wasn't sure. 'You'll be missing out on a lot, dear, if you don't get to know him. They're not babies for long. Of course I know you're very keen on this stage career.'

'Yes, I am, Aunt Grace, and Joseph's fine with Mam, he is really.' Nancy didn't seem to be offended by Grace's plain speaking, but then she never was, only hearing just what she wanted to hear. She was very egotistical, but in the nicest possible way. 'Now ... let me tell you about the other dress I want,' she went on, quickly changing the subject. 'You've heard of Suzanne Lenglen, haven't you?'

Grace agreed that she had. Even Grace, who had never been a sporty sort of person had heard of Suzanne Lenglen, the woman tennis star from France, three times Champion already at Wimbledon and likely to be so again this year. Sportswear was now coming into vogue, influencing fashion trends as a whole, and the Frenchwoman had caused a sensation with her wardrobe of what they were calling 'chic' – a fashionable French word – tennis dresses designed by Jean Patou. Skirts were becoming shorter, so short, in fact, that photographs of the French star in play even showed the tops of her stockings and a glimpse of bare thigh. She was instantly recognisable by the coloured bandeau she wore round her head, and Grace wasn't surprised when Nancy went on to explain what she had in mind.

'We're doing a sporty scene, you see, Aunt Grace,' she said. 'Ivy's wearing a bicycling outfit, Rose a riding costume – and I'm the tennis player. And we're going to sing "Ain't We Got Fun". She burst into song at that point.

'Though there's nothing in the larder,
Ain't we got fun.
Times are hard and getting harder...

You know it don't you, Aunt Grace?'

'Yes, I think so, dear.' Grace was beginning to

feel a trifle overwhelmed by her niece's infectious exuberance.

'So I thought I'd wear an emerald-green bandeau, like Mam'selle Lenglen does, and I want a really stylish tennis dress, something that'll knock 'em in the aisles.'

Mmm. You're not asking for much, are you, at such short notice ... Grace thought to herself, but she didn't voice the words. This one was her mother all over again, sure enough, and Grace would try to accommodate her, just as she had always done, years ago, with Hetty. She did say, tentatively, 'There isn't much time, is there, dear? Doesn't the show open next week?' Nancy agreed that it did. 'And ... don't you have a wardrobe mistress?'

'Oh yes ... sort of. There's a little woman that Sid knows in Halifax who runs things up for us but she's not a patch on you, Aunt Grace. There is a dress that would do at a pinch, but I want something really special this time. I'll have to pay for it myself, of course. I've two solo numbers this year and I've got to look my best. It'll be the first time I've sung all on my own – since I left the song-booth, I mean.'

And in the face of such enthusiasm Grace couldn't but offer to help. In the end they chose two dresses from the readymade department which needed very little alteration. The tennis dress had a knife-pleated skirt and the fashionable collarless neckline; the 'Flapper's' dress was tubular-shaped with an irregular hemline and a band of sequins round the hips. The colour, dark red chiffon, was one that Nancy said she would never have thought of.

'Red! With my hair?' she said in some disbelief.

'Why not? Anything goes these days,' Grace assured her. And when Nancy tried it on, turning this way and that in front of the long mirror in the cubicle, she had to admit that her aunt was right.

'You're a marvel, Aunt Grace,' she said, kissing her again on both cheeks. 'I can never thank you enough. I know what I'll do. I'll get tickets for the show – for everybody. For you and Uncle Edwin, and Sarah and Alex, and perhaps Mam and Joyce'll come as well. You can all come and see me.'

'That would be lovely, dear,' said Grace warmly. 'We'll look forward to it. A family outing is a wonderful idea. It's ages since we had one of those.'

Grace was thoughtful as she watched the jaunty figure of her niece almost bouncing across the floor of the shop, turning to give a cheery wave as she reached the staircase. What was it their mother used to say, when she and Hetty got too excited for their own good? 'There'll be tears before bedtime...' Nancy had always been a high-spirited girl, but this bubbling effervescence seemed too excessive to last. Grace certainly hoped that she wasn't riding for a fall.

It was during the second week of her job at Sarah's Café that Drusilla saw him. She was upstairs in the back part of the restaurant, polishing the tables and chairs, whilst Mrs Duncan was at the window end, folding the cream damask cloths ready for collection by the laundry van. Suddenly a tall figure bounded up the stairs, passing Drusilla without so much as a glance, for his eyes were already on the young woman near the window. Drusilla had overheard the waitresses gossiping and had gathered that they envied Sarah Duncan her charming and handsome husband. '… and they're so much in love it makes you go all funny to see them together,' she heard one of them say.

So this, then, was the husband. Drusilla stole a sideways glance, at the same time carrying on with her dusting. Then she looked again… The man was half-turned towards her, the light from the window showing clearly his lean features; the straight, rather long, nose and firm chin, the deep clefts which ran from his nose to the corners of his wide mouth, the shrewd grey eyes … although now they were filled with the light of love as he looked adoringly at his wife. Drusilla had remembered them, though, as being shrewd, knowing eyes, belonging to one whom, she had heard, could be ruthless when things didn't work out in just the way he wanted. For there was no doubt in her mind who this man was. She had recognised him instantly. It was the doctor from Melrose, the one who, all those years ago, had let her darling Matthew die.

The knowledge made her stop what she was doing, and stare at him and Sarah in undisguised astonishment. Fortunately they were unaware of her scrutiny. Snatches of their conversation drifted across to her, although she wasn't really taking it in.

'…Lovely surprise, darling … it's not often…'

'…Finished early … thought I'd take a wee look at my darling wife…'

Drusilla was dumbfounded at what she had discovered. She turned back to her work after a few moments; she had to keep this knowledge completely to herself. Not by so much as a word or a glance must she betray to anyone that she knew this man. For this was of supreme import-ance; this discovery put all the others into the shade. Hetty Turnbull and her grandchild, Nancy, Zachary … they all faded into insignificance now in the face of this new astounding revelation. This, then, was why Fate had put her in this place. *He* was the one on whom she had to wreak her vengeance, this doctor who had allowed her beloved son to die. And her enemy had been led right into her hands.

Why, she pondered, had she not put two and two together when she discovered that her employer's name was Duncan? Because Duncan was a common enough name, that was why, and because no one had bothered to mention to her that Sarah Duncan's husband was a doctor. And not only was he a doctor, and the one who had neglected her son, but Drusilla knew something else about him; something of such importance that she could scarcely believe it. What on earth was he doing down here in Blackpool, married to Sarah? It just wasn't possible…

Much as Drusilla wanted to avenge herself on this man – and she knew that she must – she was strangely loth to inflict any hurt on Sarah. And yet Sarah was the one who would have to be told. There was no doubt about that; it was only right that she should know. On the way home Drusilla bought a notepad and envelopes, a pen and a bottle of ink. She had never had much schooling, but Jock had taught her to read and write. It was a skill that she didn't use overmuch, but she knew enough to get by. It wouldn't take much telling, anyway. The bald facts would be enough … then retribution would be sure to follow.

Chapter 23

Sarah was finding it hard to combat the fits of depression that came upon her nowadays, especially as she knew that she really had nothing whatsoever to be depressed about. She had an adoring husband whom she loved just as much in return, affectionate parents, good friends, her own business ... everything to make her happy. And yet, at times, she was sad. The fact that she knew what was causing the sadness didn't do anything to alleviate it. She had been sad ever since Clara Donnelly had died a few weeks ago and she couldn't seem to shake it off. The old lady had had a fall at home which had brought on a heart attack and she had died in hospital a week later.

Sarah's parents and friends had uttered all the usual platitudes.

'It's a blessing really. You wouldn't have wanted her to go on suffering. She'd been crippled with rheumatism for years and the pain was getting worse.'

'She'd had a good run. Just turned eighty, wasn't she? You can't ask for more than that.'

'She wouldn't have wanted you to go on feeling sad.'

But Sarah did. Not all the time, of course. A couple of weeks ago, when her mother had paid her surprise visit to the café, Sarah remembered saying how very lucky she was, so lucky that sometimes she couldn't believe it, and she had meant it, too. To have such a husband as Alex with his thoughtfulness and kindly ways, and the love they shared together – to think of it sometimes in the daytime brought a faint blush to Sarah's cheeks – was all a very great joy to her. But at the heart of her there was this sadness which wouldn't entirely go away.

It was the thought that never again would she see her grandmother, hear her voice, share a little joke with her. It was the 'never again' that was getting to Sarah. Never was a very long time: it was forever. She was gratified that her parents seemed to understand. They hadn't said to her, as they might well have done, that Clara wasn't her real grandmother. To Sarah she had been just as much of a relation, and just as dear to her as Grandma Makepeace was on the other side of the family. Grace and Edwin had been sad too, but not as devastated as Sarah appeared to be. Her parents had said to her that it was understandable, that it was the first time she had lost anyone really close to her, apart from her Uncle Albert, and so she was bound to be feeling the pain of the bereavement. Grace had also tried to say to her, falteringly – for they didn't often talk about such deep personal matters – that perhaps she should try to believe that they would all meet again some day. Wasn't that what the Christian faith was all about? But Sarah wasn't sure that she knew what to believe about that any more. Her gran had gone; so had Uncle Albert. Sarah was thinking about him, too, a lot more lately. Where were they? What exactly had they gone to? And did they know what was going on down here? It was all a great puzzlement and Sarah found at times that her head was reeling with it. It was one subject about which she could not talk with Alex. She remembered, from a time just before their marriage, how unsure he had been about what he believed, and it was something they hadn't discussed since.

Sarah was to wonder, later, if she had been in some strange way prepared for what was to happen. At all events, the melancholia had found its way into her being and it was almost as though she were waiting for something worse to happen.

The first letter arrived at the café by the second post. Sarah, in the middle of the mid-morning rush, took a quick glance at the name and address and shoved it into her apron pocket to read later. As it happened, it was much later in the day before she got round to reading it. It had lain forgotten in her pocket until the café closed, then she had transferred it to her handbag to be perused at home when she was alone.

She looked in some puzzlement at the badly-formed writing, like that of a child, on the envelope. Who on earth could be writing to her, and at the café as well? It was usually only business letters – bills and the like – that came there. She frowned even more when she read what was written – printed, more like – on the cheap lined notepaper. Some of the words were misspelt and the blue ink was smudged. '*Yor husband is keeping a secret from you. Ask him wot he*

507

knows about Hermitage' (there had been three tries at spelling this word) *'House neer Melrose.'*

Sarah felt a spasm of fear run through her. An anonymous letter, a vile thing that she had heard of, but had never thought to receive herself. And what on earth could it mean? She scrutinised the envelope. Had it come from Scotland? she wondered. From somebody who had known Alex when he lived up there? No – the postmark was Blackpool, posted yesterday afternoon. Seeing this, Sarah felt even more alarmed. Somebody here... Not knowing why she did it she suddenly screwed up the paper and envelope and tossed them on top of the coal which the woman who cleaned for them had carefully laid in the living-room fireplace that morning. It was the first week in June, but still chilly enough for a fire and Sarah felt chilled to the marrow now. She knelt on the hearthrug and struck a match, noting how her hands were trembling, then held the flame to the folds of newspaper beneath the sticks and coal. It soon caught alight and in a few moments the frightening, horrible missive was consumed.

It didn't – it couldn't – mean anything. It wasn't worth bothering about. Anonymous letters were best ignored. It was probably some person who had a grudge against Alex; doctors attracted their fair share of enemies, she was sure. But what was the person – he or she – doing in Blackpool? Sarah tried to push it all to the back of her mind as she went into the kitchen to prepare their evening meal – Alex had not yet arrived home – but she found that it was easier said than done. The words that she had read kept

508

flashing across her mind as she gathered together the ingredients for their meal. Sausages, bacon, mushrooms – a mixed grill tonight; Alex loved a mixed grill. She decided she would say nothing to him. She would try to behave as though nothing had happened, and any preoccupation that he noticed in his wife he would no doubt put down to her continuing sorrow about her grandmother.

She had been half-prepared for another of the vile things to arrive the next day, and sure enough, it did. By the first post this time, at eight o'clock, again at the café. Sarah snatched it off the floor together with another couple of letters which, from their brown envelopes, were probably bills, and retreated into the staff toilet to read it. The wording was similar. *'Yor husband has a secret. Ask him wot he knows about a yung lady called Fiona. She used to be called Fiona Cameron but not anny more.'*

A wave of sickness engulfed Sarah, so much so that she was forced to lean over the toilet bowl, bringing up the contents of her stomach. She hadn't had much breakfast, only toast and a cup of tea; in fact she hadn't felt much like eating at all since the first letter arrived. And here was another of them. Dear God, what on earth was she to do? Sarah leaned her head against the whitewashed wall of the cubicle, feeling faint and dizzy. How on earth was she going to carry on at work today as though nothing was amiss? And later, when she had to go home and face Alex... For Sarah knew that she was too afraid to ask Alex what it was all about. There must surely be a simple explanation; Alex would be able to allay her fears as he always did, to tell her it was all nonsense… And yet she knew that she could not ask him. Not yet.

She drew back the bolt on the door, coming out of the claustrophobic, rather smelly little room into the staff cloakroom. She had a drink of icy-cold water from the tap, then took hold of the sides of the wash-basin, gripping tightly in an endeavour to stop the trembling of her limbs. She closed her eyes and forced herself to breathe deeply. She would be all right in a moment or two. There was absolutely nothing to be alarmed about; it was just the work of a cruel hoaxer, someone who, for some reason, wanted to get even with Alex. But who? And why? *What did it all mean?* Her head was spinning, but she would have to push it all to the back of her mind again, as she had done yesterday, and get on with the job in hand. Then, perhaps tomorrow, she would do something about it. She would confront Alex. For Sarah had a feeling that by tomorrow she might have something more to tell him.

Fortunately it was a very busy day at the café. This was the first week in June, and early summer visitors had now arrived in the town. Joyce and Doris and the rest of the staff didn't seem to notice her preoccupation. But Alex commented on it later that evening.

'Is something the matter, darling?' he asked. 'You're very quiet, and you've eaten hardly any of your meal. I know you've been upset about your grandmother, but it isn't still that, is it?'

Sarah shook her head and smiled at him,

though she found it difficult to make the smile reach her eyes. 'I'm all right, love. Just a bit tired, and I sometimes think I see so much food all day that I don't want to eat it at night. We've been very busy today, Alex. There are a lot of visitors in town.' She was trying to make her voice sound normal.

'Och, you mustn't go overdoing it. Sometimes I worry about you, you know. I canna help thinking it's all too much for you, all you do at the café, then coming home and looking after me.'

'I love looking after you, Alex. You know that.'

'Well, it's my turn now to be looking after you, darling. An early night for you, my lass.' He laid his hand gently on her head, stroking her brown curls. 'Off you go now and pop into bed; you look worn out. And I'll make you a nice wee drink of cocoa, just the way you like it with plenty of sugar. And how about a shortbread biscuit? To make up for that pudding you didn't eat.'

Sarah actually smiled then, feeling her love for him light up her eyes. He was such a thoughtful person; nothing was too much trouble for him. 'All right, love,' she said. 'I'll do what the doctor orders. An early night would be lovely. It's probably what I need.'

She was still awake when Alex came up to bed more than an hour later. He kissed her tenderly on the cheek, not knowing whether she was asleep or not, as she kept her eyes tightly closed. 'Goodnight, my darling. See you in the morning.'

She didn't answer, but continued to lie motionless at his side in the big double bed. She was too weary even to think, but there was still that nagging uncertainty at the back of her mind. Tomorrow, though, she would sort it out. She would talk to Alex ... tomorrow. Then, because she was so worn out, she slept.

The blue envelope on the floor of the café the following morning came as no surprise to Sarah. And neither did the words that she read later in the confines of the cloakroom. It was almost as though she had been waiting for this. Her subconscious mind hadn't so far, let the fear take on a tangible shape, but this time it was real enough and she knew that it was what she had been dreading all along. It was impossible, horrific, terrifying beyond belief; and yet she had had a good idea when she drew the familiar cheap paper from the envelope what it was that she was going to read.

'Yor husband, Alex Duncan, is not reelly yor husband at all. He already has a wife. She is in Scotland.'

Sarah waited for the sickness to engulf her again, but it didn't, neither did she feel faint. She just felt cold, chilled to the bone, deadly calm and empty inside. She knew that she couldn't carry on with her duties at the café today. They would have to manage without her, as they were well able to do. This matter wanted dealing with immediately; she knew that she couldn't wait until this evening.

Sarah pushed the letter into her handbag and, after telling a very surprised Joyce that she had something urgent to see to at home – she would explain later – she quickly walked the few

512

hundred yards to where she lived. Alex, of course, had left for the surgery, but a phone call soon located him. The young woman who took the calls for both the doctors said that Dr Duncan had just started his surgery, but she would tell him that his wife had called.

'Tell him to come home as soon as he's finished,' said Sarah, knowing full well that her voice was unusually abrupt. 'It's urgent.'

She had an hour to wait before she heard Alex's key in the lock, but she knew that it might well have been much longer. He would have been unable to leave in the middle of surgery but this had obviously been a short one, people not being as prone to ailments in the summer. It had been the longest hour of Sarah's life. She was only thankful that she was on her own as it was a day when her cleaning lady didn't come.

'Darling, whatever is it?' Alex's face was full of concern as he entered the living room and saw her sitting, motionless, in one of the fireside chairs. 'I couldna come any sooner, but Miss Cartwright said you sounded upset. Are you feeling ill, my love?' He knelt at her side and his arms went round her, and Sarah felt herself relaxing against their comforting strength; but not for long. She stiffened her body, not exactly pushing him away but he dropped his arms, looking at her anxiously.

'No, I'm not ill, Alex,' she said. 'Just … worried. Scared out of my mind. Here – read this. It's the third one I've had.' She thrust out the letter to him which had been tucked down the side of the chair.

He stood on the hearthrug, frowning as his eyes scanned the paper, then she heard his gasp of horror. 'Oh God ... no!' He quickly sat down in the chair opposite her as though his legs would no longer support him. She watched the colour drain from his face and an agonised, haunted look come into his eyes. 'No, no...' he muttered again, closing his eyes, and his face told her all she needed to know, all that she had dreaded, had told herself was impossible...

'It's true then?' she said, her voice scarcely audible.

Alex shook his head, not yet looking at her. 'No.' Hope resurged in her then, to be just as quickly extinguished as he went on to say, 'It ... *was* true. I did have a wife – Fiona – but not any more. She's dead, Sarah. She's dead.' He looked at her then, pleadingly, his eyes dark with anguish. 'You're my wife, Sarah. I only ever loved you. Please believe me.'

'But ... why didn't you tell me. I don't understand.' Sarah was shaking her head slowly, in bewilderment. 'You were married before ... but why ever didn't you say so? I wouldn't have minded. But to have found out like this...' It wasn't, however, as bad as she had first anticipated, thought Sarah. The woman was dead. He had just said so. 'At first I thought it meant that–' she went on. Alex wasn't answering. He was staring at the floor now as though he were afraid to look at her. Suddenly an awful thought struck her. 'When did she die?' she said, almost too scared to ask the question.

'Last year,' said Alex flatly. 'June, last year.'

514

'Last year? And we were married in October … the year before.' Sarah's voice petered out to a mere whisper in her disbelief. 'Oh my God, Alex. We're not married at all.'

'We are married, Sarah.' Alex's voice was forceful, almost angry. 'Didn't that vicar marry us, say that we were man and wife?'

'But not if– We can't be, not if it's true that–'

'Och! What difference does it all make anyway? Words spoken in church. You're my wife, Sarah. You should know by now how much I love you. That's what makes a marriage – love, not some church ceremony. And … I love you, Sarah.' The look in his eyes, behind all the pain and anguish, was one of undoubted love. Sarah almost felt sorry for him, but she was cold inside and she knew she had to have an explanation. Her mind still couldn't grasp the enormity of it all.

'I remember you didn't want a church ceremony,' she said coolly. 'Now I understand why. Don't you think you'd better tell me about it?' She knew that her voice sounded much more calm than she was feeling.

'Whoever wrote this,' Alex stabbed angrily at the letter, 'hasn't got her facts right. Och, I'm pretty sure it's a woman,' he said, at Sarah's questioning glance. 'She thinks that Fiona's still alive, but she's not.'

Sarah could almost have laughed if the matter hadn't been so grave. 'You're missing the whole point, aren't you, Alex? She was alive when we were married. In fact, we're not married. Don't you think you'd better tell me about it?' she repeated.

'I grew up with her,' Alex began in a monotone. 'We lived in the same village, but her parents had a good deal more money than we ever had. She was almost one of the gentry, was Fiona Cameron.'

Sarah listened, stupefied, as he told his story. They had been young; Alex, in fact, had still been at medical school when they had married. He had always been aware that Fiona was a very highly strung girl, but had no idea at the time of their marriage of the strain of mental instability that ran through the family, which was the reason the Camerons had had only the one child. She had been committed to care before Alex joined the Army in 1914 but, as her parents were wealthy, they had been able to afford a private nursing home for her, Hermitage House, rather than see her sent to the mental asylum, which was what happened to so many. When he returned from the war in 1919, Fiona's violent attacks had increased and she hadn't even known who he was. Both her parents had died during the war years, but she was well cared for by fully trained nurses and doctors.

'The best care we could afford, Sarah,' Alex told her, almost defiantly. 'There was a lot of animosity, of course, between me and her parents, a lot of harsh words spoken... I thought they should have warned me. It seemed as though they were glad she was getting married – and no longer their sole responsibility, you see. But they had to take charge again when I joined the Army. And then ... they died.'

'The poor girl. How awful,' said Sarah in a

whisper, in spite of the hurt she was feeling.

'Aye, it was very sad, but she didn't know anything about it. And I could no longer feel anything, you see – except pity. Any love that I did have for her had died, long before. It had been killed in the early days of our marriage when she became so … strange. But I did all I could for her, and that was to see that she was well looked after. There was a trust fund left by her parents, and added to by myself, to see to all her needs. They told me, when I came back after the war, that it wasn't just her mental state. She had … she had a growth as well. It couldn't be very long…'

'Oh no, this is awful!' Sarah burst out again.

'She didn't know me. She hadn't known me for years,' said Alex in a low voice, as though trying to excuse himself.

He had decided to get right away, to make a new life for himself, and in the summer of 1919 he had seen the advert for the post in Blackpool. He gave instructions that he was to be kept informed of the situation at Hermitage House, but there was nothing further that he could do. There was no useful purpose to be served by his remaining in Scotland, although he had gone back very occasionally to see his wife. What he hadn't anticipated was meeting Sarah and falling helplessly in love; so much so that he had to have her, at any price.

'But why … *why*? Why didn't you explain? I would have waited, Alex. I loved you!' She didn't notice that she had used the past tense.

'I was afraid of losing you, my darling,' said Alex

simply. 'And does it matter so very much? We are married in our hearts, aren't we? You couldn't belong to me any more fully if we went through a dozen ceremonies. And no one knows…'

'Someone does know,' said Sarah, pointing to the letter. 'Someone who obviously dislikes you or me. And it's a criminal offence, bigamy.' She felt herself shuddering at the word. 'A criminal offence.'

Alex's face bleached. 'Don't say that, Sarah! I can't think of it like that. And surely … they couldn't? It isn't as if she's still alive.' He sounded confused. 'Who the hell can it be?' he went on, raising his voice now. 'Someone who's on holiday down here, I suppose. Someone who's been in the café … caught sight of me. Put two and two together … and made five as it happens.' Alex was almost talking to himself. 'I thought I was safe enough down here. I hardly ever come into contact with the holidaymakers.'

'You hardly ever come into the café,' said Sarah darkly. 'Is that why, Alex? Because you thought you might be recognised?'

Alex gave a deep sigh. 'I don't know. Subconsciously, maybe, that might have been the reason. I don't know, Sarah. It's all such a blasted mess. I could kill whoever wrote this, upsetting you, making you unhappy.'

'It's you who is making me unhappy,' said Sarah tonelessly. 'I trusted you, Alex. I honestly believed that you were one person who would never let me down.'

'I'm sorry,' he muttered. 'What else can I say but … I'm sorry. I'd have given anything not to have this happen.'

'Not to be found out, you mean.'

'Sarah, for God's sake, don't say things like that,' cried Alex. 'I love you. Don't you believe me? I love you so very much–'

'I don't know what to believe any more,' said Sarah. Another thought struck her. 'June,' she said, speaking very deliberately. 'You said that your ... that Fiona died last June. Wasn't that when your uncle died? Your uncle Andrew who lived in Edinburgh? Yes, I remember now.' She was speaking more quickly. 'I said I would go with you, to the funeral, and you wouldn't let me. And now I know why. It wasn't your uncle who had died at all. It was ... her.' She looked at him searchingly. 'Perhaps there *is* no Uncle Andrew at all.'

'I do – did – have an Uncle Andrew,' replied Alex, 'and he is dead, as I told you. But you're quite right, Sarah. When I went up to Scotland last June, it was because Fiona had died. I'd been expecting it ... and it came as a relief, as you can imagine. I had to go and sort things out – as her next of kin, you see.'

'So you lied to me.'

'What else could I do, my love? I'd have given anything for you not to find out, to be hurt like this, but I did it because I loved you so much. When I met you I couldn't bear the thought of losing you ... then I had to on with the deception.'

'And what about your uncle? When did he die?'

'A few months before. When I told you I was going to sort out his affairs ... he'd died then. I knew, you see, that it couldna be long before Fiona went as well, and I would want a good reason for going up to Scotland again.'

'So you lied to me again. You deceived me, Alex. You've been deceiving me all along. Our marriage – no, not a marriage, our ... time together – it's been nothing but a pack of lies.'

'You can't believe that, Sarah. You *mustn't* believe it.' He came and knelt at her side and for the first time in their marriage, which she now knew was no such thing, Sarah could see a trace of tears in his grey eyes. Alex didn't normally cry; he had many of the qualities of a dour Scotsman. But he had been gentle, too, and considerate and loving and Sarah had been so sure that she could trust him, with her love ... with her life. Now she felt that her heart was breaking. She forced herself to remain silent, impassive.

'Listen to me, darling,' he said, seizing hold of her hands. 'We'll get married again. We could go over to Preston, or somewhere where no one knows us, and get married in a Registry Office. We only need a couple of witnesses.'

'And who could we ask? You wouldn't want anyone to know.'

'I'll think of something. Please, darling, please. Let me try to make amends, although nothing will convince me that we're not married, you and me.'

'No, Alex. I can't.' Sarah sat back in the chair, pulling her hands away from his.

'What d'you mean, you can't? You can't ... what?'

'I can't go through another ceremony – not yet,

perhaps not ever. I don't know. I've got to have some time on my own, time to think. Leave me alone now, please.' She looked straight into his clear grey eyes, that she had once thought were so honest and true, and she could see from the torment there that he did, indeed, love her. What she felt for him she didn't honestly know. The overriding feeling at that moment was one of extreme hurt and a desire to be alone. 'You have your visits to do, haven't you?' she asked calmly.

'Yes, I have, but I can't leave you on your own, not now.'

'Leave me, please, Alex,' she said again. 'I'm asking you to go ... now.'

'Very well, my darling.' Alex looked troubled as he stood hesitantly in the doorway. 'I'll see you later this afternoon, hmmm? And please think about what I've said.'

Sarah didn't answer and Alex, after an anguished look at her, went out of the room. He hadn't kissed her, the first time in their 'marriage' that he had failed to do so on leaving her; but Sarah knew that this was due to her own aloofness and not because of any lack of feeling on Alex's part. She heard the front door close behind him; then she put her head in her hands and wept.

Chapter 24

Grace and Edwin Donnelly had both been shocked at Sarah's news. It was to their home that she had gone on that afternoon in early June, visibly shaken and disturbed, but able to talk calmly and rationally enough to Grace and, later, to Edwin. Fortunately it was a Wednesday afternoon, half-day closing, and Grace was at home and it wasn't long before Edwin had joined them. Sarah told them the whole story, omitting nothing; she had never had any secrets from her parents and, in this case, half-truths certainly wouldn't suffice. They both agreed, though somewhat reluctantly, that Sarah must stay there for a while in her old home, in her old room. Their reluctance was because they were so sad at the turn of events, not because they didn't want their daughter back home again.

'Until things are sorted out,' said Edwin, and on hearing that, tears came into Sarah's eyes for the first time since entering her old home.

'Sorted out?' she cried. 'I fail to see how they can be sorted out, Father. Alex has deceived me. All along he's been cheating me. To pretend that he was single … to go through a marriage that he knew was just a sham. I find that very hard to forgive. In fact, at the moment I can't forgive him at all.'

'But surely, my dear, you could try to think

about what Alex has suggested,' said Edwin. 'To get married again, quietly. You must know how much he loves you. Nobody who has seen you together could be in any doubt about that.'

Sarah gave him a reproachful glance. 'It sounds as though you're siding with him, Father. Can't you see what he's done? How much he's hurt me? I can't believe—'

'Of course I can. He's behaved badly; there's no question of that. Like you, I find it hard to believe, especially of someone like Alex. Your mother and I both liked him so much. We thought he was just right for you, and all this has come as a terrible shock to us, just as it has to you. But surely something can be salvaged. You can't ruin your life, my dear, because of wounded pride. Try to … to come to terms with it. I know he's done wrong, but try to forgive him. Try to find a way out. There must be a way.'

Sarah shook her head, her eyes brimming with tears as she looked at her father. 'I can't,' she said in a whisper. 'Not yet. I'll be grateful if you'll let me stay till I decide what to do. I can't live in the attic over the café like I did before. Doris is there now, sharing with Joyce, as you know, and there wouldn't be room. Besides, I couldn't stay there. Not now…'

'Of course you can stay here, dear,' said Grace, her expression sad beyond belief. 'As long as you wish. What about your work – the restaurant? Are you going to feel up to it?'

'I'll have to, Mother. I don't have much choice. The staff are all very good and they'll be managing perfectly well today while I'm not there,

523

but I'll have to go back. Just so long as I don't have to see Alex.'

Grace and Edwin exchanged sorrowful glances. 'What are you going to say, dear?' asked Grace tentatively. 'About ... all this? People will be curious about you and Alex.'

'The least said the better.' Sarah gave a slight shrug. 'Just that Alex and I have had a disagreement, I suppose. I don't know.'

'But you never do quarrel, do you, love? You were the most perfect couple. Oh dear!' Grace was clasping and unclasping her hands in agitation. 'This is just too awful.'

Finally they decided that the rest of the family – that is, Grandma and Grandad Makepeace and the Gregsons – must be let into the secret, however unpalatable the truth might be. Everyone else, the staff at the restaurant, friends and acquaintances, would be told nothing at all and just left to draw their own conclusions – which no doubt would be that Sarah and Alex had not been quite the loving couple they had seemed to be on the surface. And they mustn't forget, Sarah pointed out to her parents, that there was someone else who knew the truth; someone who was obviously not in possession of all the facts, but who knew enough to cause trouble if they so wished.

'Have you any idea who it might be? Any idea at all?' Sarah shook her head at her father's question. How could she possibly know who it was? Edwin had agreed that it was probably a holidaymaker who had quite possibly returned home by now. It was unlikely that they would hear any more about it, he added with forced optimism. He insisted, in spite of Sarah's protestations, that he would take her to the café each morning in his motorcar; but he had to let her have her own way about returning each evening on the tram.

When she had gone to her room later that evening, Grace and Edwin sat together in their drawing room, united in the sadness they were both feeling for their beloved daughter, but both strangely quiet. They were each preoccupied with their own thoughts but, such was the closeness of the bond between them, each was aware of what the other was thinking. But they didn't give voice to these thoughts. The unhappy time in their relationship was never spoken of now, buried deep as it was beneath the flood of happy memories that their years together had brought. There were times, however, when they each thought about it, and it was one of those times now.

Grace was remembering how Edwin had abandoned her, suddenly in order to marry someone else – a marriage that, as it happened, had never materialised. And how she had sought consolation with Walter Clayton... There could be no regrets, though, about that, because that marriage had given Grace her darling daughter; the daughter who was now in the midst of so much unhappiness herself. As Grace had listened to Sarah's appalling tale earlier in the day she had found herself thinking of a terrible parallel. Jane Eyre and Mr Rochester, his mad wife confined to the attic... Would it have been better, she wondered, if

Sarah's marriage had been prevented at the altar, as had happened in the book? No, probably not. Sarah had had nearly two years of married bliss before she had found out the terrible truth, and no one could ever take that away from her. But this was real life, not a romantic story. Whoever it was that said the truth was stranger than fiction had certainly been right. And the truth was that her daughter had been living with a man who was not her husband. Edwin, though, seemed to think that it could all be sorted out, and Grace was of the same opinion. She had had a deep regard for Alex Duncan and this had shattered her faith in him; but he loved Sarah, and wasn't it said that love could conquer all?

Edwin was also remembering the time when he had been faithless to his beloved Grace, the only woman in the world he had ever truly loved. And for this reason he couldn't find it in him to condemn Alex too readily. What the fellow had done was wrong, some would say wicked, and many a father would be after the blackguard with a shotgun. But that was not in Edwin's character. He was sure there was a way out of all this mess, provided the writer of those vile anonymous letters didn't cause any more trouble. Who? he asked himself. Who the devil could it be?

This was the question that he pondered with Grace, knowing full well there could be no answer, as they sat together in the twilight of the June evening.

'I could kill whoever has done this to Sarah,' he cried. 'Who, in heaven's name, can it be? She seems to have no idea. If it wasn't for this wicked person she'd still be happy with Alex.'

'And still ignorant of the truth, Edwin,' Grace pointed out. 'We've got to admit, whether we like it or not, that Alex did deceive her. If it hadn't been for that letter she might never have known.'

'Yes, I suppose so.' Edwin looked puzzled. 'And would that have been better or worse, I wonder? They say that ignorance is bliss. It's a pretty kettle of fish at all events, but we've got to give Sarah all the support we can – guard her against wagging tongues. There's bound to be gossip, of course.'

'It's all so very sad.' Grace was looking pensive. 'I was so looking forward to us having grand-children, weren't you, Edwin?' She gave a wistful smile. 'Sarah's our only chance. Not like our Hetty with her three … and she's got a grandchild already.'

'And that was another misfortune,' remarked Edwin. 'At least, it could have been, but it seems to have worked out all right. All families have their problems, Grace, one way or another. I suppose we've become complacent; we'd perhaps thought we were immune from trouble, it's escaped us for so long.'

'We've been happy, darling, haven't we?' Grace's glance was tender but sorrowful. 'Perhaps we've had too much happiness.'

Edwin shook his head. 'No, I'm sure life doesn't work like that; so much grief for one, so much happiness for another. It's largely what you make it, Grace … and we've made one another happy, my dear. And so will Alex and Sarah, you'll see, when they get through all this.'

'D'you think they ever will, Edwin?'

'I'm sure of it. We've just got to be there to help them, both of them.' Edwin spoke positively, but how much of his confidence was assumed for her benefit, Grace didn't know. For her part, she felt very unsure as to how things would work out. Her daughter was devastated. Grace had never seen such bleakness in anyone's eyes and she felt that it would be a long time before Sarah could find it in her heart to forgive Alex for what he had done.

And still the question remained, tormenting Grace and giving her no peace. Who was it that wanted to cause the young couple so much grief? When she found out, the following week, Grace had the shock of her life.

Alex, too, was devastated when he returned home later on that fateful day and found Sarah gone. There was the briefest of notes from her, saying that she was going to stay with her parents for a while and that he hadn't to try to get in touch with her. She didn't want to see him, not yet; she wanted time to think. Alex knew, however much it hurt him, that he must respect what she had said. The pain he had brought to her by his deception was incalculable. He had acted foolishly and recklessly because he had been so much in love with her, but in the end it was Sarah, his beloved wife, who was suffering most of the distress. Yes, wife, he thought to himself defiantly, because that was how he regarded her and always would, whatever might happen. He was distressed, too, but he had always lived with the knowledge of his duplicity, aware that there was a chance, however remote, that it might be discovered.

He made no attempt to go to Park Road to see Sarah. All the same, he wanted to keep a watchful eye on her, to satisfy himself that she was all right – as all right as she could be under the circumstances, and not lying ill in bed or too grief-stricken to go to work. Should there ever be such an emergency, he trusted Grace and Edwin to get in touch with him. His feelings of guilt resurged when he thought of Sarah's parents. Such lovely, praiseworthy people in every way, and he had betrayed them, just as he had betrayed their daughter. They had trusted him with their only child and he had let them down.

Alex had to make as sure as he could that his movements and his surveillance of Sarah went unnoticed. There was a tram-shelter on the other side of the road, opposite Sarah's Café, and it was there that he stood, sometimes in the morning, sometimes in the afternoon, after making sure that his motorcar was parked well out of sight round the corner. He felt like a spy, some undercover agent in a detective story, he thought wrily, and could almost have laughed at himself if he hadn't felt so sick at heart. He saw Sarah getting out of Edwin Donnelly's Humber saloon a couple of times in the morning; and he had seen her in the late afternoon leaving the café and walking, alone, to the tramstop on the opposite side of the road from where he stood. He had been tempted to go to her, to plead with her to come back to him, but he had stayed his ground, knowing instinctively that the time was not yet ripe.

It was whilst he was keeping a watch on Sarah, during his second week without her – for thus was he reckoning the days – that he saw the tall, dark woman emerge from the door of the café. Alex frowned, peering more closely, for the woman seemed familiar to him, but from where, from when, he couldn't quite recall. She started to cross the road towards him and as she turned her head sideways, her dark eyes on an oncoming car, recognition dawned: like a blinding flash it came, and with it the realisation that this was the person who had wreaked such havoc in his life. It could be no other. And Alex knew why... He felt sick as the truth dawned on him. This woman had wanted to get even with him, to pay him back for something for which, in her twisted mind, she had held him responsible all those years ago.

But what on earth was she doing here, in Blackpool, in Sarah's Café? The last time he had seen her she had been in Melrose. What was her name? Murray ... her husband had been Jock Murray, the carpenter. Alex knew that the man had died, although the couple hadn't used his services since that time when the boy had died. She had had a fancy sort of name ... Priscilla, was it? Alex racked his brains. Something like that. No – Drusilla, that was it! Drusilla Murray. She was a gipsy, or had been until she married Jock Murray and began to lead a more settled life.

She had passed out of Alex's sight now, heading

towards the promenade, but Alex stayed where he was, lost in his recollections. He hadn't seen much of the Murrays over the years and he had thought very little about them. But it was obvious that she, Drusilla, had known about him. Not everything – she was unaware that Fiona had died – but enough to make mischief. For he had no doubt in his mind now that it was Drusilla Murray who had written those letters. He had seen the look of hatred in her eyes when the boy had died and had known that she blamed him … although he had been called out too late, much too late. Quite clearly she was a vindictive, unforgiving woman who had recognised him and seen a way of getting back at him.

But what was she doing here, in Sarah's Café? A cleaner, perhaps? Alex had taken little heed of the women who worked for his wife. There had been someone there that day, not so long ago, when he had called in to see her, but he had taken no notice, so engrossed had he been with Sarah … as always. Sarah was coming out of the café now, walking slowly – dejectedly, he thought – towards the tramstop. Alex's heart ached with love for her, but he stayed where he was. Tomorrow, though, he would watch again, at the same time. If Drusilla Murray was a cleaner, as he suspected, then he would doubtless see her again.

To say that Grace was surprised to see Alex walk into Donnelly's store, into her fashion department, was an understatement. She had known that she would have to confront him sooner or

531

later or – more to the point – he would have to confront her. She still retained a high regard for Alex, in spite of what had happened, and felt that his integrity was such that he would not be afraid to meet her and Edwin. Now, face to face with him for the first time, Grace was at a loss for words. But it was Alex who did most of the talking.

'Grace … I must talk to you. It's most urgent. I had to see you – alone. That's why I didn't come to your home. I have to tell someone, and I thought about you.'

Grace ushered him into her office. It was lunchtime, a quiet period in the store. Alex expressed, first of all, his regret for what had happened.

'I know it must be hard for you to understand, or forgive,' he said, 'but I do love Sarah, very much.'

Grace nodded soberly. 'We've never had any doubts about that, Alex.' There seemed, then, to be nothing else that she could say. Recriminations would be pointless. His next words took everything else out of her mind.

'I've found out who it is, who wrote those dreadful letters … and I'm no' sure what to do. I'll have to get her away, right away from Sarah, but I'm so afraid of making matters worse.'

Grace listened in astonishment to Alex's story of the woman he had known so long in Melrose; how her child had died and she had blamed Alex, how she must have borne a grudge all these years. And the woman was now working as a cleaner at Sarah's Café.

'She was a gipsy, you see,' Alex explained. 'She

532

tried all sorts of homemade remedies on the wee laddie. It was a tragic case, but there was nothing I could do. By the time they called me it was too late.'

'A gipsy, you say?' Something stirred in Grace's mind, something which had happened not all that long ago. 'You don't remember her name, do you?'

'Aye, indeed I do. I remember because her husband was the village carpenter. She was Mrs Murray. Drusilla Murray.'

'Drusilla,' Grace whispered the name. 'Oh dear God, not Drusilla … after all this time. But how could it be? It couldn't possibly be her.' Grace was talking almost to herself. She remembered now, quite clearly, what Sarah had called that woman in the café. 'Thank you, Mrs Murray,' she had said. But the woman had given her first name as Pearl…

'Grace, whatever's the matter?' Alex was staring at her in concern. 'You've gone as white as a sheet. Whatever is it? You can't … you don't *know* her, do you?'

'I think so, Alex,' said Grace faintly. She felt, indeed, that she was going to faint with the shock of this discovery. So the woman in the café had been Drusilla after all. She had felt sure, at the time, that she had recognised her, just as she, Drusilla, must have known full well for whom she was working. 'A long time ago,' Grace went on, almost disbelievingly, 'we knew a gipsy girl. She was called Drusilla…'

Grace felt herself reviving a little as she told Alex the story. He had known that Hetty

Gregson had been married to a gipsy called Reuben, who was Zachary's father. It was part of family lore and no secret was made of it; except that there had always been some mystery surrounding Reuben's death. But it was the first time Alex had heard of Reuben's cousin.

'My poor sister used to be frightened to death of her,' said Grace musingly. 'She used to say Drusilla had the Evil Eye. She always blamed her for Reuben's death, but nothing could ever be proved. We thought Hetty was just being fanciful.'

'But … you say you saw her in the café, Grace – that you half-recognised her. Didn't you suspect, when you heard about the letters, that they might be from her?'

'No, why should I?' Grace shook her head. 'I'd convinced myself that the woman wasn't Drusilla. And I had no idea about her connection with you – how could I? It's just a coincidence – a dreadful coincidence – that she should know you … and our family as well.' Grace shuddered. 'She must have seen it as too good a chance to miss. To revenge herself on *all* of us. Hetty used to say that Drusilla hated her. This hasn't harmed Hetty, not personally, but it's the same family … and we've always been very close.'

'But what can we do, Grace?' Alex was looking at her despairingly. 'She mustn't be allowed to do any more harm to Sarah.'

'I'll tell Edwin.' This was always Grace's solution to any problem. 'He'll know what to do. And – Alex…' Grace looked at him fondly. 'Thank you for confiding in me. To come at all took real courage. Now ... don't you think it's time you went to see Sarah? I think she might listen to you by now. My main concern is to see the two of you back together again.'

'And married?' Alex's face was sombre.

'And married, too, of course,' Grace replied unsmilingly.

'It's my main concern as well.' Alex sighed. 'I'll try, but I have a feeling it might be a wee while yet before she'll listen to me.'

Grace watched the gradually dawning horror on her sister's face as she told her the incredible story. She had known that she must tell Hetty. Now she saw all Hetty's colour drain away and a fearful look come into her eyes. 'You say that Drusilla's here ... in Blackpool?' She looked round anxiously, as though the women was about to walk through the door. 'That it's her who wrote those terrible letters? I just can't believe it. After all this time! And to think that she knew Alex as well – it's frightening. What on earth are we going to do?'

'Oh, we've already done it; at least as much as we can do,' said Grace, with an optimism she was far from feeling. 'Edwin's been round there, to Sarah's Café, and given the woman her marching orders, on Sarah's behalf, of course. He gave her a week's pay – and some extra, in lieu of notice – and told her they didn't want to see her near the place again; that she'd caused his daughter a lot of distress and that there was no point in denying it. And he told her she'd got her facts wrong – that Alex's wife had died a few years ago. A slight

535

rearrangement of the truth, but what does it matter? And he said he'd get the police if she caused any more trouble.'

'And what did she say?'

'Oh, she just mumbled something to the effect that she was going anyway. She'd done what she had to do. Edwin says it was the mention of the police that really seemed to put the wind up her. She gave him a funny look, he said. Stared right into his eyes. It made him feel … peculiar, and you know that Edwin isn't given to fanciful ideas.'

Hetty gave a visible shudder. 'I remember only too well how she could look at you. She frightened the life out of me many a time. But what on earth was she doing here, in Blackpool?'

'That's something we may never know,' said Grace. 'Let's hope we've seen the last of her.' She turned as the door of the living room opened. 'Ah, here's Zachary,' she said brightly. 'Hello, dear. Your mother and I were just having a chat. Had a hard day, have you? You look tired.'

'Hello, Aunt Grace.' Zachary nodded at her. 'Yes, I've been up since five, so I reckon I'm a bit whacked.' He looked curiously at Hetty. 'What's up, Mam? You look a bit … odd, like. Is something the matter?'

The two sisters exchanged meaningful glances, and then Hetty said, 'I think we'd better tell him, Grace. Sit down, Zachary. It's only right you should know. I know you've been concerned about Sarah…'

Zachary's reaction to the tale of the gipsy-woman was very surprising. Hetty, who had

536

begun the story, started way back in time, telling him of his father's cousin, Drusilla, 'a real troublemaker, if ever there was one,' and how she had turned up again in Blackpool.

'Oh, my God, no!' breathed Zachary. He closed his eyes as if in pain. 'I was hoping you'd never need to know...'

'Zachary, what on earth are you talking about?' Hetty snapped at him. Grace could tell her sister was still very much on edge.

Zachary shook his head as though he couldn't quite take it all in. 'I met her, Mam,' he began. 'This ... Drusilla. I met her on the prom, and she started talking to me. She thought I was Reuben, you see – my father.'

'When was this?'

'Oh, last March, I think. I'm not quite sure.'

'But why on earth didn't you tell me?'

'I dunno, Mam. I just didn't.' Zachary paused before going on. Then, 'Mam, d'you remember the time you thought our Joseph was missing?'

Hetty nodded. 'Yes, I do indeed, lad.'

'Well, it was her – Drusilla – that had taken him.'

'*What!*'

'Aye. She'd made off with the pram and our Joseph in it, and I happened to see her on Queen Street. We didn't half have a barney, I can tell you, Mam.'

'And you never said.' Hetty was looking at him in amazement. 'You never told me.'

'No, well, I didn't want to upset you, like. I knew you'd go potty if you found out what had really happened, so I let you think I'd taken him

537

to the shop with me.'

'You took all the blame, you mean.' There were tears in Hetty's eyes as she looked at her son. 'I went mad at you, if I remember rightly.'

'Aye, you were a bit narked.'

'And all the time it was her. Oh, my God! My poor baby. When I think what might have–' The tears brimmed out of Hetty's eyes now and began to run down her rosy cheeks. Grace was glad to see her colour had returned. 'Zachary, I'm sorry. I'm so sorry.'

'Yes, that was a very thoughtful thing to do, dear.' Grace smiled warmly at her nephew. 'To try to save your mother all that hurt.'

'Oh, it was nowt.' Zachary shrugged. 'I was blazing mad, though, when I saw her with our Jo, I can tell you. I told her to bugger off... Sorry, Aunt Grace.' He grinned at her. 'No, I didn't exactly say that, but I told her not to show her face round here again. I tried to handle her a bit carefully, like, because I was afraid of what she might do. I reckon she's pots for rags myself. Any-road, you were telling me, Mam. How did you find out about her? How did you know she was here?'

When Zachary heard about Drusilla's latest movements, about how she had been working at Gynn Square and how it was she who had written the letters to Sarah, dismay and alarm were written all over his face.

'Oh no ... no! What have I done? Not Sarah. She tried to harm Sarah.' He put his head in his hands. 'And it's all my fault.'

'Zachary, whatever are you saying?' Grace leaned forward intently. 'This isn't your fault at all. How can it be? As far as I can see, you averted a terrible tragedy with little Joseph. Goodness knows what might have happened. You weren't to know that Drusilla would go and get a job at the café.'

'But if I'd told Mam in the first place…'

'I can't see that it would have made any difference, can you, Hetty?' Grace looked at her sister and Hetty shook her head. 'No, you just saved your mother a lot of unnecessary heartache,' said Grace. 'I'm sorry she's had to know about it now, but we always stick together in our family.'

'I told that Drusilla woman a lot about us, though,' fretted Zachary. 'She was quizzing me, I suppose, although I didn't realise it. She wanted to know about you, Mam.'

'Aye, no doubt she would,' said Hetty grimly.

'I never told her about Joseph, though. She must have found that out for herself. But I mentioned that Aunt Grace was married to Edwin Donnelly … and I told her that Sarah had a café on Gynn Square. But I never mentioned Alex. Oh my God, what have I done?' Zachary cried out again.

'Nothing, lad. You've done nothing,' said Hetty kindly, 'so don't start fretting about it. It sounds as though you had a rare old chinwag though, the pair of you.'

'I never thought of it like that' said Zachary. 'I just thought she was a lonely old woman. A bit barmy, like, but lonely. I was only trying to humour her. I'd no idea she would try to… D'you think that's why she came down here, to try and make trouble for us all?'

Hetty nodded. 'It seems that way. Did she tell you how long she'd been here?'

Zachary frowned. 'Now let me see. No, I don't think so. She told me she'd been living in Scotland for a long time and that her husband had died – and her son as well; she told me about him – and she'd decided to visit her old haunts. That's what she said, her old haunts.'

'Haunts is right,' said Hetty, shuddering again. 'She's like a ghost from the past. I never thought to see or hear from her again.'

'And I'm sure you won't,' said Grace in a matter-of-fact voice. 'Edwin's told her to clear off, so let's hope she's done just that.'

'I'd told her before that she'd better get herself back to Scotland,' said Zachary, 'but she took no notice. She'll damn well take notice of me this time, though.' He clenched his fists, looking determinedly at his mother and aunt. 'I've a good mind to go round to Banks Street right now–'

'Banks Street?' interrupted Hetty.

'Aye, that's where she said she was living.'

'But that's only just round the corner! She was so near, and I never knew.'

'P'raps just as well, Mam,' said Zachary. 'I don't know the number, but I'll find her, don't you worry. If I could get my hands on her, right now...'

Grace was alarmed at the blazing hatred in her nephew's eyes. 'Leave it till tomorrow, dear,' she said placatingly. 'I think you'll find that Drusilla's already got the message. You'll probably discover that she's gone.'

'I hope so. For all our sakes, I hope so,' Zachary

muttered. He stared unseeingly across the room for a moment, before meeting his aunt's eyes. 'How's Sarah?' he asked in a quite different voice. 'Is she all right?'

Grace sighed. 'As all right as can be expected, I suppose, under the circumstances.'

'Her and Alex – they're not...?' he asked diffidently.

'Back together again? No, I'm afraid not.' Grace shook her head sadly. 'I tried my best. Alex came to see me, about all this business with Drusilla, and I advised him to call round and see Sarah. I thought she might listen to him by now, but I was wrong. She's still insisting that she wants some time away from him. In fact, Alex is going away for a while.'

'Going away? Where to?' asked Hetty. It was the first time that she, as well as Zachary, had heard of this.

'He's taking a post as locum up in Northumberland – Hexham, I believe. The young doctor up there is going off on a training course and they want a relief doctor to fill in for about three months. He wouldn't have decided to go, of course, if there had been any chance of him and Sarah getting back together. But he seemed to think it was the best thing to do under the circumstances. He phoned me up to tell me as soon as he had decided.'

'And what does Sarah think about it?' asked Hetty.

'She doesn't seem to care very much. Alex also told me that she put the phone down on him. She refused to talk about it. I think it was a spur-of-the-moment decision on Alex's part. I must admit that I thought at first that he was running away from trouble again, like he did over his ... over Fiona. But I suppose it will be for the best, all things considered. It will stop the gossip if we can say that he's had to work away for a few months. And Dr Mason's recently taken on a young trainee doctor, you know, so that makes it look as though Alex's absence has been planned for a while.'

'Does Dr Mason know about ... everything?' asked Hetty.

'I'm not sure. Alex must have said something to him, but I don't know how much Dr Mason knows. Alex may still stay here, of course, if he can get Sarah to change her mind and – and marry him. But I've never known that daughter of mine to be so obstinate about anything as she's being about this.'

'She's got good cause, Aunt Grace,' said Zachary, who had been listening intently and saying nothing. 'It must have been a terrible blow to her. The dependable Dr Duncan, of all people. Every woman's hero...'

'That'll do, Zachary,' said Hetty quietly.

'No, I see your point, dear.' Grace gave him an understanding look. 'You're sure to feel indignant on her behalf. We all did, at first, but now ... well, we just hope it can all be sorted out, eventually. Alex hopes, if he does have to go, that a spell apart may do the trick. The old saying of absence making the heart grow fonder, I suppose.'

'Can I go and see her?' asked Zachary suddenly.

'Our Sarah?' Grace looked at him in some surprise. 'Well, of course you can, dear. You don't need to ask, surely.'

'No, but well … I thought she might be a bit embarrassed, like.' Zachary seemed somewhat ill-at-ease himself. 'With people talking and all that.'

'But you're family, aren't you, dear? Yes, I'm sure she'd be pleased to see you.'

'She's still at your place, is she, Aunt Grace? She'll not be moving back to her own house, when Alex … if Alex goes away?'

'I can't speak for Sarah,' said Grace slowly. 'All I can say is that I have a feeling she'll be with us for quite a while.' She turned to look at Hetty. 'She was a great one for having her independence, was our Sarah. I remember when she first opened the café; she couldn't wait to have her own place. And now … now it just seems as though she wants looking after again, as though she's afraid of being entirely on her own.'

'She's been badly hurt, poor lamb,' sighed Hetty. She stopped, glancing upwards as a noise of bumping and banging came from the room above.

Zachary grinned and cast his eyes towards the ceiling. 'That's His Lordship waking up. He lets us know, doesn't he, Mam? Shall I go and get him?'

'Yes, please,' said Hetty. 'I was just thinking we'd been peaceful too long.' She turned confidently to her sister as Zachary left the room. 'I must say he's been much better with our Joseph lately. And d'you know, come to think of it, it all started from that time when I thought he'd gone off with him. Oh Gracie … if only I'd known.'

'Just as well you didn't, as your Zachary told you. He's much improved, Hetty,' Grace went on, gesturing towards the room above, from where they could hear the child's voice shouting: 'Zac! Zac!' 'I think this could well be a turning point with you and Zachary. I know he's been … difficult, but I was really impressed by what he was telling us, how he didn't want you to be hurt.'

'Yes, he's been much more thoughtful all round, just lately,' said Hetty. 'I put a lot of it down to him having his ladyfriend back in Blackpool. She's a grand girl, is Ivy, and she's good for our Zachary. I think we might be hearing wedding bells there quite soon. Isn't that right, dear?' she went on as Zachary re-entered the room carrying Joseph in his arms. 'I was just telling our Grace about you and Ivy; you're thinking of getting married at the back end, aren't you?'

'There's nothing settled yet, Mam. Honestly, you women! You never let a fellow have any peace.' He grinned at Grace, giving a slight wink, and she could see in that instant the appeal that this young man might have for the girls.

'I was only repeating what Ivy said.' Hetty sounded flustered. 'And you know you've been waiting ages for her to make up her mind.'

'It's up to both of us, Mam, and we haven't made our minds up yet, not properly … not about the date. Anyroad, what about this outing we're supposed to be having next week?' He seemed to want to change the subject. 'Is it still on? Nancy's got the tickets and I know she's looking forward to us all seeing the show – so is Ivy. Are you going, Aunt Grace?'

'I think so, Zachary. I don't see why not,' said Grace, but hesitantly. She stroked little Joseph's auburn curls as he stopped by her chair, his big blue eyes staring curiously into her own. He didn't seem to be quite sure who this lady was. 'The image of his mummy, isn't he?' she remarked, 'and his gran. Yes, Nancy was saying she would like Edwin and me to come to the show, when she came in about her dresses. But that was before…' Grace bit her lip. 'Still, there's no reason why we shouldn't go. I'll try to persuade Sarah to come as well, but as I've said, I can't speak for her. What about you, Hetty? And Mother and George? Are you all going?'

'Yes, if we can get someone to look after this little scallywag.' Hetty lifted Joseph on her knees, laying her cheek against his soft curls. 'That's always the main consideration. I thought I might ask Alice and Henry if they'd oblige. They'd happen be glad of a chance to see Joseph. He's their great-grandchild as well.'

'So there should be quite a big party of us,' said Grace, rising to her feet. 'It'll be a nice change. It's ages since we had a family get-together. No, I'll see myself out,' she said, as Hetty made to get up. 'I know you've a lot to do.' She smiled at little Joseph. 'Mummy will be home soon, won't she? And Aunty Ivy, and they'll be wanting their tea.'

Hetty gave a slight frown. Grace wasn't sure

whether it was her use of the word 'mummy' that had done it or whether Hetty was thinking of all the work that had to be done preparing the visitors' teas. Grace hadn't meant to be tactless; she never knew quite what to call people in this household.

'Aye, they'll be wanting their teas, right enough, all of 'em,' said Hetty. 'They're always ready to eat me out of house and home when they've had a matinée. But sandwiches is all they'll get, and a meal tonight when they've done both houses.'

'Sounds like hard work, Hetty,' Grace remarked, stooping to kiss her sister's cheek. 'I don't know how you do it, I'm sure. Now, don't you go worrying any more about Drusilla. Put her out of your mind. I'm only sorry you had to know, but it wouldn't have been fair to keep you in the dark.'

'Yes … Drusilla,' Hetty murmured, snuggling the child on her knee closer to her. 'Who'd have thought it, after all these years? You never knew what that monkey 'ud get up to next. But your Uncle Zachary told her, didn't he, my pet? Nobody's going to hurt our little lad, no they're not…'

'I'll settle her, Aunt Grace,' said Zachary as he held the door open for her. Grace was pleased to see the improvement in the young man's manners; at one time he would have left her to see herself out. 'Drusilla, I mean. I'll make sure she'll not come sniffing round again, not round any of us.'

'Be careful, Zachary,' Grace warned him again. 'Don't go losing your temper.'

'Don't worry,' Zachary replied cheerfully. 'I know how far to go. But you're probably right, Aunt Grace. The bird will most likely have flown.'

Chapter 25

But if the gipsywoman was still in Blackpool, Zachary was determined to find her. He started, the following morning, knocking on doors at the top end of Banks Street and it wasn't until he had gone all the way down one side and halfway up the other that he found her. And then it seemed that he had almost been too late; for when the landlady showed him into the attic room he saw Drusilla dressed in her black coat and hat – in spite of the warmth of the late June day – with two shabby bulging holdalls at her feet.

'Going somewhere, Drusilla?' Zachary kept his tightly clenched fists at his side and his voice was low. He didn't want an irate landlady showing him the door, but he was going to have his say.

'Reuben!' Drusilla's eyes were wary and she took a step back. 'You didn't tell them, did you? You promised you wouldn't...'

'It's Zachary, not Reuben,' he said evenly.

'Yes ... Zachary. I meant Zachary. You didn't tell them, did you?'

'If you mean the police...' Drusilla gave a frightened gasp at the word. 'No, I didn't tell them. But it would have damned well served you right if I had. Pinching our kid ... then causing all that trouble for my cousin and her husband.'

'He's not her husband! How can he be her husband? He's got a wife in the lunatic asylum.

And that lovely lady, that cousin of yours, she's too good for the likes of him. I only wanted to save her.'

Zachary was inclined to agree with her. Sarah *was* too good for the likes of Alex Duncan, and for a moment he almost felt an empathy with Drusilla. But she had made Sarah desperately unhappy, and that he could never countenance. 'He is her husband! You got your facts wrong, didn't you?' he lied, just as Edwin Donnelly had done before him. 'And you've just about wrecked their marriage with your damned interfering. I told you to clear off back to Scotland and my Uncle Edwin told you an' all, but you took no notice. Why didn't you go, eh?'

'Had to serve my notice, didn't I?' said Drusilla gruffly. 'At the other place. I needed the money.'

'Well, you're going this time, and I'm going to make jolly sure that you do.' Zachary picked up her bags, one in each hand. 'Come on, Drusilla. 'You've a train to catch, haven't you?' He pushed open the door with his foot. 'Go on. Let's be having you. I'll see you to the station, make sure you get there all right.'

'I'm not going yet.' Drusilla stood her ground in the centre of the room. 'You can't make me, Reuben Loveday. You can't tell me what to do. You always tried to, but you can't. Anyway, there's not a train till two o'clock.'

'There's a train in half an hour, and I know 'cause I work there.' Zachary motioned with his head towards the door. 'Go on, get moving. You'd better, I'm warning you, or else I'll tell–'

That was enough for Drusilla. She gave him a

549

cowed look and hung her head as though defeated, then quickly went out of the door and down the three flights of stairs. They didn't speak on the way to the station. Zachary slowed his brisk steps to keep apace of Drusilla's shambling walk, but they couldn't get there fast enough for him. Not until he saw her safely on the train bound for Scotland would Zachary feel safe.

He waited while she bought her ticket then saw her to a corner seat in a compartment where there were two other women. He humped her bags on to the luggage rack, then, somewhat hesitantly, he held out his hand. 'Goodbye, Drusilla,' he said in a firm voice which held more than a trace of kindness and concern. 'Take care. It's for the best, you know.'

Drusilla nodded. 'Goodbye … Reuben,' she said. A weird little smile played round her lips and her eyes seemed to be boring into him, right into the depths of his soul. A shiver ran through him as he jumped off the train and strode away down the platform.

Drusilla Loveday would not be told what to do. She never had and she was not going to start now. She waited until the young man's figure had disappeared, beyond the barrier, right across the station, then she got to her feet.

'Forgot something,' she mumbled, pulling at the strap that opened the door and stepping out on to the platform.

'The train'll be going in a few minutes, love,' a woman called after her in warning. 'Mind you don't miss it.'

'What about your luggage?' shouted a man who was just entering the compartment.

''Spect she's just gone for a magazine,' said the woman. 'She'll be back. Cutting it fine, though.'

But a few moments later when the guard had waved his flag and blown his whistle, the woman hadn't returned. The man shrugged. 'There's one born every minute,' he mumbled, opening his *Daily Express*.

Drusilla, head down, muttering to herself, was now hurrying back along Dickson Road...

'Well, we've seen the last of Drusilla, you'll be pleased to know.' Zachary smiled at Sarah as he sat down in the chair opposite her. 'She's on her way home to Bonnie Scotland.' He looked at his wrist-watch. 'She should nearly be there by now, I reckon.' He told her briefly what had taken place and Sarah breathed a heartfelt sigh.

'Thank goodness for that. And thank you for all you've done, Zachary. My mother was telling me how concerned you were, and about little Joseph as well. Just fancy that! I can't believe that she knew so much about us all. When I employed her she seemed such an ordinary sort of woman; a bit shabby. I felt sorry for her – I was sure she needed the money.'

'You didn't notice anything ... peculiar about her, then?'

'Not particularly. Her eyes were a bit strange – she'd an odd way of looking at you – but I must confess I didn't take all that much notice. You never do–' Sarah had been going to add 'of cleaning ladies', but she didn't. It wouldn't be strictly true, anyway. The reason Sarah hadn't taken too much notice was because she had been preoccupied, that melancholia that had started with her grandmother's death creeping up on her, as though she were waiting for something worse to happen.

She had been unaccountably pleased to see Zachary on the doorstep this afternoon. She had the house to herself as it was her half-day, and Grace and Edwin were at the store. Zachary told her he had checked with her mother and found that she would be at home. Now they sat in the drawing room whilst Mrs Jolly, the housekeeper, made them a cup of tea. It was nice not to have to dissemble, thought Sarah, as she looked at Zachary's friendly, familiar face. Here was someone, a member of the family, who knew the whole sad story, and she sensed that he would not say too much about it to hurt her, to rub salt into a wound that was still raw. He might have done at one time, but Zachary had changed. Her mother had told her, in some surprise, that he seemed to be a much more considerate young man now; and Sarah, looking at him, thought that this was true. When she was a girl – many moons ago now, it seemed – she had viewed him with the veiled eyes of love. Then, when the veil had been ripped away, she had caught a glimpse of what others had seen all along – a rather self-seeking, at times uncaring sort of person. And Sarah had realised, on meeting Alex, that her love for Zachary had been based mainly on girlish hopes and dreams, together with a very strong family feeling. This, though, seemed to be a new Zachary.

'Alex has gone, then?' he asked hesitantly as Sarah poured out the tea that Mrs Jolly had placed on a small table.

'Yes – and I must admit it's a great relief,' said Sarah. 'It was all the pretence that was getting to me. Knowing that people were talking – and it's only natural they would – about us not living together. Now we can say, quite truthfully, that Alex has gone to work away for several months.'

'I'm very sorry, Sarah,' Zachary murmured, looking down at his feet in some embarrassment. 'It's the first time I've mentioned it to you, but I do know about it, of course. I had to come and see you.'

'I'm glad you did,' said Sarah warmly. 'I don't have to pretend with you. It's so difficult with people like Mrs Jolly...' she nodded towards the door '...and people I work with, and Father's staff ... so many people, and they all must think it's very odd. We thought the best thing to do was to say as little as possible and hope it'll all be a nine days' wonder.'

Zachary gave a grin. 'That's one of Gran's expressions, isn't it? And you know what else she always says: "While folks are talking about you they're leaving someone else alone".'

Sarah laughed. 'That's true. It's human nature to gossip, I suppose, but it's not so good when you're the target for it.'

'No, it must have been awful for you,' said Zachary softly. 'Always wondering if someone would find out the truth. But now Drusilla's gone there's no chance of that.'

'The truth,' Sarah repeated thoughtfully. 'Yes, I

suppose when you think about it logically what Alex did was a criminal offence. I told him so, when I first found out, but he seemed to think that he'd done nothing really wrong, especially after his ... after Fiona died. It was as though he had blinkers on. I always knew that he loved me.'

'I daresay he did have blinkers on, Sarah, where you were concerned,' said Zachary gently, 'and who could blame him?' Sarah looked away, uneasy at his intense gaze. 'Nobody'll find out now, though,' he went on, more normally. 'You can rest assured on that score.'

'It's the hurt, too,' Sarah continued, finding that she did, at last, want to talk a little about it. 'I can't get over the hurt he's caused me. Someone I loved and trusted so much letting me down so completely. Even my mother and father don't seem to understand fully how I feel. They think we can just ... get married again, patch matters up and get on with our lives as though nothing has happened. But it's not as simple as that. I can't. I know I can't do that ... not yet.'

'D'you feel as though you're still married to him?' asked Zachary.

'I don't know.' Sarah shook her head in a bewildered manner. 'Part of me does. We were so happy together. We really were very happy, Zachary,' she repeated, looking at him keenly. 'But always it comes back to this ... hurt. There's a deep ache inside me – not a physical pain, but a real pain all the same – and it won't go away. I can't forget.'

'D'you still love him?' Zachary's tone was abrupt.

'Yes ... I still love him,' Sarah sighed, 'but I couldn't go on living with him. Not after all the lies and deception, even though he insists that it was all because he loved me. No – I know we have to stay apart for a while, and this job in Northumberland seems to be the answer, I suppose.'

'D'you think you might be trying to ... to punish him, maybe? To make him suffer for what he's done to you?'

Sarah looked at Zachary in surprise and in admiration, too. She had never known him, before, to be so perceptive. 'I think you may have hit the nail on the head,' she said quietly. 'Perhaps, deep down, that's what I'm doing, although I hadn't realised it. At least I'm coming to terms with it all a bit more now, even though it still hurts like mad. And the family have been wonderful. There's not a soul knows outside of the family, and I know it'll stay that way. You and Joyce and Gran ... and everyone; it's so good to know that everybody cares so much about me.'

'I've always cared, Sarah. I don't want you to think that I ever stopped caring.' Zachary was looking at her intently again in a way that made her a little uneasy. 'When we ... when we split up that time, I told you I still cared, and I do. I wish ... sometimes I wish that that had never happened. I wish we could be friends again – more than friends, like we used to be. It's not impossible ... is it, Sarah?' His deep brown eyes now held the look that she had so often searched for in the past ... and failed to find. It was there now, though, a look that told her that he really did care. 'And now that you're on your own, I'd like to – oh hell, Sarah! – I'd like to look after you.'

Sarah smiled at him, very sadly. 'It's sweet of you, Zachary, but you don't really mean it, you know. A lot has happened since that time, and you've got your Ivy now.' Zachary looked down at his feet. 'You're just feeling sorry for me, and I appreciate it, honestly I do. But you've your own life to lead, and a grand girl to share it with you.'

'Damn it all, Sarah.' Zachary was looking at her despairingly. 'I ... I love you!'

How often Sarah had waited to hear those words in the past and they had never been spoken. Now that they were she had no doubt but that Zachary meant them, or thought he did, but it wouldn't do. Herself and Zachary – she had known for a long time that it would never have been right. 'And I love you too, Zachary,' she said softly. 'But as a cousin and a very dear friend, and if you think about it you'll realise that that is what you feel for me.'

'But ... what will you do, Sarah? You're on your own again. You're not ... damn it all, you're not even married any more. You need somebody.'

'I'll survive.' Sarah sighed. 'As I told you, I've a good family and I've a thriving business and my health and strength. Everything I need, you could say.'

'And ... Alex?'

Sarah closed her lips in a grim line before she spoke. 'We'll see,' she said. 'I ... don't know. But there's Ivy for you, isn't there?' She smiled at him. 'And she's a certainty. Oh come on, Zachary,' she went on, as he didn't reply, 'if ever there was a girl that was right for you it's Ivy Rathbone. She adores you, anybody can see that, and she's good for you, too.'

'So everybody keeps telling me.' Zachary gave a grimace. 'She can see right through me, and that's a fact.'

'Is that such a bad thing? To know someone's faults and still go on loving them?' Sarah stopped, aware of what she had just said. 'Maybe it's myself I should be talking to,' she said, almost under her breath. Then, 'You love her, don't you Zachary?' she went on. 'I'm sure you do. You've had enough to say about her dangling you on a string, not wanting to give up her stage career.'

'Yes, I care about her,' said Zachary. 'I suppose I must love her. I meant it, though, when I said I loved you. I do.' He looked puzzled.

'It's possible to love more than one person,' said Sarah. 'There are different kinds of love. But Ivy's your girl.'

'Aye, she is. I realise that. Though I must admit I've got a bit fed up of waiting while she's prancing around on the stage. I suppose I've been a bit selfish really… I've not been entirely faithful to her.' Zachary paused, looking awkwardly down at the floor.

'You do surprise me!' He looked up again at the irony in Sarah's voice, then grinned at her, as cheekily as ever.

'Anyroad, the concert party are back in Blackpool, and Ivy with them,' he said, 'so that puts an end to my carryings-on.'

'And you're glad to have her back,' said Sarah firmly.

'Yes ... s'pose I am. We're having a family outing in a couple of weeks to the pier show. Has Aunt Grace told you?'

'Yes, she's mentioned it,' replied Sarah guardedly.

'There'll be Mam and Joyce and me, Gran and Grandad Makepeace, your mam and dad ... and you'll come as well, won't you, Sarah?'

Sarah hesitated. Then, 'Yes, I do believe I will,' she said. 'It's ages since I heard Nancy sing, and your Ivy. Yes, why not? I think it might be a great idea. And it'll certainly help to stop the wagging tongues if it's seen that I'm going out and about as normal.'

They chatted for a little while about family matters, and when he was leaving Zachary kissed her gently on the lips. 'Take care, Sarah,' he said, very concernedly. 'You're looking a bit pale. You are all right, aren't you, apart from...?'

'Perfectly all right,' she assured him. 'As you say, "apart from" ... and that's sure to have taken its toll, isn't it? Yes, I'm fine, and all the better for having talked with you. Thank you for coming, Zachary.' She reached up and kissed his cheek. 'See you soon.'

She smiled to herself after he had gone. It had been good to see her cousin again.

It was the day after Zachary's visit to Sarah that Hetty saw the piece in the *Evening Gazette*. Zachary took little notice at first as she started to read it out at the tea-table. His mother was in the habit of reading out loud bits and pieces that she saw in the local newspaper and they were usually of no consequence.

'There's been an accident on Dickson Road,' she began. 'I know myself how busy it's getting with the trams an' all. It's them that cause the problems, cluttering up the roads. I sometimes have to wait ages before I can get across with our Joseph in the pram. It wasn't a tram, though. Seems it was just a bicyclist that caused it...'

Zachary mumbled in agreement, just to show that he was listening, but he was more concerned with filling his mouth with his mother's delicious homemade Eccles cakes. His ears pricked up, though, as she began to read the passage.

'"Police are anxious to get in touch with anyone who can identify the woman who was so tragically killed in the accident. Witnesses say that she walked into the road without looking and collided with a bicyclist. She fell to the ground, striking her head against the kerb, and was found to be dead on arrival at Victoria Hospital. Police say that she was a woman of about fifty years of age, dark-haired and dark-eyed with a swarthy complexion and she was shabbily dressed in a black coat and a black felt hat. She was not carrying a handbag, so there was no means of identifying the body..."'

Zachary stopped with his cake halfway to his mouth, staring at his mother in disbelief. 'It's her,' he spluttered, through a mouthful of crumbs.

'What? Don't talk with your mouth full Zachary. What did you say?'

Zachary swallowed hastily. 'It's her,' he repeated. 'Drusilla. It must be. It can't be anyone

559

else. Dark hair, shabbily dressed, Dickson Road… It's got to be her!'

'Don't be silly, Zachary. How can it be? Drusilla's in Scotland. You told me yourself you saw her on to the train.'

'I saw her get on the train … but I didn't see it leave. It's her, Mam, I know it is. You've told me yourself she's as crafty as a cartload of monkeys. She must have got off again.'

'Oh, come on, lad. Be reasonable. You're letting your imagination run away with you. There must be lots of women who fit that description.'

But nothing would move Zachary from the conviction he had that this woman was Drusilla. 'There's only one way to find out, Mam,' he said, 'and that's to go and see. And there's no time like the present. I'll get on my bicycle now and go to the hospital.'

Hetty sighed. 'I think you're being silly but I know nothing'll shake you once you've got a bee in your bonnet. You'd best go to the Police Station first, though, hadn't you?'

It was, of course, Drusilla, as Zachary had known all along it would be, although why on earth she should have got off the train was a complete mystery, one they would never solve.

'Aye, it's her. It's my aunt,' he said quietly, as the doctor drew back the sheet from the sallow, marbled face. 'Well, not my aunt exactly. She was my father's cousin. A sort of aunt, I suppose.'

Zachary had seen hundreds of corpses on the battlefield; they had frequently featured since then in his nightmares; but it was the first time he had seen the body of someone who had died in what might be called normal circumstances. There was a livid bruise, black and blue and yellow, near her temple, partially covered by her lank greasy hair, and Zachary knew that she must have fallen with some force for the blow to cause her death. He turned away, feeling a moment's compassion for the woman, even though she had caused such havoc in his family.

But the police took some convincing that he really did know her. It was understandable, Zachary supposed. It was such a strange tale, of a second cousin turning up after twenty-five years, someone whom he had never known about before. He told the police nothing about the trouble she had caused, save to say that she had worked for a time for his cousin, Sarah, and that Edwin Donnelly, who was his uncle, would be able to confirm his story.

Edwin was a prominent citizen of the borough and he soon affirmed what Zachary had said. A long-distance call to the police in Melrose, Scotland, verified that Drusilla Murray had been missing from her home since last March and that no one knew of her whereabouts.

'My goodness, this is a tale and a half,' said Hetty, in some disbelief, when Zachary returned home much later that evening, accompanied by Edwin. 'The trouble that woman's caused us, and we're still not rid of her, even now she's dead. And I know I shouldn't say it, but I'm glad an' all, glad she's gone. She won't get up to any more mischief now, and that's for sure. And you say you're going to see to the funeral Zachary? Why should it be you, for heaven's sake?'

'I offered, Mam. Seems there's no one else,' said Zachary simply. 'Well, she's probably got lots of relations up and down the country, but gipsies are hard to track down and the woman's got to be buried. Soon.'

Edwin joined in now. It was he, together with the police, who had decided on the course to follow. 'We're going to get in touch with a solicitor up in Melrose,' he said, 'to sort out Drusilla's affairs. We don't know, as yet, whether she had her own home, or any possessions. In fact, we don't know the first thing about her.'

'Except that she was a load of trouble,' said Hetty, almost under her breath.

'And I've offered to help Zachary with the funeral arrangements here' Edwin went on. 'It'll be very simple, of course. We'll take her to Layton Cemetery...'

'There's a plot at Marton,' said Hetty tonelessly. 'There's only ... only Reuben in it. You can put her there, if you like. I suppose it's only fitting she should lie alongside one of her own kin, and we don't know where the rest of 'em are. Don't expect me to come, that's all.'

'No ... no, we don't,' said Edwin sympathetically. 'I'll go with Zachary. I doubt if there'll be anyone else there, apart from the clergyman.'

'It's uncanny,' said Hetty, in a faraway voice. 'It's incredible. She fell, and banged her head on the kerb ... and it killed her. That's exactly what happened to Reuben.'

'What?' said Zachary. 'What are you saying, Mam? What do you mean?' It was the first time he had heard anything about the circumstances

562

surrounding his father's death.

'I never told you, lad. There didn't seem much point. Your father … Reuben … he fell and hit his head, but it was inside, on the steel fender. And she hit her head on the kerb. It seems as though the wheel has gone full circle…'

There were only three people at the graveside, Zachary, Ivy and Edwin, as the vicar intoned the finals words of the burial service. Zachary threw the clods of earth on to the coffin; then he stood motionless as his uncle and the vicar walked back up the path. His eyes were fixed on the single spray of red roses, the only tribute for a woman who, he imagined, had in her youth been like a full-blown rose herself. His mother had told him how she had used to dress in red with golden circlets dangling from her ears.

'We brought her to this,' he said, as Ivy took hold of his hand. 'All of us. Me, Edwin, my mam … Sarah, too, I suppose. We never really had time for her.'

'Zachary, what on earth are you saying? You know that isn't true,' Ivy protested. 'Your mother will tell you – Drusilla was her own worst enemy. She brought it on herself. It's a tragedy, yes, but it's no one's fault. It just happened.'

'Aye, I suppose so,' said Zachary resignedly, 'and we'll never know why. But, like my mam says, the wheel's gone full circle. There's a certain … rightness in it. She wanted Reuben and she couldn't have him. My mam's been telling me all about that, this last day or two. But now, when she's dead, she's got him, at last.'

The tears came to his eyes as he read the wording on the simple gravestone. *Reuben Loveday, the dearly loved husband of Henrietta. Died May 25th, 1898, aged 26 years. Rest in peace.*

'Come along, love,' said Ivy gently, squeezing his hand. 'You've done all that you can do.'

'Yes, and life is for the living, isn't it?' He smiled at her. 'I've heard my gran say that, many a time. And we've a lot of living to do, haven't we, Ivy?'

Chapter 26

Nancy stood near the window of her bedroom, her mouth opened wide, peering anxiously inside with the aid of a mirror. Yes, her throat was a little red but not, thank goodness, swollen at all. If she had a good gargle with salt and hot water she should be all right. These summer colds were always the worst, and trust her to get one when she wanted to be at her best. It was tomorrow night that all the family was coming to watch her and she had been looking forward to it for so long. Nancy, like all artistes, loved the adulation of an audience; she wondered whether her family would be more or less critical because they knew her so well. At all events, she wanted to be at the very peak of her performance. She'd heard that Barney Bellamy might be coming along as well and she wanted him to see how much she had improved since she sang for him on the Golden Mile. It was three years since she had first met Barney, and what a lot had happened since then. Who would have thought, at that time, that she would have a successful stage career ahead of her or that she would, by the time she was twenty-two, be the mother of a fifteen-month-old boy.

At the thought of Joseph she frowned slightly. She put her tortoiseshell-backed mirror down on the dressing table and flopped on to the bed, making the springs of the old brass bedstead creak. The boarding house was bursting at the seams, with the concert party, plus a few visitors on Wakes' Weeks from the inland towns, and the members of the Gregson family. And the daughter of the house, as usual, was banished to the attic to sleep on a lumpy flock mattress, whilst her son slept in his cot in his grandmother's room. Nancy wasn't sure why she should feel so resentful. She had been glad enough for her mother to care for Joseph in the beginning and, as Mam said, it made sense for the child to go on sleeping in the room that he was used to. But she couldn't help feeling a bit peeved when she saw him trotting around the house hand in hand with her mother. He hardly ever seemed to leave her side, or, more correctly, her mother hardly ever let him out of her sight. That was understandable after that carry-on with the gipsy cousin who had turned up after all those years. Nancy, quite rightly, had been told all about that, but she hadn't attached any blame to Hetty. It was coming to something if you couldn't leave a child sleeping peacefully in his own front garden without some crackpot turning up and taking him.

No, Nancy knew that Joseph was in safe hands with her mother. He was everybody's 'blue-eyed boy', metaphorically as well as physically. Even Zachary had started making a fuss of him now, tossing him up in the air and catching him and making him scream with laughter. It was Zachary who was teaching the little boy to say 'Mummy' and 'Gran', pointing to the child's respective relations, and Nancy was very grateful to her

566

brother for this. It hurt more than a little when she heard her mother say to Joseph, 'Show Nancy your new shoes,' or some such thing, never: 'Show Mummy.' It seemed to be only Hetty who did this, although, in all fairness, Nancy had never heard her mother refer to herself as the child's 'mummy'. There was little doubt, though, that this was how Hetty often thought of herself and Nancy was pleased that Zachary was trying to put the matter straight in Joseph's mind. Zachary was a much nicer person these days, Nancy found herself thinking.

Her thoughts soon flitted away from the vexed problem of her child, as they often did when she could find no solution, back to herself and the forthcoming performance. She would have to try and save her voice tonight and not sing out too lustily, or she might find that she had none left at all for tomorrow night's show. It might be as well if she were to ask Sid if she could leave out her solo number, 'Ma, He's Making Eyes at Me,' just for tonight.

Nancy's cheeks were flushed, but as she looked at her reflection in the dressing-room mirror the following day, she tried to tell herself that it was due to excitement and not because she might be running a temperature. She had gargled frequently since yesterday and, as there had been no matinée, had spent most of the day resting in bed. A few doses of aspirin had taken away most of the pain in her throat and she was determined that she was going to push it all to the back of her mind and give the performance of her life. She hadn't said a word to anyone about how she was feeling; even her mother thought she was only 'resting up' in preparation for tonight. She had decided, on second thoughts, to sing her solo number the previous night, but she had been aware that it had lacked her usual verve and exuberance. Nobody, however, had made any comment. Nancy thought that Sid might have told her that she was not up to her usual standard, but he hadn't seemed to notice.

'Sounds like a full house tonight,' said Ivy, coming into the dressing room. 'I've just been on stage and I can hear the hubbub from the audience. Funny how you can tell, isn't it even when the curtains are closed, that it's standing room only.'

'As full as that?' said Nancy. 'Good gracious!'

'Pretty near, I would say,' Ivy replied. 'Of course, there's an extra special crowd in tonight with all our lot. They'll take up nearly a full row, won't they. I know you got a lot of tickets.'

'Eight,' said Nancy. 'There's Mum and Joyce and Zachary, Gran and Grandad, and Aunt Grace, Uncle Edwin and Sarah. That is, if Sarah decides to come. Zachary said she would, but you never know if she might change her mind again. Aunt Grace was telling Mam that she's very much up and down at the moment... Poor Sarah. But it just goes to show that you can't trust fellows, not any of 'em.'

'Yes, poor Sarah,' said Ivy, though not commenting on Nancy's last remark. Ivy was the only person outside of the family who knew about Sarah and Alex, and this was because she was

Zachary's fiancée. 'I like Sarah. I always have, though I know that Zachary's still got a soft spot for her.'

'Not any more, has he?' Nancy looked surprised. 'As far as I can see he's potty about you. He's been pretty decent one way and another just lately, has our Zachary. You've worked wonders with him, Ivy.'

'Don't know that it's me.' Ivy shrugged. 'But I must admit he's been a lot better. He seems to be thinking of other people more instead of himself. He was marvellous over all that business with his cousin, the gipsywoman. It's funny … I always knew he was a selfish so and so, but I couldn't help loving him. Anyway, we've "named the day", as my mother puts it.'

'Gosh! Have you?' Nancy gave her friend an odd look. 'Definitely? Our Zachary never said.'

'We've only just decided,' replied Ivy. 'I've written to tell my parents, and Zachary's told your mother, so you're the next to know.'

'When is it going to be?'

'October. That'll give me a chance to wind down a bit after the show finishes here.'

'Are you getting married in Blackpool?'

'No … Halifax.' Ivy grinned. 'I'm a Yorkshire lass, tha knows. But I'm hoping you'll all come across the Pennines to the wedding. We thought it was about time,' she went on. 'I'm twenty-six now. Almost on the shelf, you could say, and Zachary's only a year younger. You know that, of course.'

Ivy stopped abruptly, noticing the blank look in Nancy's eyes and the fixed smile on her face. Yes

… Ivy recalled how Nancy had vowed, after that episode with Clive Conway, that she would never get married, never have any more to do with men, in fact. And, so far, she hadn't. It wasn't likely, therefore, that she would be eager to listen to someone else's ramblings about weddings and such-like.

'So I'll be hanging up my shoes when this lot's finished,' Ivy concluded.

'You're giving up your stage career?'

'Yes, I think it would be as well,' said Ivy, in a matter-of-fact voice. She didn't want to say too much about finding a little place to rent, settling down and looking after Zachary – starting a family, maybe – which was what she had suddenly decided she wanted to do.

'So we'll have to find someone else for the Trio,' said Nancy, looking woebegone. 'Oh Ivy, I will miss you.'

'Go on with you! You'll still see me. I'll be your sister-in-law, won't I?'

'Oh yes – how funny. Does Rose know yet?' asked Nancy.

'No, not yet. Or Sid, so keep it under your hat, there's a love. I'll tell them soon. It's time Rose was getting herself back here, too. We'll be on in about fifteen minutes. After the opening number there's only Sid, then it's us. And Rose hasn't got all her clobber on yet.' The Trio's first appearance was a sporting scene, and Ivy pointed to Rose's brown leather peaked riding hat and crop lying on a chair. 'I bet she's chatting to Toni Tarrant somewhere. They seem to be always together just lately.'

'I'll go and find her,' said Nancy, jumping up from the stool. She peered in the mirror, pursing her red lipsticked mouth. 'Mmm, I think I'll do. I want to have a peep through the curtains to see if all our lot are there.'

Ivy laughed. 'It's not a Sunday-School concert, you know. You're supposed to be a real trouper.'

'What d'you mean, supposed to be? I am a real one,' Nancy retorted. 'I should be, after two years. Ta-ra, won't be long.' She fluttered her hand at Ivy as she went through the door.

Ivy was thoughtful for a moment. Nancy was very flushed tonight, not a healthy flush either, but Ivy knew better than to ask her if there was anything the matter. She would only deny it. Her solo number last night, though, had lacked its usual sparkle and her voice never powerful at the best of times, had sounded strained. Too many second-rate performances and Sid would not be pleased...

The trouble started near the beginning of the programme, whilst Sid was singing. The audience, an almost capacity one tonight, had applauded enthusiastically at the end of the opening number, a sextet of long-legged girls in short skirts and fishnet tights who had joined the troupe just for the season. Sid had thought that this was a good omen – the opening scene was often a reliable yardstick for the rest of the show – but he was soon to be proved wrong. It was when he reached the end of the first verse of his opening song:

'... In havens unfrequented that a busy life forgets,
The fishermen of England ... are working at the
  nets,'

that he was exhorted in a boorish voice from the
back of the theatre to 'Go and join 'em, mate!'
This was followed by jeers of laughter and
raucous cheers from the same quarter. Sid tried
to take no notice and there were several
indignant shouts of 'Shush!' and 'Let him get on
with his song.' Sid had every intention of singing
his song – he had put up with rough crowds
before, though not very often, thank goodness –
but he could feel the veins standing out on his
forehead and the perspiration running down his
face and he was aware that his fists were tightly
clenched.

When he sang of his 'Little Grey Home in the
West', the crowd at the back told him, in no
uncertain terms, to go there and stay there.

'Though the road may be long,
In the lilt of a song,
I forget I was weary before...'

Sid soldiered bravely on to cries of, 'Not half as
weary as we are, mate, listening to this load of old
rubbish!'
Sid was not afraid of boors and troublemakers
who, if he guessed correctly, had been put up to
this, although for the life of him he couldn't
imagine why. He knew that this was a grand little
show and they had had nothing but appreciative
audiences so far. Sid could give as good as he got.

After all, he was in charge of the company and it was up to him to make a stand. He finished his song then, standing four-square in the centre of the stage, he roared, 'If the gentlemen at the back don't shut their mouths I'll be happy to come and do it for them.'

'Good for you, Sid...'

'You tell 'em, mate...'

'I should think so, indeed...'

He left the stage to cheers and tumultuous applause.

He was worried, though, more for the women of the company than for himself, if this hullabaloo were to continue. His wife, Florence, had a fear of any rough stuff, and he could see that Ivy, Rose and Nancy, waiting in the wings, were very apprehensive. Especially Nancy; her green eyes were fearful and her cheeks were flushed. Sid knew that she wasn't well. She hadn't been up to scratch last night, although he hadn't had the heart to tell her so. She was a game little thing and he had felt sorry for her after that carry-on with Clive Conway. She was an adequate-enough performer now, although carried along largely by Ivy and Rose; and still, after two years with the company, she was very naïve, seeming to regard it all as a glorified chapel concert. This could break her, if they carried on with their funny business.

'It's all right,' he whispered to the Trio. 'I've told 'em. I've sorted 'em out. I don't think they'll try again. Go on, girls. Give 'em all you've got.'

Sarah, in her seat near the front of the theatre,

was feeling very uneasy.

'It's the Trio next,' she whispered to Zachary, who was sitting beside her. 'I hope everything'll be all right.'

'Should be,' Zachary hissed. 'That Sid looks as though he'll stand for no nonsense. Anyway, if they start again we can get the manager to sort them out. Your dad'll tell him, won't he?'

'I'm sure he will. Shhh... They're here now.'

Things were not too bad to start with. The Trio's opening number, 'In the Good Old Summertime', was greeted warmly by the audience, the majority of whom seemed to be wholly on the side of the girls, determined to give them all the support they needed. The anxiety showed on the faces of the Trio, but by the end of the number they had visibly relaxed and were appearing much more confident. They all looked very dashing in their sporting outfits; Ivy in cycling knickerbockers and a double-breasted jacket, Rose in riding gear, and Nancy a veritable Suzanne Lenglen in the tennis dress she had chosen from Donnelly's fashion department.

They were well into their stride now.

'In the meantime, in between time,
Ain't we got fun...'

they assured the audience with their dazzling smiles and rolling eyes.

Sarah had been holding her breath, but now she let it go in a long sigh. They had got through the song without interruption. It was going to be all right. It was during the reprise, however, that

574

the trouble started again. This time the girls each had a solo line. Ivy and Rose got through theirs without any mishap, but when Nancy declared, in a somewhat quavery voice,

'There's nothing surer,
The rich get rich and the poor get poorer...'

it was then that the uproar recommenced at the back.

'Sing up, darlin'. We can't hear yer!'

'We don't want to, do we?'

'She can't sing, anyroad...'

Nancy bit her lip, stepping back into line with the other two, but she was obviously shaken. The rest of the scene consisted of dancing and various actions to represent the three sports. The girls performed it very well, but a feeling of restlessness had by now pervaded the audience, many of whom were turning round to see who was making all the fuss at the back.

'Father, can't you do something?' Sarah pleaded to Edwin, who was on the other side of her.

'I fully intend to,' he said. 'I'll just wait till the end of this act, then I'll go and find the manager.'

But the manager was not in his office and no one seemed to know his whereabouts. He was, apparently, a somewhat elusive character, very rarely around when he was needed. There were two attendants on duty, but they didn't seem to be attending to very much and, from their puny appearance, Edwin thought it unlikely that they would be much use. One of them did, however, disappear out on to the promenade and came back a few moments later with a policeman.

Edwin slid back into his seat. 'Should be all right now,' he told Sarah. 'We've got a policeman.'

'Good gracious! Fancy having to resort to that,' said Sarah. 'Poor old Nancy. And she was so looking forward to tonight.'

'It seems to have settled down,' said Zachary, giving her a comforting smile. 'Don't worry, luv.'

The last act had passed without interruption. It was Mervin the Marvel and Maria, and they had performed their tricks to an appreciative hush from the audience, even from the back row. Charlie Chinn the comedian and Albertino the juggler followed, and there was still no disturbance. By the time the interval came it seemed as though the Law, with all its pomp and dignity, had had the desired effect. The policeman, with a cautionary, 'Just watch your step, lads,' to the youths on the back row, decided that he was superfluous. It must have been high spirits, he thought to himself. Young men on holiday in Blackpool often got a bit too big for their boots. He'd put the wind up them, though, right enough.

'Whew! That was nasty, wasn't it?' said Hetty to Grace during the interval. 'Our poor Nancy. I'd like to have gone up there and given them a piece of my mind. Why d'you suppose they were doing it? Couldn't be personal, could it? Not against our Nancy...'

'Of course not,' said Grace consolingly. 'They've stopped now, haven't they? Just forget it, Hetty, and enjoy the rest of the show. I must say it's very good, all of it.'

Sarah looked round at the Eastern Pavilion. This was the theatre at the landward end of the pier. The Indian Theatre, which had stood at the other end of North Pier since 1878 had, last year, been totally destroyed by fire. Sarah remembered how she had visited this self-same theatre three years ago with Nancy – before that young lady had been part of the company, of course – and seen almost the self-same show. Summer variety shows didn't vary much and this was virtually the same company, except that Clive Conway had been replaced by Toni Tarrant and there was a new group of chorus girls. The songs and sets and costumes were all different, but the content was, by and large, the mixture as before. And the seats were still as uncomfortable, thought Sarah wrily, wriggling a little. She recalled, too, the conversation she had had with Nancy on that occasion, something about unfortunate performers who were given 'the bird'. Sarah shuddered. It had been a near thing with Nancy tonight, but the evil moment seemed to have passed. Perhaps the troublemakers had gone, or else had decided to pipe down. She said as much to Zachary and he agreed with her.

'Yes, I think we've heard the last of them, thanks to your dad. Like an ice cream?'

But Sarah had spoken too soon and this became apparent almost immediately after the start of the second half of the show. The opening chorus was allowed to proceed without disruption, then Sidney Marchant took the stage once more. He was an impressive figure in his full evening dress, and it was obvious from his stance that he was very proud of himself; but he was greeted with shouts of derision.

'Look at 'im, all done up like a dog's dinner.'

'More like summat out a' Burton's window.'

There were angry mutterings from other parts of the audience.

'Shush, will you? Let him sing.'

'We've come to hear him, not you lot.'

Sid cast a baleful look towards the back row before he started his song.

'Love, could I only tell thee
How dear thou art to me...'

He struggled through to the end, but it was obviously taking a lot out of him. His face was red and his eyes were bulging and Sarah feared that he was going to burst, like an overblown balloon. She felt more and more scared as he ploughed through his next number, 'Love's Garden of Roses', to the accompaniment of scuffles and murmurings, though no outright jeering, from the rear of the audience. But Sarah's fears were chiefly for Nancy, who she knew would be coming on again shortly. She was anxious for Ivy, too, of course, but Ivy was made of sterner stuff than her cousin, who had already had one terrible setback in her stage career.

She got hold of Zachary's arm. 'What shall we do? It's starting again.'

'It seems to me that it's Sid they're getting at,' whispered Zachary. 'Wait a bit. It might die down.'

And it did, during Toni Tarrant's act and Charlie Chinn's second performance. Then it was time for the Trio to appear again. Sarah was, by this time, almost sick with fright. The girls looked stunning, though, in their Flappers' dresses, and she applauded enthusiastically with the rest of the audience as they danced the Charleston and the Black Bottom. Nancy was clearly in her element now, the fringe on her dark red dress gyrating wildly round her hips as she swung her long bead necklace in time to the music. Ivy and Rose looked equally fetching, Ivy in a bright royal blue which made her blonde hair appear fairer than ever and Rose in emerald green. A dazzling trio, with quicksilver movements and perfect rhythm and timing, they completely captivated the audience. Zachary was leaning forward in his seat, enthralled by his bewitching Ivy. Sarah slowly let her breath out again. Perhaps her fears were groundless after all.

And then Nancy stepped forward into the spotlight. It was time for her solo spot, the part of the show that Sarah knew her cousin had been looking forward to the most, though dreading it as well. She stood there in the centre of the stage, looking very tiny and very alone, as the five-piece orchestra played the introduction. Then she started to sing.

'Ma, he's making eyes at me,' she began, opening her green eyes wide as she stared across at the rows and rows of seats.

'Ma, he's awful nice to me,
Ma, he's almost breaking my heart…'

She stopped then, putting her hand to her throat as though she were choking. Sarah, in sympathy, put her hand up to her own mouth. Oh lor, whatever was the matter? It was all quiet at the back, for the moment, but perhaps what had happened before had unnerved her. Go on, Nancy go on, Sarah willed her. You can do it...

'I'm beside him,
Mercy let his conscience guide him...'

But her voice was tinny and strained and it was clearly an effort for her to sing at all. A sympathetic audience might go along with her, but would this one? Sarah buried her face in her hands, terrified for what might happen next.

'Ma, he wants to marry me,
Be my honey bee...'

But it was too much for Nancy. Her voice had by now almost completely gone. From the rear of the theatre came the inevitable jeers.
'Get off home to yer Ma...'
'Aye, geroff. We've heard enough...'
'Get the juggler back on...'
'Aye, let's have the fellow with the big balls...'
There were bursts of lewd laughter as Nancy stood stock-still in the centre of the stage, not even attempting to sing now. Her mouth was wide open and the tears were streaming out of her eyes as the orchestra, watching her and not sure what to do, ended the song on an unfinished cadence.

'You're horrible, horrible!' yelled Nancy. Her voice was hoarse, but there was enough strength left for her to shout: 'I hate you! I hate you! Why can't you leave me alone? You've gone and spoiled it all...' She stamped her foot, and Sarah thought, in that moment, that her cousin looked like a little girl who had failed to get her own way. Nancy, in fact, had never really grown up at all. Then, suddenly, she bolted to the side of the stage. Ivy tried to restrain her and Rose ran from the wings at the other side, but Nancy was too quick for them. She almost fell down the steps leading from the stage, then she fled up the centre aisle towards the back of the theatre. Through the double doors, across the wooden planks of the pier and through the iron turnstile ... right into the path of an oncoming tram. There was a squeal of brakes and a sickening thud; and when her horrified family arrived on the scene it was to see Nancy's unconscious form lying by the edge of the tramtrack.

Chapter 27

Inside the theatre it was pandemonium for a few minutes, until Sid took the matter in hand, as calmly as he was able. Nancy's frantic family, all eight of them, had stood as one and hurried after her, and throughout the audience groups of people were standing up and turning round to see what was happening. Sid gave a signal to the orchestra to start playing again and whispered to Ivy and Rose that they must carry on as well as they could in Nancy's absence. Then he marched down the centre aisle, a formidable figure at the moment in his rage, in spite of his lack of height.

'You lot – OUT!' he bellowed to the group of youths on the back row. There were five of them, a couple looking no more than about sixteen years of age, and all, by now, realising that they had gone far enough. It was only meant to be a bit of a lark – and they were getting well paid for it, too – but they had never dreamed it would cause all this rumpus. Sid seized hold of one pimply youth by the scruff of his neck and yanked him out into the aisle, then he put his boot into the retreating behind of another; assisted, at last, by the two attendants who had decided it was up to them to look as though they were earning their money. Sid rubbed his hands together in a peremptory manner as he strode back to the stage. Many of the troupe considered him to be rather a pompous little man, but he would certainly go up in their estimation after tonight's showing.

He waited until Ivy and Rose had finished singing Nancy's abandoned number, then he stood in the centre of the stage and raised his hands, asking for silence. 'Thank you, ladies and gentlemen,' he said. 'Just a little contretemps, nothing more, and it's all been settled. Now – *let the show go on*!' He hadn't time, just now, to concern himself with what had happened to Nancy, but her family was with her. They would take care of her.

Nancy was still lying motionless at the edge of the tramtrack, her distraught mother kneeling beside her. 'Nancy! Nancy, love, speak to me,' Hetty cried, cradling her daughter's head in her arms. 'Oh, Nancy. Wake up, love.'

'Be careful not to move her,' said Edwin gently, stooping down beside them. 'You don't know what... It's best to leave her very still, until the ambulance comes. They've sent for one.'

'Don't you tell me not to touch my own daughter,' Hetty snapped. But she did let go of her head and shoulders and took Nancy's hand instead, feeling in fear and trembling, for the pulse. She turned frightened eyes towards her brother-in-law. 'Edwin. Oh my God, Edwin. I can't feel anything. I think she's–'

Edwin took Nancy's limp hand, closing his eyes as though he were praying as he knelt there. 'Yes,' he said, after a few moments. 'There *is* a pulse – very faint, but she's still alive. She'll be all right, Hetty. The ambulance will be here soon. They'll take care of her.'

The rest of the family stood in a frightened group just outside the pier entrance. Quite a crowd had gathered by this time and there were already three trams caught in the traffic jam, which could go no further until the ambulance arrived. There was an outcry from Zachary as he saw the group of youths dashing through the turnstile.

'Just let me get my hands on the bastards,' he yelled, taking a step towards them.

But Sarah restrained him. 'No, leave it,' she said, pulling at his arm. 'It won't do any good, getting yourself into bother. Look, the policeman's here now.'

The policeman who had abandoned his post earlier in the evening, was now in evidence again. He strutted importantly up to the troublemakers and could be seen talking earnestly to them, before they all walked off along the promenade.

'He won't do anything,' said Zachary bitterly. 'Just give 'em a caution, I suppose. I can't tell you what I'd like to do to 'em. They might've killed my sister.'

'Don't say that, Zachary,' said Sarah, feeling very frightened. 'I don't suppose for one moment that they meant this to happen. They didn't know she was going to panic and run in front of a... Oh Zachary, she will be all right, won't she?' She buried her head against his tweed jacket and he put his arm round her.

'Course she will,' he said, though his voice lacked conviction. 'Look, the ambulance is here now.'

584

The crowd was hushed as the porters lifted the still-unconscious form of Nancy and carried her into the van. 'I'm going with her. I'm her mother,' said Hetty, and the ambulancemen nodded. 'Aye, that's right, love. You come along with her.'

And there was nothing that the rest of them could do but go home and wait. At least, that was what the Grandparents and Grace and Edwin decided to do. The younger members, Sarah, Zachary and Joyce, went back into the theatre. Not that they had any desire to see the rest of the show, but they knew that they must tell Sid what had happened. And Zachary was anxious to be with Ivy.

Hetty had been advised by the doctor to go home and rest, with the promise that she would be contacted immediately, should there be any news. She hadn't heard anything, but she was there at the hospital at ten o'clock the following morning. The boarding house – the visitors, the pros, the whole lot of them – could go hang as far as Hetty was concerned; her mother and the two girls were there to see to things. Her only concern was for her daughter. Even Joseph, for the moment, had taken second place, being cared for by his great-grandmothers. There were two of them, both equally anxious to do a bit of 'spoiling'.

They were normally quite strict about visitors at the hospital – only two to a bed, and only at certain times – but this was something of a special case as the patient had not yet regained consciousness. Nancy was breathing normally, Hetty was glad to see, as she sat there quietly at her bedside. Her daughter had been lucky, the doctor told her this morning, very lucky indeed. The tram had dealt her a glancing blow, but on the body, fortunately, not on her head. They thought she had a cracked rib, which should soon mend as she was a strong, healthy girl, and various bumps and bruises, but, as far as they could see, no internal injuries and no injuries to the head. Her whole system, though, had been given a shock and sleeping was Nature's way of letting her come to terms with it. It was just a matter of time...

A multitude of thoughts rushed through Hetty's mind as she waited at her daughter's side. Accidents were becoming more and more common in the busy crowded streets. At one time it had been runaway horses; now it was motorcars and trams. Hetty had never cared for the trams, great lumbering things they were, although they were a part of Blackpool and she supposed they had come to stay. How long would it be, though, before they decided to do something about the unguarded tramtrack, where visitors, who were not used to such transport, wandered on to the rails? She could foresee many more accidents. This hadn't been a visitor though. This had been her darling daughter, fleeing in a panic from a situation with which she was unable to cope. Hetty feared that Nancy never would be able to cope with such traumas, that she was, in fact, not at all suited to the precarious life of a trouper. She had tried to warn her, right at the beginning, but Nancy would never listen.

This was the second accident to affect their family in a very short time. And how haphazard the outcome of such accidents could be, very much in the lap of the gods, as folk were apt to say. Or, more accurately, thought Hetty, in the hand of the one God; for though she seldom went to church, Hetty did believe that God was in control and that He was able to shape the affairs of His children … if they asked Him. She couldn't understand why Drusilla should have been killed by what seemed to be a single blow to the head. Or Reuben. Never would she understand why Reuben had been taken from her. But sometimes you didn't have to question; you just had to go on. As she had gone on, without him, for so many years. Even though she had had Albert and her three children, Hetty had never stopped thinking about her first beloved husband. The pain of her loss had lessened, of course, over the years, but Reuben had been much in her thoughts recently with all that business with Drusilla.

But her daughter, who had been involved in what could have been a much worse accident, had escaped with minor injuries. If only she would wake up… Hetty closed her eyes now and prayed as fervently as she had ever prayed in her life that Nancy would do so.

It was about noon when Nancy opened her eyes, to a glorious midsummer day with a faint breeze rippling the white curtains at the window. That was what she noticed first, a white fluttering, like a seagull in flight, at the edge of her vision. There was a faint cry, too, of a seagull, bringing back memories of the sea, the sand, a long pier stretching out over the ocean. Nancy frowned, trying to remember … but it had gone. No, it wasn't a seagull – how silly of her – it was a curtain flapping in the breeze. But it wasn't her curtain, or her window, and the green painted ceiling was not her ceiling, the familiar sloping rafters of the attic bedroom. This ceiling was much higher. Where on earth was she? Then her eyes alighted on the person at her bedside, a dumpy figure in a navy and white spotted dress that looked familiar, with a halo of untidy reddish hair. It seemed like a halo in that moment with the sunlight glinting through it. And anxious green eyes, very loving ones, staring down at her. Nancy frowned again. It was so hard to remember… Then recognition dawned.

'Mam,' she said softly. 'Hello, Mam. Where am I?'

'You're in hospital, dear,' said Hetty, bending down and kissing her daughter's cheek. She stroked the tendrils of hair that curled over her forehead. 'You had a little accident and they brought you here. And I've been waiting for you to wake up.'

Nancy smiled and nodded, but she still couldn't remember. It didn't matter, though. It was very comfortable here, in this bed. As she lay still she became aware of a slight pain in her left side, just above her waist, and her legs were aching too. It was good to see Mam though. But there was someone else who should be there, someone she wanted to see very badly. A memory returned then, with blinding clarity, of big blue eyes, soft ginger curls, a chubby, dimpled face breaking out in an infectious grin, a tiny hand nestled inside her own...

'Where's Joseph?' she asked, raising her head from the pillow. 'I want to see my little boy.'

Nancy didn't see the slight tightening of her mother's mouth, nor could she know anything of the jolt that her words gave to Hetty. And when Hetty answered it was in the tenderest tone that her daughter had ever heard. 'And so you shall, my love. Joseph'll come to see his ... his mummy just as soon as we can arrange it.' Hetty turned as the door opened. 'Look, here's the nurse come to see how you are. She's woken up, Nurse. Isn't that wonderful?'

'It hurt, Gracie. I don't mind telling you it hurt,' said Hetty to her sister a few weeks later, 'and I certainly wouldn't admit that to anyone else. I know it was mean of me – real rotten – but I felt as though I didn't want to give him back to her. I'd come to think of him as mine – just mine – and I didn't want to lose him. I've already lost so much,' she added quietly. 'There, I bet you think that's terrible, don't you?'

'No, indeed I don't,' said Grace emphatically. 'You've been marvellous with that little lad. No one could have done more for him. And, when all's said and done, your Nancy dumped him on you, didn't she? Oh yes, she did,' she went on, as Hetty tried to protest. 'And what else could you do but bring him up as though he were your own?'

'And now she wants him back. Well, she's got him back,' said Hetty, giving a shrug. 'There's no doubt about that. You should see the pair of them – as thick as thieves they are now. She's taken him down on the sands this afternoon with his new bucket and spade, so I thought I'd come and see my dear old sister. I know you'll understand, Grace, if no one else does. But then I wouldn't tell all this to anyone else, would I?'

'You can say anything you like to me, Hetty. You always have done and I hope you always will. And I'll tell you what I think. I'm really glad you're making some time for yourself at last. You've been tied to that boarding house long enough. Start delegating the work a bit more. Engage more staff – you can afford it, can't you?'

Hetty nodded in agreement.

'Well, there you are then,' Grace said triumphantly. 'And as far as Joseph's concerned … what has happened is only right, you know. Nancy's his mother. I know she's only just waking up to the fact, but it's all for the best in the long run. You and I, Hetty…' Grace smiled, a trifle sadly '…we're getting rather old, aren't we for coping with young children?'

'I wouldn't call forty-five old,' Hetty retorted.

'No, of course not – but on a permanent basis, I mean,' said Grace. 'You know what our mother has always said about grandchildren; that you can have the pleasure of them without the responsibility. And little Joseph's his mother's responsibility now. Try to see it that way, Hetty.

And you haven't lost him, you know. How could you? There's always a special link between grandmothers and their first grandchild.'

'Hmmm. Can't say I've noticed it with Mam and Zachary,' observed Hetty wrily. 'I think she's always regarded him as a damned nuisance. And so he was at one time, I've got to admit it.'

'He's much improved though now, Hetty. I don't think I've ever seen such a change in anyone,' said Grace.

'Yes, you're right.' Hetty nodded. 'And it was because of Zachary – I realise it now – that I made so much of young Joseph. My own lad had been such a bitter disappointment to me, though I didn't want to admit it to anyone, not even to myself. And then, when our Nancy's baby arrived, it was as though I was given a second chance. I could have a fresh start, with another little lad.'

'And now you've got the first one back,' said Grace, smiling consolingly at her sister. 'Your Zachary – you and he are the best of friends again, aren't you?'

'Yes, we're getting on better than we have for ages.'

'And you've a wedding to look forward to, and there'll be more grandchildren, no doubt. Take pleasure in it all, Hetty. And take a bit of time for yourself. It's wonderful, isn't it, that Nancy's made such a speedy recovery. It could have been so much worse.'

Hetty knew that what her sister said made sense, all of it. And Nancy had started to get better, it seemed, as soon as she set eyes on her son. He had trotted into the hospital ward, that same afternoon, hand in hand with Zachary, clutching in his little fist a bunch of bright orange marigolds picked from the garden of Sunnyside.

'For you, Mummy,' he had said, thrusting them into Nancy's face. 'Get better, Mummy.' He had been schooled by Zachary, a doting uncle now to the little lad, who had once been so indifferent. Yes, things were changing all round and it must be for the better. It must be, Hetty told herself as she saw the tears of joy in Nancy's eyes at the sight of her baby son.

Nancy had stayed in hospital for a week and since then she had been taking things quietly at home. It was now the last week in July, the height of the season in Blackpool, and Nancy was almost back to normal. There had been no mention, though, of her returning to the show. Yes, the height of the season, thought Hetty, and here she was, in her sister's elegant drawing room, drinking tea from eggshell china in the middle of the afternoon. Wednesday afternoon – Grace's half day, to be sure – but a time when Hetty, normally, would have been up to her eyes in baking, or mending, or some such chore. But she felt only a momentary flicker of guilt. Hetty was realising, not before time, that there were other things in life besides work.

'Yes, our Nancy's getting along fine now,' she said, in answer to her sister's remark.

'Any talk of her returning to the show?'

'No. She's never mentioned the accident or anything that happened that night. It's as though she's blotted it out of her mind. Sid's been to see her, and so have a few other people from the company, and she chats brightly enough with them, but there's no talk of her going back. Ivy was telling me they've got another girl in the Trio to replace Nancy. And they'll need another one an' all before long, when Ivy and our Zachary get married. You know what they always say – "the show must go on". Between you and me I don't think our Nancy'll go back to the stage at all.'

'Perhaps she was never really cut out for it?' said Grace.

'I've known that, right from the beginning,' said Hetty. 'I tried to warn her that it wouldn't be easy, but you know our Nancy. She never would listen. And in the end I decided it was best just to let her go. She had to find out for herself, make her own mistakes … like you and I have had to do, Grace. Anyway, I'm going to do as you say. Try to take things a little more easily. Enjoy my grandchildren. Our Joseph, and the others, when they come.'

'Yes … grandchildren.' A wistful, almost pained expression came over Grace's face and Hetty immediately felt remorseful. Here she was, harping on about her own problems, and there was Grace with this awful business of Sarah and Alex still unsettled. No wonder Grace looked pensive at the mention of grandchildren.

'I'm sorry,' Hetty said now. 'Hark at me going on like this, and you with worries of your own. How is Sarah? Any news of Alex? They're no nearer a reconciliation?'

Grace shook her head sadly. 'No, and it seems to me as though they never will be. Our Sarah's unmovable. I've never known her to be so determined about anything.'

Sarah woke with a start. She had been dreaming and, as always, her dream was of Alex. This time, though, it had been even more real than usual and when she awoke it was with a feeling of desolation. She had watched him walk away from her and she was on her own again. She found that she was almost crying with disappointment and yet, what else could she expect? In her dream, just as in real life, she had told him to go; she wanted to be on her own. And now she had been on her own for three months ... and never had she felt more lonely. Sarah knew, in that moment, that she couldn't stand it any longer. She would have to go to him. She loved him. Dear God, how she loved him! The thought struck her like a blinding revelation, as though it was something she had never considered before. And yet, deep down, she had always known that she loved Alex; she would love him for ever, in spite of the hurt he had done her and the humiliation she had suffered. Suddenly, in an instant, all that hurt had vanished, and in its place was this deep yearning to be with him. Right now, this very day, this hour, this minute... Sarah knew that she couldn't bear to be apart from the man she loved for another second.

But such thinking was arbitrary. There was the rest of the night to get through, somehow. And if she set off as early as possible the next morning, it would still be a good few hours before she arrived in Northumberland. She couldn't go without leaving instructions at the café and packing a few belongings. Sarah sprang out of bed and carried her small clock over to the window to check the time. Twenty past three! Why did the time seem to stand still when you wanted it to move quickly? It was another three hours before she needed to be up and doing, but Sarah knew that it would be impossible for her to sleep through the rest of the hours of darkness, not with this newfound realisation taking control of her.

She crept down to the kitchen and made a pot of tea, as noiselessly as she was able, then she sat by her bedroom window waiting for the dawn. It was a long time since she had seen the sunrise; and now, as she watched the sun appearing between the rooftops of the houses opposite, painting the sky in glowing tones of pink and orange, it was as though she were seeing it all with new eyes. A warmth flooded through Sarah as she sat there and thought about Alex, where formerly there had been nothing but bitterness. She remembered opening her eyes in the attic bedroom, on that fateful occasion when the new young doctor had been called in to minister to her. She had seen his steadfast grey eyes looking so concernedly into her own and she had fallen immediately in love with him ... as he had with her. She had known then, inexplicably – absurdly, some might have thought – that she loved him and would love him for ever.

All around her, for the last few weeks, there had been signs of 'togetherness'. Sarah had tried not to be jealous of this, but to rejoice with the people concerned as they took delight in their relationships. There were Zachary and Ivy, deliriously happy together as they looked forward to their wedding; Nancy and little Joseph, taking great pleasure in the close kinship they had only just awoken to; her mother and father ... but they had always been a couple of love birds; it was just that Sarah was noticing it more after having lived apart from them for a while; Grandma and Grandad Makepeace, a devoted couple if ever there was one, a second marriage for both of them, but one in which each tried to put the other first. Only Aunt Hetty was alone, but she seemed more contented these days, no longer so possessive about her grandson, and actually spending more time on her appearance and going out occasionally to enjoy herself. Whilst Sarah, with a numbness deep inside her that nothing could alleviate, had taken refuge in her work. The café and restaurant were both thriving; she had taken on more staff to cope with the seasonal rush, which was now drawing to an end, and there was a fulltime cook in charge of the menus. Sarah knew that they would be well able to cope in her absence, which should be only a few days, as long as it took to sort things out with Alex.

As she watched the daybreak Sarah experienced a moment of panic. Supposing Alex no longer loved her or wanted her? She had been very stubborn and he couldn't be blamed, surely, for changing his mind? Or supposing, after her long journey, he wasn't there? She had his address; he had insisted on sending it to her, although she recalled now, with a stab of guilt, that she hadn't even acknowledged his letter. He might well have moved from there, or decided to stay in Northumberland for ever, maybe? But commonsense took over from vague imaginings. Hadn't he said he would always love her? He had only gone away because she had rejected him and his pleas to put things right. Wherever he was she would find him.

It was early afternoon before she left Blackpool. There had been various matters to attend to at the café and an explanation to be given to Joyce; she was the only one in Sarah's confidence and would be in charge whilst she was away. Then she had called at her home – her previous home, the one she had shared with Alex – to pick up some warmer clothes. It was September now and the nights and early mornings were decidedly cooler; probably they would be even more so in the hills of Northumberland.

She leaned back now in her corner seat, watching the flat landscape of the Fylde flash past the window. When she left Lancaster, where she had to change trains, the flat green fields would give way to gently rolling hills and stretches of moorland, and greystone houses would take the place of the redbrick. Sarah knew little about the town of Hexham, where she was bound, except that it stood on the River Tyne and that there was an Abbey there. But all she cared about was that this was the town where she would find Alex, her beloved husband. No ... that wasn't strictly true, but it was a matter that could easily be put right. The feeling of him had been with her very strongly when she called at their

597

home in North Shore. He was there, in the very ambience of the place. She had felt that she could almost have touched him and now she couldn't wait to see him again. Her mother, she recalled, had shown no surprise on hearing what Sarah was about to do. Grace had just smiled serenely and said, 'I'm sure you're right, dear.' And Edwin, departing for work had said, 'Jolly good.'

Now it was up to her. She crossed her fingers tightly, and closed her eyes, too, as the train rushed into the blackness of a tunnel. Please, please let me find him. Let it be all right.

It was dusk when she finally arrived in Hexham. A taxi took her to the address she gave and as it drove away she stood uncertainly on the pavement, her small case at her side, staring up at the tall greystone house. It was near the Abbey, one of a terrace of similar three-storeyed, solid-looking houses which had the air of belonging to prosperous business people. Sarah felt a momentary qualm. She had no idea what she was coming to, whether this was the house of the doctor with whom Alex was working, or the surgery, or whether he was just lodging here. Taking a deep breath she opened the iron gate and walked up the short path to the green-painted front door. The letterbox and doorknocker gleamed with recent polishing and the stone step was well-scrubbed. Sarah was impressed, and when the door opened and she caught a glimpse of the deep red carpet and highly polished stair banisters she felt that her welcome here must be a cordial one.

'Good evening,' said the woman who stood on

the threshold. 'Can I help you?' She was short and stout with somewhat untidy gingerish hair and a friendly smile. She reminded Sarah of her Aunt Hetty, except for the colour of her eyes. This woman's eyes were blue and they were looking at Sarah intently, though in quite an amiable way.

'Good evening, madam. I hope you can help me,' replied Sarah. 'I'm looking for Dr Duncan. Dr Alexander Duncan. I believe he's staying with you, but I'm not sure–'

'Aye, he's staying here all right.' The woman nodded. 'But I'm afraid you're out of luck, my dear. Dr Duncan went away this morning.'

Sarah could almost have wept with disappointment and it must have shown on her face because the woman reached out and took her arm. 'You look as though you've had a shock, dearie. And me leaving you there on the doorstep. How rude of me… Come on in, my dear.' The woman lifted up Sarah's case and ushered her into the hallway. Then she looked at her more searchingly. 'You've come a long way to find him, have you? And you are…?'

'I'm his … I'm Mrs Duncan,' said Sarah faintly. 'I've come from Blackpool. If you could perhaps tell me where he's gone, then I could–'

The woman's eyes softened. 'Aye, I can indeed. That's the very place he's gone to – Blackpool. He left this morning. He told me he had some business to sort out and he'll be back in a day or two.'

Sarah's mouth dropped open in astonishment. That was incredible! She had come all this way to find him, and Alex had gone. Why had he gone? To find her – to try to talk her round? Sarah hoped against hope that this was the reason for his visit to Blackpool and that he hadn't gone for an entirely different reason; to terminate his partnership with Dr Mason, for instance.

'But … I've just come from there,' Sarah said stupidly. 'If only I'd known. Does he … is he lodging here? This isn't the doctor's house, is it?'

The woman gave her an odd look, and well she might, thought Sarah; coming here and saying she was Mrs Duncan, but not knowing the first thing about her husband. 'No, dearie, it's not the doctor's house. That's just down the road. Dr Duncan's lodging here with me. I'm Mrs Appleyard. Connie Appleyard.' She held out her hand. 'I'm very pleased to meet you. And I know you're Mrs Duncan all right. The doctor's got a lovely photo of you up in his room.' She nodded slowly, all the while looking closely at Sarah. She's no doubt thinking we're a couple of silly fools who can't sort out our affairs, thought Sarah as she shook hands with the woman. She felt that Mrs Appleyard was owed some sort of an explanation.

'There's been a mix-up,' she said. 'We seem to have got our wires crossed. I should have written, but I thought I'd give him a surprise. I'm just wondering what is the best thing to do now. Perhaps you could tell me of a small hotel, Mrs Appleyard, where I could stay for tonight. Then tomorrow, perhaps … I'm not quite sure what to do tomorrow.'

'No, indeed I won't,' replied Mrs Appleyard

600

vehemently. 'You're staying right here, my dear, in your husband's room. Where else would you stay? And if you'll take my advice, you'll send him a telegram first thing in the morning. It's too late to do anything tonight. Now, come along, dear. I'll show you to your room. You must be exhausted after that long journey.'

'Thank you, you're very kind,' replied Sarah. She suddenly realised how hungry she was. It was early evening now and she hadn't had a bite to eat since lunchtime. 'I'm sorry to trouble you, Mrs Appleyard,' she said, feeling that she was being a dreadful nuisance, 'but could you possibly make me a sandwich, please? Just cheese or something simple.'

'I'll do more than that.' Mrs Appleyard smiled, showing the dimples in her rosy cheeks and Sarah thought how appropriate her name was. 'Your husband always has his evening meal with me, and it's almost ready now. So you can have his share tonight. Come down as soon as you're ready, dearie.'

The room seemed to be permeated with an aura of Alex. His tartan dressing gown hung behind the door and a couple of his pipes rested on a pipe rack beside a well-thumbed copy of *Ivanhoe*. It was a comfortable room with one bed – a double one, Sarah noticed – two easy chairs, a well-filled bookcase, and a sturdy gent's wardrobe and a chest of drawers. On the top of it stood, as Mrs Appleyard had said, a framed photograph of herself, one that Alex had taken on the first morning of their honeymoon in the ruins of Bolton Abbey. It looked, at the moment, like a typical bachelor's room, thought Sarah with a pang of sadness. Mrs Appleyard told her, over a delicious meal of steak and kidney pie, that she took only one gentleman lodger at a time – a professional gent – to help with the expense of maintaining the house. This had proved increasingly difficult, she said, since her husband had died a couple of years ago. Sarah could tell that she was curious about her lodger – and about his wife, who had appeared so suddenly out of the blue – but she was too polite to ask any questions. And there were certain matters which could never be disclosed.

Sarah slept well, tired after the traumas of the day. She was at the post office soon after it opened at nine o'clock the following morning. *Am here in Hexham. Stop.* the telegram read. *Will await your return. Stop. I love you. Stop. Sarah.* Then there was nothing she could do but wait. It was pointless now to have fears or misgivings, but still they niggled at her. Did Alex still love her? Or did he intend to stay here in Northumberland and make a new life without her? Perhaps he had started to do so already. No … that couldn't be so; her photo in his room refuted that. Oh stop, stop!' she cried to her over-active mind as she wandered away from the warmth of the September sunshine into the cool dark silence of the Abbey church. Mrs Appleyard had told her to be sure to see the Abbey, founded by St Wilfrid and with what was reckoned to be the finest Anglo-Saxon crypt in England. Sarah gazed, with only partially-seeing eyes, at the Roman altars, the stone caricatures of St Christopher and St George and the dragon, and the medieval screens and panels. Then she sat down in a pew and closed her eyes, her head full of a fervent, though wordless, prayer.

It was market day and the colonnaded shelter near to the Abbey was crowded with local farmers and market gardeners selling their wares; fruit and vegetables, new-laid eggs, jars of homemade lemon curd and jam. There was a multitude of other stalls too, with brightly coloured cotton materials, pots and pans, tin toys and wooden dolls, boiled sweets and trays of treacle toffee. Sarah, as a rule, loved markets, but today she knew that she mustn't linger.

How long would it be, she wondered, before he arrived? Her journey the previous day had taken several hours. Alex, though, would be in his motorcar. She assumed that he would set off back as soon as he heard from her. She felt that she could hardly swallow for the tension in her throat; nevertheless, she managed to partake of a cup of tea and a ham sandwich from a market stall before she wandered back to the tall grey house across the road. She picked up one of Alex's books, one of the Waverley novels, and tried to read, but the words were a meaningless jumble, her restless mind refusing to make sense of them. She put the book down and laid on the bed, on top of the billowy eiderdown. She closed her eyes, trying to still her mind, and in a little while she slept.

When Sarah opened her eyes it was to see a pair

of kindly, yet grave, grey eyes regarding her. For a moment she was transported back in time to another occasion when the same face had looked down at her. She hadn't known, then, who he was, but she had fallen in love with him in an instant. The face was now a familiar one and she loved him still; she loved him more than ever.

'Alex… Oh, Alex.' Her arms reached out to him, then there was no need for any more words as his arms encircled her and his lips came down upon hers in a tender kiss. There was still no need for words as they, gently at first, then more ardently, made love.

'Why didna ye tell me?' Alex asked afterwards, running his hand caressingly over the slight bulge in Sarah's stomach, indiscernible when she was fully clothed, but obvious to someone who knew her and loved her as much as Alex did.

'There hasn't been the chance,' replied Sarah, feeling very guilty. She knew only too well how stubborn she had been. 'I … I haven't seen you for ages.'

'I'm here now,' said Alex tenderly. 'When is it?'

'February. It must have happened just before we… Oh Alex, I'm so very sorry. I've been so stupid.'

'Hush, hush, my darling,' said Alex, kissing away the tears that were brimming from her eyes. 'There's no need for that. But I think it's time I made an honest woman of you, don't you?'

Sarah nodded, too choked to speak.

'Sarah, my darling … will you marry me?'

She nodded again, then at last managed to find her voice. 'Oh yes, Alex. Of course I will.'

Explanations came much later. Sarah learned how Alex had woken suddenly in the night, just as she had done, knowing that he couldn't bear to be apart from her any longer. He had a couple of days' holiday due to him, and so he had dashed off to Blackpool. It had been Grace who had told him that Sarah had done the self-same thing.

'I was coming back, my love,' he said, 'even before I got your telegram, but I couldna drive all that way back the same day. Your mother's happy.' He smiled at her. 'I can see she's very happy about us. Does she know...?' Gently, almost reverently, he touched her stomach again.

'No – at least, I haven't said anything. But she's been giving me some very searching looks lately.'

'Aye, Grace is a very discerning lady.' Alex nodded slowly. 'I think ye'll find she's made a pretty shrewd guess. And the doctor?'

'Yes, I've seen our family doctor, but I've told him to keep mum. He knows we've been having ... problems.'

'Problems that can soon be remedied, my love.' Alex kissed her again. 'I have some good friends here. Friends who know not to ask too many questions. All we need is a special licence and a couple of witnesses. You can stay, can't you, darling, for as long as it takes?'

'Of course I can,' replied Sarah. 'For a few days, certainly. But you've still several weeks to do here, haven't you?' Having found him again, Sarah knew that she didn't want to be apart from him, not for an instant.

Alex smiled at her glum face. 'Only three, and

they'll soon pass, my darling. Then we'll be together for ever and ever.'

'For ever and ever,' said Sarah softly, and his arms went round her again.

They stood at the window as the daylight began to fade over the rooftops of the little town. The early sunshine had given way to squally showers and a high wind, a harbinger of the coming autumn. But as they looked at the darkening sky over the Abbey church, there, in the midst of all the greyness, was a silver lining to the cloud.

The publishers hope that this book has given you enjoyable reading. Large Print Books are especially designed to be as easy to see and hold as possible. If you wish a complete list of our books please ask at your local library or write directly to:

Magna Large Print Books
Magna House, Long Preston,
Skipton, North Yorkshire.
BD23 4ND

This Large Print Book for the partially sighted, who cannot read normal print, is published under the auspices of

THE ULVERSCROFT FOUNDATION

THE ULVERSCROFT FOUNDATION

... we hope that you have enjoyed this Large Print Book. Please think for a moment about those people who have worse eyesight problems than you ... and are unable to even read or enjoy Large Print, without great difficulty.

You can help them by sending a donation, large or small to:

The Ulverscroft Foundation, 1, The Green, Bradgate Road, Anstey, Leicestershire, LE7 7FU, England.
or request a copy of our brochure for more details.

The Foundation will use all your help to assist those people who are handicapped by various sight problems and need special attention.

Thank you very much for your help.